The Science of Learning

A Systems Theory Perspective

Robert T. Hays, Ph.D.

BrownWalker Press
Boca Raton, Florida

The Science of Learning:
A Systems Theory Perspective

Copyright © 2006 Robert T. Hays

BrownWalker Press
Boca Raton, Florida
USA • 2006

ISBN: 1-59942-415-0 (paperback)
ISBN: 1-59942-416-9 (ebook)

www.BrownWalker.com

Table of Contents

Chapter 8:
   Categories of Learning Outcomes, Instructional Events,
   and Instructional Objectives 193

Chapter 11:
Research on the Effectiveness of Instructional Games 251

List of Tables

List of Figures

List of Figures
(continued)

Preface

Many people are talking about the "science of learning" and "scientifically-based" education research. For example, the "No Child Left Behind" legislation (U.S. Congress, 2001) mentions "scientifically-based research" over 100 times (Richardson, 2002; Slavin, 2002). To effectively apply science to the study of learning, persons in the instructional field need to understand science and how the scientific method is used in the study of learning and the development of instructional applications. The goal of this book is not to make every reader a scientist. It is rather to help each reader appreciate and more fully understand science and how it is applied to the study of learning and the development of instruction. Above all, it is intended to help readers to think more "scientifically" about learning and instruction.

What is the Science of Learning?

The *Science of Learning* is the body of knowledge derived through scientific research about the way that people learn, the factors that affect learning, and the ways in which instructional methods and technology can be used to facilitate learning. The Science of Learning helps us plan, develop, and deliver effective and affordable instruction. The Science of Learning also provides the methods to evaluate whether the instruction meets its learning objectives.

The Purpose of This Book

The purpose of this book is three-fold. It will help the reader understand the role of science in the study of learning processes and the development and evaluation of various approaches used to enhance learning. It also will help the reader think more scientifically, whether he or she is a scientist, an instructional developer, or an instructional program manager. It will help any of these instructional practitioners understand how science and the scientific method are used to generate data that support specific instructional practices. Second, it provides an introduction to systems theory and introduces two system-based models: a systems model of the learner and a systems-based model of instruction. Third, these models are used to organize summaries of learning research and the use of instructional media to help the reader integrate these data and transform them into a "body of knowledge." The book is not intended to provide specific prescriptions for classroom practices or instructional designs, although some of these will be discussed to help explain various learning theories and concepts. Other books (e.g., Mayer, 2002; Clark, R. C., 2003; and Clark, R. C. & Mayer, 2003) provide ample guidance on specific instructional approaches such as classroom management techniques or instructional methods.

Data, Information, and Knowledge

When discussing research results, an important distinction should be made between the terms *data*, *information*, and *knowledge*. Davenport and Prusak (1998) provide a useful discussion about the relationship among these concepts. Acknowledging that the word data is plural, but choosing to use the more popular singular form, they define data as, "a set of discrete, objective facts about events" (p. 2). These facts include the results of many different experiments and research efforts on learning and the effects of instruction. However these results alone are insufficient to build the knowledge base for the science of learning. "There is no inherent meaning in data" (p. 3). Data can be considered as raw material, which provides "no judgment or interpretation and no sustainable basis of action" (p. 3). To do this, we need to understand the meaning of the data. We need information.

Information is derived from data, but goes beyond facts to: 1) change the way someone perceives something and 2) to have an impact on his or her judgment and behavior. "Information is meant to shape the person who gets it, to make some difference in his outlook or insight" (p. 3). Davenport and Prusak (1998) suggest that data can be transformed into information by adding meaning to the facts through several methods:

- *Contextualizing*: knowing for what purpose the data were gathered
- *Categorizing*: knowing the units of analysis or key components of the data

- *Calculating*: analyzing the data mathematically or statistically
- *Correcting*: removing errors from the data
- *Condensing*: summarizing the data into a more concise form

Researchers and theorists have used the data on learning to develop a variety of theories and models of processes that contribute to learning. Many of these theories and models are discussed in the following chapters. Information on learning effects is still not sufficient for our purposes. The science of learning requires a knowledge base.

"Knowledge is a fluid mix of framed experience, values, contextual information, and expert insight that provides a framework for evaluating and incorporating new experiences and information" (Davenport & Prusak, 1998, p. 5). Knowledge derives from information through another level of transformation. This transformation happens through methods like the following:

- *Comparison*: relating the information about one situation to other situations
- *Consequences*: determining the implications of the information for decisions and actions
- *Connections*: relating bits of knowledge to each other
- *Conversation*: determining what various people think about the information

Media, such as this book help humans communicate information to help each other develop knowledge.

Knowledge is still not the highest level we can hope to achieve. If we cogently use our knowledge, we may reach the level of wisdom. This book uses systems theory to organize discussions of the important data on learning, instructional media, and instructional design. It is hoped that these discussions help the reader to transform and synthesize these data into information. The book also suggests methods and recommendations for applying this science of learning knowledge base in a wise manner. Our wisdom will be judged by whether our efforts help learners achieve their learning goals.

Organization of the Book

The book is organized into four major sections. The first section, *Using Science to Study Learning and Develop Instruction*, includes three chapters. Chapter 1, *The Process of Science*, is a discussion of the purpose and process of science and how the scientific method helps us learn more about the world. Chapter 2, *A Scientific Approach to Instructional Development*, focuses on how the scientific method is applied to the study of learning and presents an introduction to systems theory and a systems model of the learner. This model is used in Section II as a way to organize and integrate summaries and discussions of learning research and instructional approaches. The third chapter, *Learning and Education Research and Myths about Learning and Instruction*, is a discussion of the similarities and differences between learning and education research and includes a presentation of some prevalent, yet erroneous beliefs about learning and instruction.

Section II, *Empirical Research on Learning*, includes five chapters that summarize the data generated from major learning research efforts and theoretical approaches. Chapter 4 is titled *Research on Physiological and Simple Learning*. It summarizes what we know about the physiological basis of learning and memory and how simple learning mechanisms seem to work. Chapter 5, *Research on Complex Learning: The Cognitive Domain*, is a discussion and summary of research on complex learning in the cognitive domain. It includes discussions of information processing models of learning and summaries of recent research on metacognition. Chapter 6, *Research on Complex Learning: The Motor and Affective Domains*, includes discussions and summaries of data that have been generated from studying the learning of complex motor tasks and the use of techniques to alter the learner's emotional reactions to instruction (affect). Chapter 7, *The Learning System*, provides an overview of the research results presented in the previous chapters. The systems model of the learner is used to organize this overview and to help the reader integrate and better understand the data. Following the overview of learning data, a model instruction as a communication process is presented as a way to discuss how our knowledge of learning can help us facilitate instruction and make it more effective. Chapter 8, *Conditions of Learning Outcomes*,

Instructional Events, and Instructional Objectives, introduces the reader to Gagné's theory of instructional design and the important events that must occur in effective instruction. It then provides summaries of taxonomies of instructional objectives and instructional techniques in each of the three domains of complex learning: cognitive, motor, and affective.

Section III, *Research and Issues on the Use of Instructional Media*, includes three chapters on methods and approaches used to aid instructional communication. Chapter 9, *Instructional Media: Issues and Approaches*, opens this section. It provides an explanation of the debate on the use of instructional media that has been ongoing for over twenty years. It also includes a summary of some of the research data on the effectiveness of instructional media. These summaries include data from laboratory, classroom, and field research on the use of a variety of instructional media (e.g., computer-based instruction, instructional simulations, and instructional games). Chapter 10, *Research on Instructional Simulations*, provides definitions of important terms in the field of instructional simulations, a historical review of the use of instructional simulations, and summaries of research on the effectiveness of these approaches. It also includes a discussion of the concept of simulation fidelity as a method to determine the characteristics of an instructional simulation. Chapter 11, *Research on the Effectiveness of Instructional Games*, concludes this section. It provides summaries and discussions of research to determine if instructional games are effective instructional aids and when to choose a game over other instructional methods.

Section IV, *The Science of Learning and the Art of Instruction*, is the final section of the book. It includes two chapters. Chapter 12, *Evaluation of Learning Outcomes*, is a discussion of the important methodological decisions that must be made if one wishes to evaluate the outcomes of instruction to determine if learning has occurred. It provides methodological recommendations about how to scientifically determine the effectiveness of instruction in terms of improved learner performance. The final chapter, *Applying the Science of Learning*, summarizes recommendations that can help readers apply the science of learning to design effective instruction. It illustrates some of these recommendations by discussing a successful instructional development project, the first virtual environment training system fielded by the U.S. Navy. Finally, the chapter closes with a few concluding remarks that highlight important recommendations discussed in the body of the book.

Section I
Using Science to Study Learning and Develop Instruction

During the last several centuries, science has helped humans to gain a great degree of understanding about and control over their environment. The main tool of science is the scientific method, a controlled process used to accumulate knowledge and test its accuracy. This section includes three chapters that examine the scientific method and how science is used to help us understand learning and develop effective instruction. The first chapter focuses on the methods and processes of science and how people can think more scientifically. Chapter 2 discusses how the scientific method is applied to the study of learning and the development of instruction. It also presents an introduction to systems theories and a systems model of the learner that will be used to help organize and integrate subsequent summaries of learning research. Chapter 3 examines the similarities and differences in research on learning and research on education. It also includes a discussion of pervasive, yet incorrect assumptions about learning and instruction (myths). The chapter concludes with an introduction to methods to evaluate the scientific quality of learning and education research. More detailed discussions and recommendation on the evaluation of instructional outcomes are provided in Section IV, Chapter 12.

Chapter 1
The Process of Science

The *Science of Learning* is the body of knowledge derived through scientific research about the way that people learn, the factors that affect learning, and the ways in which instructional methods and technology can be used to facilitate learning. There are three parts to this definition. First, the science of learning is a body of knowledge. Second, it is not just any knowledge. Rather, it is knowledge about how people learn and how to enhance the learning process. Finally, this knowledge is derived from scientific research data. The quality and utility of empirical data depend on the scientific quality of the research from which they were derived. These data are transformed into knowledge by integrating them using learning theories and models. This book uses systems theory as the integrative perspective.

The Science of Learning is used to plan, develop, and deliver effective and affordable instruction. It also is used to evaluate whether the instruction meets its learning objectives. However, to effectively apply the science of learning, one must develop the worldview that allows one to think "scientifically." Some basic rules of scientific thinking are presented next. Then, we will examine how science and the scientific method help us in our search for "truth" in the realms of learning and instruction.

Basic Rules of Scientific Thinking

Science is more than methods and the data they generate. These are important and are discussed below. However, science is also a way of thinking and of making decisions. Here are a few basic rules (Beveridge, 1957) that anyone can use to think more "scientifically."

1. *Maintain a healthy level of skepticism.* Don't believe everything you hear. Demand evidence that demonstrates the effectiveness of instructional approaches and require demonstrations of instructional products that will justify their claims.

2. *Consult original sources (e.g., publications) whenever possible.* Don't trust someone else's summary,

interpretation, or explanation of a research effort (p. 14). Read it yourself and make your own interpretations.

3. *Don't jump to conclusions* on the basis of opinions or insufficient data (p. 74). If it sounds too good to be true, it probably is.

4. *Always be ready "to abandon or modify our hypothesis* as soon as it is shown to be inconsistent with the facts" (p. 66).

5. *Do not draw general conclusions from one experiment.* "Experimental results are, strictly speaking, only valid for the precise conditions under which the experiments were conducted" (p. 35).

6. *Apply Occam's Razor.* This is the maxim of parsimony (first stated by William of Occam in the 14th century): given alternative explanations for some phenomenon, the simplest explanation is usually to be preferred.

Science and the Scientific Method

Humans have always wondered about their place in the universe. They have sought to understand themselves and the world around them by applying various approaches to the examination of the environment and their internal states. Science is the most successful of these approaches. We have made incredible progress in our understanding and control of our environment because science works. As Francis Bacon, widely regarded as one of the earliest proponents of the scientific method, put it, "The lame in the path outstrip the swift who wander from it" (quoted in Beverage, 1957, p. 3). The "path" of science is very narrow—it requires the use of precise vocabularies, carefully developed definitions, reproducible measurement techniques, and open communication among scientists. To stay on the path, we must carefully apply the techniques of science and use these methods to identify and correct our errors. We need to remain on the path of science because we need to build and expand our body of knowledge of how people learn and how to apply instructional techniques to make learning more efficient. If we do not follow the path of science, we are left with speculation, biases, and fads—not the most efficient way to ensure improved performance.

Science Defined

Science (from the Latin *scire*, to know) deals with knowledge. Science is defined (Webster's New Collegiate Dictionary, 1977) as:

1. Possession of knowledge as distinguished from ignorance or misunderstanding.
2. Knowledge covering general truths or the operation of general laws especially as obtained and tested through scientific method.

It is only since the seventeenth century that the scientific method, as we know it today, has played a major role in the search for knowledge. In earlier times, other methods were used to test the truth of our conceptions of reality. "*Scientia* in the classical world meant reasoned disclosure of something for the sake of the disclosure itself. Up to the seventeenth century such disclosure consisted largely of classifications of things that were qualitatively different, but after Galileo it became the search for nature's quantitative laws" (Smith, 1982/1989, p. 83). The goal of the science of learning is to apply the scientific method to the factors that influence learning to help us use these results to design more effective instruction.

Four Ways to Search for Truth

Wallace (1971), based on W. P. Motague's (1925) *The Ways of Knowing*, stated that there are four major ways of generating and testing the truth of empirical statements: authoritarian, mystical, logico-rational, and scientific. The *authoritarian mode* seeks and tests knowledge by referring to those who are socially defined as qualified producers of knowledge (for example, oracles, elders, archbishops, kings, presidents, or professors). By relying on these authority figures, one does not have to worry about testing the truth of statements about reality. It is assumed that, because of their social status, authority figures have special knowledge in their area or expertise and will communicate that knowledge to others.

The *mystical mode* is partly related to the authoritarian. However, the authoritarian depends essentially on the social position of the knowledge-producer. On the other hand, the

25

mystical mode depends on the manifestations of the knowledge-consumer's personal "state of grace," and on his or her personal psychophysical state. Thus, an individual receives knowledge directly and the "truth" of the knowledge is judged by the strength of the accompanying emotional, physical, and psychological manifestations. Some experiences are felt to be so "real" that one would never question them. However, problems occur when we try to communicate the reality of such an experience to another individual who did not share the experience.

In the *logico-rational mode*, an individual judges whether statements are "true" by evaluating the procedure whereby the statements were produced. This procedure centers on the rules of formal logic.

Finally, the *scientific mode* relies on a combination of the observational effects of the statements in question, with a secondary reliance on the procedures (methods) used to generate them. The scientist rejects authority and mystical revelation as the basis for truth in favor of the collective search for truth using the scientific method (Wilson, 1952, p. 21).

The Scientific Method

The modern sense of science arose in the seventeenth century with the focus on empiricism and the development of the scientific method. This approach was extremely successful in augmenting humans' control over their environment. It was so successful that most people no longer question its validity. The essence of the scientific method is that scientists collaborate with one another in their search for "truth." To communicate effectively, scientists must speak the same language. Before examining the scientific method itself, the next sections discuss communication using the language of science.

The Language of Science

Scientists and philosophers have long struggled with how to accurately communicate with one another. How does one scientist give an account of behavior that another scientist can understand? Will the words that I use mean the same things to you as they mean to me? Will my account of a phenomenon enable you to understand it and possibly recreate it for your own purposes?

If scientists only needed to communicate an emotional or poetic description of behavior they could rely on "poetic license" without worrying about accuracy. If scientists only needed to describe a chronology of events they would only concern themselves with historic precision (e.g., the correct ordering of events). However, scientifically accurate communication must be more mathematically and logically precise than these other two approaches.

The philosopher Charles Morris (1938) described a system that can help us understand scientific language. He called his system *semiotics*, or the study of signs. A sign is a physical representation of a thing other than itself (e.g., words represented by ink on a page or sound waves produced in the throat). His system includes two sub-areas, *syntactics* (the relation of different signs to each other) and *semantics* (the relations of different signs to the objects to which they refer).

Syntactics. Syntactics deals with the formal rules for manipulating signs, the way signs are related to each other. For example, the rules of language tell us how to put words (signs) together to make grammatically correct sentences. Science often needs more precise languages than the spoken or written word. It finds such precision in the languages of logic and mathematics.

Logic and mathematics have their own rules for relating signs together. For example, the mathematical equation $M = \sum X/N$ can be manipulated in various ways according to the rules of arithmetic and algebra (e.g., $NM = \sum X$ or $N = \sum X/M$). These rules allow us to move the signs into different combinations even if the signs don't actually refer to anything. This example, as the reader may already have recognized, is the formula for the arithmetic mean, where M equals the mean, $\sum X$ is the sum of all the individual scores obtained, and N is the number of scores.

To summarize, "syntactics is concerned with the establishment and use of agreed-on rules by which we can relate signs (symbols or words) to each other so that there is no ambiguity about what we are doing" (Beck, 1978, p. 12). By following syntactic rules, scientists are more precise in their communication of signs. In addition, they also need to be precise in how they assign meaning to signs. They do this by following agreed rules of semantics.

Semantics. The term *semantics* refers to the rules we use to connect a sign to an object or event. It concerns the problem of definition. The simplest way to define something is to use the *ostensive* definition—to point at it. For example, saying "That is what I mean by a *cat*" while pointing to a cat. Since we cannot always point to something, other methods have been developed to help scientists define their concepts. One of the most universal methods used in science is *the operational definition*.

Operational Definitions and Converging Operations. Bridgeman (1927) suggested that we define the meaning of something in terms of how we measure it. For example, we define the term *length* by the procedures for measuring length (e.g., by laying down a standard rod repeatedly and counting the number of times it takes to go from one end of an object to the other). A scientist operationally defines a concept by describing in detail the operations that he or she will use to measure it.

Gardner, Hake, and Eriksen (1956) observed that a single set of operations rarely isolates just one concept. Rather, they suggested that we must use a series of operations to *converge* on a concept. Beck (1978) explains converging operations using the concept of response bias. In early studies of perception, researchers presented various stimuli to subjects very quickly using an instrument called a tachistoscope. It was often found that subjects had a higher recognition threshold (time to recognize the stimulus) for certain emotion-arousing stimuli (e.g., off-color words). Some assumed that these results were due to perception effects and several complex psychological mechanisms were postulated to explain them. However, Postman, Bronson, and Gropper (1953) believed that the results might be caused by response bias. Before showing the stimuli, they told different groups that recognizing the target words were either signs of good or poor mental health. A control group was given no instructions. The former "good mental health" group was quicker to "recognize" the words than the control group and the "poor mental health" group was slower than the control group. Thus, these experimental operations converged on the concept of response bias rather than on a perceptual explanation for the phenomenon.

A Simplified Model of the Scientific Method

Using the language of science, each scientist can more easily understand the results of other scientists and communicate his or her results to them. The quality of their results usually depends on how well they follow the principles of the scientific method Figure 1.1 is a simplified and idealized depiction of the scientific method (adapted from Graham, 1977; and Wallace, 1971). In actual practice, the scientific method may occur quickly or slowly, with a high degree of formalization and rigor, or informally and intuitively. It may be the result of the interaction of many scientists or through the efforts of one scientist. It sometimes only occurs in the scientist's imagination, or sometimes in actual fact.

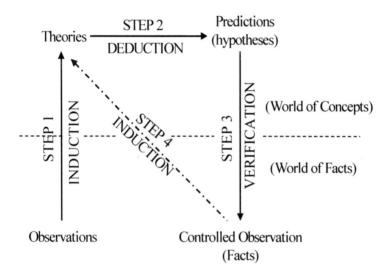

Figure 1.1:
A Simplified Model of the Scientific Method

The scientific method is a never-ending cycle that continuously improves upon its explanations. It can be subdivided into four stages or steps. Although any given scientist might start at any point in the cycle, for purposes of this discussion we start with *observations* of events in the world. If these events are observed often enough or by more than one person, scientists begin to see relationships among the events. In step 1, the scientist uses *induction* (the process of establishing general principles from specific observations) to develop some empirical generalizations about the observed events. For example, a scientist might use a barometer to record the changes in air pressure over several days and summarize these observations into an empirical generalization (e.g., on sunny days the pressure is higher than on rainy days). Similarly, we might observe that learners receiving one-on-one tutoring perform better on exams than learners in a group classroom setting (Bloom, 1984; Chi, Siler, Jeong, Yamauci, & Hausmann, 2001).

Empirical generalizations, in turn, are items of information that can be synthesized into a *theory* or "an interconnected system of ideas composed of abstract concepts and rules for relating these concepts to the observed facts" (Graham, 1977, p. 8). For example, the scientist might derive a concept of air pressure and precipitation from his or her empirical generalizations. These may result in the generation of a theory that storms are more likely under conditions of low air pressure. Following our learning example, we might generalize that tutoring is more effective because the learner has more opportunities to interact with the instructor than in a regular classroom.

In Step 2, a theory may be used to suggest further relationships or predictions about conditions in the real world through the method of *logical deduction*. The scientist deduces that if he or she measures low air pressure, a storm is likely. Or we might deduce that increasing the opportunities for interaction in a computer-delivered course will result in improved learning. Forming this deduction into a *hypothesis*, the scientist can then, through the process of *verification* (Step 3), test its relationship to reality by making new, controlled observations. The goal of the controlled observations is to minimize sources of error in the verification test (usually an experiment). If sources of error are not minimized, we have no way of knowing that the observed effect is the result of the variable of interest rather than other unknown variables (Winer, 1962, pp. 9-13). These controlled verification tests may result in a new informational outcome: namely, a decision to accept or reject the tested hypothesis.

As mentioned in the preceding section on the language of science, an important sub-step in developing and testing a hypothesis is the development of an *operational definition*. This is the definition of a hypothesis "in terms of the operations and observations to which it refers" (Sutherland, 1989, p. 292). Thus, a scientist must explain, in detail, the methods, equipment, and other operations used to test the truth of the hypothesis in the real world. For example, intelligence is often defined by how people perform on an intelligence test or hunger as the length of time since last eating.

Care should always be taken to examine the logic behind the operational definitions in any research effort when interpreting the data that result from the effort. Continuing our previous examples, the scientist would need to clearly define how he or she would measure air pressure. Air pressure might be operationally defined by describing how it is measured using a specific devise like a barometer. To investigate the effectiveness of enhanced instructional interactions, the instructional researcher would need to clearly define instructional interaction and how he or she would measure it. Then, two versions of the computer-delivered course, with different levels of instructional interaction (as operationally defined), could then be developed and used to determine if learners are more successful when experiencing the higher interaction version.

Finally, in Step 4, the results of the controlled observations are interpreted and are then used to inductively support, modify, or reject the theory. This may lead to the development of new hypotheses that can be further tested as the cycle continues.

The majority of this book is inductive. It uses systems theory to organize the large body of empirical data that has been generated from many learning research efforts. It is hoped that this theoretical perspective can help the reader understand existing learning data and also to help researchers deduce new hypotheses and design new experiments to generate additional data to advance our understanding of learning and instructional processes. One should not assume that this idealized description of the scientific method is always followed. However, the general approach of science, since the seventeenth century, has been to strive for this ideal, toward the generation of testable theories through empirical observation.

Scientific Theories. As discussed above, the scientific method uses theories to create hypotheses that can be tested in the real world. Toulmin (1953) explained how scientific theories can never explain everything by comparing a scientific theory to a map. One uses a map to describe an area of reality (e.g., the geographical terrain). The map may not show every rock or stream or may include information, like latitude and longitude that is not found on the terrain itself. Maps of a city may show sewer lines, power lines, streets, or population density. Which map shows the real city? None of the maps are "real," but each is a representation of particular items or events and each is useful for its purpose. Scientific theories also describe a portion of reality for a specific purpose.

In a scientific theory, observable events are summarized by "mapping" them into theoretical terms. "Concepts are defined in terms of particular observable events (semantics) and the theory states how the concepts are related to each other (syntactics). Predictions are made on the basis of this syntax" (Beck, 1978, p. 15). For example, Hull (1943) proposed that performance is determined by motivation and learning. His theory is summarized in his famous equation $E = H \times D$, where E is excitatory potential (performance), H is habit (learning) and D is drive (motivation).

Beck (1978, p. 16) used Hull's equation to explain the relationships between observations, definitions, and theoretical concepts. Figure 1.2 illustrates these relationships. Hull's theory is shown on the top row. These theoretical concepts are defined by specific control procedures and measurements. The controls are the *independent* variables (IV) in the experimental situation and that which is measured is the *dependent* variable (DV). If we hold one independent variable constant (e.g., H) while we systematically change the value of the other (D), the measured outcome should tell us how D affects the dependent variable (E). If the theory does not predict the outcome, we may need to change the syntax, add new concepts, eliminate old concepts or scrap the theory. Although Hull's theory did explain some data on learning in animals, subsequent research has demonstrated that Hull's theory is not sufficient to explain many diverse learning phenomena. In recent years, scientists have begun to recognize that their methods of observation and the types of theories they choose to test are highly dependent on their current orientation or scientific paradigm.

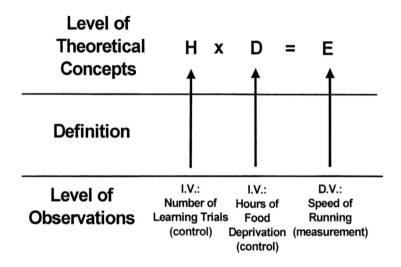

Figure 1.2:
Relationships among Observations, Definitions, and Theoretical concepts in Hull's Theory of Behavior

Scientific Progress through Paradigms

In the early 1960s, a small book written by Thomas Kuhn rocked the scientific world. This book, *The Structure of Scientific Revolutions*, was a discussion of how science is not the pure, objective enterprise in which we would like to believe. It is created by humans and is affected by our imperfections like any other human endeavor.

Kuhn (1962/1970) distinguishes between "normal" science and "revolutionary" science. He appropriated the word *paradigm*, meaning an accepted model or pattern, to refer to the accepted world-view of normal science. A paradigm provides the basis for "the intertwined theoretical and methodological beliefs that permits selection, evaluation, and criticism" (Kuhn, 1962/1970, p. 17). The accepted paradigm defines which theories are "important" and should be used to guide research. If a theory falls outside the normal paradigm, it is often ignored by many scientists. For example, during the 1940s and 1950s, most psychologists thought behavior was merely responses to stimuli (the behaviorist paradigm). As more data were accumulated, many observations indicated that different organisms (or individuals) often responded differently to the same stimulus. This led to a shift toward a more cognitively oriented paradigm during the 1960s.

The role of *normal science* is to maintain the accepted paradigm, which narrows its area of interest and provides the context for its accepted theories. A paradigm is like a "prism" through which certain phenomena are included for inquiry while others are excluded. Thus, scientists may not seek information that will contradict their accepted world-view because they are so locked into the current paradigm.

Revolutionary science occurs through the observation of anomalies that contradict the theories of the accepted paradigm. However, normal science is organized to ignore most of these anomalies. Only when enough anomalous information is observed do scientists begin to question the accepted paradigm and perhaps replace it with a new paradigm. This is a critical point. Science always requires a guiding paradigm. "To reject one paradigm without simultaneously substituting another is to reject science itself" (Kuhn, 1962/1970, p. 79).

We may therefore characterize science as progressing through a series of revolutionary shifts that result in whole new world-views. We also need to remember that "a scientific theory is usually felt to be better than its predecessors not only in the sense that it is a better instrument for discovering and solving puzzles but also because it is somehow a better representation of what nature is really like" (Kuhn, 1962/1970, p. 206). In the area of learning, a major shift in paradigms occurred when behaviorism gave way to more cognitively oriented theories and instructional approaches. General Systems Theory (von Bertalanffy, 1968) and subsequent systems theories (discussed in the next chapter) may also be viewed as a new paradigm.

The Nature and Purpose of Science

The nature of science has been described as consisting of three levels: objectivity, prediction, and control (Smith, 1982/1989, p. 83). *Objectivity* is defined in the sense of consensual or inter-subjective agreement, not in the sense of mirroring the way things are in themselves, or what has been called the "camera theory of knowledge." For example, two persons walking in a shopping mall may "see" very different things. A child "sees" candy and toy stores, but his mother "sees" clothing stores and gift shops. Neither view is entirely correct, but both can agree that they are at a mall. *Prediction* refers to the ability of science to forecast the occurrence or progression of some type of phenomenon. *Control* is the ability to produce, end, or change the course of some phenomenon.

By the end of the twentieth century, the general consensus was that the purpose of science was to provide explanations of natural phenomena (including human phenomena like learning) with a special emphasis on the ability to predict and control, and hence to manipulate the physical environment (Rubenstein, Laughlin, and McManus, 1984). In general, the closer one moves toward control, the more "scientific" one becomes.

One of the goals of the science of learning should be to help us understand how instruction can be designed to increase the success of the learner. It should help us determine which specific instructional approaches should be applied to help learn specific knowledge and skills. It should then help us evaluate and improve instructional designs and applications. Whenever we apply the scientific method to learning and instructional issues we need to be aware of and control for possible mistakes. The next section is a summary of some of these possible mistakes.

Possible Mistakes in Science

Scientists are human beings and can make mistakes like anyone else. This is true in general as well as for the science of learning. Wilson (1952) and Babbie (1975) discuss some of the mistakes that can lead scientists to make unwarranted conclusions or recommendations. Many of these are interrelated and can combine to lead to even larger mistakes.

Inaccurate observation: Mistakes can be made during measurement, data collection, and data analysis. Scientific procedures are specifically designed to reduce these errors. Although not 100% effective, "the care with which scientific observations are made is an important norm of science" (Babbie, 1975, p. 14). One example of problems with observation is the use of untrained raters judging the performance of learners. This approach is often used in aviation training. An experienced pilot may be "assigned" the duty of rating pilot trainees without being trained on a standardized rating methodology. Such subjective ratings may differ across different trainees or different raters. This makes it difficult to determine how the trainees compared to one another and whether a specific instructional approach is effective.

Overgeneralization: This occurs when the scientist imagines broad patterns on the basis of relatively few specific observations. Overgeneralization can be of two forms. First, the results can be mistakenly applied to a population that is different from the population that was tested. An example, which will be discussed in Chapter 3, is the overgeneralization of research results from children in the classroom to applications of computer-based instruction for adult learning. Secondly, conclusions can be drawn that are not supported by the data. Perhaps the chief safeguard against overgeneralization is replication of research efforts (sometimes under slightly varied conditions). An example of this type of overgeneralization is the assumption that because young people play a lot of video games, electronic games should be used more often in computer-based instruction even though very little data exist to support this assumption (see Chapter 11).

Selective Observation: Scientists can yield to the temptation to focus on future observations that correspond with the pattern they have concluded to exist and ignore contradictory observations. This is sometimes found in literature summaries that are used to justify an experiment. One clue that should make one suspicious is a bibliography with a preponderance of the author's own references.

Deducing Unobserved Information: Scientists are sometimes tempted to explain away ambiguous or contradictory observations on the basis of their preconceived notions rather than observed data. This can sometimes lead to selective data collection until the preconceived notion is "supported."

Illogical Reasoning: Sometimes scientists fail to apply clear logic or use illogical reasoning. One example is confusing necessary and sufficient conditions. For example, just because a victim of a certain disease always loses weight does not mean that anyone losing weight has a given disease. Confusion can also occur when two events are falsely related as cause and effect when both are actually the result of a third factor. For example, researchers may find that cigarette smokers are often depressed and may illogically conclude that smoking causes depression. Additional research may find that a third variable (e.g., neuroticism) is a cause of both smoking and depression. Another example of illogical reasoning is explaining contradictory data with the trite phrase "the exception that proves the rule." Illogical reasoning can be avoided by applying systems of logic consciously and explicitly (e.g., probability theory can sometimes explain "exceptions").

Premature closure of Inquiry: Scientists want to be "successful." Sometimes this desire, combined with some of the above mistakes, can lead scientists to "positive declarations of success" before they have fully explored the area of interest.

Ego Involvement in Understanding: As human beings, scientists can sometimes succumb to egotistical defensiveness regarding their own ideas and conclusions. A full commitment to the norms, rules, and methods of science can help scientists to recognize their own errors.

Guiding Principles of the Scientific Method

To guard against the mistakes discussed above, Wilson (1952), Beveridge (1957), Tart (1973) and Valiela (2001) provide some basic guiding principles of the scientific method to which a scientific investigator must be committed.

1. *Good Observation*. Scientists continuously search for better ways to observe the world. Controlled observation is the only way that we can be assured that our hypotheses concerning the causal effects of one variable (e.g., practice) on another (e.g., learning) is supported. What the scientist chooses to observe is dictated by his or her scientific orientation, or

paradigm. This orientation makes the scientist selective. "It is necessary to limit what is to be observed to a portion of the universe small enough to be encompassed" (Wilson, 1952, p. 22). Beyond this, the observer's own characteristics also affect the phenomena observed. Physicists recognized in the early twentieth century that the act of observation altered the process under study. Behavioral researchers have more recently realized that there is no such thing as a "detached observer," since scientists are affected by their own biases regarding the phenomenon under study (Rosenthal, 1966). Some of these biases can be overcome by the public nature of scientific observation. Other biases can be overcome by using experimental designs such as the "double blind," where the experimenter does not know which subjects receive the experimental treatment and which subjects serve as controls.

2. *The Public Nature of Observation.* Scientific observations should be public in the sense that they can be repeated, or replicated by other trained observers. "The essence of any satisfactory experiment is that it should be reproducible" (Beveridge, 1957, p. 23). Replication is the major means of increasing our confidence in the results of any single investigation. "A scientific observer is never afraid to allow others to view the phenomena in which he is interested. He should welcome checks and repetitions of his work as adding to their certainty" (Wilson, 1952, p. 23). Unfortunately, most scientific journals only publish "original" research rather than replications of previous research.

3. *The Need to Theorize Logically.* Theories must logically and consistently account for the things a scientist has observed. "We require that the actual facts be reported, that we are told how the facts were obtained, and that the reasoning used to reach a conclusion from the facts shown be explicit" (Valiela, 2001, p. 5). Changing the basic assumptions of a theory can change a scientist's explanation of the same data. For example, an increase in the observed suicide rate among a certain group could be explained as a result of its members' lack of self-concept. This psychologically oriented theory focuses on the individual. An alternate explanation of the same data, from a social perspective, might locate the causal

factors for increased suicide rate in the breakdown of the supporting societal mechanisms.

4. *Testing of Theory by Observable Consequences.* Scientists test theories by using them to predict certain outcomes and then determining whether the outcomes can be verified by observation. There is no necessity that the outcomes produce physical effects. Any effect, even those that occur in the human mind can be used to test a theory as long as these effects change something that is observable. For example, even though we can not locate a specific new thought in someone's brain, one can infer that learning has occurred if an individual is able to demonstrate a new skill or item of knowledge.

Beveridge (1957) and Graham (1977) provided several summary principles to help people think more "scientifically." Scientific thinking is not just important for scientists. It is just as important for those trying to interpret and implement the results of scientific investigations to improve learning.

Always consult original articles. One should never assume that the data cited in a secondary source are correct or that they have been interpreted correctly. Read the original article and then interpret the data yourself to determine if you agree with the original conclusions and if they can be applied in your specific situation.

Only view experimental results as valid for the precise conditions under which the experiments were conducted. Be very careful about drawing conclusions that go beyond the data. Do not jump to conclusions based on insufficient evidence. It is easy to confuse facts with their interpretations. A fairly extensive amount of data is needed before any generalizations can be made.

Don't regard any confirmed hypothesis as true. Think of it as, at best, partially true.

Be ready to abandon or modify a hypothesis as soon as it is shown to be inconsistent with the facts.

Always try to state the problem as precisely as you can in terms of observable or measurable events.

Chapter 2
A Scientific Approach to
Instructional Development

Why do we need to apply science to the development of instruction? Because it works! In the last four hundred years, science has helped us make enormous strides in our understanding of the world around us. Just as in investigations of the physical world, science is the most efficient method to seek knowledge about human learning and methods to improve learning. This author believes that all instruction should be systematically developed and based upon scientifically derived data. Instruction should also be evaluated using the scientific method so that there can be agreement on how it was evaluated and on whether it was effective. Using science to develop and evaluate instruction will help us avoid wasting money and other resources on ineffective instructional approaches.

The Scientific Method and the Instructional Systems Development

It can be argued that the scientific method is the intellectual foundation for all subsequent system process models (e.g., Instructional Systems Development, acquisition processes, manufacturing processes, etc.). Iterative steps, that serve to self-correct and improve understanding, are the guiding principles of the scientific method. These are also the goals of most system process models. Systems theory is the organizing perspective for this book. Before discussing Instructional Systems Development (ISD), we first examine the defining characteristics of systems and systems theories.

Defining Characteristics of Systems

Although specific definitions of systems differ (e.g., Churchman, 1968; Koestler, 1969; Laszlo, 1972; Ruesch, 1969; van Gigch, 1978; Wright, R., 1989), a system can be defined by the following characteristics:

41

1. Systems are bounded sets of *interrelated parts*, such that changes in one part will cause changes in the other parts. This has important implications for instructional interventions. Without an understanding of the entire instructional system, an intervention may cause unwanted changes in other parts of the system.

2. Systems act to maintain their *internal consistency* even in the face of external changes. Related to the first characteristic, systems act to balance themselves by resisting changes. Thus, an instructional intervention may be counteracted by these changes in other system parts or other interacting systems.

3. The *emergent qualities* of a system cannot be explained by mere addition of parts. Rather, these qualities must be explained by and examination of the relations and interactions within the system. Thus an instructional system cannot be merely "assembled." It must be designed explicitly to result in positive learning outcomes.

4. Systems are always *embedded in a hierarchy of subsystems and suprasystems*, and interactions occur between systems levels at all times. Every system is a component (subsystem) of a larger system. The larger system, which includes the system of interest is called a suprasystem. Figure 2.1 illustrates this relationship. It is also likely that a system may be affected by multiple suprasystems (see Figure 2.2). It is important to understand these relationships because instructional interventions may be counteracted by policies or actions of one or more suprasystems. For example, a new instructional simulation may not prove effective because an overriding policy, such as time limits on course length, may result in insufficient practice time for learners. It is important to identify and understand the interactions between system components and levels in any instructional system to ensure that an instructional intervention performs in the manner it was intended.

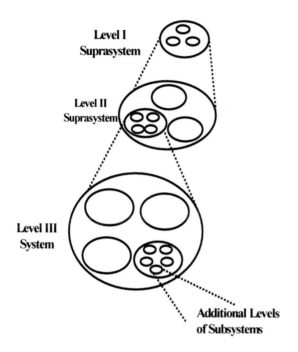

Level I
Suprasystem

Level II
Suprasystem

Level III
System

Additional Levels
of Subsystems

**Figure 2.1:
Levels of Systems**

5. Systems take inputs of information or energy and convert them (using internal processes) to outputs. Any system process (including learning) can be described in terms of input, throughput (central processes), and output. This three-phase description will be used to discuss a variety of learning issues and processes throughout the remainder of the book.

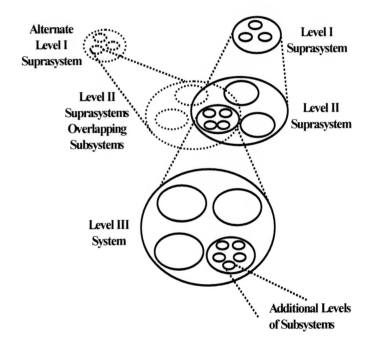

Figure 2.2:
Interactions among Systems

Systems Theories

Systems have been recognized, if not labeled as systems, at least since Aristotle began his study of living organisms (Gaines, 1978). Darwin studied the interactions of living systems in the process of natural selection (Darwin, 1952). Psychophysicists (those who study the measurement of sensation) have studied the actions and interactions of various systems within the organism in their study of sensation and perception (Gibson, 1966; Schiffman, 1976). Psychologists have used systems concepts to understand the variables that operate in organizations (Katz & Kahn, 1978).

General Systems Theory (GST) is a term coined by biologist Ludwig von Bertalanffy (1968) to describe the theoretical approach to understanding complex biological systems. Systems approaches have been successfully used in a wide variety of areas, including cybernetics (Wiener, 1948), communication theories (Shannon & Weaver, 1949), automata theory (von Neumann, 1956), fuzzy set theory (Bellman & Zadeh, 1970), and Living Systems Theory (Miller, J. G., 1978).

Living Systems Theory postulates that all living systems include 19 critical subsystems that conduct processes that are essential to the continued viability of the system. It also postulates this is true no matter which type of system is examined, from the cell to the multinational system. Table 2.1 lists and describes the 19 critical subsystems and Table 2.2 shows examples of the 19 subsystems at the level of the organism and the group. These 19 subsystem processes are relatively simple in lower level systems (e.g., the cell), often carried out by a single component. However, in more complex systems (e.g., the organism or the group) these processes are "shredded out" to multiple components, which combine in various ways to carry out the processes (Miller, J. G., 1978). When we begin to examine the learning process, we can expect to encounter "multiple sub processes which are mapped upon multiple structures" (p. 26).

In the 1950s and early 1960s, systems theory and systems analysis began to be applied in the fields of training and education (e.g., Miller, R. B., 1954; Kershaw & McKean, 1959; Hoehn, 1960). In 1975, the military services adopted the Instructional Systems Development (ISD) approach to organize and guide the development and procurement of all military training systems (Branson, Rayner, Cox, Furman, King, & Hannum, 1975).

Incomplete or mixed applications of ISD have led some people to conclude that it is not an effective method to develop instructional products (see the discussion in Chapter 3). However, considerable evidence has demonstrated the negative consequences of fragmented training development. For example, Hritz and Purifoy (1980) reported that information from training requirements analysts is often inadequately transferred to training device

Table 2.1
The 19 Critical Subsystems of a Living System

Subsystems Which Process Both Matter-Energy and Information

1. **Reproducer**, the subsystem which is capable of giving rise to other systems similar to the one it is in.

2. **Boundary**, the subsystem at the perimeter of a system that holds together the components, which make up the system, protects them from environmental stresses, and excludes or permits entry to various sorts of matter-energy and information.

Subsystems Which Process Matter-Energy	Subsystems Which Process Information
3. **Ingestor**, the subsystem which brings matter-energy across the system boundary from the environment.	11. **Input transducer**, the sensory subsystem which brings markers bearing information into the system, changing them to other matter-energy forms suitable for transmission within it.
	12. **Internal transducer**, the sensory subsystem which receives, from subsystems or components within the system, markers bearing information about significant alterations in those subsystems or components, changing them to other matter-energy forms of a sort which can be transmitted within it.
4. **Distributor**, the subsystem which carries inputs from outside the system around the system to each component.	13. **Channel and net**, the subsystem composed of a single route in physical space, or multiple interconnected routes, by which markers bearing information are transmitted to all parts of the system.
5. **Converter**, the subsystem which changes certain inputs to the system into forms more useful for the special processes of that particular system.	14. **Decoder**, the subsystem which alters the code of information input to it through the input transducer or internal transducer into a "private" code that can be used internally by the system.
6. **Producer**, the subsystem which forms stable associations that endure for significant periods among matter-energy inputs to the system or outputs from its converter, the materials synthesized being for growth, damage repair, or replacement of components of the system, or for providing energy for moving or constituting the system's outputs of products or information markers to its suprasystem.	15. **Associator**, the subsystem which carries out the first stage of the learning process, forming enduring associations among items of information in the system.

Table 2.1
(continued)

Subsystems Which Process Matter-Energy	Subsystems Which Process Information
7. **Matter-energy storage**, the subsystem which retains in the system for different periods of time, deposits of various sorts of matter-energy.	16. **Memory**, the subsystem which carries out the second stage of the learning process, storing various sorts of information in the system for different periods of time. 17. **Decider**, the executive subsystem, which receives information, inputs from all other subsystems and transmits to them information outputs that control the entire system. 18. **Encoder**, the subsystem which alters the code of information input to it from other information processing subsystems, from a "private" code used internally by the system into a "public" code, which can be interpreted, by other systems in its environment.
8. **Extruder**, the subsystem that transmits matter-energy out of the system in the form of products or wastes. 9. **Motor**, the subsystem which moves the system or parts of it in relation to part or all of its environment in relation to each other.	19. **Output transducer**, the subsystem which puts out markers bearing information from the system, changing markers within the system into other matter-energy forms which can be transmitted over channels in the system's environment.
10. **Supporter**, the subsystem which maintains the proper spatial relationships among components of the system, sot that they can interact without weighting each other down or crowding each other.	

Table 2.2:
Examples of the 19 Critical Subsystems
in an Organism and a Group

Subsystems Which Process Both Matter-Energy and Information		
	Organism	**Group**
Reproducer	Eggs, sperm, sex glands	Persons that produce implicit or explicit charter for group.
Boundary	Epidermis, fur, hair, artifacts (hat, coat, astronauts suit)	Membership committee, sergeant-at-arms, artifacts (room, building, wall)

Subsystems Which Process Matter-Energy			Subsystems Which Process Information		
	Organism	**Group**		**Organism**	**Group**
Ingestor	Mouth, jaws, artifacts (stomach tube, syringe)	Refreshment committee, budget manager who accepts fund transfers	**Input Transducer**	Components of all sensory modalities (e.g., eyes, ears, chemoreceptors), artifacts (radio receiver).	Lookout, scout, artifacts (e-mail)
			Internal Transducer	Postsynaptic regions of neurons	Subgroup or person who receives information about group tasks and conveys it to decider
Distributor	Blood & lymph vascular systems	Person who passes out tools to work group, artifacts (delivery truck)	**Channel and Net**	Network of neurons, hormones (conveyed by blood and lymph systems)	Each group member who communicates to other members, artifacts (written messages)
Converter	Mouth, teeth, digestive system	Chopper of wood, butcher, artifacts (hand tools)	**Decoder**	Retinal bipolar and ganglion cells, cochlear bipolar cells	Guide, interpreter, radar man

**Table 2.2
(continued)**

	Subsystems Which Process Matter-Energy			Subsystems Which Process Information	
	Organism	**Group**		**Organism**	**Group**
Produ-cer	None known at this level. Processes are dispersed downwardly to the level of the cell.	Cook, tailor, maintenance technician	**Associator**	Specific components not known	Laterally dispersed to members who associate bits of information, artifacts (databases)
Matter-Energy Storage	Fatty tissues, liver, bone marrow	Stock clerk, spare-parts man	**Memory**	Brain processes (specific components not known).	Secretaries, treasurers, artifacts (notes, computer files).
			Decider	Areas of the cerebral cortex; artifacts (e.g., calculator).	Chairperson, selected specialists.
			Encoder	Areas of the cerebral cortex (e.g., temporo-parietal area of dominant hemisphere).	Persons composing letter, briefing, or statement presenting views of group.

procurement personnel. This is sometimes because the requirements analysts are transferred to new jobs before their information has been communicated. Caro (1977) observed that the lack of systematic instructional development reduces program effectiveness because curriculum designers are out of touch with end-user needs. Kaufman (1990) observed that various personnel involved in different aspects of instructional program development do not share vocabularies and "mind sets." This often results in conflicting goals and orientations. The use of specific terminology

Table 2.2
(continued)

	Subsystems Which Process Matter-Energy			Subsystems Which Process Information	
	Organism	**Group**		**Organism**	**Group**
Extru-der	Kidneys, rectum, breathing passages, sweat glands	Janitor, "bouncer"	**Output Trans-ducer**	Exocrine glands, inferior frontal cortex of dominant hemisphere of human brain, artifacts (pencil, radio transmitter, computer network)	Subgroups or individuals who deliver reports or statements for the group (spokesman, publicity agent, chairman)
Motor	Muscles, bones and joints, legs, artifacts (cane, cart, automobile)	Artifacts (bus, truck, plane), may be laterally dispersed to persons who plan and execute group movement			
Suppor-ter	Skeleton, tendons, muscles, artifacts (chair, platform)	Person(s) supporting others in group, artifacts (e.g., room car, furniture)			

that has been agreed upon by all persons, as advocated in the scientific method and the language of science, can help avoid these types of conflicts.

Some studies have demonstrated the advantages of ISD and systems approaches to training development. For example, Tracey (1984) demonstrated that by applying a complete requirements analysis, the Army could cut a significant number of non-essential tasks from its Electronic Equipment Repair Supervisor course. Rose and Martin (1988) showed how a computer-based requirements analysis tool which "forced" analysts to use a systematic approach helped reduce the cost of an Air Force maintenance trainer by several million dollars. Flanagan (1984) summarized a systematic analysis effort that helped the American Red Cross reduce the course time from 10-20 hours to 7.5 hours. Furthermore, the resulting course also enabled the learner to successfully complete 88% of learning objectives compared to only 47% from the previous longer course. Markle (1967) showed how course times were shortened in a first aid and safety course after applying ISD methods. Campbell, Feddern, Graham, & Morganlander (1977) reported that an aircrew training program was more effectively designed when ISD methods were followed. An additional example was described by Steinberg, Avner, Call-Himwich, Francis, Himwich, Klecka, and Misselt (1977). They reported that quality PLATO lessons could not be produced unless the authors took a systematic approach. Without the application of ISD methods, the courseware authors failed to complete lessons on time or focused on the use of graphics and other computer factors that produced instructionally ineffective lessons.

Hays discussed a variety of system concepts that affect the quality of training systems (1992) and web-delivered instructional products (2001). Foremost among these system concepts is:

> *Any instructional program or product is part of a larger instructional system. A change introduced by the instructional program can affect the system as a whole. Likewise, other system processes or components can modify or negate the effects of an instructional program.*

This is why it is vitally important that instructional policy, design, and implementation decisions be guided by a system perspective and by principles derived from the science of learning. Furthermore, the implications of these decisions should be understood from a system perspective (e.g., be guided by principles that address and account for system processes and effects). The consequences of "falling off of the path" of science when developing instruction include:

- Establishment of ineffective instructional policies
- Delivery of ineffective instructional products
- Wasted resources (time and money)
- Increased customer skepticism (e.g., "This didn't work, why try it again?")

Instructional Systems Development

Instructional Systems development (ISD) is a controlled process for designing instructional systems and evaluating their effectiveness. An instructional system can be defined as follows:

> ***An instructional system*** *is the planned interaction of people, materials, and techniques, which has the goal of improved performance as measured by established criteria.*

These criteria are usually established by educational standards and on-the-job requirements (Hays & Singer, 1989; Hays, 1992). Table 2.3 lists the major elements of an instructional system under the three categories mentioned in the above definition.

Table 2.3
The Major Elements of an Instructional System

People	Materials	Techniques
• Students (trainees) • Instructors (teachers) • Course/content Developers • Computer programmers • Administrators • Logistics Managers • Subject Matter Experts • Instructional consultants • Instructional Aids, Equipment, & Simulator Developers • On-the-job Supervisors • Instructional System Researchers	• Instructional content • Instructional Aids, Equipment, & Simulators • Instructional Requirements Documents • Evaluation Instruments • Instructional Development Tools (e.g. authoring systems)	• Instructional Design Approaches • Instructional Strategies and Techniques • Development Methods • Instructional Aids, Equipment, & Simulation Design Methods • Needs Analysis Techniques • Effectiveness Evaluation Methods • Performance measurement tools • Instructional quality evaluation methods • Return on Investment Analysis Methods

The *interactions,* which take place in instructional systems occur during the development cycle and during the delivery of instruction. ISD is a process that consists of a series of iterative steps, phases, or stages. Various authors have summarized the ISD process using different numbers of steps (e.g., Bransford, Rayner, Cox, Furman, King, & Hannum, 1975). Figure 2.3 shows a four-stage depiction of the ISD cycle and some correspondences between its four stages and the steps of the scientific method (Figure 1.1).

The instructional development cycle normally begins with an analysis of instructional needs. This corresponds to the first step of the scientific method, induction, or observation of the real world. Next, a program of instruction is developed. This stage is often

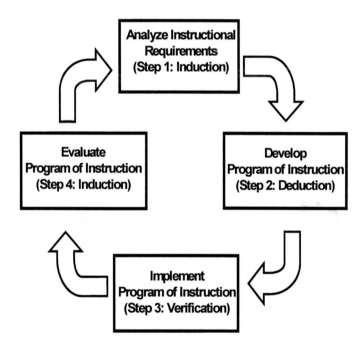

Figure 2.3:
Correspondences between the Stages of Instructional Systems Development and the Steps of the Scientific Method.

separated into design and development (this separation results in the acronym ADDIE as opposed to ADIE). Development corresponds to the second step of the scientific method, deduction, or developing ideas about how the program of instruction is expected to work. The implementation of the program of instruction corresponds to the third step of the scientific method, verification. Here the program is tried out in an instructional context to verify whether the program can be implemented (e.g., are the facilities sufficient, does all software work, will policy allow implementation). Finally, when implemented, the program of instruction is evaluated. This corresponds to the fourth step of the scientific method, induction based on controlled observations. This takes us back to the beginning of the instructional system development cycle where we can apply what we have learned to improve the instructional program or future programs. In Chapter 13, a successful instructional development project (the Virtual Environment for Submarine Ship Handling Training) will be summarized to illustrate one ISD cycle.

This conceptualization is for illustrative purposes only. One should not regard these correspondences as exact. However, the guiding principles behind the scientific method are the same as those behind the ISD process. Both are cyclic and never ending. Both rely upon logical reasoning, controlled observations, and iterative improvements.

A Systems Model of Learning and Instruction

Living Systems Theory (Miller, J. G., 1978) maintains that all living systems, from the cell to the multinational organization, are "open systems composed of subsystems which process inputs, throughputs, and outputs of various forms of matter, energy, and information" (p. 1). All the people and organizations involved in any aspect of instructional development or delivery are engaged in system processes.

Structure, Process, and Emergents

Before discussing instructional processes, it is useful to understand the relationship between the *structure* of a system and its system *processes.* "The structure of a system is the arrangement of its subsystems and components in three-dimensional space at a given moment in time: (Miller, J. G., 1978, p. 22). This structure supports and may be affected by the process or processes in which the system engages. The structure "may remain relatively fixed for a long period or it may change from moment to moment, depending upon the characteristics of the process in the system" (p. 22). It is the system's processes that determine how and if the system will change. "All change over time of matter-energy or information in a system is *process*" (p. 23, author's emphasis).

In complex systems, various processes sometimes "shred out" across multiple structures. "Shred out" is a term coined by James Grier Miller to describe how various structures in a complex system share different roles to complete a given process, somewhat like a sort of division of labor. "Each process is broken down into multiple subprocesses, which are mapped upon multiple structures, each of which becomes specialized for carrying out a subprocess" (Miller, J. G., 1978, p. 26). Sometimes, these system processes, especially in complex systems like human learners, can result in new unanticipated system characteristics called *emergents.* Miller explains that emergents arise because "a measure of the sum of a system's units is larger than the sum of that measure of its units" (Miller, J. G. 1978, p. 28). This is sometimes stated as *the whole is greater than the sum of its parts.* We can conceive of learning as an emergent characteristic of the learner that is a result of the instructional process. Learning "appears to involve qualitative restructuring and modification of schemata; it has an emergent quality" (Glasser & Bassok, 1989, p. 634).

Many theories of learning attempt to describe and further our understanding of the processes that are involved in learning. Far fewer theories focus on the structures involved in learning. There are at least two reasons for this: (1) only recently have scientific techniques been available to examine specific areas of the brain to determine how they are involved in learning; and (2) it is likely that multiple brain structures interact during learning and performance. Keeping the above structure and process issues in mind, the next section discusses process analysis as it is applied to instructional systems and specifically the system called *the learner.*

Process Analysis

An analysis of the characteristics and interactions among instructional system processes is a useful method for understanding the variables involved in instruction and learning. Often process analyses follow an information processing approach by defining processes by examining their inputs (how and what information enters the process), their throughputs or central processes (what is done with the information), and their outputs (how and what information leaves the process). Each instructional system activity can be better understood by examining its unique inputs, throughputs and outputs. The learner, as a system, receives inputs (information to be learned), transforms and stores that information (using a variety of central processes), and produces some output (e.g., demonstrated knowledge or skill). Instruction can be characterized as various interactions with the learner during each process phase. Some of these interactions are illustrated in Figure 2.4.

The middle column of Figure 2.4 shows the three learning process phases: input, central, and output. As mentioned above, any system process, including learning, can be described using these three process phases. The left column highlights these learning process phases from the perspective of the learner. The input to the learner is the information that he or she must learn. The learner's central processes include the variety of learning mechanisms that mostly occur internal to learner. These mechanisms operate on the input information to organize it in such a manner that it can be stored and later retrieved when needed. As we shall see in later chapters, a large segment of the research on learning has sought to understand these learning mechanisms. The learner's performance is the output that helps us determine if learning has occurred. If learning has been successful, the learner is able to demonstrate new knowledge or skills.

Learner	Process Phases	Instructional Focus
Information to be Learned	Input	Design of Instructional Content
Learning Mechanisms	Central (Throughput)	Application of Instructional Techniques
Performance	Output	Evaluation of Learning

Figure 2.4:
Learning as a System Process

The right side of Figure 2.4 shows the main focus of some instructional activities that target the learning process in each phase. The instructional content (learner input) must be designed so the learner will be able to take it into his or her system. This may require specifically organizing the information to make it relevant to the learner so it allows him or her to relate it to previously learned information. The instructional information must be delivered using some combination of instructional techniques that will assist the learner to successfully process the instructional information (central processes). This is where various instructional techniques or instructional media are applied. Finally, the learner's performance must be evaluated (learner output) to determine if he or she has successfully met the objectives of the course.

These processes phases interact with one another in complex ways with a number of factors acting to constrain these process interactions. In his analysis of communication, Ruesch (1969) referred to these constraining factors as "screens, which may prevent messages from being properly directed, quantified, or encoded" (p. 151). One goal of researchers in the science of learning is to more fully understand and beneficially control learning processes. An analysis of processes activities and screens can help organize and understand many of these learning system processes. To aid in this analysis, a systems model of the learner is presented and discussed in the next section. This model will be used throughout the remainder of the book to help the reader to organize and understand subsequent discussions of learning theories and data from the perspective of the learner.

The Learner as a System

Learning is a complex phenomenon as we shall see in subsequent chapters when we review the many learning theories and the large amount of empirical data that support them. In order to help the reader more easily understand the many interrelated factors that explain learning, a learner-centered model is presented below. "A model is a simplified representation of the real world. Models are created by speculating about processes that could have produced the observed facts. Models are evaluated in terms of their ability to predict correctly other facts" (Lave & March, 1975, p. 19).

Figure 2.5 shows a model of the learner, depicted as a system showing input, central, and output processes (Ruesch, 1969; Miller, J. G., 1978). The learner is always changing, so he or she is represented in the figure as a sphere, revolving in time and space. The information to be learned (input) is shown on the left side of the figure. The input arrow shows that the information must enter the learner. However, this input must first make it through the learner's *input screen*. This screen includes the learner's perceptual mechanisms, his or her level of attention, level of motivation, any preconceptions or biases about the material to be learned, and any distractions that the learner experiences.

As will be seen in subsequent reviews of learning research, the reduction or elimination of distractions is one of the major issues in the design and delivery of instruction. For example, based on the results of a comprehensive meta-analysis of the major factors that affect learning, Wang, Haertel, and Walberg (1993) concluded that proximal factors (those close to the learning environment such as classroom management) are more important for learning than distal factors (those more distant from the learning environment such as school board policies). Among these proximal factors, the minimization of distractions and interruptions was shown to be important.

Learning involves complex patterns of information. Many areas of learning research have demonstrated that successful learning depends in large measure making the information to be learned meaningful to the learner. The distinction between information and meaning can help us understand the importance of meaningful learning.

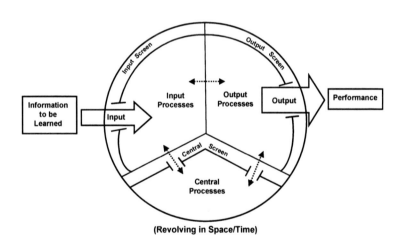

Figure 2.5:
A Systems Model of the Learner

Information is a relatively simple concept. It is "the degrees of freedom that exist in a given situation to choose among signals, symbols, messages, or patterns to be transmitted" (Miller, J. G.,

1978, p. 11). The smallest unit of information is the binary digit or bit of information. A bit "is the amount of information which relieves the uncertainty when the outcome of a situation with two equally likely alternatives is known" (Miller, J. G., 1978, p. 11). Paul Revere's message from the Old North Church is an example of a bit of information (1 if by land, 2 if by sea). On the other hand, *"meaning* is the significance of the information to a system that processes it: it constitutes a change in that system's processes elicited by the information, often resulting from associations made to it on previous experience with it" (Miller, J. G., 1978, p.11). Let us continue with our example of Paul Revere. The meaning of the lights in the church tower involves how the receivers of the message interpreted it and took actions to prepare to defend against the British. Likewise, the meaning attached to incoming instructional information sets limits on how the learner will subsequently process the information to support performance.

The learner's input screen is the initial point where the meaning of the information is determined and decisions are made on how it will be processed. Figure 2.5 shows the three main processing areas (input, central, and output). The dotted arrows indicate that each of the processing areas continuously interact with each other, exerting various influences on the information to be learned.

The interactions between the input and central processes are influenced by a central screen. This screen is controlled by various encoding processes and previously learned information. The learner's output (performance), shown on the right side of Figure 2.5, is influenced by his or her output screen. This includes how well the learner has practiced a skill or how effectively he or she understands how the learned information can be applied in a real-world setting. Each of the learner's screens (input, central, and output) will be discussed in the reviews of learning research where appropriate.

As mentioned earlier, Living Systems Theory (Miller, J. G., 1978) assumes that any system (including the learner) includes subsystems that conduct the various processes that maintain system viability. Basic definitions of these subsystems are shown in Table 2.1 and some examples of each subsystem at the level of the organism and the group are shown in Table 2.2. Figure 2.6 elaborates on the systems model of the learner by adding the subsystems that are most involved in learning.

As shown on the left side of Figure 2.6, the information to be learned is brought into the learner by the *input transducer*: the sensory subsystem which brings information into the system and changes it into forms suitable for transmission within it. The input transducer continuously interacts with the learner's input screen. The input screen is, to some degree, under the control of the *decider*: the executive subsystem, which receives inputs from all other subsystems and transmits to them information outputs that control the entire system. The decider is shown in the middle of Figure 2.6 to indicate that it is involved in all system processes (input, central, and output). The decider is important in coordinating the direction of attention and in motivating the

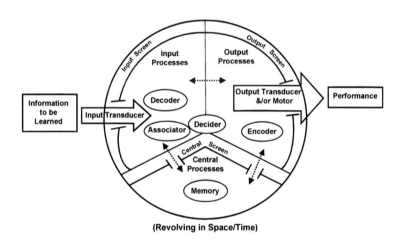

Figure 2.6:
Subsystem Processes in the Learner

learner to maintain his or her attention on the information to be learned. We can conceive of the decider as regulating the size of the opening in the input screen to allow the input transducer to bring the information into the system. This control is not always conscious because the input screen is also affected by the learner's preconceptions, biases, and internal and external distortions or distractions.

61

Once the information to be learned is passed through the input screen, several input processes begin to work with the information. These processes are shared among several subsystems and as will be discussed in later sections, the information must be held long enough for these processes to act on it. The *decoder* is the subsystem, which alters the code of information input to it into a "private" code that can be used internally by the system. Once in a usable code, the *associator* carries out the first stage of the learning process by forming enduring associations among items of information in the system. This usually consists of relating the new information to existing information already stored in the learner's memory. The interaction of previously stored material with the input processes is shown as a two-way arrow between the input processes section and the central processes section. Some theories, such as schema theory (Alba & Hasher, 1983) or theories of mediation processes (Klatsky, 1975, p. 178) postulate that these decoding and association activities begin as soon as or even before the information begins to enter the system. In this sense, they also regulate the input screen.

After the new information is decoded and associated with existing information it is passed on to the learner's central processes for storage. This storage function (memory) is shown in the central processes section of Figure 2.6. However, the information must first pass through central screen before it can be acted upon. *Memory* is the subsystem, which carries out the second sage of the learning process, storing various sorts of information in the system for different periods of time. The central screen may be affected by distractions and biases that are influenced by the information already stored in memory.

If the stored information is allowed to pass through the central screen to the output processes it is then transformed so it can be output by the learner. The first of these transformations is accomplished by the *encoder*, the subsystem which alters the code of information input to it from other information processing subsystems, from a "private" code used internally by the system into a "public" code which can be interpreted by other systems in its environment. After the information is encoded, the two subsystems, which output the information as performance are the output transducer and the motor. The *output transducer* is the subsystem, which puts out information in forms that can be transmitted over channels in the system's environment. The *motor* is the subsystem, which moves the system or parts of it in relation to part or all of its environment or moves components of its environment in relation to each other. One might distinguish these two subsystems as primarily dealing with either knowledge (output transducer) or skills (motor). However, as we shall see in the following chapters, no form or output is exclusively one or the other.

Many theories have been developed about how learning system processes function and an abundance of empirical data have been generated to support or refute the theories. A system-oriented, "learner-centric" perspective, based on Figures 2.5 and 2.6 will be used to help organize subsequent discussions of influential learning theories and summaries of empirical data on learning. In all cases, the interpretation of the research results will ask questions like, "how does this affect the learner?" or "how will this help the learner perform at a higher level?" Before beginning the discussions of empirical research, the next chapter discusses the differences and similarities between learning and education research and some of the pervasive myths about learning that are not supported by empirical data.

Chapter 3
Learning and Education Research and Myths about Learning and Instruction

In Chapters 1 and 2, we discussed science and the scientific method and its relationship to system theories and development models like Instructional Systems Development (ISD). Next, we turn to the way science examines the learning process and some of the myths about learning that science can debunk.

Learning and Learning Theory

Learning is defined in three ways (Webster's New Collegiate Dictionary, 1977):
1. The act or experience of one that learns
2. Knowledge or skill acquired by instruction or study, and
3. Modification of a behavioral tendency by experience.

For our purposes, learning can be defined as *a change in the internal state of the individual that is inferred from a relatively permanent improvement in performance as the result of instruction and experience.*

This definition includes five parts:
1. *Internal states* that are *inferred*. Learning involves the storage of memories or skills. Researchers differ on their theories of how this storage works. They do not differ in their agreement that these internal states can only be *inferred* from the behavior of the learner.
2. *Change.* Learning involves changes in these internal states that are inferred from changes in behavior.
3. *Permanent.* The changes from which we infer learning are long-term. A change that only lasts a short time (e.g., the effects of drugs or fatigue) is not evidence of learning.
4. *Improvement.* Learning is inferred when the individual demonstrates new or improved knowledge or skills. If no improvement can be demonstrated, learning cannot be inferred. (It is possible to learn incorrect information or skills, but this is due to the instructional method or

instructional content, not because a given individual learns differently).

5. *Experience*-based. Learning depends on what the learner has experienced (e.g., reading a book or watching an instructional video). Changes in behavior that are due to physiological states (e.g., fatigue, injury, drug effects) are not examples of learning. Furthermore, learning depends, not on what is done to the learner (instruction), but rather it depends on how the learner interprets what he or she experienced.

The parts of this definition will be discussed in greater detail in subsequent sections of this book.

Where Did the Term "Science of Learning" Originate?

People have understood some of the principles of learning for thousands of years. This understanding helped humans pass on their knowledge and skills in many areas, from philosophy to the principles of warfare. B. F. Skinner (1954) was one of the first modern researchers to use the phrase "science of learning." He argued that the principles of learning discovered through science could be applied to improve the methods used in the art of teaching. This orientation has inspired many learning researchers since that time. For example, Simon (1981) called for the development of a "linking science" between psychology and instructional practice (cited in Pintrich, Cross, Kozma, & McKeachie, 1986). Glaser (1982) also advocated that the design of instruction foster the acquisition of performance based on our knowledge of how learning occurs.

Most modern behavioral scientists view *learning theory* as "a systematic statement of principles that explain learning, in general, as a relatively permanent behavior change, independent of maturation and such temporary 'performance' factors as fatigue and sensory adaptation" (Lippman, 1973, pp. 144-146). The principles derived from learning theory help us develop new and improved methods to enhance learning.

Research on Learning and Research on Education

There are at least two major divisions within the science of learning. One is the research on the mind, memory, and the general topic of learning. The second is research in the field of education. Although both share some of the same characteristics, they differ in some of their methods, the variables under investigation, and our ability to generalize their research findings. For example, much of the data that has been accumulated in psychological research has used college students as their subjects. On the other hand, much of the data collected in education research has used grade school children as their subjects. Care must be taken when attempting to generalize from one of these populations to the other and when interpreting data as general "rules" of learning.

Does Science Have a Place in Educational Research?

In recent years, some educators and scientists have disagreed on the role of science in educational research. One view is that educational research does "not belong to science alone" (Eisner, 1997, p. 5). Rather, it should also look to "arts-based" research as a source for understanding and improving education (Barrone, 2001). Examples of arts-based research include case studies, fictional narratives based on the author's experiences, and other qualitative forms of inquiry.

The alternate view maintains that educational research should be "firmly within the domain of science" (Mayer, 2000, p. 38). Mayer (2000; 2001a) provides two justifications for his position: 1) to maintain self-correcting progress for educational theory; and 2) to maintain the reputation of educational research as a scientific enterprise. He suggests a way to reconcile the disagreement. "Scientific research can involve either quantitative or qualitative data; what characterizes research as scientific is the way that data are used to support arguments" (Mayer, 2000, p. 39). He also maintains that "educational researchers should agree to base their discussions on evidence and reasoned arguments rather than on opinion and stance" (p. 30).

Mayer's view is echoed by educational researchers (e.g., Merrill, Drake, Lacy, Pratt, & the ID2 Research group, 1996). It is also becoming the dominant view of educational policy makers. For example, Slavin (2002) points out that the "No Child left Behind" legislation (U.S. Congress, 2001) mentions "scientifically-based research" over 100 times. It further defines such research as "rigorous systematic and objective procedures to obtain valid knowledge" (quoted in Slavin, 2002, p. 15). This author agrees with Mayer that learning outcomes are too important to leave to chance or opinion. Furthermore, only by applying the principles of science and the scientific method can we efficiently and effectively develop new and effective educational approaches and policies (Anderson, J. R., Greeno, Reder, & Simon, 2000).

Common Characteristics of Learning and Education Research

The National Research Council's Committee on Scientific Principles for Education Research (Shavelson & Towne, 2002) maintains that scientific research on learning and scientific research on education share several characteristics with each other and with scientific research in general:

1. The accumulation of scientific knowledge is accomplished through fits and starts (p. 45-46). Often researchers go down "blind alleys" and have to regroup and start again. The good news is that the scientific method leads to "self-correction" as new methods, empirical findings, and theories emerge.
2. Knowledge accumulation is contested (p. 46). Scientists should be skeptical observers and should ask critical questions, which challenge research results through constructive dialogue with their peers. It is the norms of the scientific community that help move from critiques to scientific consensus.
3. Generation and accumulation of scientific knowledge is based on "the interdependent and cyclic nature of empirical findings, methodological developments, and theory building" (p. 48). This refers to the ideal scientific method discussed in Chapter 1.

4. "Studying humans is inherently complex" (p. 48). Although the main principles of science apply to all fields, research on learning and education (as well as other research in the behavioral and social sciences) "is qualitatively more complex than inquiry in the natural sciences" (p. 48). This is because humans bring their unique beliefs, actions, volition, and other characteristics to the research. This makes it more difficult to isolate causes and their effects through controlled research. Humans also change over time, making it more difficult to replicate individual research efforts.

Given these common characteristics, scientists and educators should share the goal of understanding the processes and conditions of learning with the goal of implementing instructional methods that will result in more effective learning. Unfortunately, many policy makers, educators, and even some scientists believe in a variety of myths about learning that are not supported by empirical data. The next section discusses some of the most pervasive of these myths.

Myths about Learning and Instruction

As in every other field of endeavor, persons in the field of learning and education can share a variety of misconceptions. In learning and education, these misconceptions often take on the mantle of "truth." These misconceptions are so pervasive that they have become "myths." These myths are shared by a large number of individuals in the instructional field and exert a strong influence on the formulation of instructional policies, the design of instruction, and the implementation of instructional products.

Myth 1: Instructional Design is "Scientifically" Based

Recently, there has been an increasing level of interest in the "scientific" basis for instructional design. For example, in the 2002 "No Child Left Behind" (NCLB) legislation, the phrase "scientifically-based research" appears over 100 times in the law (Richardson, 2002; Slavin, 2002). However, Valerie Reyna, deputy director of the Office of Educational Research and Improvement, suggested in an NCLB meeting that schools have largely based their practices on "tradition, superstition, and anecdotes" (quoted in Richardson, 2002, p. 1). This view is echoed by Mestre (2001) in his testimony before Congress. "The problem here is that too often 'best practices and materials' are based on accepted practices and folklore rather than on scientific evidence from the science of learning" (p. 4).

The weak influence of research on educational practice is also recognized by the Committee on Learning Research and Educational Practice of the National Research Council (Donovan, Bransford, & Pellegrino, 2000). The Committee cites two major causes for this weakness.

The first cause is that *educators generally do not look to research for guidance*. This is largely attributed to the different orientations, vocabularies, and goals between researchers and educators. Many educators feel that "research has largely been irrelevant to their work" (Fleming, 1988 cited by Donovan, et al., 2000, p. 6). In some cases, research can directly influence classroom practice, but only when teachers and researchers collaborate in the design of experiments or when interested teachers take it upon themselves to review research and incorporate the resulting ideas in their classroom practice.

The second cause is that *the direct link between research and practice is mediated and filtered by four other arenas.* These four arenas are:

1. Developers of educational materials supply the tools that teachers must use. These developers "need to understand and incorporate the principles of learning into their products if teachers are to successfully change their practice" (Donovan, et al., 2000, p. 7).
2. Most pre-service and in-service teacher and administrator education programs do not include relevant research, so many teachers and administrators are not aware of the recommendations from the research.
3. Policy makers at the national, state, and local levels usually are not aware of or do not understand the implications of research for changing teaching methods and materials. Therefore, the policies may actually undermine efforts to improve these methods and materials.

4. The public (including the media) can sometimes support instructional approaches that do not have a solid research foundation or not support those that do.

Similar issues and outside constituencies exert influences on instructional practices outside the classroom. For example, the implementation of web-based training is strongly influenced by the information technology community. Their focus is on computer-centric issues rather than on learner-centric issues. This focus on the tools to deliver instruction diverts resources away from efforts to use research results towards the improvement of the quality of instruction.

Myth 2: Someone Can "Own" the Science of Learning

Not long ago, the author was discussing the science of learning with a colleague. In the course of the discussion, the statement was made that a certain organization "owned" the science of learning. Of course no one can "own" science or the scientific method. However, this myth is often the result of an organization's "mission statement." The organization may be in charge of implementing science of learning principles within its larger, parent organization, but this is not the same as "owning" it. Science is a public enterprise and only works when individuals collaborate to share and cross-check their data and methods. All individuals in the organizations that work with the science of learning should be "stewards" of the science of learning, not "owners." Each steward needs to help persons involved in any facet of instructional development or procurement to think more scientifically and to make their decisions based upon the empirical data that is available on learning rather than upon the latest fad or marketing presentation. These empirically based decisions should be the rule for all events in the ISD process. This includes using only empirical data generated in earlier ISD phases to support efforts in subsequent phases. The mission of learning research organizations should be to facilitate collaboration on learning research and to enhance the dissemination and evaluation of new instructional methods and techniques that result from this research.

Myth 3: Every Published Article is "Scientific"

People often believe that any article that is published is "scientific." It is assumed that the publisher and reviewers ensure that the authors followed scientific procedures and that their conclusions are supported by data. This is not always the case. Authors and publishers make mistakes and have their own agendas (e.g., publish or perish). Furthermore, these agendas may conflict with the scientific method (e.g., only publish original articles not replications). This is especially true with the increase of articles in web journals and self-published articles, which may not be peer reviewed.

Two recent studies illustrate the need for readers to consult original articles and draw their own conclusions about the quality of the data and the methods used to collect them. Garcia-Berthou and Alcaraz (2004) sampled papers from two highly respected journals. They found that at least one statistical error (e.g., rounding, transcription, or typesetting) was found in 38% of the articles in *Nature* and 25% of the articles in *BMJ*. They conclude that "the quality of research and scientific papers needs improvement and should be more carefully checked and evaluated in these days of high publication pressure" (p.7).

The second study examined errors in the citations in published articles (Simkin & Roychowdhury, 2003). Using a stochastic modeling process to track patterns of citation errors led these researchers to conclude that only about 20% of citers actually read the original article. The best recommendation is to read the original article yourself and form your own conclusions based on the quality of the science behind the results.

Myth 4: Information, Instruction, and Learning are Synonyms

Many people use the terms information, instruction, and learning interchangeably. Some believe that any source of information (e.g., a web site or a news report) is also instruction. Some have even advocated designing computer-based and web-delivered instruction to resemble the scrolling information screens used on many news programs. They believe that more information is always better. People can learn from information, but it is uncontrolled and unstructured learning, producing unpredictable results. Winner (as cited in Iseke-Barnes, 1996, pp. 16-18) distinguishes between information and knowledge. He maintains that only when information is interpreted and related through critical thought and understanding does it become knowledge. It is the structured processes of helping the student transform information into knowledge that constitutes instruction.

A distinction also needs to be made between instruction and learning. Instruction is the structured presentation of information to the learner. The learner must process the information. Hopefully, learning is the outcome of this processing. As will be discussed in Chapter 6, we can only infer that learning occurred by measuring the performance of the learner. The control of the learning experience, including controlled assessment, is an essential feature of instruction. Without this control, we can't be sure that the student learned what is required from a given instructional approach or product.

Instruction, as a minimum, must include the following four elements. First, instruction must be designed to support specific instructional objectives, which are determined by job requirements. Second, instruction must include the opportunity for a learner to interact with the instructional content in a meaningful way. Third, the student's performance must be assessed to determine if he or she has learned what was intended. Finally, the results of the assessment must be presented to the student in a relevant and timely manner to either reinforce correct actions or to provide remediation for incorrect actions. If these four elements are not present, we are not dealing with instruction and learning will be uncontrolled. Merrill (1997) presented a slightly different categorization of instruction (i.e., knowledge structure, presentation, exploration, practice, and learner guidance), but made essentially the same point.

Myth 5: Instruction Should Consider Learning Styles

Very often proposals for the design of new instructional materials include statements such as "We will tailor the materials to the learning styles of the learner." The notion of learning styles seems fairly intuitive. People are different. They have different experiences, physical and mental capabilities, interests, and learning goals. Do these differences indicate that people have different "learning styles?" Many educators and researcher would answer in the affirmative and large numbers of articles have been published advocating various models of learning styles and instruments that purport to measure them. For example, Coffield, Moseley, Hall, and Ecclestone (2004a; 2004b) found that 1004 research articles on David Kolb's experiential learning theory were published between 1971 and 2000. Comparable numbers of articles have been published about many other learning style models.

Because there is so much interest in learning styles and so many different approaches, Frank Coffield and his associates (2004a; 2004b) conducted a comprehensive review of the literature on learning styles to assess supporting research and implications for the practice of instruction. They categorized the learning style models and provided detailed summaries of the 13 most influential and representative models. These summaries included assessments of the research evidence that either supports or contradicts the models. They concluded that the research on learning styles "can, in the main, be characterised [*sic*] as small-scale, non-cumulative, uncritical and inward looking" (Coffield, et al., 2004a, p. 135). They also found "a serious failure of accumulated theoretical coherence and an absence of well-grounded findings, tested through replication" (2004a, p. 136). One of their most illuminating findings is that "the field is bedeviled by vested interests because some of the leading developers of learning style instruments have themselves conducted the research into the psychometric properties of their own tests" (2004a, p. 137). In the opinion of this author, as long as there is money to be made with "learning style" instruments, there will be strong advocates for their use. Unfortunately, these advocates can offer few, if any, empirically based advice on the design of instruction.

Stahl (1999), commenting on the area of reading instruction, succinctly captures the issue: "The reason researchers roll their eyes at learning styles is the utter failure to find that assessing children's learning styles and matching to instructional methods has any effect on their learning" (p. 1). He goes on to give the following recommendation: "...we have other things that we know will improve children's reading achievement. We should look elsewhere for solutions to reading problems" (p. 2).

Merrill (2000) provides a cogent discussion of the relative importance of learning styles and instructional strategies. He acknowledges that students differ in their interests and other cognitive, affective, and physiological factors. However, he observes that "many research studies have demonstrated that, regardless of the learning style of the student, when the goal of the instruction, as measured by tests that are consistent with this goal, are consistent with the strategies used to teach this goal, then learning is optimal" (p. 1). Within a given instructional strategy, certain parameters may have to be adjusted to the needs of particular students. For example, some students may need more examples to grasp a concept. Merrill's bottom line is:

> Appropriate consistent instructional strategies are determined first on the basis of the type of content to be taught or the goals of the instruction (the content-by-strategy interactions) and secondarily, learner style determines the value of the parameters that adjust or fine-tune these fundamental learning strategies (learning-style-by-strategy interactions). Finally, content-by-strategy interactions take precedence over learning-style-by-strategy interactions regardless of the instructional style or philosophy of the instructional situation. (Merrill, 2000, p. 4)

John Hattie (1999), in his inaugural lecture as Professor of Education at the University of Auckland, presented data from 180,000 studies that assessed the effects of instructional innovations over a 10-year period. The data indicate that the top three influences on learner achievement are reinforcement, the learner's prior cognitive ability, and instructional quality. Innovations related to learning styles, such as the affective and physical attributes of the learners and the individualization of instruction (e.g., matching instruction to learner attributes) are among the least effective innovations. Markham (2004) summarized the data on learning styles in the following statement. "There is, in effect, no data in the research literature that shows that learning styles are related to any learning outcomes, either qualitative or quantitative" (p. 1).

Myth 6: Instruction Should Consider Hemispheric Specialization

Somewhat related to learning styles, there has been a large amount of speculation about the existence of "left-brained" and "right-brained" people and the need to tailor instruction to their specific needs. The research of Gazzaniga (1967; 1970) and other researchers (e.g., Nebes, 1974; Sperry, 1968) showed that when the two halves of the brain were surgically separated, activities performed with one hand or objects seen with only one eye were not remembered by one half of the brain. However, this does not support the idea that people have different "types" of brains and require different learning strategies. As Norman (1976) explains

> ...the strong, oversimplified separation of processing styles implied by some people working in these areas probably does not exist. The two hemispheres are strongly interconnected... Furthermore, sheer logic alone indicates that the distinction between two modes of thought or consciousness simply isn't that strong. Just as...all representations must be both prepositional and analogical, so is all thought both analytic and synthetic. (p. 216)

Commenting on the unifying theme among articles on lateralization of brain functions in a special issue of *Current Directions in Psychological Science*, Banich and Heller (1998) state that "the direction of future research in lateralization of function lies in exploring how the hemispheres act as complementary processing systems and integrate their activities" (p. 1).

Tailoring instruction to the needs of students is a laudable goal. Students have different abilities, interests, and levels of motivation. Instruction should attempt to meet these different needs. However, inventing "left-brained" and "right-brained" people does not lead to improved instructional outcomes.

Myth 7: Computer-based Instruction Can Produce a "Two Sigma" Shift

In recent years, some policy makers in the Department of Defense have stated that converting traditional classroom instruction to self-paced, web-based instruction can result in a two standard deviation (two sigma) improvement in performance. This statement is based on the results of a study by Bloom (1984) in which he compared traditional classroom instruction for children to one-on-one tutoring. Although Bloom did find a two-sigma improvement for those children who were tutored, this does not mean that web training or any other type of training will result in the same level of improvement. This is a prime example of the misuse of scientific data to make policy decisions. It squanders the potential of well-designed web-based instruction to improve learning and performance by assuming that the mere use of the web will achieve these results.

Myth 8: ISD Doesn't Work

Instructional Systems Development (ISD) has been advocated by instructional development experts at least since the military mandated its use (Branson, Rayner, Cox, Furman, King, & Hannum, 1975). However, many instructional managers and sponsors maintain that the ISD process does not result in effective instructional systems and products. Some of these individuals lament the time and other resources needed to accomplish the many tasks required for a complete ISD approach. Others believe that ISD may work on some instructional programs, but does not work for their program, whether it is computer-based instruction or web-delivered instruction.

Doubts about ISD have been voiced since the earliest days of systems approaches to training (SAT) in the 1950s and 1960s (Montemerlo & Tennyson, 1976). While serving as a prototype for subsequent ISD approaches, SAT programs were criticized because they relied so heavily on subject matter experts. Simplified models, methods and techniques were developed with the hope that non-experts could successfully apply them to instructional development. The assumption was that "if training program design experts could formalize models of the methods and techniques that made them successful, then laymen could follow these models and produce the same result at lower cost" (Montemerlo & Tennyson, 1976, p. 10). Between 1960 and 1975, over 100 SAT manuals were produced. Unfortunately, these manuals only told the layman what to do, not how to do it. When used by inexperienced personnel, these SAT manuals did not result in effective and efficient instructional programs (e.g., Ricketson, Shulz, & Wright, R. H. 1970). The managers that expected the SAT manuals to work concluded that a systems approach was not an effective way to develop instruction. Many of the problems associated with ISD result from the unrealistic expectation that it will make instructional development easy for non-experts.

ISD works if it is worked scientifically. The main problem with ISD is that it is seldom fully applied. Instructional programs often suffer from the fragmented development that ISD is supposed to correct, but usually due to strict schedules and limited budgets, critical ISD steps are skipped or not completed. Merrill, Li, and Jones (1990) observed that one of the main limitations of instructional development is the failure to integrate the various developmental phases. This lack of integration has been shown to compromise the potential of instructional approaches. Many of these integration problems are due to lack of communication. Some examples from the field of instructional simulation include:

1. Simulator and curriculum design specialists who are out of touch with the requirements of the end user (Caro, 1977). This is usually the result of an incomplete user requirements analysis and lack of continued interaction with users during development.

2. Inadequate transfer of information from training analysts to simulator procurement personnel. This is often the result of long lead times in the procurement process and the turnover of personnel who have this critical information. It can also result from the "pass through problem" (Kane & Holman, 1982), which occurs when persons sign off on forms without ensuring that the information on the form is correct and complete.

3. Lack of shared vocabularies and conflicting goals among instructional developers and managers (Kaufman, 1990). A better understanding of the ways each group contributes

to the entire instructional development process would improve the effectiveness of ISD.

Many events must occur to successfully apply ISD. An overview of a successful instructional development project is provided in Chapter 13 to illustrate some of these important events in one ISD cycle.

Belief in the above myths about human learning and instructional development can reduce the effectiveness of instructional programs. Avoiding these myths can help ensure a more effective learning environment. In addition to discounting these myths, it is very important that instructional developers, managers, and policy makers carefully evaluate the quality of research supporting all instructional approaches prior to advocating their implementation. The next section discusses several principles that can help in these evaluations.

How to Evaluate Learning and Educational Research

There are several well-accepted principles that can guide individuals when evaluating the quality of learning and education research efforts. Most of these principles follow from the application of the scientific method (see Chapter 1) and use of well-designed evaluation procedures (see Chapter 12). Several of these principles were documented in a report prepared for the U.S. Department of Education's Institute of Educational Sciences (Department of Education, 2003) by the Coalition for Evidence-Based Policy (sponsored by the Council for Excellence in Government). The report enumerates guidance for identifying educational practices (interventions, strategies, curriculums, or programs) that are supported by rigorous evidence and distinguishing these from those that are not. One of the appendixes of the report provides the guidance as three steps.

Step 1: Look at the Strength of Evidence

The first step is to determine if the practice is supported by "strong" evidence of effectiveness. The designation of "strong" evidence is based on a combination of quality and quantity of the evidence. Quality evidence is collected from research that uses randomized, controlled trials. The reported results should clearly describe the intervention and the random assignment process. This description should include: (a) who administered the intervention, who received it, and what it cost; (b) how the intervention differed from what the control group received; and (c) the logic of how the intervention was supposed to affect the outcomes.

The quantity of "strong" evidence means that data should be generated from more than one study or from a study that collected data from more than one site (e.g., two school settings or classrooms). In general, more data from more sources is usually better.

Step 2: If There is Less than Strong Evidence

The intervention may not be supported by "strong" evidence. For example, there may be flaws in the randomization process. Nevertheless, the intervention should at least be supported by "possible" evidence of effectiveness. "Possible" evidence includes data collected from two groups that were closely matched (e.g., in terms of academic achievement levels, demographics, or other characteristics). The study should follow all other requirements other than randomization (e.g., it clearly described the intervention, used valid outcome measures, and reported tests for statistical significance).

Studies that do not meet the threshold for "possible" evidence of effectiveness include" (a) pre-post studies, because the effect might have occurred even without the intervention; (b) comparison-group studies with poorly matched groups; and (c) "meta-analyses" that combine the results of studies which do not individually meet the threshold for "possible" evidence.

Step 3: Drawing a Conclusion from the Evidence

If the intervention is neither backed by "strong" or "possible" evidence, one should conclude that it is not supported by meaningful evidence of effectiveness. If this is the case, one should not implement the intervention unless other "strong" or "possible" evidence is either found or generated.

The above discussion is very brief and only provides a hint at the efforts required to make informed decisions about the quality of educational research. It is strongly recommended that the reader consult the original (Department of Education, 2003) for additional details on this process.

There is a large amount of empirical data that has the potential to help instructional program developers and managers provide more effective instructional products. The following chapters summarize some of the most important examples of this research. The reader should refer to the above discussion and also the information provided in Chapters 1 and 12 to guide them in evaluating these research summaries. This information can help the reader determine how much credence to give the results of each study and how much they can generalize from these results to their specific instructional context.

Section II
Empirical Research on Learning

This section provides summaries of the major empirical research that forms the knowledge base upon which the science of learning rests and how this research supports specific instructional designs and approaches. It includes five chapters. Chapter 4 focuses upon research that examines the physiological basis for learning and memory and research on simple learning mechanisms. Chapters 5 and 6 provide summaries of research on complex learning in the cognitive, motor, and affective domains. In Chapter 5, research that was conducted primarily in the cognitive domain is summarized. Chapter 6 includes summaries of research that was conducted in the motor and affective domains. Each research summary contains a discussion of how the research relates to the systems model of the learner and how the results contribute to our understanding of instructional design and instructional approaches. Chapter 7 uses the systems model of the learner to organize overviews the research results summarized in the earlier chapters. A communication model of instruction is also presented to emphasize how the science of learning can be applied to remove some of the barriers to effective instruction. Chapter 8 presents summaries of Gagné's theory of instruction and Bloom and associates' taxonomies of instructional objectives in each of the three domains of learning. It also includes discussions of how these instructional objectives are supported by the empirical knowledge base.

In the Preface there was a discussion about the relationship among the terms data, information, and knowledge. It was argued that data must be converted to information before it can be used to increase our knowledge. In Chapter 2, a similar distinction was made between the terms information and meaning. Meaning was defined as the significance of information to a system that processes it. The chapters in this section summarize data on various types of learning and use the systems model of the learner to help the reader transform these data into information. The systems model of the learner is also used to help analyze this information to assist the reader in transforming the information into knowledge.

Chapter 4
Research on Physiological and Simple Learning

People have been investigating how we learn for centuries. Only in the last few hundred years have these investigations been guided by the principles of the scientific method. To aid in the understanding of learning research and learning data, it should be remembered that any system process, including learning, involves a combination of structures and processes. In some cases, researchers have focused on the hypothesized structures that support learning (e.g., the study of the brain and the nervous system). In other cases, researchers have focused on the processes involved in learning (e.g., the effects of reinforcement). No single research thrust, theory, or model explains everything about the learning process. Rather, each adds to our overall understanding of learning and instruction.

This chapter and the two following chapters provide summaries of important learning theories and research results. The systems model of the learner is used to organize these research summaries from a learner-centric perspective. In Chapter 7, the model is used to provide an overview of these research results and help to organize them in a manner that can help guide us in the design of effective instructional programs and products.

The Physiological Basis of Learning and Memory

To demonstrate that something has been learned, it must be remembered. Therefore, "memory of any sort must be based on some change within the individual as learning occurs" (Fernald & Fernald, 1979, p. 163). Some scientists refer to this change as a *memory trace* that is located somewhere in the nervous system of the learner. However, we have only limited understanding what specific structures and processes are changed. Some psychologists make no assumptions about these structures and processes by merely speaking of *associative strength*. By this they mean "the probability that a given response can be reproduced when an appropriate stimulus is present" (Fernald & Fernald, 1979, p. 163).

As mentioned earlier, Living Systems Theory defines the *associator* as "the subsystem, which carries out the first stage of the learning process, forming enduring associations among items of information in the system" (Miller, 1978, p. 65). These association processes probably involve both physiological changes (as discussed below) and the formation of associations among items of information (cognitive associations, discussed in this and the next chapter).

Physiological Change Hypothesis

Some researchers think that memory is a result of physiological changes such as a realignment of molecules in the nervous system. Penfield and his associates (Penfield, 1958; Penfield & Perot, 1963) provided some spectacular evidence from brain surgery that supports this hypothesis. During operations for epilepsy, researchers stimulated various points in the patients' cerebral cortex with weak electrical currents. For example, when one point was stimulated in this manner, the patient reported detailed memories of sights, sounds and other details from past experiences. Stimulation of other points in the patient's cortex brought forth memories of other experiences. Some scientists interpret the results of electrical stimulation of the brain (ESB) to suggest that memories are somehow stored in the brain as permanent records that can reappear or be reproduced when solicited by the appropriate stimulus. If this is true, forgetting is a failure of retrieval not storage.

Subsequent scrutiny of Penfield's ESB-induced "memories" has revealed that they included major distortions or factual impossibilities (Squire, 1987). For example, the person who remembered being in a lumberyard had never actually been to one. The reconstruction hypothesis (that memory is assembled or reconstructed from prior acts and experiences) was suggested by Bransford & Franks (1971) as a cognitively based alternate explanation for Penfield's data. They pointed out that the reproduction experiments provided no convincing evidence that the patient's experience was a memory rather than a fantasy, or that it was accurate or complete. "These ESB-induced recollections were hallucinations, dreams, or loose reconstructions of events rather than exact replays of the past" (Weiten, 2004, p.

210). Taking these different viewpoints into consideration, we are led to conclude that at this time there is no unambiguous evidence that memories are stored in specific areas of the brain.

Biochemical Explanations

Experiments with planarians (flatworms) suggest that there is some biochemical basis for memory. McConnel (1962, 1973) conditioned the worms to contract their bodies when exposed to a bright light. He then fed these trained worms to other worms. These new worms learned the original conditioning task faster than control worms. Although these results suggest that memory can be transferred through chemistry, "these experiments have not been verified" (Fernald & Fernald, 1979, p. 164). Attempts to provide such verification have had difficulty replicating McConnel's results (Rilling, 1996; Morange, 2006).

Another line of biochemical research indicates that memory formation results in alterations in synaptic transmission at specific sites. Researchers have studied conditioned reflexes in a simple organism (a sea slug). This research, which earned Eric Kandel a Nobel Prize, showed that conditioned learning in the sea slug results in an increase or decrease in the release of neurotransmitters by pre-synaptic neurons (Kandel & Schwartz, 1982; Kennedy, Hawkins, & Kandel, 1992). Kandel believes that these durable changes in synaptic transmissions may be the building blocks of more complex memories. These results are very tentative because of the risk in generalizing from mollusks to humans.

Alterations in hormone levels shortly after an organism has learned a new response have been shown to affect memory storage. Depending on the specific hormone and amount of alteration, memory can be either facilitated or impaired (McGaugh, Roozendall, & Cahill, 2000). McGaugh (2000) theorized that hormones affect memory storage by modulating activity in the amygdala and various neurotransmitter systems in the brain.

The Neural Circuitry of Memory

Some research indicates that specific memories may involve localized neural circuits in the brain (Thompson, 1989; 1992). Rolls (2000) summarized research indicating that different brain systems are involved in different types of memory. For example, research on primates indicates that the orbitofrontal cortex and the amygdale are involved in learning stimulus-reinforcer associations and may also play a role in emotion and motivation. Another brain system in the temporal cortical area may be involved in learning invariant representations of objects. A system in the hippocampus seems to be implicated in both episodic memory (memory for events) and the learning of special relationships. Still other systems, located in the fontal and temporal cortices seem to be involved in short-term memory.

Steinmetz (1998) demonstrated that a rabbit's memory of a conditioned eye blink response creates unique, reusable pathways along which signals flow in the brain. The key link in this circuit is a microscopic spot in the cerebellum, a structure in the hindbrain. When this spot was destroyed, the conditioned stimulus no longer elicited an eye blink response even though the unconditioned stimulus still did. This does not mean that the cerebellum is the key to all memories. Other memories may create different pathways in other areas of the brain.

The existence of specific neural circuits for memories is also supported by research on long-term potentiation (LTP). LTP is "a long-lasting increase in neural excitability at synapses along a specific neural pathway" (Weiten, 2004, p. 288). Researchers have produced LTP by sending a burst of high-frequency electrical stimulation along a neural pathway (Racine & deJonge, 1988). This indicates that natural events may produce the same type of potentiated neural circuit when a memory is formed.

Memory formation may stimulate the growth of new neural circuits. For example, Greenough (1985) found that new branches in the dendritic trees of certain neurons emerged in rats that learned to run a series of mazes. These additional dendritic branches may lead to the formation of new neural pathways to store new learned information.

Brenda Milner and her colleagues studied how head injuries can result in certain types of amnesia (Corkin, 1984; Milner,

Corkin, & Teuber, 1968). One well-known case, a man referred to as H. M. has been studied since the 1950s. H. M. had surgery to relieve epileptic seizures. During the surgery, parts of his brain were inadvertently destroyed. This resulted in the total loss of his long-term memory. H. M. can remember nothing that has happened since 1953 (other than the most recent 20-30 seconds of his experiences). After many years of study by a variety of researchers, it has become clear that the hippocampal region (including the hippocampus, dentate gyrus, subiculum, and entorhinal cortex) and adjacent regions all have roles in long-term memory. It appears that memory involves multiple brain regions and circuits.

Instructional Implications from Recent Brain Research

In 1989 President Bush proclaimed the 1990s the "Decade of the Brain." Brain science is a rapidly growing field and as Wolfe and Brandt (1998) observe, "we have learned more about the brain in the past 5 years than in the past 100 years" (p. 8). However, they also observe that neuroscientists are "wary of offering prescriptions for using their research in schools" (p. 8). Two of the reasons for this degree of caution are:

1. Much of neuropsychological research has been conducted on animals or memory-impaired humans (Squire, Knowlton, & Musen, 1993). It is difficult to translate these findings directly to recommendations for instructional practices.
2. Findings from brain research are still at a rather "simplistic level" (Fitzpatrick, quoted in Wolfe & Brandt, 1998, p. 8)

Even so, there are several neuroscientific findings that do have implications for instructional practices. For example:

*   The brain changes physiologically in response to the environment as a result of experience. An "enriched" environment probably leads to better learning. "The trick is to determine what constitutes an enriched environment" (Wolfe & Brandt, 1998, p. 11).
*   Intellectual ability (IQ) is not fixed at birth. Early intervention programs can prevent children from having low IQs and mental retardation (Ramey & Ramey, 1998).

However, this is not only true for children. Research also shows that the brain remains somewhat malleable throughout life, responding to stimulation into old age (Thompson & Nelson, 2001).

- Some abilities are acquired more easily during certain periods of development. For example, learning a second language is easier before age 10 than later in life.
- Learning is strongly influenced by emotion. The stronger the emotion associated with an experience, the stronger the memory of that experience (Goldman, 1995). However, LeDoux (1996) observes that if an emotion is too strong (e.g., if the situation seems threatening), then learning may be decreased.

Simple Types of Learning

No one knows how many different types of learning there are. Researchers have developed a number of schemes to categorize various types of learning to help organize research results and aid our understanding of learning processes. Regardless of the specific type of learning, it is likely that "their underlying principles may be quite similar, even identical" (Brown, & Weiner, 1979, p. 108). One useful categorization of learning types is to organize them as simple or complex. Simple learning types include: two types of non-associative learning (habituation and sensitization) and two types of simple associative learning (classical and operant conditioning). Much of the research on these types of simple learning has been conducted using animals, but most researchers assume that similar processes also operate in humans.

Habituation

Habituation is "a primitive form of learning in which an instinctive or well-learned response diminishes in intensity when the stimulus normally eliciting the response is presented at frequent and regular intervals" (Brown, & Weiner, 1979, p. 670). Habituation is considered a non-associative type of learning because the stimulus is not paired with any specific response.

More complex learning involves forming associations between stimuli and responses.

Habituation has been demonstrated in a wide range of animals. For example, it has been found in snails (Humphrey, 1933), birds (Hinde, 1954), and fish (Kandel, 1976). One explanation for habituation is that it provides an evolutionary edge for the animal. Since it is impossible to respond to every stimulus, it is important for survival that an animal notes and deals with new and unfamiliar stimuli. Old or routine stimuli can usually be ignored without placing the animal in danger.

Habituation has important implications for the design of instruction. As will be discussed below, maintaining a student's motivation and attention is an essential component in effective instruction. In terms of the systems model of the learner, habituation can affect the permeability of the learner's input screen. Instructional information that is presented in the same manner over and over again may decrease the learner's reaction to it. This may make it more difficult for the information to enter the system. To help the learner avoid becoming habituated to the material being presented, well-designed instruction probably should include a variety of presentation methods and media.

Sensitization

In habituation, the animal becomes less sensitive to repeated stimuli. In another type of non-associative learning, called *sensitization*, the animal becomes more sensitive to stimuli. Sensitization is defined as "a primitive form of learning in which a stimulus comes to evoke a response more frequently, and with greater intensity, as a result of a state of alertness induced by events not directly paired with the stimulus" (Brown & Weiner, 1979, p. 676). An example of sensitization is hearing every noise in your house after watching a scary movie. The noises are not directly paired to the events in the movie, but still they keep you awake.

Like habituation, sensitization can affect the learner's input screen. Novel presentation methods or specific cues that sensitize the learner to important information may help open the input screen. Using techniques to stimulate sensitization can help designers improve the quality of instruction by helping ensure that the instructional information enters the learner for further processing.

Gould (1986) reviewed both field observations and laboratory experiments on animals. He concluded that both habituation and sensitization, along with associative trial-and-error learning appear to be the building blocks of more complex forms of learning. We now move up this hierarchy of complexity by examining the first level of associative learning, conditioning.

Conditioning

Conditioning is a term applied to two forms of simple associative learning. Both forms are believed to be involved in more complex learning processes. The Russian Ivan P. Pavlov (1849-1936) was the first researcher to study the first form, *classical conditioning*. Pavlov observed that when food was presented to a dog, the dog responded with the "automatic" response of salivating. Later, when Pavlov presented two stimuli (e.g., food and the sound of a bell) almost simultaneously, the dog would begin to associate the two stimuli together. After a number of pairings, the dog would salivate to the sound of the tone alone.

Figure 4.1 is a diagram of the process of classical conditioning. In the top section of the figure, before conditioning, the unconditioned stimulus (UCS) elicits an unconditioned response (UCR), but the neutral stimulus (NS) does not. During conditioning, the neutral stimulus is paired with the unconditioned stimulus. Each time the dog is shown meat powder, a tone is also sounded. The dog comes to associate the sound of the tone with the meat powder. After conditioning, the sound of the tone alone elicits the response. The neutral stimulus has become a conditioned stimulus (CS) and the response to it is a conditioned response (CR).

The second form of conditioning, *operant* or *instrumental conditioning*, was extensively studied by two Americans, E. L. Thorndike (1898; 1931; 1932) and B. F. Skinner (1938; 1954). Thorndike (1932) described this type of conditioning as the "law of effect." He meant that "the effect of a behavior (its consequences) determines whether that behavior will occur again" (Beck, 1978, p. 124). Contrary to classical conditioning where the

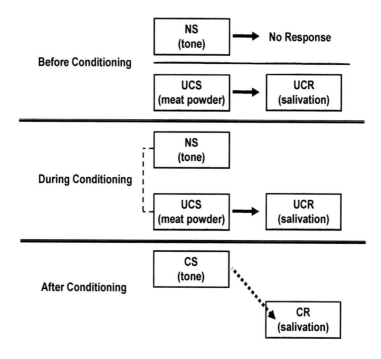

Figure 4.1:
The Process of Classical Conditioning

subject has no control of the stimuli, operant conditioning provides reinforcements (rewards) for specific behaviors (e.g., pressing a bar or taking a certain path in a maze). Thus, the subject's actions (operants) are instrumental in gaining the reward. Research has also demonstrated that separate responses can be linked together into larger and larger units through a process called *chaining* (Lubar, 1973).

There is sometimes confusion about the terms reinforcement, reward, and punishment. Reinforcement always strengthens behaviors. However a reinforcer can be either positive or negative. A *positive reinforcer* is any event (i.e., stimulus) "which serves to strengthen responses preceding its occurrence" (Baron, Byrne, & Kantowitz, 1978, p. 120). Positive reinforcers increase the probability that an individual will respond again in the way he or she responded prior to experiencing the reinforcer. This is what most people think of as a reward. If the reward is withdrawn, the response will gradually decrease until it eventually ceases. This process is called *extinction*.

A *negative reinforcer* is any event "which strengthens responses leading to its termination or removal" (Baron, Byrne, & Kantowitz, 1978, p. 120). In negative reinforcement, the organism strengthens behaviors that allow it to avoid or terminate uncomfortable or annoying stimuli. When a negative reinforcer is removed, the individual is more likely to behave the way he or she did prior to the removal of the aversive stimulus. On the other hand, *punishment* always reduces behaviors. A punisher is some type of unpleasant stimulus that follows a behavior. Its unpleasantness reduces the likelihood that the organism will behave in the same manner.

Figure 4.2 illustrates the differences between positive reinforcement, negative reinforcement and punishment. The top row of the figure illustrates positive reinforcement. When a rat presses the lever, it is presented with food. This increases the rat's tendency to press the lever. On the other hand, the second row of the figure illustrates negative reinforcement. In this case, the rat experiences a shock until it presses the lever. This behavior turns the shock off and results in an increased tendency for the rat to press the lever. Both types of reinforcement increase the tendency to emit a behavior.

Punishment, as illustrated in the bottom row of Figure 4.2, tends to decrease behavior. In this example, the rat experiences a shock each time it presses the lever. This results in a decrease in the tendency for the rat to press the lever.

In summary, there are two ways to increase the likelihood of a behavior: (1) provide a reward (positive reinforcement) or (2) remove an aversive stimulus (negative reinforcement). In contrast, there are also two ways to decrease the likelihood of a behavior:
(1) provide an aversive stimulus (punishment) or (2) take away the rewarding stimulus that follows (is contingent on) a response. The data on classical and operant conditioning were so persuasive that the resulted in behaviorism reigning as the primary paradigm in psychology for almost 40 years.

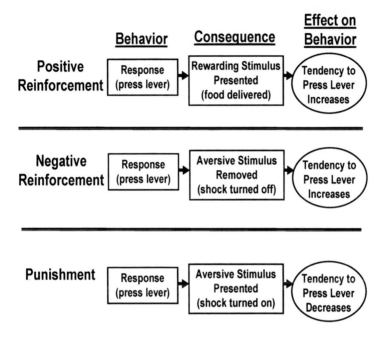

Figure 4.2:
Positive and Negative Reinforcement and Punishment

Behaviorism, especially Skinner's work, was the main impetus for the "programmed learning" movement. This approach was very popular from the late 1950s through the 1970s and is still followed by some instructional developers today. Essentially it is a self-instructional process where the learner uses various forms of instructional materials (e.g., textbooks, mechanical apparatuses, or computers) to move through instructional content. The learner is presented the content in small stages and is immediately reinforced for correct performance. Although programmed learning had many advocates, it is difficult and costly to produce good programs and often learners tire of the technique (Vitro, 1973). It is probably best thought of as complementary to rather than a replacement for other approaches.

95

Behaviorism, as exemplified by conditioning and stimulus-response research dominated the psychology of learning in the 1950s. Some researchers have continued to collect empirical data on conditioning since that time (see Staddon and Cerutti, 2003 for a review that focuses on reinforcement schedules). However, the focus of learning research began to change in the late 1950s and early 1960s. In his 1959 review of learning research, Kendler observed that theorists were beginning to try to handle the influences of motivation and perception in their theories of learning. As we shall see in the following chapters, these and other cognitive issues have become central in more recent research on complex learning. This represents a paradigm shift as discussed in Chapter 1.

Chapter 5
Research on Complex Learning:
The Cognitive Domain

Many researchers classify complex human behavior into three broad and interrelated domains: cognitive, motor, and affective (e.g., Gagné, 1973; Bloom, 1956; Krathwohl, Bloom, & Masia, 1964; Harrow, 1971; Magill, 1980). As we shall see in the discussions that follow, these three domains should not be regarded as mutually exclusive. Many of the same learning processes occur in each domain. This division is used in this and the following chapters because many instructional approaches focus on one of these broad categories of behaviors. It should also be noted that although a large amount of learning research has been conducted in either the cognitive or motor domains, much of this early research was conducted prior to the conceptual division into three domains. In other words, many early researchers were examining learning in general, not specifically cognitive or motor learning. This chapter provides summaries of some of the most important research in the cognitive domain, which primarily involves intellectual activities or thinking. Almost as early as humans recognized that they could think, people began to wonder how the thinking process works.

Associationism

One of the earliest and most enduring theories of thinking and learning is associationism. "According to this doctrine, when one idea occurs in thinking, its occurrence is likely to evoke other associated ideas to which it is linked" (Siiter, 1973, p. 18). Associationism arose in opposition to theories that the mind consisted of "innate" ideas that order rather than arise from sensory experience. Plato and Descartes championed the innate view of the mind. Aristotle began to question this view, but it was Thomas Hobbes (1588-1679) that proposed associations as a distinct alternative to innate ideas. Many philosophers expanded on and advanced the associationist view, including: John Locke (1632-1704), Bishop Berkeley (1685-1753), David Hume (1711-

1776), James Mill (1773-1836), and his son John Stuart Mill (1806-1873). Near the end of the nineteenth century, Alexander Bain (1818-1903) presented "the last comprehensive attempt to explain all psychological functions with associations" (Siiter, 1973, p. 19).

Although associationism is no longer viewed as a feasible explanation of all behaviors, many of its ideas are still important in modern theories of learning. "Associative learning should be the foundation for our understanding of other forms of behavior and cognition in human and nonhuman animals" (Wasserman & Miller, 1997, p. 573).

Association is especially important in the first stage of the learning process when an individual is initially developing the cognitive structures that will facilitate learning additional material. As we shall see in subsequent discussions of learning research, associations are also important in retrieving learned information. For example, Gillund and Shiffrin (1984) propose that recognition of learned information is "affected by the strength of inter-item associative relations and associations between items and context" (Johnson & Hasher, 1987, p. 643; see also Anderson, J. R. & Bower, 1972, 1974).

In general, people are motivated to associate by: receiving rewards, avoiding punishments, or both. Two important assumptions about the forming of associations are:

1. Associations take place over time and build up as a person "experiences repeated instances in which the information input and response output are temporally connected" (Miller, 1978, p. 409).

2. The formation of associations requires both reinforcement (a stimulus that increases the likelihood of repeating a response that preceded its occurrence) and knowledge of results (information about the response).

The formation of associations is so important for the functioning of living systems that Miller (1978) labeled one of the subsystem processes that are critical to system viability the *associator*. As we shall see in subsequent reviews of learning theories and research, the formation of associations is a component of almost every learning process. Associations are also important in the retrieval (recall) of information that has been learned. We will see that the "strength" of the associations among new and existing information is often the major factor in determining if someone will later be able to use the learned information. In many of the research summaries presented in later sections we shall see the importance of associations and the associator process.

Insight Learning

The formation of associations can occur over time or can suddenly appear. When an organism suddenly forms an association it is often called *insight learning*. "Insight or the rapid apprehension of relationships between objects and events, is regarded by many psychologists as a learning process quite different from—and more complex than—simple operant conditioning" (Brown & Weiner, 1979, p. 159).

The first systematic study of insight learning was conducted by Köhler (1925) while he observed the behaviors of apes in the Canary Islands. One of his star performers was an ape named Sultan. Over time, Köhler observed Sultan learn to use a stick to pull bananas from outside his cage. Later, Köhler gave Sultan two hollow bamboo rods and placed the bananas far enough from the cage that neither rod was long enough to reach them. Sultan began toying with the rods until their ends became accidentally aligned. Snap! Sultan proceeded to fit the rods together and haul in his reward. This sudden formation of a new association is the hallmark of insight.

These experiences led Köhler to believe that learning was more complex than the simple stimulus-response formula popular at the time. He felt that learning consisted of a "constellation of stimuli-organization-reaction to the results of organization" (Köhler, quoted in Gredler, 2005, p. 54). In other words, insight occurs when existing stimuli are organized and reorganized into new patterns of associations.

Some evidence suggests that insight may depend on familiarity with the various elements of a problem (Birch, 1945). Insight may involve a combination of several learned behaviors through operant conditioning or other types of learning. Once enough separate behaviors have been learned for the individual to "catch on," insight may occur. Thus, it is likely that insight learning involves multiple subsystem processes. Minimally, these processes probably include the input transducer, the decoder, the associator, the decider, and memory.

Learning Lists of Items

One of the earliest experimental research programs on learning was conducted by Ebbinghaus (1885). He studied how people learn lists of words (often nonsense syllables). His methods set the stage for many subsequent researchers. Some of the terms and methods he developed include:

1. The observation that learning takes place over a series of *trials*.
2. That learning could be quantified through the *measure of savings*. This refers to how much work is needed to relearn after a given amount of time has elapsed.
3. The *retention interval*, or the time between initial learning and retention. He found that the amount of information that is forgotten increases with time.

Learning lists of items or words is often referred to as rote learning. One area of rote learning research is called *serial learning* or "learning items in a particular order" (Brown & Weiner, 1979, p. 166). Research in this area has identified several learning effects, such as:

1. The *primacy effect*, which shows that a higher percentage of items are recalled from the beginning of the list.
2. The *recency effect*, which shows that the highest percentage of items are recalled from the end of the list.
3. The *von Restorff effect*, which shows that "a novel or unexpected item is learned quickly, even when it comes in the middle of a list" (Brown & Weiner, 1979, p. 166)

Another type of rote learning is called *paired-associate learning*. It is "learning to respond to the first item in a pair by giving the second" (Brown & Weiner, 1979, p. 166). Examples of paired-associate learning include:

1. Learning a foreign word (e.g., mañana for tomorrow)
2. Learning to pair someone's name to their face
3. Learning a synonym (e.g., ruminate for ponder)

Reid, Brackett, and Johnson (1963) investigated the influence of associations (relationships) among words on the ability of learners to remember the words. They found that subjects who were given the opportunity to group the words into some generic class were better able to remember the words than subjects who only were required to remember unrelated words. This finding has been replicated many times in various contexts. For example, Einstein and Hunt (1980) found that learners who performed a taxonomic categorization or pleasantness rating of terms during learning performed better on recall tasks than learners who did not perform these semantic orienting tasks. Furthermore, learners who combined both semantic orienting tasks demonstrated better recall than either task alone. Ritchie and Beal (1980) found that the recall of unrelated concrete nouns was better when learners formed detailed images corresponding to the words.

Applying the terminology of the systems model of the learner, evidence on the effectiveness of forming meaningful associations indicates that the learning of word lists involves, at least, interactions between the processes of the associator and memory.

Information Processing Approaches to Learning

During the late 1950s and early 1960s, the emergence of computers offered useful models or metaphors to describe human learning. In fact, computer or information processing models became so pervasive that by 1988, Estes could state that "the learner is not a bunch of reflexes but rather a highly sophisticated information processor" (Estes, 1988, p. 90). Information processing models describe learning processes using terms such as:

1. *Encoding*, or putting information into a system. This may include modifying the information so it is in an appropriate form for the system.
2. *Storage*, or storing information in the system. Things may happen to stored information (e.g., it may be changed by subsequent information or lost).
3. *Retrieval*, or the action of getting at the stored information

All three of these processes are important and work together during learning. Furthermore, any of these three processes may break down, resulting in a failure to remember.

There are two basic assumptions in information processing approaches (Broadbent, 1963; Haber, 1969; Klatsky, 1975):

1. *The stage assumption*: processing can be broken down into sub-processes or stages and information can be remarkably transformed as it goes from one stage to another. Craik and Lockhart (1972) distinguished between the stages by referring to them as "levels of processing." They assumed that the greater the "depth of processing," the greater the degree of semantic or cognitive analysis and the greater the probability of remembering an item of information.

2. *The limited capacity assumption*: we can identify limits on human capacity to process information at each stage of processing.

Klatsky (1975) also observed that these information processing approaches are cognitive in character. They assume that humans are active seekers of knowledge and processors of information. In these views, perceiving and remembering are acts of construction, by means of which people actively build mental representations of the world.

Figure 5.1 is a simplified depiction of the stages of learning and memory (adapted from Atkinson & Shiffrin, 1968). Much of the following discussion will refer to this figure. The reader should see similarities between Figure 5.1 and Figures 2.5 and 2.6 (the systems model of the learner). One difference between the models depicted in these figures is that the stages of learning and memory only deal with how information is entered into memory and how existing memory affects this process. The systems model of the learner also deals with how memories are retrieved and expressed as performance.

On the left side of Figure 5.1 is some object or item of information in the outside world. The object enters one of the sensory registers of the individual. The sensory registers are where incoming information is held for a very brief period in veridical form. That is, as a faithful reproduction of the original stimulus— before it is recognized and passed on through the system. Sperling (1960) conducted some of the first research on the *visual register*. "Sperling's results demonstrate the existence of a form of immediate visual storage that is highly accurate but that decays very rapidly" (Klatsky, 1975, p. 25). The image stored in the visual register is sometimes called an *icon*.

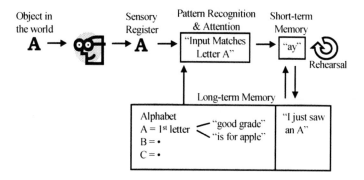

Figure 5.1:
A Model of the Stages of Learning and Memory

Moray, Bates, and Barnett (1965) found that humans also have an *auditory register*, where auditory information is temporarily stored. The auditory analogue of the icon is sometimes called the *echo*. Research on these two sensory registers has found a *modality effect* or "the difference in recall corresponding to a difference in the modality (auditory or visual) of presentation" (Klatsky, 1975, p. 36). This modality effect has also been demonstrated in studies of the allocation of resources for the performance of multiple tasks (Wickens, 1984; Wickens & Hollands, 2000). This multiple resource theory will be discussed below in the section on processing systems.

In terms of the systems model of the learner (Figures 2.5 and 2.6), the sensory registers can be regarded as one of the regulators of the learner's input screen. No information can be learned if it is not "sensed"—if it is not allowed to enter the learner through the input screen.

Pattern Recognition and Selective Attention

The next stage in the information processing model, as depicted in Figure 5.1, is where the information, temporally held in the sensory register, is processed so it can be entered into memory. This is done through a combination of *selective attention* and *pattern recognition*. Selective attention and pattern recognition are functions of the learner's input screen and also his or her decider, decoder, and associator subsystem processes.

Norman (1976) maintained that attention is the study of limitation and selection (p. 3). "Selective attention makes it possible for you to focus on, or tune in, the relevant information, filtering out the rest" (Klatsky, 1975, p. 15). The decider, as the executive subsystem, adjusts the learner's input screen to filter incoming information by distinguishing more "important" information from information that has less relevance for the learner. This process helps ensure that only the important information is brought into the limited-capacity system.

Once the information is allowed in, *pattern recognition* is used "to convert raw information (like visual forms or patterns of sound), relatively useless to the system, to something meaningful" (Klatsky, 1975, p. 15). This conversion process involves the decoder, which converts the information into a form that is "private" to the learner. In other words, into a form that has personal meaning and relevance. This is accomplished in concert with the associator and memory, which allow the formation of associations between the new information and information previously learned. Thus, pattern recognition matches the incoming sensory information with previously learned information that is stored in long-term memory (LTM). This is shown in Figure 5.1 where the visual form is recognized as the letter "A." LTM and short-term memory (STM) are discussed below.

Cherry (1953) presented different information to either ear of experimental subjects (the *Dichotic Listening Task*). She found that the subjects attended to one channel and rejected the other. However, they could switch easily between channels and gained some general information from the rejected channel. However, Moray (1959) found that subjects did not retain information from the rejected ear.

Broadbent (1958) developed one of the first models of selective attention, called the "filter model." It proposed that selective attention acts like a filter, blocking out some channels and letting only one through. Broadbent's model was later shown to be inadequate by experiments demonstrating that attention can jump back and forth between channels to follow the meaning of a message (Gray and Wedderburn, 1960). These experiments "rejected the Broadbent's idea that attention was based on the physical characteristics of sensory channels and suggested that psychological attributes played an important role in selection" (Norman, 1976, p. 25).

Triesman (1964) collected additional data that showed the inadequacy of Broadbent's model. Her data showed that sensory cues alone were not sufficient to explain selective attention. Rather incoming verbal information undergoes a series of "tests." The first tests distinguish among inputs on the basis of sensory and physical cues. Later tests distinguish among syllabic patterns, specific sounds, individual words, and finally, grammatical structure. She further maintained that all tests are relevant and are all prebiased or presensitized by existing stored information. On the basis of these data, Triesman (1969) proposed a modification of Broadbent's model. She proposed that attention acts more like an attenuator that turns down the volume on unattended channels without blocking them out. Norman (1976) elaborated on this approach by suggesting that all channels impinging on the processing system get enough analysis to activate a representation in LTM. "At that point, selective attention takes effect, for selective attention corresponds to the full recognition of attended-to patterns" (Klatsky, 1975, p. 61). This is the "pattern recognition" shown in Figure 5.1, which, for Norman, corresponds to attending to the pattern. Once attention has been directed toward the recognized pattern it can be processed and moved into memory.

The investigation of expert performance is an area of research that has examined the role of pattern perception. Expert performance has been defined as "consistently superior performance on a specified set of representative tasks for a domain" (Ericsson & Lehmann, 1996, p. 277). Research on the performance differences between experts and novices demonstrated that in many areas of expertise any skilled activity "was the result of acquiring, during many years of experience in their domain, vast amounts of knowledge and the ability to perform pattern-based retrieval" (Ericsson & Lehmann, 1996, p. 275). Thus, associations are strengthened when experiences are stored in memory and interrelated. These associative relationships in memory then interact with the associator to facilitate the pattern recognition that regulates the learner's input screen. Further interactions between the associator and memory are then involved in the formation of new associations between the new material and information already in memory.

Not only are experts better at recognizing patterns in important information, but they are also better at organizing that information for later retrieval. Chi, Feltovich, and Glaser (1981) examined the differences between experts and novices in solving physics problems. They found that novices emphasized the surface features of the problem (e.g., springs, pulleys, or inclined planes) while the experts focused on the principles of physics (e.g., momentum). This is consistent with theories of skill acquisition (e.g., Anderson, J. R., 1993; Fitts & Posner, 1967) "in which knowledge is first acquired and then organized into appropriate actions that, with further practice, individuals can access automatically through pattern-based retrieval" (Ericsson & Lehmann, 1996, p. 276). In the next chapter these theories will be examined in greater detail in summaries of research in the motor domain.

Processing Systems

The processing systems that categorize, associate, and transform information so it can be moved into memory can be classified as data driven (bottom-up) or conceptually driven (top-down). Norman (1976) maintained that human processing can't be explained by either bottom-up or top-down alone. Rather both are essential and must take place simultaneously (p. 41). Palmer (1975) provided evidence for the interaction between these two types of processing. Using simplified drawings, Palmer found that facial features could be recognized when shown in the context of a profile, but not recognized out of context. If additional detail was added to the features (e.g., internal structure), they were more readily recognized. Thus, the physical representation of the features (bottom-up processing) seems to work in conjunction with information about context (top-down processing) to recognize and classify information. As Norman (1976) stated, "ambiguous perceptions get interpreted in completely unambiguous ways, depending on the context surrounding them" (p. 41). Top-down and bottom-up processing data provide additional support for the existence of continuous interactions between the associator and memory.

It was mentioned above that it has been demonstrated that humans have two types (or modes) of sensory registers: visual (Sperling, 1960) and auditory (Moray, et al., 1965). Wickens and his colleagues (Wickens, 1984; Wickens & Hollands, 2000) have proposed that humans process information based on the types of resources necessary to encode, process and respond to incoming information. This *multiple resource theory* differs from some previous processing theories (e.g., Kaneman, 1973), which proposed "that there is a single pool of...resources, available to all tasks and mental activities" (Wickens, 1984, p. 293). Single resource theory assumes that more difficult tasks performed at the same level of competence demand more resources. However, Wickens maintained that single resource theory cannot account for data from dual-task interference studies. "Examples abound in which interference between tasks is predicted not by their difficulty but by their structure" (Wickens, 1984, p. 300). For example, Wickens (1976) found that performance on a manual-tracking task (like flying an airplane) was more disrupted by a concurrent task requiring a similar type of response (maintaining constant pressure on the stick) than by an auditory signal detection task. This was found even though the auditory task was judged by subjects as being more difficult and presumably would demand more resources.

These types of data led Wickens to propose multiple resource theory. "The multiple resource view argues that instead of one central 'pool' of resources with satellite structures, humans possess several different capacities with resource properties. Tasks will interfere more if more resources are shared" (1984, p. 301). If we apply multiple resource theory to learning we can assume that the way to-be-learned information is presented can either interfere with (demand competing resources) or aid shared processing (demand separate rather than common resources).

Short-term Memory

The amount of time a pattern is held in a sensory register is so brief that it cannot be actually be called memory. The first stage of memory is a store called *short-term memory* (STM). In Figure 5.1, STM is shown on the top right. Here the pattern of the letter "A" has been recognized and is being held in STM as "ay." In system terms, the associator has formed a link between the new information and existing information. However this linkage is ephemeral due to the limitations of STM.

STM is limited in two important ways:
1. How long something can be held in STM
2. How many separate items can be held in STM

Two processes primarily control how long a piece of information can be held in STM before it is forgotten: *passive decay* and *interference* (Peterson and Peterson, 1959). Both processes affect the strength (amount of information present or the completeness of the information) of the item to be remembered. Passive decay occurs because the strength of the item simply declines with the passage of time. It is called passive because there is no specific cause for this decline in strength. However, passive decay can be avoided through rehearsal (repetition) of the item. The circular arrow on the right in Figure 5.1 represents this activity.

Rehearsal can be divided into two operations: maintenance rehearsal and elaborative operations (Craik & Lockhart, 1972; Craik & Watkins, 1973). *Maintenance rehearsal* is simply keeping an item in STM until it can be used (e.g., repeating a phone number until the call is made). In *elaborative operations* one actually organizes the material by forming meaningful connections and associations among items. Bjork (1975) and Bjork and Jongeward (1975, cited in Norman, 1976) found that both types of rehearsal were effective for immediate retention (with maintenance rehearsal showing slight superiority), but for longer intervals, elaborative processing showed clear superiority. Thus, maintenance rehearsal is better for holding information in STM, but elaborative operations are better for facilitating long-term remembering. Referring to elaborative operations, Norman (1976) stated that "what is done at the time of learning probably is a crucial determinant of what will later be retrievable" (p. 127). Thompson and Tulving (1970) went even further. They suggested that memory retrieval is entirely determined by what happens when the memory is stored. "They argued that no cue, however strongly associated with the item to be remembered, can be effective unless the to-be-remembered item is specifically encoded with respect to that cue at the time of storage" (Norman, 1976, p. 127).

An item in STM can also be forgotten because of interference when a new item enters STM. This new item can displace the first item or interfere with (confuse) its representation in STM because of similarity to other items in LTM (e.g., "ay," the letter versus "aye," meaning "yes"). Interference in STM has been shown to follow patterns predictable on the basis of the meaning of the information (Shulman, 1972). For example, Shulman's subjects were instructed to memorize a list of words. Then they were given a "probe" word and asked to say whether it "matched" a word on the list. On some trials, "match" meant "identical to" while on other trials it meant "means the same as." The subject was signaled just before the probe occurred as to which meaning of "match" applied to that trial. Often the subject in the "identical" trial made errors by identifying a synonym instead. Klatsky (1975) suggested that the errors were due to semantic confusion, indicating that the subject stored the meanings of the words and used these semantic patterns to accomplish the task.

Baddeley (1972) challenged this explanation. He argued that the semantic confusions are the result of the retrieval techniques and rules stored in LTM. If the subject's retrieval rules are for remembering a series of letters, the subject might confuse "H" with "8" simply because he or she thinks that the sound "ay" is in reference to a sequence consisting of letters.

George Miller (1956) documented the second limitation of STM, how many items can be held at one time, in his famous article "the magical number seven, plus or minus two." Miller summarized the results from several studies that showed, on average, between five and nine separate items could be held in STM at one time. He further showed that by organizing the items of information into sequences or chunks, this limited span of immediate memory could be expanded. For example, more numbers can be held in STM if they are grouped or chunked (like the digits of a telephone number). When this strategy is applied, each chunk of information is processed much like a single digit.

The chunking principle has been extended beyond holding items in STM. For example, chunking of lesson content has been shown to help inexperienced learners, but provided no advantages to experienced learners (Pollock, Chandler, & Sweller, 2002). This may be because the experienced learners have already formed meaningful associations between incoming information and existing information. These associations may override the benefit of chunking.

STM as "Working Memory"

The original concept of STM as a simple rehearsal buffer is regarded by many as inadequate. For example, the original model focused on the phonemic (verbal) encoding of information and on decay as the process responsible for loss of information. Subsequent research has shown that STM is probably more complex than this conception (Bower, 2000). Alan Baddeley (1986; 1992; 1999) proposed more comprehensive, modularized model of STM that characterizes it as "working memory."

Baddeley's model of working memory handles a greater number of functions and depends on more complicated processes than previous models of STM. Figure 5.2 shows a diagram of Baddeley's model of working memory. According to the Baddeley's model, working memory consists of 4 components:

1. The *phonological rehearsal loop*, which represents all of STM from the original model. This component is active when one uses recitation to temporarily hold on to information (as depicted by the curved maintenance rehearsal arrow).

2. The *visuospatial sketchpad*, which allows one to temporarily hold and manipulate visual images (like mentally rearranging the furniture in your home).

3. The *executive control system*, controls deployment of attention to handle the limited amount of information one uses at one time when engaging in reasoning and decision making (e.g., when one weighs the pros and cons of something). In terms of the systems model of the learner,

these processes are controlled, in large part, by the decider.

4. The *episodic buffer*, which is a temporary, limited capacity store that allows the various components of working memory to integrate information and serves as an interface between working memory and long-term memory. This is one of the functions of the associator.

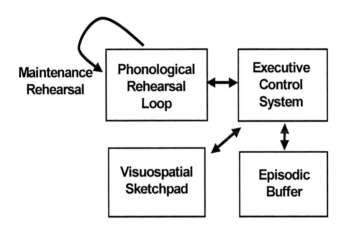

Figure 5.2:
Short-term Memory as Working Memory

The double-headed arrows in Figure 5.2 depict the interactions between the various components of working memory. As the arrows show, all of the components interact with the executive control system. Although more complex, Baddeley's model still includes the two key characteristics that originally defined STM—limited capacity and short storage duration. The other components and processes in working memory may be supported by future research or new conceptions may be developed. Nevertheless, we can be fairly certain that information to be learned must somehow move from this short-term store to the more permanent store labeled long-term memory (LTM).

The systems model of the learner does not make an explicit distinction between STM and LTM. As we have seen, STM includes some of the functions of the associator as well as some of the functions of the memory subsystem. However, the main function of memory is long-term storage of information, one of the capabilities that is usually thought to be located in LTM.

Long-term Memory

Long-term memory (LTM), represented in the bottom portion of Figure 5.1, is the deeper storage area where all learned information is stored. Klatsky (1975, p.18) maintains that the preponderance of research suggests that there are two important hypotheses concerning LTM:

1. *LTM is a permanent store of information.* One forgets, not because the information is lost, rather because it cannot be retrieved.
2. *Information in LTM can be coded in many ways.* Each item of information can be reached in a multitude of pathways.

As mentioned in the discussion of STM, rehearsal can be used to maintain items in STM. Rehearsal also has implications for LTM. The data examined by Atkinson and Shiffrin (1968) strongly suggest that the longer an item is rehearsed in STM, the more likely it is to be remembered later (i.e., retrieved from LTM). Rundus (1971) also found strong support for this effect. In addition, he found that the items that the subjects rehearsed tended to be affected by their long-term knowledge. That is, a new word was more likely to be rehearsed if its meaning fit in with the current rehearsal set. For example, the word "sparrow" was more likely to be rehearsed if it was included in a set of words like "robin," "canary," and "wren." It was less likely to be rehearsed if it was included with words like "bread," "eggs," and "cheese." Thus, there is a strong link between LTM and STM, based largely on the associator subsystem process.

Craik and Watkins (1973) found that the amount of rehearsal alone does not always affect later recall. They found that interpretation of the information is more important than mere repetition of an item to hold it in STM. The kind of rehearsal that does lead to long-term recall is an *elaborative process* where items are mediated, associated with one another, and enriched through contact with information in LTM. To be most effective, elaborations should "reflect on the significance of what is to be remembered" (Horton & Mills, 1984, p. 367). Stevenson (1981) and Bradshaw and Anderson, J. R. (1982) showed that memory for sentences was improved when the elaborations reflected cause or effect as compared to neutral or unrelated elaborations. Stein, B. S. and Bransford (1979) found that elaborations only improved performance when they clarified the precise significance of a target word in each sentence. For example, when a sentence like "The fat man read the sign" was elaborated as "The fat man read the sign warning of thin ice," recall of "fat" was facilitated.

Research on rehearsal helped build the foundation for an important learning concept. *New information is not learned in isolation.* The information is recognized, classified, and associated with information already in LTM. The term *mediation* refers to this use of LTM to relate previously learned information to information currently being processed (Klatsky, 1975, p. 71). Linking such new information to prior knowledge has been shown to be one of the major factors associated with successful school learning (Wang, et al., 1993). This is another indication of the importance of the associator.

Ruth Clark (Clark, R. C., 2003, p. 122) discusses research that supports five methods to help learners' link new information with existing knowledge:

1. Ask effective questions.
2. Give practice assignments.
3. Train learners to self-question.
4. Promote self-explanations of problem-solving steps.
5. Provide collaborative learning assignments.

Each of these methods helps establish associative links with the learner's memory. Thus, it is likely that the associator and memory are the primary subprocesses involved in elaboration and mediation.

Types of Long-term Memory

Tulving (1972) distinguished between two types of LTM: semantic and episodic memory. *Semantic memory* stores specific factual information and all of the information we need to use language. This information includes: the rules of grammar, the meanings of words, chemical formulas, math rules, and "facts" that do not depend on a particular time or place (Klatsky, 1975, p 132, Norman, 1976, p. 187). This type of memory is very resistant to forgetting.

The second type of memory mentioned by Tulving is *episodic memory.* This type "holds temporally coded information and events, information about how things appeared and when they occurred.... It stores things that depend on context" (Klatsky, 1975, p. 132-133). Episodic memory is in a constant state of change and is therefore more susceptible to modification because new information is constantly coming in.

After 30 years of research on episodic memory, Tulving (2002) concluded that episodic memory is not only a different type of memory. It is "a neurocognitive (brain/mind) system, uniquely different from other memory systems" (p. 1). He reviews evidence that episodic memory is uniquely human and, according to episodic theory, "evolved out of semantic memory" (p. 6). Some of this evidence comes from research on amnesia conducted in the 1950s. This research showed that there were two kinds of amnesia that Nielsen (1958) called temporal amnesia (loss of memory for personal experiences) and categorical amnesia (loss of memory for acquired facts). These two types of amnesia seem to differentially affect episodic and semantic memory. Nielson observed that "either may be lost without the other" (Nielsen, 1958, p. 15, cited in Tulving, 2002, p. 12).

Modern brain imaging studies also support the notion of separate brain systems. Brain scans indicate that episodic and semantic memory systems may encode information in different brain areas. The hemispheric encoding/retrieval asymmetry (HERA) model assigns episodic information encoding to the left prefrontal cortex and retrieval of episodic information to the right prefrontal cortex. Although this model also assigns semantic encoding to the left prefrontal cortex, semantic memory retrieval is "seldom observed in the right hemisphere" (Tulving, 2002, p. 18, citing Cabeza & Nyberg, 2000; Nyberg, 1998).

Bransford, Barclay, and Franks (1972) examined the question of whether persons could more easily remember the semantic structure of sentences or the overall situations that the sentences described. They found that their subjects more readily remembered the situations rather than the specific structure of the sentences. These results support the idea that memory is constructed from the meaning of information, not its specific structural characteristics.

Context Effects

In addition to the research on context effects in recognizing images discussed above (Bjork, 1975; Bjork & Jongeward, 1975), research using word lists has also shown that the context in which a stimulus occurs is very important in determining its ultimate classification. Miller, Heise, and Lichten (1951) found that "when the words formed meaningful sentences, they were much more readily identified than when they were arranged into random strings: the context formed by the sentence facilitated the recognition of the words" (Klatsky, 1975, p. 56). Even when learners supply their own context, they often recall better. Slamecka and Graf (1978) showed that people remembered words they generated themselves better than people who were simply presented the words. Tulving and Thompson (1973) emphasized the importance of restating the encoding context at the time of retrieval. Horton and Mills (1984) reviewed numerous research efforts that showed "strong support for this principle" (p. 373).

Context is also important when people attempt to learn how to operate a device. In a classic study, Kieras and Bovair (1984) demonstrated that learners who first learned a model of how a device works prior to learning a set of operational procedures outperformed learners who only learned the procedures by rote. The group that learned the device model not only learned the operating procedures faster, they also retained them more accurately, executed them faster, and simplified inefficient procedures more often than the rote group. "This study points to the performance benefits of building a deeper understanding" (Clark, R. C., 2003, p. 151).

Network Models of LTM

Klatsky (1975) maintained that no model of LTM was "totally adequate" (p. 132). However, additional research indicates that it is organized as a network of associated bundles of information. One of the first indications of this comes from research on the "tip-of-the-tongue phenomenon" (Brown & McNeill, 1966). This occurs when one can almost remember something, like a word, but can recall its synonyms, the number of syllables it contains, its initial sound, or other related pieces of information (generic recall). This research leads one to believe that information in LTM is somehow connected to other information in LTM.

"Tip-of-the-tongue" research, as well as the concept of semantic memory and evidence of context effects has led to the development of several network models of LTM (e.g., Quillian, 1969; Anderson, J. R. & Bower, 1972; 1973; 1974). Network models of semantic memory "depict LTM as a vast network of associated concepts" (Klatsky, 1975, p. 134). These models posit that different kinds of associations can be formed between items of information and that concepts are thought to have meaning by virtue of their associations to other concepts.

Bousfield (1953) showed that persons recalling lists of items tended to cluster the items into groups based on their similarity. Even when the items were not presented in organized groups, people tended to remember them in clusters belonging to the same category (e.g., animals, names, vegetables, etc.). Bower (1970) maintained that these clusters of information are organized in LTM as a conceptual hierarchy. "A conceptual hierarchy is a multilevel classification system based on common properties among items" (Weiten, 2004, p. 273). According to Bower, recall can be improved if the information is organized into a conceptual hierarchy.

Another scheme that some believe helps organize knowledge is called a semantic network. A *semantic network* consists of nodes representing concepts, joined together by pathways that link related concepts. Meyer and Schvaneveldt (1976) used semantic networks to explain why thinking about one word (e.g., butter) may make it easier to remember another word (e.g., bread). Collins and Loftus (1975) maintained that people's thoughts naturally go from one related word to another. These theorists called this process *spreading activation* within a semantic network. They assume that the connections (strength of activation) between words becomes weaker as it travels farther from the original words somewhat like ripples decrease in size as they radiate away from a rock tossed into a pool of water.

Connectionist and parallel distributed processing (PDP) models of memory are inspired by the way neural networks appear to handle information. For example, studies of visual perception have shown that the human brain seems to depend extensively on PDP (e.g., Wurtz & Kandel, 2000). This involves simultaneous processing of the same information that is spread across networks of neurons. According to connectionist and PDP theorists (McClelland, 2000; Smolensky, 1995), cognitive processes depend on patterns of activation in highly interconnected networks that resemble neural networks. A PDP network consists of a large number of interconnected nodes. These nodes may be inactive or may send either inhibitory or excitatory signals to other nodes. A specific node's level of activations depends on the weighted balance of these inhibitory and excitatory inputs from many other nodes. PDP models assume that specific memories are the result of particular patterns of activation in these networks (McClelland, 1992). These models differ from semantic networks because a piece of knowledge is not just connections between concepts. Rather, it is a pattern of activation across an entire network. The information depends on the strength of connections, which is why PDP models are called "connectionist."

Interference Models of LTM Forgetting

Tulving (1972) suggested that semantic knowledge is not as easily forgotten as information stored in episodic memory. Various models explain forgetting in LTM as a result of interference among items in episodic memory. Some of the models are grounded in the stimulus-response (S-R) tradition and explain forgetting in terms of reduction in "habit strength" over time (e.g., Melton & Irwin, 1940; Underwood, 1948). Other models equate forgetting with extinction (unlearning) of associations because of interference (e.g., Briggs, 1954, 1957). Slamecka (1968) found that some cues, expected to help recall, actually interfered with recall. He gave subjects some words from a list they had just learned. Instead of helping them to remember the rest of the words on the list, the subjects that received the "cue" words did worse. He concluded that the plan for future retrieval was developed while the list was being learned. Once developed, anything that interfered with the plan resulted in confusion and poorer recall. This explanation is not universally accepted, but there is considerable agreement that "cues can have negative effects" (Baron, Byrne, & Kantowitz, 1978, p.164.)

Forgetting may not simply involve the loss of strength or interference of associations among individual items of information stored in LTM. For example, Postman, Stark, and Fraser (1968) hypothesized that interference occurs at the level of whole response systems, not single associations. Things get even more complicated when we look at one of the earliest studies of forgetting and natural language.

Bartlett (1932) conducted a study of memory using a legend of Native Americans from North America called "War of the Ghosts." In his study, Bartlett asked his subjects to read the story twice and then tested their free recall after various delays (e.g., 15 minutes, 2 months, and 2½ years). Bartlett found that the subjects made systematic errors in their recall of the story. He proposed that these errors were the result of the subjects trying to fit the story into their existing mental structures. Bartlett labeled these existing mental structures *schemas*, which he defined as "active organization of past reaction" (Bartlett, quoted in Gredler, 2005, p. 204). These schemas operate on an individual's responses in any situation. This may explain why Bartlett's subjects forgot the aspects of the story that did not fit in with, or were incompatible with or actually generated interference with the schemas that form their LTM structure.

Alba and Hasher (1983) stated that schemas serve three functions:

1. Schemas provide a framework into which new data must fit in order to be comprehended.
2. They serve as a guide for goal-directed activities and searches of the environment.
3. They fill in gaps in information received from the environment.

Brewer and Treyens (1981) conducted an experiment that demonstrated the influence of schemas on visual and perceptual memory. They designed a room to look like a graduate student's office, but included items that did not fit the "schema" of a graduate student's office (e.g., skull, toy top, picnic basket). Each subject was asked to wait in the office for a few minutes then he or she was escorted to another room. Here, they were asked to write down his or her recollection of the first room. A total of 88 objects were listed by one or more subjects, of which 19 were not found in the room (e.g., books, filing cabinets, pens, lamps). The researchers concluded that schema knowledge became integrated with actual information about the room. Therefore, schemas can aid recall, but can also produce errors.

Similar evidence led Bransford, Barclay, and Franks (1972) to observe that forgetting can sometimes consist of remembering more, not less, than was presented. They concluded is that memory is "constructed." This view has become one of the main foundations of the "constructivist" theories of learning (see Driskell, Olsen, Hays, & Mullen, 1995 for a brief overview of the constructivist approach).

Loftus (1979; 1992) provided additional support for the idea that memories are constructed through her research on the "misinformation effect." She found that the memories of eyewitnesses could be changed depending on the way the questions were constructed. For example, Loftus and Palmer (1974) showed subjects a videotape of a car accident. The subjects were then questioned as if they were giving eyewitness testimony. One group was asked "How fast were the cars going when they *hit* each other?" The other group was asked "How fast were the cars going when they *smashed into* each other?" After a week the subjects' recall of the accident was tested. They were asked whether they remembered seeing broken glass at the accident site (there was none). Those that had earlier been asked about the cars *smashing into* each other were more likely to "recall" broken glass.

Remembering

In addition to research that examined processes of forgetting, research has also examined processes that facilitate remembering. As discussed above, items can be remembered for only a limited amount of time when they are held in STM. However, once stored in LTM there appears to be no limit to how long something can be remembered.

Three things must occur if one is to remember something (Klatsky, 1975, p. 171): encoding, storage, and retrieval. *Encoding* is primarily an STM (associator and decoder) process where information is put into a form compatible with internal LTM storage. This is thought to involve *mediation* or "certain processes that intervene between the presentation of a stimulus and the overt responses to the stimulus; these processes are not predictable from the stimulus by itself" (Klatsky, 1975, p. 178). Several types of mediators have been identified:

1. *Natural Language Mediators*, which apply information about natural language such as spelling and meaning.
2. *Sentence Mediators*, which convert information into sentences.
3. *Image Mediators*, which help one recognize and categorize shapes and patterns.

As mentioned above, the mere rehearsal of information does not automatically lead to improvements in recall (Craik & Watkins, 1973). After information has been encoded, it is stored in LTM until it is retrieved (remembered). Both storage and retrieval are facilitated if the information to be learned is organized and related to existing information in LTM (Bousfield, 1953, Bousfield & Cohen, 1955). Furthermore, organizations, once formed, tend to persist and new learning builds on these organizations or structures (Tulving, 1962; 1963). As Norman (1976) put it, "the best way to learn new material seems to be to use it in a meaningful way" (p. 114). For example, Bahrick and Hall (1991) found that individuals who took high-level mathematics courses in college remembered their high school algebra for almost half a century. On the other hand, persons who performed as well in high school algebra, but took no college mathematics courses, performed at only chance levels. Thus, if one uses what has been learned, there appears no limit to how long it can be remembered. This indicates that memory interacts with the learner's output processes (the encoder, output screen, output transducer, and motor) to strengthen existing associations.

Recognition versus Recall

Shepard (1967) demonstrated that there are two types of remembering: recognition and recall. Furthermore, recognition performance is extremely high relative to recall. This means, for example, that when a person is shown a list of several items, it easier to recognize that one of the items has been remembered than to recall the same item without seeing it on the list. This difference has been explained using the *Threshold Hypothesis*. It assumes that both recognition and recall depend on the strength of the items in memory and the threshold that must be reached to retrieve the information. It is assumed that the threshold for recognition is not as high as that for recall. Klatsky (1975, p. 276) maintained that the threshold hypothesis is inadequate to fully explain these differences. She felt that recall and recognition either depend on different mechanisms (the *Dual-Trace Hypothesis*) or that recall includes recognition as a subprocess (the *Dual-Process Hypothesis*). She cautioned that the interrelationships between recognition and recall are intricate and not fully understood (p. 223). Care must be taken by instructional developers to ensure that the instruction targets which type of remembering is needed.

Rules for Efficient Memorization

Various techniques have been developed to improve memory. Norman (1976) observed that "they all have similar bases: they teach the user to pay attention and to learn how to organize" (p. 131). He suggested four rules for efficient memorization (pp. 154-155):

1. *Small basic units.* The material to be learned should be divided into small, self-contained sections, with no more than four or five individual items in any section. This is because of the limited capacity of STM. Once the items have been encoded into LTM, new material can be added.
2. *Internal organization.* The sections must be organized so that the various parts fit together in a logical, self-ordering

structure. This structure then becomes an aid to forming associations and retrieving information.

3. *External organization.* Some relationship must be established between the material to be learned and material already learned, so that one fits neatly within the other. This is a requirement of the retrieval process because the associations provide a starting place for searching memory.

4. *Depth of processing.* Any mental activity performed on the material such as forming images or putting it into mental settings or stories, increases the depth of processing, thereby automatically helping to form and strengthen the relevant connections that improve retrievability.

Status of the Modal Model of Memory

The assumption of the existence of distinct sensory, short-, and long-term memory modes has been labeled the *Modal Model* (Healy & McNamara, 1996). Probably the earliest articulation of the modal model was by James (1980). He proposed two distinct memory stores, primary and secondary. James described *primary memory* as that which is held momentarily in consciousness and *secondary memory* as unconscious but permanent. Atkinson and Shiffrin (1968) expanded this conception by adding a sensory store. They relabeled primary memory as short-term memory and secondary memory as long-term memory. Others have suggested modifications of the basic modal model. For example, Baddeley (1999), as discussed above, suggested that short-term memory consists of several components and is better categorized as working memory. After reviewing numerous research efforts, Healy and McNamara (1996) concluded that "the modal model is still useful as a means to frame current literature on verbal learning and memory" (p. 168).

Metacognition

In the late 1970s and 1980s researchers began to examine the "higher-order processes involved in the selection and management of specific activities in learning and thinking" (Gredler, 2005, p.

233). These activities include knowledge about one's cognitive functioning and how to improve it. In general, the term *metacognition* has been applied to thinking about thinking.

According to Gredler (2005) there are two key components of metacognition; "(1) knowledge about and awareness of one's own thinking and (2) knowledge of when and where to use acquired strategies" (pp. 233-234). Knowledge about one's own thinking involves an awareness of one's capabilities and limitations and awareness of learning difficulties and remedial actions. Knowledge of when and where to use learning strategies involves knowledge about the task to be learned and the situations for which particular learning strategies are appropriate.

Differences in Metacognitive Capabilities

Differences in metacognitive capabilities have been found by examining the differences between younger and older children and the differences between novices and experts. Young children often are not aware of the broader purpose of instruction. For example, they may think that the purpose of reading is to pronounce all the words correctly rather than to understand the information in the reading assignment (Alexander, Schallert, & Hare, 1991).

Another difference between young and older children is that younger children are sometimes unaware of the demands of the task or the factors that influence task difficulty. For example, Karmiloff-Smith (1979) found differences between the ways children constructed toy railroad tracks. The younger children (ages 4-5) picked up pieces of track at random and arranged them in that order. Older children (ages 8-9) first sorted the pieces of track into straight and curved and then systematically selected the pieces from each group to complete the loop.

A third difference between young and older children is their ability to monitor their own learning performance. Younger children have not developed the skills to monitor their comprehension and detect their own errors they also often lack the knowledge of when and where to change learning strategies.

Differences between Novices and Experts

As previously discussed under the topic of pattern recognition, experts are better at detecting the patterns among important task cues and are better able to use the patterns to help retrieve information from memory (e.g., Chi, et al., 1981). However, based on an extensive review of research on expert performance, Ericsson and Lehmann (1996) concluded that, in addition to pattern recognition, expert performance "reflects many different types of complex mechanisms acquired to meet the specific demands of the tasks in a domain of expertise" (p. 290).

One of the mechanisms used by experts is better application of metacognitive skills. For example, researchers in the area of reading performance (e.g., Gredler, 2005) have found that experts understand the general goals of reading and studying and can allocate their time and effort to more difficult tasks. Novices, on the other hand, do not change their reading behavior for different types of content and do not slow down for difficult passages.

A second difference between experts and novices is that experts monitor their performance more often than novices. Thus, the experts become aware of and use "fix-it" strategies when they encounter problems before the problems become major. Two examples of these strategies are looking back at prior text to establish and clarify context and the pause-and-reflect strategy to strengthen associations between the new material and information already in memory. Finally, experts are more flexible than novices in applying strategies. Novices tend to use a single strategy while experts use different strategies in different circumstances and adapt their strategies to different kinds of texts and task demands.

Experts also differ from novices in their problem solving capabilities. This is because experts have more knowledge of the subject area and are better able to organize and access that knowledge. Schoenfeld (1987) demonstrated these differences by comparing the problem-solving approaches of expert and novice mathematicians. The novices latched onto a possible solution and worked it until time expired. Experts, on the other hand, tried many different approaches and discarded those that lead to blind alleys.

Britton, Stimson, Stennett, and Gülgöz (1998) found that learning from text is enhanced if the learners have higher domain knowledge. This domain knowledge enables them to make more connections among pieces of information. They also found that the experts' self-monitoring skills, specifically their ability to detect when their mental representation was not coherent, led them to seek extra connections among pieces of information.

Metacognitive Skills of Better Learners

Some research has demonstrated that better learners apply the metacognitive skill of self-explanation. Stark, Mandel, Gruber, and Renkl (2002) studied how bank apprentices used training materials that included worked examples (step-by-step procedures) related to accounting. The learners displayed three study profiles. About one third of the learners used a superficial approach (primarily repeating the information in the example). About half of the learners used an elaboration approach in which they explained the examples to themselves, focusing on important principles. A small portion of the learners (about 12%) used metacognitive monitoring strategies where they explicitly pointed out to themselves if they did not understand an example. The learners who elaborated performed better on a posttest than the superficial group. However, the learners who used the metacognitive monitoring techniques performed better than either of the other groups.

Not all things to be learned are centered on thinking. Many physical skills also need to be learned. The next chapter summarizes learning research, which has sought to understand how we learn motor skills like playing tennis or riding a bike. It also discusses research that examined how the emotional (affective) state of the learner can affect the learning process.

Chapter 6
Research on Complex Learning:
The Motor and Affective Domains

The previous chapter summarized learning research in the cognitive domain. Research on complex learning has also been conducted in the motor and affective domains. This chapter summarizes learning research in these domains. Although the research summarized in this chapter was initially focused on motor and affective issues, the reader should remember that the results are not exclusive to these domains. The results of much of the research in the motor and affective domains also have implications for learning in all three domains.

The Motor Domain

Motor behavior involves movement. In fact, the systems model of the learner labels the output processes for these types of behavior the motor. However, the motor domain is often referred to as the *psychomotor* domain because almost all motor behaviors also involve a mental or cognitive component. The definitions of several critical terms in motor research will aid the reader in understanding the following research summaries and discussions.

Some Key Terms in Motor Research

Although some of the following terms are used in the other domains, the definitions below focus on their role in the motor domain.
1. *Skill*: Motor researchers use the term *skill* in two ways. First, motor skills can be defined as "acts or tasks that require movement and must be learned in order to be properly performed" (Magill, 1980, p. 11). A second way the term is used is as "a qualitative expression of performance" (p. 11) connoting *proficiency*. This means that the performance on a given task can range from awkward to polished, from lousy to professional. Proficiency can be expressed in terms relating to the

productivity of the performer (e.g., he hits 80% of the targets) or characteristics of the person's performance (e.g., consistency of performance, use of meaningful cues to initiate or guide performance, or ability to anticipate required responses).

2. *Ability*:   An *ability* is "a general trait or capacity of an individual that is related to the performance of a variety of motor skills by being a component of those skills' structure" (Magill, 1980, p. 13). Fleishman (1972, 1978) is largely responsible for our understanding of the relationship between human abilities and the performance of motor skills.

3. *Movement Pattern*: This term refers to "basic elements or components of movement that are generalizable to the specific demands of a particular motor skill" (Magill, 1980, p. 14). For example, the movement pattern of kicking is a basic component of punting a football, kicking a soccer goal, or kicking a field goal in football.

4. *Motor Learning*:   As defined above, the general term learning refers to some form of behavioral change in an individual as the result of instruction and experience. In the motor domain, learning can be defined as "an internal change in the individual that is inferred from a relatively permanent improvement in performance of the individual as a result of practice" (Magill, 1980, p. 14). It is important to distinguish between the terms *motor learning* and *motor development*. The study of motor development is concerned with how a child learns motor skills and develops abilities as he or she matures. For example, a researcher in motor development might be concerned with how a child develops the ability to jump by gradually becoming stronger and more coordinated at different ages. Motor learning is specifically concerned with how motor skills are learned by mature performers.

5. *Motor Programs*: A motor program is set of commands from the central nervous system to the muscles of the body to perform a specific movement. "The set of commands will be carried out completely, even if the sensory feedback system indicates midway through the movement that the movement should be altered" Magill,

1980, p. 190). Although there is no direct evidence that motor programs exist, "there are certain response situations which cannot be explained any other way" (p. 191). Motor programs seem to be activated for complex movements after they have been learned enough to become automatic.

6. *Sensory Systems*: It is not possible to perform motor skills without sensory information being detected by the performer. *Vision* is considered to be the primary sense in most skills. The *auditory* sensory mode (hearing) is also involved in many motor skills. *Kinesthesis* is information that is sensed about the movement of the limbs. *Proprioception* is a broader term that includes sensing the position of body parts and also the forces and pressures on the body or its parts. Finally, *tactile* or *cutaneous* information is about objects detected through the skin. Most often this information comes through the fingers and hands, but the feet, body, and head can also be used to detect such information for some tasks.

Categories of Motor Skills

Motor skills have been classified into categories on the basis of at least four classification systems (Magill, 1980, p. 17).

1. *Precision of the Movement*: Motor skills can be classified as *gross motor skills* (those involving large musculature as the primary basis for movement) or *fine motor skills* (those that require the ability to control the small muscles of the body).

2. *Distinctiveness of Beginning and End Points*: A motor skill that has distinct beginning and end points (e.g., throwing a ball or hitting the key on a computer keyboard) is categorized as a *discrete motor skill*. If discrete motor skills can be put together in a series, the resultant skill is classified as a *serial motor skill*. Playing the piano can be considered as a serial motor skill because the discrete movements of striking the piano keys must be accomplished in a definite serial order. On the other hand, a motor skill that has no distinct beginning and end points is called a *continuous motor skill*. Steering an automobile,

tracking a blip on a radar screen, or running are all examples of continuous motor tasks, in that the beginning and end points of the task are determined by the performer, not specified by the task itself.

3. *Stability of the Environment*: E. C. Poulton (1957) classified a task as *open* if the environment was ever changing and unpredictable. If the environment was stable (predictable), he classified the task as *closed*. Gentile (1972) suggested that these terms were better used as anchor points of a continuum. On the closed end of the continuum are tasks like bowling, golf, archery, where the stimulus in each task waits to be acted upon by the performer. For example, bowling pins are not going to fall down until the performer acts. On the open end of the continuum are tasks that take place in a changing environment where the performer must act upon the stimulus according to the action of the stimulus. Examples of these are hitting a baseball or tennis ball. The baseball player or tennis player must adjust his or her behavior to the ball's spatial and speed demands. Closed tasks are sometimes called *self-paced tasks* and open tasks are sometimes called *externally-* or *forced-paced tasks*.

4. *Feedback Control*: The fourth classification system is "based on how and when the sensory feedback that results from all movements can be used by the performer in the production of that movement" (Magill, 1980, p. 20). *Closed-loop skills* are those where the feedback information can be used to adjust the action during the movement itself. An example of a closed-loop task is serving a tennis ball. Tasks where feedback must be remembered and applied to the next response require *open-loop skills*. These skills occur very quickly and the performer must respond with little opportunity to adjust behavior during the response. An example of an open-loop task is hitting a baseball. If the batter swings and misses the ball, he or she must wait for the next pitch to apply the available feedback.

Learning versus Performance

The distinction between learning and performance "has been of critical importance in the evolution of learning theory" (Estes, 1988, p. 85). *Performance* can be thought of as *observable behavior*. Learning, on the other hand, is not directly observable, but must be *inferred* from a person's behavior or performance. In order to infer that learning has occurred: 1) the performance change should be persistent (it should not last for just a short time); and 2) the performance should show increasingly less variability over time.

Just knowing how to do something does not mean that one is motivated to perform. Hull (1952) and Spence (1956) developed theories that introduced motivation as an important factor in the performance of learned skills. Although their theories and "laws" have been shown to be incapable of explaining all factors in learning, the distinction they made between learning and performance still influences most learning theories.

Motivation

The word motivation is related to the word "motive." Motive comes from the Latin word, *motivum*, meaning "a moving cause." Thus motivation is concerned with determining the causes of behavior and what influences those causes. Magill (1980) defined motivation as "the causes of the initiation , maintenance, and intensity of behavior" (p. 298).

As discussed previously, psychologists have long understood that a person must be motivated to perform. In most cases this is also true of learning (one exception is incidental learning discussed below). A student usually must be motivated to learn. The following discussion looks at some of the theories of motivation and the research that supports them.

Locke (2000) argued that motivation includes four key concepts:

1. *Needs*: the requirements of physical and psychological health;
2. *Values*: that which one considers good or beneficial and acts to gain or keep;

131

3. *Goals and Intensions*: the situationally specific form of values, the specific object or aim of an action; and
4. *Emotions*: the form in which one experienced automatized value appraisals.

Thus, "the term 'motive' combines values and emotions; a motive is the desire for a goal or value" (p. 411). Furthermore, Locke argued that motivation affects actions in three ways. First, it affects the facts we choose to act on by focusing attention and action on value- and goal-relevant behavior. Second, the value and goal aspect of motivation affects the intensity of the action based on how important the value is held to be. Finally, it affects the persistence of action, or how effort is sustained over time. Motivation appears to be controlled, or at least influenced by the decider, which coordinates the processes of several other subsystems, including memory, the associator, the input transducer, and the input screen. This coordination helps maintain the learner's motivation by keeping attention focused on relevant instructional information. Motivation is such an important factor in learning that a substantial amount of research has been devoted to understanding its effects.

Reinforcement as Motivation

There are many theories of motivation (Beck, 1978). Many of the early theories centered on the concept of reinforcement and what the organism found reinforcing. For example, Hull's (1943) theory maintained that "drive reduction is the necessary condition of reinforcement" (Beck, 1978, p. 129). For Hull, a *drive* is a hypothetic energizing state brought about by some biological *need* (e.g., lack of food results in the hunger drive). According to Hull's theory, the energizing effect of a drive "motivates" the organism to seek a way to reduce the drive.

Some motivational theories have focused on arousal as a reinforcing factor in motivation. Arousal or activation theory (Berlyne, 1960; Hunt, 1965) assumes that individuals strive for an optimal level of stimulation (arousal). If an individual is either over- or under-stimulated, he or she will be motivated to return to the optimal stimulation level. Dember and Earl (1957) proposed that "there is an optimal level of stimulus complexity which is reinforcing for each organism and that organisms vary in the level of complexity that is optimal" (Beck, 1978, p. 137). Furthermore, they maintained that organisms tend to respond to stimuli that are a little more complex than previous stimuli. Once the organism has become familiar with the new stimuli (e.g., learned the appropriate responses), it will tend to prefer even more complex stimuli. This effect probably involves habituation and sensitization, as well as other processes that affect the learners input screen (e.g., selective attention based on previously learned associations).

Hunt (1963) proposed that information itself can arouse, activate, and motivate. He argued that information can either provide too much or to little incongruity, which in turn, leads to arousal. The organism is then motivated to reduce the arousal level. The stimulation provided by information can be aversive if it is either too complex to be processed or too simple and therefore boring. This concept is a major factor in Csikszentmihalyi's (1990) theory of "flow." His theory is discussed later in the section on research in the affective domain.

The Effects of Consistency and Change on Motivation

The Russian physiologist, E. N. Sokolov (1960) proposed that sensory inputs, which arouse attention may habituate if presented frequently. This assumption is shared by several motivational theories that focus on the effects of consistency and change. One of the most famous theories is Festinger's (1957) theory of cognitive dissonance. Dissonance is said to occur when two beliefs are incongruent or lead to contradictory conclusions. When applied to learning, it is important that items of instructional information be logically related to one another so they do not create contradictions. These logical relations aid in the formation of meaningful associations and, in turn, facilitate the storage of these associations in memory.

Learners have certain expectancies about the material they intend to learn. Aronson (1968) suggested that dissonance occurs when these expectancies are violated. Such expectancies can involve the way instructional materials are presented and also how the learner's performance is rewarded or remediated.

Intrinsic and Extrinsic Motivation

Some researchers, especially in the field of industrial psychology, distinguish between intrinsic and extrinsic motivation (Lepper & Greene, 1975; Lepper & Malone, 1987). *Intrinsic motivation* refers to activities that are rewarding in and of themselves. These activities might include games, puzzles, or creative endeavors such as art and music. *Extrinsic motivation* refers to reinforcement from some external agent. For example, an extrinsic motivator might be money received for completing a task.

It has been shown that providing extrinsic rewards for a task that is intrinsically motivating may actually decrease performance. One study (Anderson, R., Manoogian, & Reznick, 1976) compared the effects of money, a "good player" award, and verbal praise on the performance of nursery school children. Both the money and the "good player" award reduced the amount of time the children spent drawing pictures, but verbal praise produced an increase. Other research also supports these results (e.g., Calder & Staw, 1975; Notz, 1975).

Need for Achievement

The need for achievement has been shown to be a powerful motivating factor. Murray defined it as a desire or tendency "to overcome obstacles, to exercise power, to strive to do something difficult as well and as quickly as possible" (Murray, 1938, pp. 80-81, quoted in Beck, 1978, p. 317).

Atkinson (1964) refined Murray's ideas about achievement motivation into the framework of *expectancy-value theory* (Lewin, 1935; Tolman, 1959). In Atkinson's theory, the probability that one will engage in achievement-oriented behavior is a balance between the tendency to succeed and the tendency to avoid failure. Thus, persons will tend to engage in tasks where they expect to succeed and tend to avoid tasks where they expect to fail. It is therefore important that learning tasks maintain this expectancy balance in order to sustain the learner's motivation to continue learning.

Learning as Motivation

Ausubel (1968) observed that the relationship between motivation and learning is not unidirectional. Sometimes, students can begin the learning experience and that experience can itself lead to higher levels of motivation and thus to further learning. Thus, if the instructional material is engaging and relevant to the student, he or she is more likely to be motivated to continue learning.

Incidental Learning. A line of research that demonstrated that learning can occur in the absence of motivation examined *incidental learning*. For example, Dickinson (1978) demonstrated that persons could learn an arm-positioning task even if they were not specifically told to learn it. However, this research also showed that the incidental learners performed more poorly after a 5-minute retention interval. Thus, it appears that intentional learners may retain learned skills longer than incidental learners.

Goals as Motivation

Another line of research has shown that establishing an appropriate level of aspiration or goal to be achieved is an effective means to motivate behavior. For example, Latham and Locke (1987) found that "goal setting is a simple straightforward and highly effective technique for motivating employee performance" (p. 132). Magill (1980) used the terms "goal setting" and "level of aspiration" interchangeably. He defined both terms to mean "the level of performance on a task which a person expects to achieve in the future" (p. 319). According to Locke (2000), goal setting theory argues that "specific, difficult goals lead to better performance than 'do best' or easy goals and that goal effects are moderated by feedback and commitment" (p. 415).

Nelson (1978) studied the motivating effects of goal setting on performance of a motor task. He gave four groups different goals to achieve in an elbow flexion strength test (actual performance norm, fictitious norm, an obtainable performance goal, or nothing). The results showed that the three groups given goals to achieve (realistic or not) performed better than the group with no goals.

135

Locke and Bryan (1966) demonstrated that goal setting is important for both performing and learning a motor skill. Two groups were asked to learn a complex task requiring them to use both hand and foot controls to match two sets of light patterns. One group was told to "do your best" and the other was given a specific goal to strive for. The specific goal group out performed the other group and also learned the task faster.

Efforts to attain goals can be reduced by frustration. Frustration often occurs when goal-directed activity is blocked (in other words, the performer's output screen is closed). Beck (1978) maintained that goal-directed responses can be blocked by either barriers (external physical objects or internal states) or deficiencies (lack of the necessary ability to attain the goal). Besides these blockages, frustration can also be aroused by the lack of rewards or by rewards that differ from those expected. However, frustration is not this simple. Beck (1978) pointed out that in addition to the cessation of goal-directed activity, frustration can sometimes lead to increased effort (the frustration effect). However, this effect is probably temporary and cannot be expected to sustain performance over longer periods of time.

Magill (1980) provided several guidelines for setting goals.

1. *Set objective goals.* Goals should be stated in terms of a number or some other objective form rather than "do your best."

2. *Set goals that are meaningful.* The goal should have meaning to the person. For example, asking a student to hit 6 out of 10 targets is not as meaningful as stating that 6 out of 10 is an above average score.

3. *Set goals that are obtainable.* Challenging, yet obtainable goals tend to increase motivation. However, an unobtainable goal may lead to failure and poorer performance (Nelson, 1978).

4. *Set goals according to individual differences.* All students do not have the same physical and mental abilities nor have they shared the same experiences. An instructor must determine goals for each individual so they can exert maximum effort toward an achievable goal.

5. *Set goals on the basis of past experience.* Students who have succeeded in the past will usually expect to succeed

in the future. Instructors need to individualize student goals so they can develop a pattern of success.

Keller's Model of Instructional Motivation

Keller (1979, 1983) developed a theory of instructional motivation that incorporated many of the instructional variables and issues discussed above. A diagram of Keller's model is shown in Figure 6.1. Following the tradition of field theory (Lewin, 1935), the model describes the influences of the person and the environment on the behavior of the learner. The three major variables in the model are motivation, performance, and instructional influence. The model identifies variables as either output or input variables. The output variables are distinguished as effort, performance, and consequences. "*Performance* means actual accomplishment, whereas *effort* refers to whether the individual is engaged in actions aimed at accomplishing the task" (Keller, 1983, p. 391, authors emphasis). Therefore, effort is an indicator of motivation while performance is a measure of learning. This measurement ties performance to consequences as the results of performance.

The model identifies two types of input variables: person inputs and environmental inputs. The person inputs are related to how the learner reacts to instructional conditions. They include the learner's motives (values) and expectancy, his or her abilities, skills, and knowledge, and how he or she evaluates the consequences of performance. The model assumes that "motivation is a multiplicative function of values and expectancies, that is, a person will approach activities or goals that are perceived to be personally satisfying and for which the person has a positive expectancy for success" (Keller, 1983, p. 394). The learner's motives (values) and expectancy are derived from his or her cognitive evaluation of the consequences of performance, as shown by the dotted lines in the figure. "Consequences are related to motivation because they combine with cognitive evaluation...to influence changes in one's personal values or motives" (Keller, 1983, p. 391). Initially, this is probably the result of the learner's evaluation of the consequences of past performance on similar tasks. As instruction proceeds, this evaluative loop influences the learner's motives and expectancy for subsequent learning and performance.

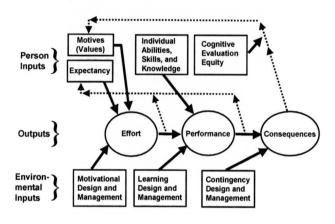

Figure 6.1:
Keller's Model of Motivation, Performance, and
Instructional Influence

The model categorizes environmental inputs as variables involved with: motivational design and management, learning design and management, and contingency design and management. The *learning design* variables are those that influence instructional approaches, such as how ideas are sequenced and related together by the instructional content (Reigeluth & Stein, F. S., 1983) or how specific instructional approaches are used to present the content (Merrill, 1983). The contingency design variables are those that influence how the consequences of performance are communicated to the learner. For example, the use of feedback, rewards, and remediation are all contingency design variables. Keller does not elaborate on these environmental inputs because many other researchers have made them their focus. Rather, he focuses on the third category of environmental inputs, motivational design variables. This focus led him to develop the ARCS model of instruction.

The ARCS Model of Instruction

Keller (1983, 1987) developed a comprehensive approach to the design and management of instructional motivation. The ARCS model refers to the four basic categories of motivational conditions: attention, relevance, confidence, and satisfaction.

Attention (originally labeled *interest*) "refers to whether the learner's curiosity is aroused, and whether this arousal is sustained over time" (Keller, 1983, p. 395). The model refers to different types of arousal and recommends various techniques to increase each type. *Perceptual arousal* can be increased by using novel, surprising, incongruous and uncertain events. *Inquiry arousal* can be increased by stimulating information seeking behavior by posing questions or problems or having the learner generate questions or problems to solve. Interest can be maintained by varying the elements of instruction (e.g., switching between information presentation and learner activities that allow them to interact with the content).

Relevance "refers to the learner's perception of personal need satisfaction in relation to the instruction, or whether a highly desired goal is perceived to be related to the instructional activity" (p. 395). Relevance can be increased by providing the learner with concrete examples, with which the learner is familiar (e.g., related to their previous experiences and values). Relevance can also be increased by presenting goal oriented statements and objectives and by explaining the utility of the instruction for the learner's present and future uses.

Confidence (originally labeled *expectancy*) "refers to the perceived likelihood of success, and the extent to which success is under learner control" (p. 395). Instruction that is designed to enable the learner to succeed can increase confidence. The instruction should be challenging, but not overwhelming. The learner should see that his or her expended effort directly influences the consequences by receiving relevant and meaningful feedback about their efforts. Instruction that presents realistic performance requirements and meaningful evaluation criteria can increase learner expectations.

Satisfaction "refers to the combination of extrinsic rewards and intrinsic motivation, and whether these are compatible with the learner's anticipations" (p. 395). Providing the learner with opportunities to use their newly acquired knowledge or skills in a real or simulated setting can increase satisfaction. Then, providing feedback with either reinforcement to sustain the desired behavior or remediation to correct undesired behavior. At all times, the learner should perceive that the outcomes of his or her efforts are consistent with their expectations.

Keller (1987) observed that motivation is "a means to an end, not an end in itself" (p. 7). The purpose of motivational strategies is to "stimulate the motivation to learn, and not detract from the learning process" (p. 7). In order to help ensure that this is the case, Keller (1987) recommended that the ARCS model be applied at each phase of instructional systems development. He suggested the following activities:

- *Define Stage*: Classify the problem; analyze the audience motivation, and prepare motivational objectives.
- *Design Stage*: Generate potential strategies for each motivational objective and select those that are appropriate. The strategies should: (1) not take up too much instructional time; (2) not detract from the instructional objectives; (3) be feasible within the time and money constraints of the planned instruction; (4) be acceptable to the audience; and (5) be compatible with the chosen delivery system.
- *Develop Stage*: Prepare motivational materials and integrate them with the instruction.
- *Evaluate Stage*: Conduct formative (try-out) evaluations of motivational materials and assess motivational outcomes as well as instructional outcomes. Motivation should be assessed with direct measures, such as persistence, intensity of effort, emotion, and attitude.

The reader is encouraged to consult the original sources (e.g., Keller, 1983, 1987) for details on the ARCS model because motivation is so important in the learning process.

A Test of the ARCS Model. Recent research tested the effectiveness of a computer-assisted instruction (CAI) course that was designed using the principles of the ARCS model (Song & Keller, 2001). Three types of CAI were designed and presented to different groups of learners. Motivationally minimized CAI contained the minimal number of motivational strategies.

Motivationally saturated CAI included a large number of motivational strategies, which were presented to all learners, regardless of their motivational needs. Motivationally adaptive CAI provided motivational strategies targeted to the immediate needs of each learner. In this condition, motivated learners were not presented with motivational strategies that might distract them. The learners' levels of motivation and attention were continuously assessed during instruction. Results showed that the motivationally adaptive CAI was more effective than either of the other approaches.

Inferring Learning

The only way to determine if learning has occurred is to measure the output of the learner system to determine if there is a change in the performance of the learner. Newell and Simon (1972) eloquently stated this position. "The study of learning, if carried out with theoretical precision, must start with a model of a performing organism, so that one can represent, as learning, the changes in the model....If performance is not well understood, it is somewhat premature to study learning" (pp. 7-8, quoted in Glaser & Bassok, 1989, p. 633).

"The inference that learning has occurred is generally based on performance curves and retention tests" (Magill, 1980, p. 39). A *performance curve* (sometimes called a *learning curve*) is a graph showing a person's performance scores in a learning situation. It is an "illustration of learning over the practice time in which the performance is occurring" (p. 40). Figure 6.2 shows two hypothetical performance curves. In this hypothetical example, the performance of two groups has been measured as they practice hitting a target. One group received verbal motivation and the other did not. These hypothetical performance curves show the effect of verbal motivation on performance over time (this is a real effect, but the data shown here are hypothetical).

According to Magill (1980), two characteristics, shown in any performance curve, should be considered in order to make any inference about learning. "First, the curve should show an *increase in the performance score* over the practice trials...Second, the curve should show a *decrease in the variability of the performance score* as the number of practice trials increases" (p. 44, author's emphasis).

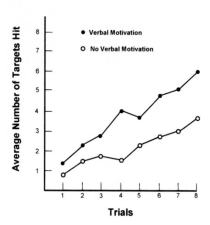

Figure 6.2:
Hypothetical Performance (Learning) Curves

A *retention test* is another means of inferring learning from performance. In this case, a test of the motor skill is administered at the end of the practice session and again after some period of time following practice of the skill. The difference between these two scores is an indicator of performance increase. Another performance test is administered at some later time, after no additional practice of the skill. "If there is a positive difference between that score and the score on the first practice day, you can be certain that learning has occurred" (Magill, 1980, p. 45).

Self-efficacy as a Predictor of Learning

Some researchers have used individuals' perceived self-efficacy as a predictor of learning and in some cases even as a measure of learning. "Perceived self-efficacy refers to a belief in one's capabilities to organize and execute the actions necessary to manage particular situations...in the academic sphere, it refers to the belief that one can perform particularly academic tasks successfully" (Gredler, 2005, p. 354).

Bandura (1995) stated that there are four types of influences that affect an individual's self-efficacy beliefs: mastery experiences, vicarious experiences, social persuasion, and reduction of physiological and emotional stress.

1. *Mastery experiences* refer to the individual's past successes in similar types of activities. Bandura (1995) cautioned that mastery experiences should not only consist of easy successes. These can lead individuals to expect quick results and become discouraged by failures. Mastery experiences should also involve "acquiring the cognitive tools for creating and executing appropriate courses of action to manage ever-changing life circumstances"(p. 3). It is assumed that these tools will help individuals persevere, even when they encounter setbacks.

2. *Vicarious experiences* occur when one observes other individuals (social models) successfully performing the task. These models can demonstrate effective strategies for task accomplishment.

3. *Social persuasion* (usually verbal) can help individuals counter mild self-doubts by focusing their attention on self-improvement rather than outperforming others. Persuasion should be used in conjunction with other influences.

4. *Reduction of stress and negative emotional feelings* associated with the task can enhance self-efficacy. Individuals can learn to interpret the first signs of tension as a cue to focus their efforts.

Gredler (2005) summarized the effects of perceived high and low efficacy. For task-related behavior, those with high self-efficacy strengthen their efforts in the face of difficulties, but those with low self-efficacy slacken their efforts. The previously acquired skills of those with high self-efficacy are intensified and strengthened when they are faced with difficulties. Persons with low self-efficacy may give up the task when it becomes difficult. Those with high self-efficacy focus their efforts and attention on the demands of the task, while those with low self-efficacy often focus on their own personal deficiencies.

In terms of long-term effects, those with high self-efficacy participate in a variety of activities and experiences that aid their self-development. Persons with low self-efficacy avoid these activities and miss out on their benefits. Those with low self-efficacy experience anxiety and stress in performance situations, but those with high self-efficacy experience little stress in taxing situations. Persons with high self-efficacy attribute lack of effort as the cause for failure, but low self-efficacy persons attribute it to their personal shortcomings. Finally, those with high self-efficacy choose goals that are challenging and that sustain their interest. Persons with low self-efficacy have lower aspirations as a means of avoiding stress.

Although some research supports the notion that self-efficacy beliefs can predict learning performance (e.g., Pajares, 1996), there is also research that indicates that people tend to hold overly favorable views of their abilities (Kruger & Dunning, 1999). In four studies, participants who scored in the bottom quartile on tests of humor, grammar, and logic grossly overestimated their test performance. Although their test scores placed them in the 12th percentile, they estimated themselves in the 62nd percentile. Kruger and Dunning (1996) stated that "the skills that engender competence in a particular domain are often the very same skills necessary to evaluate competence in that domain" (p. 4 of 56). They concluded that when people are incompetent, they suffer from two burdens: (1) they reach erroneous conclusions and make unfortunate choices; and (2) their incompetence robes them of the ability to realize it.

Maki (1998) reviewed research that showed learners' ratings of their reading comprehension were only weakly correlated with their performance on objective tests of their comprehension. The learners often believe that the teaching technique is entertaining. However, the technique may have little influence on their actual cognitive performance.

It can be concluded that self-efficacy is one of many factors that influence attention, motivation, and persistence in learning a task, but it is not a sufficient method of predicting task performance. If one wishes to measure the effects of instruction, the most valid method is to measure the performance of the learners after they have completed the instruction.

Measures of Motor Performance

Since performance is the only way to determine if learning has occurred, it is important to measure performance. Magill (1980, p. 33) classified objective performance measures into four categories as shown in Table 6.1.

Table 6.1
Four Categories of Objective Performance Measures

Category	Examples of Measures	Performance Examples
Speed	Time to completion (e.g., sec., min., hr.)	Amount of time to: • Run a mile • Do 50 sit-ups • Trace through a maze
Accuracy	• Number of errors • Amount of errors • Successful attempts • Time-on/off-target • Time-on/off-balance	• How many free throws made? • How many inches off target in reproducing movement? • How long balanced on balance board? • How long stylus kept in contact with disc on pursuit rotor?
Response Magnitude	• Height (e.g., cm, in., ft.) • Distance • Velocity • Pounds • Number of Responses • Trials to completion	• How high did you do the vertical jump? • How many points did you score? • How many times did you try an offensive wrestling move?
Response Latency	Reaction time	How long did it take you to move when the football was hiked?

It is also necessary to judge the *appropriateness* of any type of performance measure of the learner's output on a motor task (or, to a great extent, for tasks in other domains). Four criteria that can be used to make these judgments are:

1. *Objectivity*: Two different people should be able to arrive at a similar score for a performance. This is not a large problem with measures like those described in Table 6.1. It is more difficult when subjective terms such as "good," "bad," or "excellent" are used instead of objective measures.
2. *Reliability*: This refers to the repeatability of the performance measure. It is an indication of the certainty that a similar performance score will be obtained if the same subject is tested a second time.
3. *Validity*: This is an indication of whether the task or performance score actually measures what it is intended to measure. For example, in measuring a motor task, one must ensure that it actually requires a motor skill, that it requires physical movement to be successfully accomplished. Then, one must consider if the measure actually reflects the factor in questions (e.g., strength, coordination, or balance).
4. *Novelty*: A novel task is "one with which subjects have had no previous experience" (Magill, 1980, p. 34). A novel task enables the researcher to focus on the variable in question (e.g., fatigue) without confounding the results with the previous experience of the subjects. Magill used the example of a basketball free throw to illustrate a novel way to measure fatigue. He suggested that having the subjects shoot with their non-preferred hand or bouncing the ball into the hoop could help avoid the confusion of different skill levels at basketball.

Stages of Learning

Many researchers have found that the learning of motor skills occurs in stages. Fitts and Posner (1967) described the learning process as involving three stages:

1. *Cognitive stage*: When the learner begins to acquire a new skill, he or she must learn important information about the skill. For example, he or she must acquire answers to the following types of questions. What is the basic task? What are the rules of the game? How do you know who wins? How do I hold the racquet? This stage

is characterized by large numbers of errors and the errors tend to be gross. It is also marked by highly variable performance.

2. *Associative stage*: The second stage of learning is centered on refining the skill. The basic fundamentals have been learned and the learner can now detect his or her own errors and work on improving performance. Errors are fewer at this stage and the performance is less variable.

3. *Autonomous stage*: In the third and final stage of learning the skill has become almost automatic or habitual. The skilled performer does not need to concentrate on individual portions of the skill. Rather he or she can concentrate on the most difficult portions or the quality of the entire performance.

Van Lehn (1996) maintains that these three stages (or phases) "also aptly describe the course of cognitive skill acquisition" (p. 515). Other models of the stages of learning have also been proposed (e.g., Adams, 1971). The main difference between these models is the number of stages they propose. What can be agreed upon is that "learning does progress in stages which can be differentiated on the basis of the amount and nature of the cognitive activity associated with the production of the response" (Magill, 1980, p. 52). Furthermore, each stage of learning requires somewhat different instructional strategies to maximize the efficiency of practice during that stage.

Practice and Skilled Performance

"One major activity separates the gifted amateur from the professional: practice" (Norman, 1976, p. 199). As indicated in the above discussion on the stages of learning, practice is essential to learning any motor skill. The amount and quality of practice must be tailored to the requirements of the skill and the stage of learning. Several researchers have demonstrated that early performance of a motor skill is an unreliable predictor of later performance (Fleishman & Rich, 1963; Welch, 1963; Trussell, 1965). It is important for instructors to realize that poor performance in the early stages of skill acquisition can lead a learner to "give up" or be removed from a team. Early phases of instruction should concentrate on the basics of performing the skill, on whether the learner has the basic abilities to perform, and whether he or she is motivated to succeed. If these initial requirements are met and the student has sufficient practice time, a more accurate prediction of later success or failure can be made.

Similar to the learning stages approach discussed above, many researchers believe that practice moves the learner closer to *procedural efficiency*. This procedural efficiency, in turn, "results in qualitative changes in knowledge structures and in changes of choice of cognitive strategies....The theoretical implication is that major metacognitive changes are an unconscious by-product of highly practiced successful performance" (Glaser & Bassok, 1989, p. 640).

Hagman and Rose (1983) reviewed 13 experiments on the retention of learned tasks in the military context. Some of their conclusions from this review include:

1. Retention can be improved with repetition (practice) both before and after task proficiency has been achieved. This supports the *overlearning principle* (e.g., more practice is usually better, even though the learner has achieved criterion levels of performance; see the next section for additional information on overlearning).

2. Retention is better when task repetitions are spaced rather than massed during training (see the next section).

3. Retention can be improved through the use of instructional methods that are tailored for the specific training environment. For example, if training is to be conducted in a military field environment, the specific variables that make this environment unique need to be determined and accounted for when designing the instructional approach.

Some Principles of Practice. Magill (1980) provided several principles to guide instructors to maximize the benefits of practice.

1. *The amount of practice affects the quality of learning although the effect is not always proportional.* Practice almost always improves performance. However, there appears to be a point of diminishing returns from practice. Researchers have studied the problem of how much practice is beneficial to optimize learning. *Overlearning* can be defined as "the practice time spent beyond the amount of practice time needed to achieve some

performance criteria" (p. 266). Melnick (1971) showed that overlearning groups outperformed a group that only practiced enough to achieve criterion performance. However, the 50% overlearning group performed as well as the 100% and 200% overlearning groups.

2. *The spacing or distribution of practice appears to affect performance rather than learning.* Practice can be provided where the amount of rest between trials is either very short or not at all (*massed practice*). It can also be provided where the amount of rest between trials or groups of trials is relatively large (*distributed practice*). An early research example of that supports this principle was conducted by Adams and Reynolds (1954). They trained four groups on a motor task (pursuit rotor) for 40 trials. Part of the time, all the learners practiced under massed practice conditions. They were then were switched to distributed practice conditions after 5, 10, 15, or 20 massed practice trials. The performance of the 4 groups was compared to the performance of a control group that only practiced under distributed practice conditions. In all cases, each group's performance reached the performance level of the control group within 3 trials. Magill (1980) concluded from this and other research that "the evidence seems rather convincing that the superiority of distributed practice over massed practice occurs as a performance attribute. When the amount of learning is taken into consideration, there does not appear to be any superiority of one over the other schedule" (p. 272). Magill postulated two reasons for these learning and performance differences. First, in massed-practice conditions, fatigue may override performance. The individual may be learning the task, but is too fatigued to perform it well. His second reason relates to theories that postulate stages of learning (e.g., Fitts and Posner, 1967; Adams, 1971; Van Lehn, 1996). Massed practice in early learning trials may limit the amount of cognitive processing the learner can dedicate to evaluation of the results of the trials. Thus, the learner is not able to modify his or her behavior based on these results. For these and other reasons, distributed practice appears to be more effective than massed practice

for learning most tasks. The National Research Council (1991) made an even stronger statement on the benefits of spaced practice. "The so-called spacing effect—that practice sessions spaced in time are superior to massed practices in terms of long-term retention—is one of the most reliable phenomena in human experimental psychology. The effect is robust and appears to hold for verbal materials of all types and for motor skills" (p. 30).

3. *Light to moderate fatigue affects performance, while heavy or extreme levels of fatigue affects both performance and learning.* Some research (e.g., Godwin & Schmidt, 1971) provided evidence that fatigue does not affect learning, but does affect performance. Other research (e.g., Carron, 1972) indicated that fatigue affects both learning and performance. Magill (1980) maintains that there may be a *threshold of fatigue* for various motor skills. If fatigue levels are kept below the threshold, practice of a new skill will probably be beneficial in the long run. However, if fatigue levels are greater than the threshold, additional practice is not advisable. "Unfortunately, no evidence has been provided in the research literature to suggest any valid criteria for determining such a threshold" (p. 277). He suggested that instructors must use their past experience and intuition to guide them in determining the amount of fatigue which their students can show before stopping instruction for that session.

4. *The decision to practice a motor skill as a whole or by parts should be made on the basis of the complexity and organization of the skill.* Early research on whether to practice whole tasks or parts of tasks was very mixed. Naylor and Briggs (1963) suggested that the issue could be resolved by considering two features of the task in question. First, one must consider *task complexity* or how may part or components there are in the task and the information processing demands of the task. The second feature is *task organization*. This refers to how the components of a task are interrelated. If the parts are intimately related to each other, it has a high degree of organization. If the parts are rather independent, the task

would be considered low in organization. In terms of these categories of tasks, Singer (1980) maintained that there are two general rules that can be applied in teaching motor skills. The first general rule centers on task complexity. Low complexity tasks that are highly organized should be trained as wholes. On the other hand, high complexity tasks with low levels or organization are good candidates for part-task training. Tasks that fall in the middle of these two continua should be trained with a combination of whole and part-task approaches. The second general rule is that "parts of a skill that are highly dependent on each other should be practiced together as a unit, but parts which are relatively independent can be practiced individually" (Magill, 1980, p. 282).

5. *Practice that occurs mentally can be beneficial to the acquisition of a new motor skill and to the performance of a well-learned skill.* Mental practice or "cognitive rehearsal of a physical skill in the absence of overt, physical movements" (Magill, 1980, p. 289) has been shown to benefit both the learning and performance of motor skills (Clark, 1960; Richardson, 1967; Oxendine, 1969).

Training High-Performance Skills

Walter Schneider (1985) discussed a number of fallacies that negatively affect the training of high-performance skills. He defined high-performance skills as those that have three characteristics:

1. Skills that require considerable time and effort to acquire (e.g., greater than 100 hours).
2. Skills that many persons fail to acquire. Training programs that produce persons with high-performance skills often have failure rates greater than 20%.
3. Skills that show substantial qualitative differences in performance between novices and experts.

Examples of high-performance skills include playing a musical instrument, flying a fighter jet, or performing as an air traffic controller. Each of these skills requires extensive training and practice.

High-performance Skill Training Fallacies. Schneider (1985) maintained that many training programs are unsuccessful because they are based on fallacies of how to train high-performance skills. Some of these fallacies include:

1. *Practice makes perfect.* Although more practice usually results in better performance, for highly complex skills, some persons show very slow acquisition rates and some never reach acceptable levels of performance (e.g., 50% washout rates for many military training programs). However Schneider did maintain that "practice on consistent component tasks does improve component skills" (1985, p. 287). He defined component tasks as "those elements of the task where the subject can make the same response to the stimulus whenever it occurs" (p. 287).

2. *It is best to train the total skill.* Related to the first fallacy, many believe that it is best to train the skill in a form similar to how it will ultimately be executed. This may be true for less complex skills. However, for very complex skills, the learner may not receive enough practice on certain components to achieve proficiency on the entire task. For example, an air traffic controller can only observe about 15 seconds of an aircraft turn during each radar sweep although it takes about four minutes to complete a 90 degree turn. Therefore, it is only possible to practice a few 90-degree turns in an hour of training time. This may not be efficient to achieve proficiency on this difficult task component. Schneider recommended structuring the training task differently from the real-world task to provide sufficient practice on difficult components.

3. *Skill learning is intrinsically enjoyable.* Some believe that learning a task provides sufficient intrinsic motivation to maintain the learner's attention. However, Schneider observed that extensive practice is often boring. He recommended that "when designing a training program, one must include motivational events to maintain active participation" (p. 288).

4. *Initial performance is a good predictor of trainee and training program success.* "In reality, initial performance

of complex skills is very unstable and often provides a poor prediction of final performance" (p. 289). This is more true as the skill becomes more complex and novel. The reader is encouraged to consult Schneider (1985) for a discussion of additional fallacies and for recommendations for how to design training programs to teach high-performance skills.

Observational Learning

The theory of *observational learning* (also called *modeling*) holds that "on many occasions it is far easier to acquire information or new responses by observing others than by pursuing an extended process of trial and error" (Baron, Byrne, and Kantowitz, 1978, p. 147). A wide variety of birds and non-human mammals show the capacity for observational learning (Thorpe, 1963). For example, Herbert and Harsh, (1944) found that cats could learn tasks by watching other cats. Kawai (1965) found that monkeys could also learn through observation. Bandura (1971) found that individuals can often avoid the tedious trial-and-error procedures often found in operant conditioning by observing and modeling correct behaviors. He referred to this as "no-trial" learning.

In addition to its role in the learning of motor skills, observational learning plays a crucial role in socialization, the process through which children acquire the many behaviors they need to function as adult members of their culture (e.g., attitudes, values, self-control, etc.). Some studies have shown that children learn more from the behaviors they observe than the words they are told (Bryan, Redfield, and Mader, 1971; Rushton, 1975).

Recently, some researchers have investigated how people learn from observing others when engaged in group endeavors. This type of observational learning has been labeled *intent participation* (Rogoff, Paradise, Correa-Chávez, & Angelillo, 2003). In this type of learning, "they observe and listen with intent concentration and initiative, and their collaborative participation is expected when they are ready to help in shared endeavors" (Rogoff, et al., 2003, p. 176). These authors reviewed an extensive body of literature that shows the pervasive nature of observational learning. More than any other type of observational learning, attention is critical in intent participation. If the learner expects to engage in an endeavor, he or she more keenly observes and listens to prepare for this engagement. The more experienced persons in the group serve as guides. They help the learner understand how to act and how to coordinate his or her actions with other persons sharing in the endeavor. Rogoff and her colleagues maintain that learning exercises that incorporate intent participation can be beneficially mixed with other instructional approaches, like classroom lectures.

Perceptual Learning

One of the first types of learning that children encounter is perceptual learning. This involves the development of perceptual associations and an internal model of the world. Some theorists (e.g., Gibson, 1966) believe that much of our thinking is influenced by "perceptual invariants" that are learned during early development.

Once learned, our "world model" can be very resistant to change. However, a type of perceptual learning where a person's view of relationships among environmental elements can change quite suddenly is known as *insight learning* (Hebb, 1949). As discussed in Chapter 4, the term "insight" was coined by Wolfgang Köhler to describe certain behaviors of apes that he observed on the island of Tenerife during World War I (Köhler, 1925). He reported that chimpanzees would pile up boxes to reach a banana hanging from the ceiling or would put sticks together to pull in fruit lying outside their cage. These solutions seemed to occur quite suddenly without apparent preparation. This phenomenon is now thought to be important in the study of problem solving.

Learning to Learn

This area of study involves the effects of early learning on later learning. Scientists have observed improvements in the ability to learn about a class of problems if one has learned about similar problems in the past. The learner has developed more or stronger associations between the new information and information already in memory. In one of the earliest studies of this effect, Harlow (1949) observed that rhesus monkeys learned "rules" from previous experiments so that they learned faster in later experiments. Harlow labeled these rules "learning sets." Additional research has confirmed Harlow's early work (e.g., Medin, 1972). One possible explanation for the monkeys' abilities is that they may have learned "to focus their attention on relevant cues and to ignore distracting cues" (Brown & Weiner, 1979, p. 163). It is now widely accepted that humans can readily transfer rules far beyond the specific task at hand. Furthermore, some hypothesize that the associations learned early in life are more permanent than those formed later (e.g., Miller, 1978, p. 99).

Information Processing in the Motor Domain

In our discussion of the cognitive domain, it was shown that information processing models have served as a major orienting paradigm for theory and research. Although not as central, information processing models have also played a role in understanding learning in the motor domain. The learning of motor behaviors was once thought to be explained as a simple stimulus-response (S-R) connection. It was believed that during practice, the bond between the S and the R becomes stronger until a learned response automatically follows a specific stimulus. "Today most human learning theorists agree that between the stimulus and the response, the learner is taking in much information and trying to make sense out of it...the learner is processing information in order to make a response" (Magill, 1980, p. 58).

Researchers in the motor domain focus on what the learner is doing while learning the proper response to a given stimulus. Figure 6.3 shows a very general information processing model used by researchers in the motor domain (Magill, 1980). The three boxes depict important areas of motor research. The reader should see similarities between this figure and Figures 2.5 and 5.1. As mentioned in Chapter 5, the information processing model most often used in cognitive learning research (Figure 5.1) does not directly address performance and feedback as does the model depicted in Figure 6.3 (and the systems model of the learner, Figure 2.5). This is because motor research has focused much more than cognitive research on the effects of performance feedback on the generation of new responses. Although the details of the processes may differ across domains and task types, a process model helps us organize and understand learning research regardless of domain.

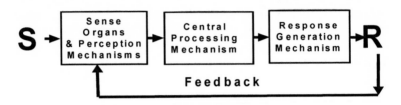

Figure 6.3:
A General Information Processing Model

Much like researchers in the cognitive domain, motor researchers investigate the distinction between *sensing* (detecting a stimulus) and *perceiving* (understanding or interpreting what has been seen, heard, touched, etc.). They also investigate how the learner attends to stimuli (*attention*) and how he or she selects among all of the stimuli available (*selective attention*). Another important area of investigation is how the learner recalls important relevant information about the task from memory. This involves the central processing mechanism and may include strategies that were used in the past and how they can be applied to the present situation. The response that is determined from the information processed (whether correct or incorrect) will be executed. Researchers study this response generation mechanism. Finally, feedback on the correctness or incorrectness of the response is used to adjust the processing of future stimuli. Researchers in the motor domain understand that "development of the ability to use feedback information is an important consideration in the learning process" (Magill, 1980, p. 62).

The Senses and Motor Skill Performance

The above discussion indicates the importance of all the information processing mechanisms. However, it is very important that we understand which sensory modes are essential to the successful performance of a motor skill. "If the learner relies too heavily on information from other modes, the performance will ultimately suffer" (Magill, 1980, p. 70). Thus, instructional designers and instructors need to know which mode the student needs to attend to for the requisite information to effectively perform the motor task. Vision has been long recognized as the "queen of the senses" (Magill, 1980, p. 71). We tend to rely on vision, sometimes to the detriment of learning important cues from other senses. In fact, sometimes we need to be taught not to rely on vision (e.g., when playing the piano or typing).

Some researchers have investigated the concept of *cross modal transfer*, or transferring what has been learned through one sensory mode to another sensory mode. Connolly and Jones (1970) investigated various types of feedback when learners were trained to draw a line of a given length. Their results indicated that transferring from the visual to the kinesthetic mode leads to more errors than transferring from the kinesthetic to the visual.

Attention

Just as we saw in the cognitive domain, learners must attend to important information in order to learn motor skills. Sternberg (1996) defined attention as "the phenomenon by which we actively process a limited amount of information from the enormous amount of information available through our senses, our stored memories, and our other cognitive processes" (p. 69, quoted in Clark, R. C., 2003, p. 66). Attention is one mechanism used by the decider subsystem to adjust the learner's input screen. The literature on attention includes the study of gaining attention (preparing for sensory information) and maintaining alertness (vigilance).

Before anyone can react to a stimulus, he or she must detect it. This is not always easy given that many different stimuli are present all of the time. Some research has shown that individuals can actually become blind to obvious environmental stimuli. This research on "inattentional blindness" has demonstrated that one's expectations can cause a person to miss important events (Simons & Chabris, 1999). The experiment used a 25 second video clip of 6 people playing basketball. Three were dressed in white and three in black shirts. Observers of the video were instructed to watch one of the two teams and count the number of times they passed the basketball among themselves. Thirty seconds into the task, a woman carrying an umbrella walked into the scene. Although easily seen on the tape, 44% of the observers failed to notice the woman. In addition, when a person dressed in a black gorilla suit walked into the middle of the game, beat its chest, and walked away, a majority (73%) of the observers did not see the gorilla when instructed to count the number of basketball passes. This minor deflection of attention was sufficient to cause the observers to miss something as obvious as a gorilla. A similar deflection of attention is well know to stage magicians who make their audiences attend to the wrong stimuli while they do their "tricks." If attention can be so easily deflected, it is important that instruction avoid distractions, which may distract learners from important instructional information.

Researchers have studied how individuals prepare to detect sensory information (*signal preparation*). Before one can prepare to detect a signal, one must be alert. *Alertness* is often regarded as synonymous with the term *activation*. As early as 1908, Yerkes and Dodson postulated that the association between a person's activation level and his or her performance resembles an inverted-U relationship as shown in Figure 6.4. This relationship has been labeled the *Yerkes-Dodson Law*. The "law" implies that for every behavior, there exists an optimal level of activation for optimal performance. This optimal level tends to be somewhere between the low and high levels of activation with poor performance resulting from either extreme of the activation continuum.

Gaining Attention

Several methods have been suggested to gain the attention of learners. With tongue firmly in cheek, Travers (1972) suggested that shouting can provide a strong stimulus that cannot generally be "blocked from entering the perceptual system" (quoted in Magill, 1980, p. 101). Two other, more subtle methods for gaining

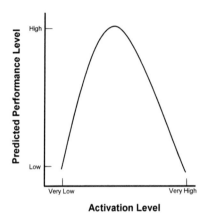

Figure 6.4:
Inverted-U Diagram According to the Yerkes-Dodson
Law

attention are to use the novelty and complexity of the stimulus. *Novelty* of a stimulus gains attention because it arouses the curiosity of the learner to direct him or her to the stimulus. Novelty may also counteract habituation effects that may reduce the learner's attention to reoccurring stimuli. Travers suggested three ways to make a situation novel: 1) using a stimulus that has not been presented recently; 2) presenting the stimulus in a new or unfamiliar context or setting; and 3) presenting a stimulus that has never been used before.

Travers (1972) cited research that suggests individuals are more likely to attend visually to an object that is more complex than to one which is less complex. For example, babies will fixate longer on a more complex diagram hanging over their heads than a simple one. People also tend to visually attend more to a person's eyes and mouth rather than any other portions of the face. This may be because these features provide more information in a smaller space.

Maintaining Attention

Once a learner's attention has been gained it is necessary to maintain that attention for some period of time. The term *vigilance* has come to be used as synonymous with maintaining attention. Many vigilance researched used the following procedure. Subjects were asked to monitor something like a radar screen until a designated signal appeared. The subject's task was to report when the signal was noticed. One of the earliest of these vigilance studies was conducted during World War II by British psychologist N. H. Mackworth. His results demonstrated that during a two-hour period, "the subject's ability to detect a specified signal markedly decreased each half hour" (Magill, 1980, p. 103).

Other vigilance studies have focused on the factors that affect a person's ability to maintain attention. For example, Wilkinson (1963) examined the effects of sleep deprivation on subjects' ability to tap a series of specified points when corresponding lights appeared in a certain order. The results indicated that most errors were committed by subjects who were sleep deprived and who performed the task in a quiet situation. The least errors were committed by subjects with normal sleep who performed in a quiet situation. With sleep-deprived subjects, a noisy environment seemed to help performance, whereas the performance of subjects with normal sleep was hindered by noise.

Broadbent (1958, chapter 6) reviewed what he termed "theories of vigilance decrement." One theory postulates that people lose attention because the surroundings are monotonous. Another suggests that if a signal is very infrequent, an individual's arousal level will deteriorate during the time of the activity. A third theory suggests that the incoming information is "filtered" in some way so that only part of the information reaches the perceptual system. Each of these theories may partially explain vigilance problems.

These theories and vigilance research data suggest several ways instructors and instructional developers can aid the maintenance of attention (in other words, maintain an open input screen). First, instruction can sensitize students to important cues that help the student prepare to detect a signal. For example, a baseball coach can instruct an outfielder to make each pitch a signal preparation event that will direct the player's attention to hit the ball. Words of encouragement or instructions directed toward the learner can also help prevent his or her attention from wandering. Thirdly, providing immediate knowledge of results after each of the signals to be detected maintained subjects' proficiency for longer periods of time. Finally, the instructional environment should never be permitted to become boring or monotonous. For example, practice drills should be kept short enough that they avoid learner fatigue and habituation.

Knowledge of Results

The concept of feedback originated in the branch of engineering known as control theory (Moray, 1981). Knowledge of results (generally abbreviated as KOR) is a special case of feedback that long been recognized that an important aspect of instruction. KOR is often used interchangeably with the term feedback. However, it is important to distinguish between these two terms. In the motor domain, *feedback* is considered as information about a response obtained from a person's own sensory system. On the other hand, KOR is information about a response that is obtainable only by means of an external source, such as a teacher, coach, experimenter, or some form of equipment. This distinction is important because KOR plays a vital role in learning motor skills and because it is a learning variable that is can be directly manipulated by an instructor or instructional developer to gain influence over all types of learning. Research in the motor domain has demonstrated that "knowledge of results (KOR) serves at least three important functions in learning: information; motivation; and reinforcement" (Magill, 1980, p. 215).

During practice, KOR is a primary *source of information*, which can be used to correct performance errors (Holding, 1987, p. 951). These corrections should then lead to improved performance. As early as 1938, Elwell and Grindley demonstrated that in motor learning KOR is more than simply a reward. Their results showed that subjects used KOR to correct their errors in each practice trial of a two-hand coordination task requiring them to line up a light in a bulls-eye. Bilodeau, Bilodeau, and Schumsky (1959) conducted a classic study that demonstrated this important role of KOR for learning. Their subjects learned to move a handle to a specific location while blindfolded. Their results showed that individuals who received no KOR did not perform very accurately over twenty trials. Subjects who received KOR on all trials improved consistently over the twenty trials. The groups who had KOR withdrawn after either two or six trials began to perform poorly after that point. Several other studies (e.g., Stelmach, 1970) confirmed these results. In fact, by the 1960's several researchers (e.g., Bilodeau & Bilodeau, 1961; Fitts, 1964; Holding, 1965) considered "KR [*sic*] as the strongest and most important variable involved in learning" (Magill, 1980, p. 220).

In addition to providing information, the second function of KOR is to provide a *source of motivation* for the learner, keeping him or her moving toward a goal. Locke, Cartledge, and Koeppel (1968) cited research evidence that shows a consistent relationship between KOR and an individual's goals, which, in turn, relates to the individual's performance.

Even though research, like that of Elwell and Grimley (1938) showed KOR was more than just a reward, "this does not eliminate the fact that KOR can also serve as a reward or reinforcement" (Magill, 1980, p. 220). A *reward* tends to strengthen the response or increase the probability that this same response will occur again. There is ample evidence from research on animal learning that supports the notion that KOR serves a reinforcement function.

Research has shown that KOR needs to be detailed enough to benefit the student, but not too precise as to create confusion. For example, Trowbridge and Cason (1932) measured subjects' attempts to draw 3-inch lines given different forms of KOR. Some subjects received "qualitative" KOR (right or wrong) while others received "quantitative" KOR (1/8 inch units, such as "plus 1" or "minus 3"). One group received no KOR and another received "irrelevant" KOR in the form of nonsense syllables. The group receiving irrelevant KOR performed worst, followed by the no KOR group, and the qualitative KOR group. The quantitative KOR group performed best. Smoll (1972) found similar results in a study where subjects learned to roll a duckpin bowling ball at 70% of their maximum velocity. Two groups received quantitative KOR (one within hundredths-of-a-second and the other within tenths-of-a-second) and a third group received qualitative KOR ("too fast," "too slow," and "correct). Both quantitative groups performed better than the qualitative group, but not significantly different from each other. Thus, there seems to be a point of diminishing returns on quantitative KOR. Rogers (1974) had subjects learn to turn a knob of a micrometer to a certain setting without being able to see the micrometer. They had to rely one of four types of KOR to learn the task (direction of error only, direction and error to the nearest whole unit, direction and error to the nearest tenth unit, or direction and error to the nearest thousandth unit). His results showed that subjects who received KOR that was too precise (thousandth unit) performed as poorly as those that received no KOR with the other two groups performing better.

Transfer of Learning

An almost universally applied principle in education is transfer of learning (often called transfer of training). According to Magill (1980), it "is the foundation of curriculum development, for it provides the basis for arranging in sequence the skills to be learned" (p. 244). *Transfer of learning* is "the effect of previous learning on new learning. It occurs successfully when a person uses knowledge from previous experience to help learn something new" (Mayer, 2002, p. 5).

Transfer of learning can be positive, negative, or neutral. *Positive transfer* occurs when a person's experience with a previous skill aids or facilitates the learning of a new skill. *Negative transfer* is the opposite; experience with a previous skill hinders or interferes with the learning of a new skill. *Neutral or zero transfer* occurs when experience with a previous skill has no influence on the learning of a new skill.

Transfer of learning is important for curriculum design because learning tasks need to be sequenced to promote positive transfer. For example, algebra should not be taught before basic arithmetic or trigonometry before geometry. The same is true for motor skills. A learner needs to master basic skills (throwing or catching a ball) before he or she can learn to use these skills in a game.

It has been argued that transfer to real-world tasks can be improved if the learner perceives that the relationship between actions and consequences in the learning situation are the same as in the normal environment (Estes, 1988). In other words, the relevance of the learning situation should be made clearly apparent to the learner. This recommendation is the result of a long history of research on transfer of learning.

The History of Transfer of Learning Research

R. E. Clark and Voogel (1985) described the history of transfer of learning research as a development from a strictly behaviorist approach to a more cognitive understanding of transfer. Thorndike and Woodworth (1901) provided the earliest empirical support for the behaviorist approach to transfer. Their research led to the development of the "identical elements" hypothesis, which states that transfer occurs when the training and application contexts are identical.

Behaviorally oriented research generated a large body of data during the first half of the 20th century. Clark and Voogel (1985) stated that "Many behaviorally based studies provide evidence that: Generally, positive transfer increases when overall training and application conditions are similar. The identical elements-transfer relationship is maintained across a variety of learning tasks and training application contexts" (p. 116).

Building on the work of Thorndike and Woodworth, researchers investigated the characteristics of learning (stimulus) and transfer (response) situations. Specifically, they sought to avoid "habit interference." Wolfle (1951) explained that "habit interference arises when partially overlapping stimulus patterns are expected to elicit different responses" (p. 1271). An example of habit interference might be stepping on the brakes at a green light because the orientation of the lights was horizontal rather than vertical as one expected.

Research up to the early 1950s seemed to justify two hypotheses about transfer. "1. The greater the similarity between two stimulating situations, the greater should be the similarity between the two responses if habit interference is to be avoided. 2. The greater the similarity between the two responses, the greater should be the similarity between the two stimulating situations if habit interference is to be avoided" (Wolfle, 1951, p. 1271). However, this led to a paradox. If responses are identical learning is facilitated, but if they are different, interference reduces learning. However, since responses can never be truly identical, how does ordinary learning occur?

Osgood (1949) attempted to resolve this paradox by constructing a three-dimensional model called the "transfer surface." In his model, the direction and degree of transfer and interference were a function of the degree of similarity between the stimuli in the learning situation and the requirements of the learned responses. Although Osgood's model did a good job of integrating the data from verbal learning research up to that time, it was almost forgotten as researchers studied other types of tasks and began to take a more cognitive approach to learning research.

Gagné (1954) questioned the necessity of exact similarity between the learning and transfer situations. Referring to several empirical studies, which deliberately changed the training situation so it differed from the job situation, Gagné concluded that the problem of effective training "was not one of making the tasks similar, but rather of arranging the conditions of practice in such a way that essential skills were most efficiently learned" (1954, p. 101).

Applying this type of cognitive interpretation to Thorndike and Woodworth, Clark and Voogel (1985) explained that by using the word identical, "they did not mean to imply exact duplication but a general similarity of contexts and problems" (p. 115). This interpretation has been supported by numerous studies of transfer. "There is considerable evidence that much of what is learned can only be applied to problems that are similar to those experienced in training" (Clark & Voogel, 1985, p. 113). This has also been demonstrated in the transfer failure of learners who read a story about a general attacking a fortress to a problem of a doctor trying to destroy a tumor (Gick & Holyoak, 1980; 1983).

Even though agreement with this "similarity" principle is widespread, Clark and Voogel observed that there is also "evidence of transfer failure in many training programs" (p. 114). They also observed that "most performance evaluations do not measure transfer beyond the training setting" (p. 113). This is a problem because performance in the training situation does not guarantee similar performance on the job. "Most research on employee training clearly shows that although millions of dollars are spent on employee training in the public sector, there is little empirical evidence linking training to improved job behavior or employee attitudes" (Haskell, 2001, p. 5 cited in Clark, R. C., 203, p. 136).

A possible explanation for the lack of transfer to job situations is the distinction between "near" and "far" transfer (Royer, 1979). Near transfer is "when performance reaches established criterion levels...in the setting defined by training" (Clark & Voogel, 1985, p. 114). In far transfer the learner is able "to apply skills in contexts that are very different than the ones encountered during training" (p. 114). This distinction is similar to Rumelhart and Norman's (1981) distinction between "procedural" and "declarative" knowledge. Procedural knowledge is situation-dependant and declarative knowledge is generalizable to various situations. Ruth Clark suggested that "transfer takes place not only on the basis of shared elements among tasks but also as a result of understanding" (Clark, R. C., 2003, p. 142).

Bransford (1979) and Nitsch (1977) cited several studies that support the view that transfer is facilitated when learners are able to practice in different contexts. This practice enables the learners to identify the important elements of the task and subtract them from the irrelevant elements of the training situation. Thus, they are able to "decontextualize" the task and perform it in various job situations.

Mayer (2004) maintained that transfer should be conceived as "specific-transfer-of-general-knowledge." He stated that the first step in designing instruction should be to clearly define the subject matter domain. Then, a cognitive task analysis should be conducted to specify the major cognitive processes required to accomplish the task. Only then, can general transfer principles be applied to the meet the specific requirements.

<u>Guidelines for Transfer</u>

Several guidelines and recommendations for the design of instruction that will help ensure that what is taught is more likely to transfer to new learning situations or real-world tasks were provided by Ellis (1965), R. E. Clark and Voogel (1985), Estes (1988), and Mayer (2002).

1. *Maximize the similarity between teaching and the ultimate transfer situation.* The ultimate transfer situation means the situation in which the learner will eventually or

ultimately use what has been learned. This can be accomplished by providing concrete activities and cues that are similar to the transfer task and require the learner to use the skills and knowledge that are required in the transfer task.

2. *Provide adequate experience with the original task.* Maximizing practice on the original task is directly related to positive transfer to the new task.

3. *Provide a variety of examples when teaching concepts and principles.* These examples should, ideally, be drawn from real-world situations that are similar to the situations where the learner will use the new skills or knowledge.

4. *Provide useful feedback.* This feedback should help the learner gain deeper understanding and/or hone their skills. It should also explain and help them understand how these skills and knowledge will be used in the transfer situation.

5. *Label or identify important features of a task.* The instructor should direct the learners' attention to those elements of the task that will most directly transfer to the subsequent task.

6. *Make sure that general principles are understood before expecting much transfer.* This will help the learner apply the principles to transfer situations that are somewhat different from the learning situation.

7. *Provide practice in different contexts to improve the learners' ability to "decontextualize" the task.* These different contexts should reflect the various aspects of the transfer situation or situations.

8. *Help the student see the relevance of the learning situation.* This can be accomplished by helping the learner perceive that the relationship between action and consequences in the learning situation are the same as in the job environment.

9. *Provide less able learners with more instructional support to achieve transfer.*

Most learning research has been conducted in either the motor or cognitive domains. Nevertheless, many have recognized the importance of affective (emotional) variables in learning. The next section summarizes research in the third (affective) domain.

The Affective Domain

Many consider affective behaviors to be a third behavioral domain (Krathwohl, et al., 1964). In fact, Underwood (1983) and Bower (1981) proposed that affective responses should be regarded as components of memory (Johnson & Hasher, 1987). Much of the research in this area has investigated how the affective (or emotional) state of the learner influences his or her success at learning and how the behavior of teachers can influence student affect.

The Influence of Student Affect on Learning

We have already discussed how learning can be influenced by motivation and attention. The discussion of motivation focused on goal setting as one of the primary means of motivating learners. The discussion of attention examined the role of alertness in preparing a learner to receive information and how to maintain the learner's attention. Research has also shown that affect influences students' receptivity to instruction and their learning success. For example, there is evidence that the affective valence (e.g., emotional attachments) of words can reduce interference in memorization tasks (Wickens & Clark, 1968).

Affect is used in psychology as a synonym for emotion or feeling (Drever, 1964). It covers a range of moods or "feeling tones" that individuals experience in various situations. Some of these affective moods can be characterized as emotion sets that each fall along a bi-polar continuum (Kort, Reilly, & Picard, 2001). Table 6.2 is a listing of some hypothetical emotion sets with descriptive labels for points along each continuum.

It should be noted that these emotion sets are not mutually exclusive, nor does the level in which an individual falls on one set correspond to the same level on any other set. Furthermore, the emotion sets probably combine in any given situation to result in the individual's overall feelings about that situation.

Table 6.2:
Hypothetical Emotion Sets and Continuum Labels

Emotion Set	Continuum Labels					
Anxiety-Confidence	Anx-ious	Worried	Uncom-fortable	Comfort-able	Hope-ful	Confi-dent
Boredom-Fascination	Ennui	Bored	Indiff-erent	Interested	Cur-ious	In-trigued
Frustration-Euphoria	Frus-trated	Puzzled	Confused	Insightful	En-light-ened	Eu-phoric
Discourage-ment-Enthusiasm	Dispir-ited	Disap-pointed	Dissatis-fied	Satisfied	Thrill-ed	Enthu-siastic
Terror-Excitement	Terrifi-ed	Fearful	Appre-hensive	Calm	Antici-pative	Excited

Receiver Apprehension

Several researchers have looked at learner anxiety as it may influence the assimilation of instructional information under the term "receiver apprehension." Receiver apprehension has been studied by communication researchers (e.g., Wheeless, 1975; Ayres, Wilcox, & Ayres, 1995; Wheeless, Preiss, & Gayle, 1997) as the anxiety associated with the process of decoding information. This anxiety may be the result of:

- Fear of encountering new information.
- Inability of the receiver (learner) to assimilate the new information because they lack the cognitive complexity.
- Lack of the necessary interpretive schemes to understand the information.
- Anxiety because they will be evaluated on how well they remember the information.

Whatever the cause or combination of causes of learner anxiety, it is likely to make it more difficult for a person to learn. From the perspective of the systems model of the learner, we would say that anxiety make the learner's input screen less permeable. On the other hand, if a learner is comfortable in the learning situation it is more likely he or she will learn more effectively because the information more easily passes through his or her input screen.

169

Flow

There are data, which show that individuals' performance in a variety of situations (including learning situations) is better if they experience the feeling that they are performing at the peak of their abilities. This feeling has been described as optimal experience or "flow" (Csikszentmihalyi, 1990). The cross-cultural study of optimal experience has shown that it is a condition that is available to everyone. Csikszentmihalyi (1990) defines *flow* as "the state in which people are so involved in an activity that nothing else seems to matter; the experience itself is so enjoyable that people will do it even at great cost, for the sheer sake of doing it" (p. 4). He further explains that an "activity" does not need to be active in the physical sense, nor does the "skill" necessary to engage in it have to be a physical skill. The experience of flow has been reported in sports, dance (& other movements), sex, yoga, the martial arts, music, tasting, thinking, and learning. People have even reported the experience of flow while at work.

The flow experience, or as Csikszentmihalyi labels it, the "phenomenology of enjoyment" (1990, p. 49), has eight major components:

1. The experience usually occurs when we confront tasks we have a chance of completing.
2. We also must be able to concentrate on what we are doing.
3. This concentration is possible because the task has clear goals, and
4. provides immediate feedback.
5. During the task, one acts with a deep but effortless involvement that removes from awareness the worries and frustrations of everyday life.
6. The enjoyable experience allows people to exercise a sense of control over their actions.
7. During the experience, one's concern for self disappears, yet paradoxically the sense of self emerges stronger after the flow experience is over.
8. During the experience, one's sense of the duration of time is altered.

When all of these elements are combined, one experiences flow.

The process of flow is diagrammed in Figure 6.5. The two main variables of the flow process, challenges and skills, are shown along the axes of the figure. The flow experience occurs in the diagonal area labeled, flow channel. One may experience flow when the task offers little challenge and one's skills are not well developed (A1). As one develops higher skill levels, the task will become boring because it no longer provides a challenge (A2). On the other hand, one may experience anxiety if the task is too difficult (A3). If, however, one gradually develops higher skill levels as the task becomes more difficult (A4), it is possible to maintain the flow experience.

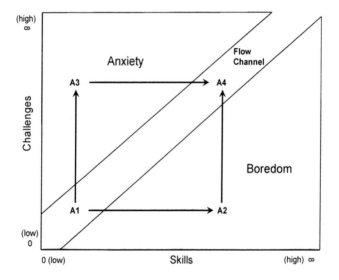

Figure 6.5:
The Process of "Flow"

How is one to learn to experience flow? Csikszentmihalyi stated that the key to flow is the process of attention. "Information enters consciousness either because we intend to focus attention on it or as a result of attentional habits based on biological or social instructions" (Csikszentmihalyi, 1990, p. 30). He feels that a person who is in control of consciousness is able to focus their attention at will. They become so involved that they are oblivious to distractions, are able to concentrate for as long as it takes to achieve their goal. This level of concentration is what all teachers hope to see in their students. There has been some research on training teachers to behave in ways that help learners feel positive affect and make them more likely to experience flow while learning.

Teaching Behaviors That Can Influence Student Affect

Individuals working in the area of communication have noted that the student-teacher relationship can neve. be free of affect (Richmond, Gorham, & McCroskey, 1987). Mehrabian (1969, p. 203) defined a teacher's communicative behaviors that "enhance closeness to and nonverbal interaction with another" as "immediacy." Andersen and Andersen (1982, pp. 110-112) cited a number of empirical studies that indicate that immediacy behaviors are likely to influence a learner's favorable attitudes toward the learning situation. Furthermore, there is some research evidence that teacher's immediacy behaviors can be modified through awareness and training (Grant & Hennings, 1971; Nier, 1979; Nussbaum, 1984).

Research on nonverbal immediacy has investigated a number of specific behaviors. For example, Heiser (1972) showed that a teacher's proxemic position influenced their students' affective ratings. Teachers who sat at, on, beside, or behind their desk were rated as low in both affection and inclusion. On the other hand, teachers who moved in front of the desk or among the students were rated as more warm, friendly, and effective. More immediacy has been shown to be communicated when people face one another directly and that people assume closer positions to those they like than to strangers or those they dislike (e.g., Andersen, Andersen, & Jensen, 1979; Byrne, Baskett, & Hodges, 1971; Mehrabian, 1968; Patterson & Sechrest, 1970).

Other areas of research on nonverbal behaviors include the effects of eye contact, smiling, and body movement. Evidence that more eye contact is associated with greater liking and more positive feelings can be found in the work of Exline and Winters (1965), Kendon (1967), and Thayer and Schiff (1974). Smiling has been shown to be an indication of both liking and arousal (Kraut &

Johnston, 1979; Mehrabian, 1981). Body movements, such as gestural activity and head nodding have been shown to be related to positive affect (Rosenfeld, 1966). Finally, overall body movement has been positively associated with the perceived immediacy of the teacher (Andersen, et al., 1979).

A small amount of research has shown that vocal expressiveness, rate, and volume are related to interpersonal liking and arousal (Mehrabian, 1981). Weineke (1981) observed that the delivery as well as the content and organization of the first lecture in university classes had an impact on students' reactions to the subject and to the teacher.

Some research has examined the clarity of teacher messages in terms of the way the teacher structures his or her instructional presentations. Smith and Land (1981) reviewed ten studies, which indicated that the presence of vagueness reduced student achievement. On the other hand, the clarity of written material has been shown to be increased by using advance organizers (Ausubel, 1960, 1963). *Advance organizers* are "subsuming concepts" (Ausubel, 1960, p. 267) that help learners mobilize the most relevant aspects of the instructional information to create the cognitive structures that facilitate learning and memory. They are "concepts introduced before material is covered which are on a more general or abstract level than the material which is to be covered" (Chesebro & McCroskey, 1998, p. 449). Advance organizers provide a conceptual structure or framework to aid the encoding of information and also help the learner activate prior knowledge and relate it to the new information.

Ausubel (1968) identified two types of advance organizers:

1. *Expository Organizers*: Are used with unfamiliar material to set the stage for learning new concepts. For example, when teaching the American Revolution, introduce stages common to all revolutions as a framework for the new information.

2. *Comparative Organizers*: Are used to aid the integration of new ideas by comparing and contrasting them with similar concepts that have already been learned. For example, atomic structure can be taught by discussing the similarities and differences between electrons circling a nucleus and moons orbiting around a planet.

Two other methods that have been found to increase clarity are the use of skeletal outlines given to students prior to lectures (Hartley, 1976) and the effective use of transitions (Cruickshank & Kennedy, 1986).

Additional research is needed not only on how teachers' behaviors influence learners' affective states, but also on how student affect can be influenced by other means. This is especially important for computer-based instruction and web-delivered instruction when a teacher (instructor) is often not available. In these cases, the design of the instructional content must "play the role" of the teacher to help learners reach and maintain the most positive affective state for the learning experience. Hays, Stout, and Ryan-Jones (2005) developed an Instructional Quality Evaluation Tool to help instructional developers and program managers ensure that their computer- and web-delivered instruction is of the highest quality. The "Tool" is discussed in greater detail in Chapter 13.

The next chapter uses the systems model of the learner to organize an overview of the research summaries presented in this and previous chapters. This overview will help the reader understand the relevance of the research and how various research areas interrelate. The chapter also includes a discussion of how the learner is part of a larger instructional system, which is analyzed using communication theories. This analysis highlights some of the important issues that are involved in improving the learning outcomes of the learning system.

Chapter 7
The Learning System

In Chapter 2 a model of the learner as a system was presented. This model was used to organize the summaries of learning research in chapters 4, 5, and 6. The following discussion uses the systems model of the learner to provide an overview and integration of the learning research previously discussed. This overview focuses on the critical processes involved in learning and the research, which has been conducted to help us understand these processes. This learner-centric overview is followed by a system-oriented discussion of the instructional process.

A Learner-centric Overview of Learning Research Data

In chapter 2, a systems model of the learner was presented to introduce the reader to the many subprocesses involved in learning. Figure 7.1 reproduces the systems model of the learner that was presented earlier in Figure 2.6. Although most learning subprocesses interact, the following summary of learning research is organized by discussing the research areas under the subprocess or subprocesses that are their primary focus. Interactions among subprocesses are discussed as appropriate. Table 7.1 lists the learning subsystem processes and learning research areas that have investigated parts of each subprocess. The chapter that summarized the research area is shown in parentheses. An overview of this research is provided in the following sections.

Input Screen

The input screen consists of a number of interactive processes that limit the amount and quality of information that is allowed to enter the learner system. The input screen may be the most important factor in learning because information must enter the learner system in learning is to occur. Many, if not all of the learner's subsystem processes affect the permeability of the input screen. Foremost among these interacting subprocesses is the decider, which limits information by allocating the learner's attentional and motivational resources. The decider will be discussed in more detail in the next section.

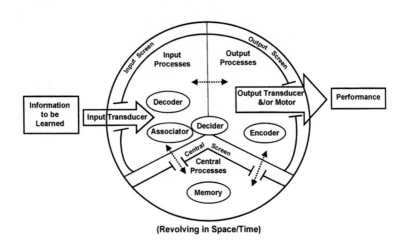

Figure 7. 1
The Learner as a System

The permeability of the input screen is directly affected by the learner's habituation and sensitization to the incoming stimuli. These simple types of learning affect how the learner reacts to incoming information (stimuli). If the information becomes routine, habituation tends to diminish the learner's responses. On the other hand, if the information is varied and relevant to the learner, sensitization may increase the learner's responses. These simple learning processes probably interact in a complex manner depending on the characteristics of the information and how these characteristics interact with other learning subprocesses. It is possible to manipulate habituation and sensitization processes through the design and presentation of instructional information. For example, using a variety of presentation methods can help avoid habituation. Furthermore, the learner can be sensitized to important information by using techniques like advance organizers (Ausubel, 1960; 1963). Additional research that directly addresses the relationships among ways of presenting instructional information and these simple learning processes is needed to derive specific guidance for instructional developers.

Table 7.1:
The Learner's Subsystem Processes and Learning Research Areas

Subsystem Process	Research Area
Input Screen	• Habituation (Ch. 4) • Sensitization (Ch. 4) • Prior knowledge (Ch. 5) • Biases (Ch. 5) • Affect (Ch. 6) • Teaching Behaviors (Ch. 6)
Decider	• Metacognition (Ch. 5) • Motivation (Ch. 6) • Attention (Ch. 6) • Vigilance (Ch. 6)
Input Transducer	• Sensory Mechanisms (Ch. 5) • Habituation (Ch. 4) • Sensitization (Ch. 4) • Conditioning (Ch. 4)
Decoder	• Selective Attention (Ch. 5) • Perceptual Filters (Ch. 5) • Biases (Ch. 5)
Associator	• Associationism (Ch. 5)
Central Screen	• Prior knowledge (Ch. 5) • Linkages (associations) (Ch. 5)
Memory	• Short-term Memory (Ch. 5) • Long-term Memory (Ch. 5)
Encoder	• Practice (Ch. 6)
Output Screen	• Practice (Ch. 6) • Motivation (Ch. 6)
Output Transducer and/or Motor	• Performance Measurement (Ch 6) • Metacognition (Ch. 5)

Other processes also interact to determine how the learner attends to and interprets incoming instructional information. Some of these include the learner's prior knowledge and his or her biases about the information and the specific behaviors of the instructor. For example, some research, discussed in Chapter 6, has shown that specific teaching behaviors can influence learner emotions (affect) to alter the learner's input screen.

Decider

The decider is the executive control subsystem. As such, it is involved to some degree in all of the other subprocesses. Although the decider does not always operate on the conscious level, it is the main arbitrator of the learner's motivation, attention, and vigilance. Data from research on each of these topics has contributed to our knowledge of how a learner allocates his or her limited resources to the learning task. In addition, research on metacognition has examined the learner's use specific techniques to monitor his or her learning and thinking and methods to improve one's ability to use these techniques. It directs the learner's application of metacognitive skills to the learning task.

Motivation research (e.g., Lepper & Greene, 1975; Anderson, R., et al., 1976) has demonstrated that external rewards are not sufficient to maintain a learner's attention o the instructional task. Furthermore, the way a learner relates the instructional information to his or her expectations (Atkinson, 1964) and goals (Locke, 2000) also appears to influence motivation as do a variety of other evaluative variables (Keller, 1983; 1987) The decider manages the associator as it forms associations between instructional information and previously learned information stored in memory.

Not only does the decider interact with input and central processes, it also interacts with output processes like the decoder and the output transducer. For example, the level of effort, which the learner dedicates to performance is regulated by the decider based on the perceived or expected consequences of the performance.

Input Transducer

The input transducer is the subsystem that brings instructional information into the learner system via the input screen. It accomplishes this by interacting with sensory and perceptual mechanisms and learning processes like habituation, sensitization, and conditioning. The input transducer interacts with the input screen, the decider, the associator, and memory. These interactions determine which stimuli are perceived or ignored and how the learner assigns meaning to the stimuli. Thus it is important that instructional designers use techniques that will make new information relevant to the learner so the input transducer will be able to transmit it into the system.

Decoder

The decoder is the subsystem that translates incoming instructional information into a form that can be used internally by the learner system. One of the mechanisms that is used in this translation is selective attention. Under control of the decider and interaction with other subsystems (e.g., memory, associator), the learner "selects" which portion of incoming information to focus upon and how to associate this information with previous knowledge. It is likely that the decoder modifies the incoming information so that it is more meaningful as the associator and memory establish relationships between previously learned information and the new information that is to be learned.

Associator

The associator is the subsystem that forms meaningful associations among pieces of incoming information and existing knowledge. As discusses in Chapter 5, associationism was one of the earliest theories of learning. As researchers have collected more and more empirical data on learning, associations among items of information has been shown to be a primary factor in most types of complex learning. The associator is depicted in the input section of the learner system (Figure 7.1), however it also functions in the other two sections of the learner system (central and output). For example, the associator and the associations among existing knowledge and new information is a regulator of the learner's central screen. Data on primacy, recency, and von Restorff effects, as well as data on paired-associate learning (Chapter 5) support this assumption.

Instructional designs that help the learner form and use associations, such as advance organizers (Ausubel, 1963) or skeletal outlines (Hartley, 1976) enhance learning. Stronger associations also enhance an individual's ability to retrieve information (Bower, 1970; Norman, 1976).

Central Screen

The central screen regulates the transfer of information between the three sections of the learner system: input, central, and output. It operates like the input screen to block or selectively allow the movement of information. The central screen is affected by the learner's prior knowledge, previous linkages (associations) among items of information under the control of the decider. Any instructional approach that enhances the formation or strengthens associations allows the central screen to be more permeable to the information from the input section or to the output section.

Memory

Memory is the subsystem process that stores information for various amounts of time. Information processing theories of memory assume stages of information transformation that enable the learner to store the information in memory (e.g., Craik & Lockhart, 1972). These theories conform to the systems model of the learner, which assumes that instructional information is transformed by the decoder and associator as discussed above. The transformation of information can result in the storage of the information for various durations, from seconds to years. The existence of distinct sensory, short-, and long-term memory modes has been labeled the Modal Model of memory (Healy & McNamara, 1996) and has been very influential in our understanding of how information is stored and retrieved.

Learning theorists do not agree that all information is stored in the same way. For example, motor memory may use different storage mechanisms than verbal memory (Fleishman, 1978; Mayer, 1980) or semantic memory may be stored differently than declarative memory (Tulving, 2000). Nevertheless, most theorists agree that learned information must be stored in some way because learners are able to retrieve and use the information.

There is also agreement that information is probably stored as some type of network of associations (Alba & Hasher, 1983; Anderson, J. R. & Bower, 1979; Wertz & Kandel, 2000). However, there are disagreements about how this network is formed and what are its specific characteristics (see Chapter 5). Nevertheless, there is little disagreement that deeper learning (i.e., the formation of stronger associations) leads to better remembering (e.g., Kieras & Bovair, 1984) and better performance (e.g., Mayer, 2002).

Encoder

The encoder transforms stored information from the learner's internal coding scheme into a form that can be used in performance. Before this information can be used, it must make it through the learner's output screen. Practice and repetition are two of the mechanisms used by the encoder. Some believe (e.g., Norman, 1976) that practice and repetition are the most important factors in learning. However, rote repetition or simple practice is not sufficient for deep learning. Effective learning requires the proper spacing of practice (National research Council, 1991) or emphasis on the relevance of the information that is repeated (Norman, 1976).

Output Screen

The learner's output screen limits the learner's options on how her or she can use learned information. For example, a learner may understand how to hold a tennis racquet and the rules of the game, but still not be able to hit the ball into the opponent's court due to an insufficient amount of practice. Likewise, the way a learner incorporates new information into memory (e.g., schemas) affects how effectively the information can be retrieved and whether it can easily move through the output screen.

Output Transducer and/or Motor

The output transducer and the motor are the subsystems processes, which the learner uses to perform. As discussed in Chapter 6, we cannot infer that learning has occurred unless the learner is able to demonstrate some change in performance. The output transducer deals primarily with cognitive (i.e., verbal) performance and the motor deals primarily with motor performance. In the cognitive realm, it has been shown that metacognitive skills (e.g., self-monitoring) can enhance performance. Thus, the output transducer seems to be regulated by use of these metacognitive skills. The motor seems to be regulated by motor programs and the practice methods used to build them.

Learning Suprasystems

The previous sections discussed the results of learning research under the subsystem processes of the learner. Like every other system, the learner is also a subsystem component of a larger suprasystem (or multiple suprasystems). Any discussion of learning and instruction is not complete unless it includes an examination of how the learner is influenced by and fits into the learning suprasystem.

One way to define the learning suprasysem is by detailing the people, materials, and techniques involved in instruction. This was done in Chapter 2 (see Table 2.3). Another approach is to identify the various individuals and organizations that combine to influence a given instructional situation like a schoolhouse. This was the approach taken by a program manager (riley, 1991) in a briefing about a schoolhouse-based aviation maintenance course. Figure 7.2 is an adaptation of Riley's illustration showing some of these interacting individuals and organizations. The figure shows each of these interactive components centering on the schoolhouse where the learner experiences instruction. However, the figure leads to the mistaken impression that all components equally support the learning situation. This is seldom the case because many of the components that influence the learning situation (in this case, the schoolhouse) are subsystems of different suprasystems. A more realistic illustration of these relationships is shown in Figure 7.3.

In Figure 7.3, the various interactive components, like instructional aids or subject matter experts, are influenced by different suprasystems. Because the suprasystems may not coordinate with one another, the developers of instructional aids like simulations may never work with the subject matter experts (instructors) who are drawn from operational units. This can result

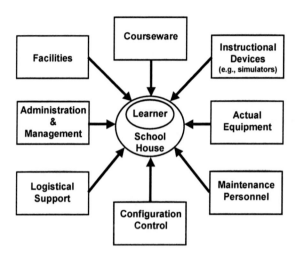

Figure 7.2:
Some Interactive Components of the Learning System

in instructors who may not fully understand how to use all of the instructional capabilities of the simulation. Similarly, courseware developers may not design their computer-based instruction products to integrate with simulation exercises. Furthermore, the school administration may be so concerned with issues like maintaining schedules that it does nothing to encourage this coordination.

To achieve its goals, the learning system must coordinate the interactions among its various components. A detailed description and analysis of each and every interacting subsystem is beyond the scope of this discussion. However, these interactions must not be ignored if the learning system is to provide effective instruction.

The remainder of this chapter will focus on the main interaction in the learning system: the interaction of the instructor and the learner. In the following discussion, the term "instructor" is used to represents the wide variety of instructional approaches (e.g., lecture, computer-based instruction, instructional games, instructional simulations). All instructional approaches attempt to emulate the strengths of face-to-face, one-on-one instruction so

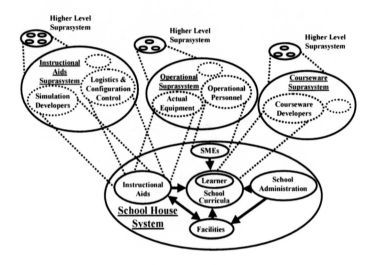

Figure 7.3:
Systems View of a School House

this will be the model presented in the next sections. The main goal of instruction is to communicate new information to the learner and to ensure that the learner has internalized (learned) the information and can demonstrate this with improved performance. The following section discusses this communication process

Instruction as Communication

Instruction can be regarded as a communication process between the instructor (representing the wide variety of instructional approaches) and the learner. It is a two-way communication process since the learner must demonstrate that he or she has learned the material by communicating new proficiency to the instructor. In order to more fully understand the instructional process as communication we will first discuss communication, then apply communication principles to the systems model of the learner and a model of the larger learning system.

The Stream of Communication

One of the founding fathers of psychology, William James, characterized consciousness (thought) as a continuous stream, which he labeled "the stream of consciousness" (James, 1890; 1892). He described it as consisting of five basic characteristics (Lundin, 1972, pp. 99-100):

1. *Consciousness is personal.* Every thought is part of one's personal consciousness. A given thought is experienced as my thought not yours. Therefore there is a gulf between one's own consciousness and that of others.

2. *Consciousness is always changing.* James explicitly disagreed with Wundt on this point. He traced the concept back to Heraclitus who regarded all things as being in a constant state of change. Heraclitus is best known for stating "all things flow, nothing abides. Into the same river one cannot step twice." James applied this philosophy to his conception of consciousness. He believed that "no state of mind or idea even if it recurred, could ever be identical with the first" (Lundin, 1972, p. 100). He viewed consciousness as a constantly flowing stream that sometimes flowed rapidly and other times seemed to hardly move at all.

3. *Consciousness is sensibly continuous.* James believed that the stream contained no breaks. There might be interruptions in the continuity of consciousness such as during sleep, but during waking life one has no trouble making connections between thoughts.

4. *Consciousness deals with objects other than itself.* James saw a clear dualism between the mind and the objects it dealt with. He pointed out that some psychologists confused the objects of thought with the thoughts themselves.

5. *Consciousness is always selective.* Sensation and perception are selective. We do not passively receive the experiences imposed on our minds. Rather, we actively

choose, from the mass of stimuli that bombard us, those to which we attend.

Since his time, there have been many that disagreed with James' characterization of consciousness. However, based on research in many areas (e.g., selective attention), we can now see that James was more accurate than not.

The process of communication can also be described as a "stream." A model of the "stream of communication" applied to instruction is shown in Figures 7.4 and 7.5. The model assumes that communication is not just a transfer of information from one person to another. It is rather a series of transformations of the information as it moves from the sender (instructor) to the receiver (learner). In instructional communication, both the instructor (sender) and the learner (receiver) are seeking a "communal awareness" or shared understanding of the information to be learned. The purpose of the stream of communication model is to look inside the "black box" of both the instructor and the learner to help understand the delivery and reception of instruction.

Figure 7.4 shows that communication in the instructional situation begins in the long-term memory (LTM) of the instructor. Part of the instructor's LTM is his or her conception of the communal awareness of the subject matter that he or she wants to share with the learner. This communal awareness is, in part, the result of the instructors training and previous instructional acts (communications) between the instructor and the learner or persons similar to the learner. The instructional information must be brought into the active consciousness (personal awareness or working memory) of the instructor through the first transformation process (T1). Once the information to be communicated resides in the instructor's active consciousness it can be transformed into a form of communication.

The second transformation (T2) converts the information into a form that can be transmitted to the learner (receiver). This transformation is influenced by the instructor's communal awareness, but as this transformation occurs, it also changes the instructor's awareness of the reality he or she is seeking to communicate. The very act of communicating changes the instructor's conception of the information. This change results in modifications to the instructor's communal awareness of the information to structure it as something that can be understood by the learner.

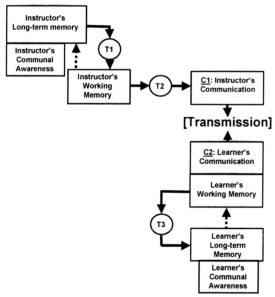

Figure 7.4:
The Stream of Instructional Communication

At this point, the instructor (sender) transmits the information to the learner (receiver). Transmission can be face-to-face using voice, touch, or gesture. The information can also be transmitted by one or some type of transmission device (e.g., video, radio, graphics, etc.). To simplify the description of the model, we can think of it as face-to-face communication.

The learner's communication (C2) is the first step in the receipt of the instructional information. The arrow points toward the transmission because the learner must have a predisposition to attend to the message. The learner can attend to the information with any of his or her five senses or combinations of the senses. In the systems model of the learner, this is describes as the opening of his or her input screen.

The process of attending to the instruction is also mediated by the learner's working memory. This is the total mass of sensory

187

and mental information that is available to the learner at a given moment. It includes the information that he or she has just received and also previously learned information retrieved from his or her LTM. If the communication stops at this point, it is just like it didn't happen. To make it exist beyond the moment of its inception, an additional transformation must occur.

Internalization of the information (learning) occurs when it is transformed (T3) into a more permanent code and stored in the learner's LTM. In this transformation, the information is incorporated into the learner's memory on the basis of his or her personal identity. The information is related to the viewpoint, needs, and goals of the learner's "me" or unique self. Because the learner's memory is complex and affects all aspects of his or her attention and ability to understand the communication, it is worthwhile to look more closely at his or her LTM.

Figure 7.5 shows some of the components of the learner's working memory and LTM. It indicates these components influence his or her personal and communal awareness. The

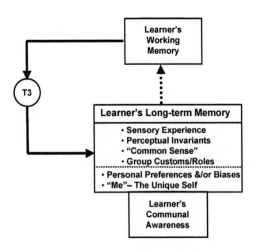

Figure 7.5:
The Learner's Long-term and Working Memory

learner's LTM includes, as a minimum, his or her sensory experiences, perceptual invariants (learned interpretations of sensory experiences), "common sense" (preconceptions about the world), and the role that the learner plays based on group customs (e.g., the "student" role). These components are affected by the learner's conception of self as a unique individual.

Figure 7.5 is oversimplified—there are many additional components of LTM that are beyond the scope of this discussion. The components depicted in the figure (and many more) interact to affect how the learner develops his or her communal awareness of the instructional situation. This communal awareness influences the permeability of the learner's input screen.

Once the instructional message has been stored in the learner's LTM the stream of communication may be regarded as complete because no further transformations are necessary. However, the communication is not truly over because the learner must now reverse roles and become the sender. He or she must now communicate an understanding of the information to the instructor who now becomes the receiver. All communication, including instruction, is a series of processes like the ones described in the stream of communication with sender and receiver continuously reversing roles and transmitting information to one another. The next section examines the instructional process in greater detail as a form of communication.

A Model of Instruction as Communication

Ruesch (1969) developed a General Systems Theory model of communication. An adaptation of this model was incorporated into the systems model of the learner (Figures 2.6 and 7.1). This communication approach will now to help examine some of the variables that affect the instructional process. Figure 7.6 shows a model of instruction as a communication process.

Two communicators, such as a learner and an instructor, do not present the same state throughout the period of communication. "The most suitable model for the conceptualization of the variability of a communicating entity is the rotating globe. Each globe receives and emits messages or engages in action" (Ruesch, 1969, p. 151). This means that each entity during instruction is continuously changing and revising their relationships to one another and among their internal subsystem processes.

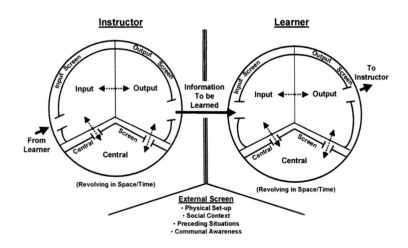

Figure 7.6:
Instruction as a Communication Process

Some of the most important components of Ruesch's communication model are external and internal screens. Internal and external screens may prevent instructional messages from being properly directed, quantified, or encoded. Only when the instructor and the learner receiver are using the same code (shared communal awareness), when interference of internal and external screens is minimized, and when the signal is capable of passing through the selective screens and filters can the instructional communication be successful. "Considering the obstacles presented by internal and external screens and the necessity for proper steering of messages and actions, it is a miracle that we communicate at all" (Ruesch 1969, p. 152).

Internal screens were examined in some detail in the discussions of the systems model of the learner. Both the learner and the instructor process information through their input, central, and output screens. Instructional communication also requires the transmission of information through external screens. Table 7.2

190

summarizes some of the internal and external screens that can distort or block instructional communications between learners

Table 7.2:
Internal and External Screens
in Instructional Communications

Screens Located Inside the Communicating Entity (e.g., learner and instructor)	Screens Located in the Field
1. **Input Screens** (control of perception)	1. **Physical Screens** (distance, time, architecture, climate)
2. **Central Screens** that control: • Data scanning (recognition) • Data processing (thinking) • Data storage (memory)	2. **Social Screens** (language barriers, rules, regulations). Includes lack of shared communal awareness.
3. **Output Screens** (control of expression and action)	3. **Organizational Screens** (lack of provisions for certain activities or message exchanges)

and instructors. External screens can be physical (like the physical distance between the instructor and the learner). These types or external screens are especially critical in distance learning. Other physical screens can be the result of the physical characteristics of the classroom (e.g., too hot or too noisy). External screens can also be social, such as differences in languages or language abilities. A lack of communal awareness of the subject matter is a type of social screen. External screens can also be the result of organizational policies like the failure to provide sufficient facilities or time for practicing the skills to be learned.

A variety of methods and aids have been developed to enhance instructional communication. These include the use of instructional media, such as simulations and games. The next chapter examines instructional methods by summarizing the categories of information to be learned, the "events" of instruction, and the instructional objectives that target different learning categories. Section III examines the empirical evidence on the effectiveness of different types of instructional media.

191

Chapter 8
Categories of Learning, Instructional Events, and Instructional Objectives

As discussed in the previous chapter, instruction is a special type of communication—intended to help a learner improve his or her performance by incorporating new knowledge or skills. A large amount of research (summarized in the previous chapters) has shown that complex learning occurs in a variety of domains of human behavior. It is incumbent on the designers of instruction to ensure that the appropriate instructional practices be applied to assist the learning of specific knowledge and skills (see Mayer, 2004). The determination of what are "appropriate" instructional practices has been a topic of discussion and research for many years. This chapter reviews two of the most useful approaches to help design and deliver instruction that meets the requirements of different types of knowledge and skills.

Categories of Learning Outcomes and Events of Instruction

Robert M. Gagné (1973; 1985) and his colleagues (e.g., Gagné & Briggs, 1979) developed a theory of instruction based on the idea that what we know about learning could be systematically related to the design of instruction. This book also supports this idea. Gagné and Rohwer (1969) summarized a large body of research that supported their theory of instruction up to that time. More recent research has continued to support the components of Gagné's theory (e.g., Mayer, 2002; Clark, 2003).

Components of Gagné's Theory. Driscoll (2002) summarized Gagné's theory of instruction as comprised of three components:

1. The types of capabilities humans can learn (categories of learning outcomes);
2. The internal and external conditions associated with the acquisition of each category of learning outcome; and
3. Nine events of instruction that facilitate a specific cognitive process during learning.

The *categories of learning outcomes* include the following:

1. *Verbal information* or knowing "that" or "what."
2. *Intellectual skills*, which are necessary to apply knowledge.
3. *Cognitive strategies* that help the learner employ effective ways of thinking and learning.
4. *Attitudes*, which are feelings and beliefs that govern one's choices of personal action.
5. *Motor skills* that require executing precise, smooth, and accurately timed movements.

Gagné assumed that each learning outcome requires different *conditions for learning* (e.g., types of instruction). For example, riding a bike (a motor skill) requires different conditions (e.g., practice) than learning the names of presidents (verbal information) or learning to solve math problems (intellectual skill). Many have advocated the completion of a detailed task analysis, to determine what must be learned, prior to developing instructional programs (e.g., Fleishman, 1972; Mayer, 2004).

Gagné believed that there are nine *events of instruction* that are necessary to facilitate the process of learning in general. Table 8.1 lists the nine events of instruction and some of the conditions of learning that help design effective instructional communications for specific categories of learning outcomes.

Taxonomies of Instructional Objectives

In addition to Gagné's instructional events and categories of learning, other researchers have developed even more detailed taxonomies of instructional objectives based on the three-fold classification of domains of human learning (e.g., Bloom, 1956; Krathwohl, et al., 1964; Simpson, 1972). The remainder of this chapter summarizes the taxonomies in each domain. This summary will help the reader understand how instruction can be designed to focus on the requirements of specific learning tasks.

Table 8.1
Nine Instructional Events and Conditions of Learning
(Adapted from Gagné & Briggs, 1979, p. 166)

Instructional Event	Capability Type and Implications
1. **Gaining Attention:** Present a new problem or situation. (Open the learner's input screen.)	• For all types of capabilities: Help the learner selectively attend to the important information and stimuli in the task to be learned. Use "interest devices" or short "teasers" to grab learner's attention (e.g., storytelling, demonstrations, incorrect performance and its consequences, why it is important).
2. **Informing the learner of objective:** Allow the learner to organize their thoughts around what they are about to see, hear, and/or do. (Help develop communal awareness.)	• Intellectual skill: Provide a description and example of the performance to be expected. • Cognitive strategy: Clarify the general nature of the solution expected. • Information: Indicate the kind of verbal question to be answered. • Attitude: Provide example of the kind of action choice aimed for. • Motor skill: Provide a demonstration of the performance to be expected.
3. **Stimulating recall of prerequisites:** Allow the learner to build on previous knowledge or skills. (Aid the formation of associations.)	• Intellectual skill: Stimulate recall of subordinate concepts and rules. • Cognitive strategy: Stimulate recall of task strategies and associated intellectual skills. • Information: Stimulate recall of context of organized information. • Attitude: Stimulate recall of relevant information, skills, and human model identification. • Motor skill: Stimulate recall of executive sub-routine and part-skills.
4. **Presenting the stimulus material:** Chunk the information to avoid memory overload. Structure material following instructional strategies (e.g., Merrill, 1997).	• Intellectual skill: Present examples of concept or rule. • Cognitive strategy: Present novel problems. • Information: Present information in propositional form. • Attitude: Present human model demonstrating choice of personal action. • Motor skill: Provide external stimuli for performance, including tools or implements.
5. **Providing learning guidance:** Provide instructions on how to learn. (Help the learner develop metacognitive skills.)	• Intellectual skill: Provide verbal cues to proper combining sequence. • Cognitive strategy: Provide prompts and hints to novel solution. • Information: Provide verbal links to a larger meaningful context. • Attitude: Provide for observation of model's choice of action, and of reinforcement received by the model. • Motor skill: Provide practice with feedback of performance achievement.

Table 8.1
(continued)

Instructional Event	Capability Type and Implications
6. Eliciting the performance: Provide opportunity to practice. (Open the learner's output screen.)	• Intellectual skill: Ask learner to apply rule or concept to new examples. • Cognitive strategy: Ask for problem solution. • Information: Ask for information in paraphrase, or in learner's own words. • Attitude: Ask learner to indicate choices of action in real or simulated situations. • Motor skill: Ask for execution of the performance.
7. Providing feedback: Analyze the learner's behavior and provide specific feedback on degree of correctness. Also provide reinforcement, or remediation. (Establish the instructional communication loop.)	• Intellectual skill: Confirm correctness of rule or concept application. • Cognitive strategy: Confirm originality of problem solution. • Information: Confirm correctness of statement of information. • Attitude: Provide direct or vicarious reinforcement of action choice. • Motor skill: Provide feedback on degree of accuracy and timing of performance.
8. Assessing performance: Test to determine if the lesson has been learned. (Complete the instructional communication loop.)	• Intellectual skill: Learner demonstrates application of concept or rule. • Cognitive strategy: Learner originates a novel solution. • Information: Learner restates information in paraphrased form. • Attitude: Learner makes desired choice of personal action in real or simulated situation. • Motor skill: Learner executes performance of total skill.
9. Enhancing retention and transfer: Help the learner use what has been learned (e.g., additional practice, similar problem situations, reviews). (Enhance associations among new information and existing information in LTM.)	• Intellectual skill: Provide spaced reviews including a variety of examples. • Cognitive strategy: Provide occasions for a variety of novel problem solutions. • Information: Provide verbal links to additional complexes of information. • Attitude: Provide additional varied situations for selected choice of action. • Motor skill: Learner continues skill practice.

The Cognitive Domain

The *cognitive domain* involves learning behaviors that have been labeled "intellectual activities" (Guilford, 1959). Bloom (1956) described the cognitive domain by ordering various mental operations from the simplest to the most complex. He divided the domain into two broad categories: knowledge and intellectual abilities and skills.

Knowledge

Knowledge "involves the recall of specifics and universals, the recall of methods and processes, or the recall of a patterning, structure, or setting" (Bloom, 1956, p. 201). Measurement of knowledge usually involves determining if the learner can bring to mind the appropriate material (recall). The instructional objectives for knowledge emphasize the psychological processes of remembering. This may also include the organization and reorganization of a problem such that it will furnish the appropriate signals and cues for the information and knowledge the individual already possesses. The key to developing a knowledge test situation is to find the appropriate signals, cues, and clues, which will most effectively bring out whatever knowledge has been stored. In terms of the systems model of the learner, these "cues" stimulate interactions among the learner's subsystem processes (e.g., the associator, memory, the encoder, the output transducer, and the output screen).

Knowledge of Specifics. Knowledge of specifics involves the *recall of specific and isolatable bits of information* with emphasis on symbols with concrete referents. This material may be thought of as the elements from which more complex and abstract forms of knowledge are built. Knowledge of specifics includes two subcategories:

1. *Knowledge of Terminology.* Knowledge of the specific symbols (verbal and non-verbal), which stand for objects or ideas. Illustrative instructional objectives for this subcategory include:

   o   To define technical terms by giving their attributes, properties, or relations.

o Familiarity with a large number of words and their common range of meanings.

2. *Knowledge of Specific Facts.* This involves knowledge of dates, events, persons, places, etc. It may include very precise and specific information (e.g., the specific date something occurred or the exact magnitude of a phenomenon) or it may also include approximate or relative information (e.g., an approximate time period or the general order of magnitude of a phenomenon). Illustrative instructional objectives for knowledge of specific facts include:

o The recall of major facts about particular cultures.

o The possession of a minimum knowledge about the organisms studied in the laboratory.

Knowledge of Ways and Means of Dealing with Specifics. This category involves knowledge of the *ways of organizing, studying, judging, and criticizing* (e.g., the scientific method, research techniques, chronological sequences, standards of judgment within a field, and also the patterns of organization through which the areas of the fields themselves are determined and internally organized). This knowledge is at an intermediate level of abstraction between specific knowledge and knowledge of universals. Knowledge of ways and means of dealing with specifics includes five subcategories:

1. *Knowledge of Conventions.* This is knowledge of characteristic ways of treating and presenting ideas and phenomena so one may communicate with workers in a specific field (e.g., usages, styles, practices, and forms). Illustrative instructional objectives include:

o Familiarity with the forms and conventions of the major types of works (e.g., verse, plays, scientific papers, etc.).

o To help learners understand the correct form and usage in speech and writing.

2. *Knowledge of Trends and Sequences.* This involves knowledge of the processes, directions, and movements of phenomena with respect to time. Illustrative instructional examples include:

o Understanding the continuity and development of American culture as exemplified in American life.

o Knowledge of the basic trends underlying the development of public assistance programs.

3. Knowledge or Classifications and Categories involves knowledge of the classes, sets, divisions, and arrangements which are regarded as fundamental for a given subject field, purpose, argument, or problem. Illustrative instructional objectives include:

o To recognize the area encompassed by various kinds of problems or materials.
o Becoming familiar with a range of types of literature.

4. Knowledge of Criteria. This is knowledge of the criteria used to test or judge facts, principles, opinions, and conduct. Illustrative instructional objectives include:

o Familiarity with the criteria for judgment of the purpose, the correctness, and the quality of written material.
o Knowledge of criteria for the evaluation of recreational activities.

5. Knowledge of Methodology involves the methods of inquiry, techniques, and procedures employed in a particular subject field as well as those employed in investigating particular problems and phenomena. This involves the individual's knowledge of the method rather than his ability to use the method. Two instructional objectives are:

o Knowledge of scientific methods for evaluating health concepts.
o Knowledge of the methods used to investigate problems of concern to the social sciences.

Knowledge of the Universals and Abstractions in a Field. The knowledge in this category involves the *major schemes and patterns by which phenomena and ideas are organized* (e.g., the large structures, theories, and generalizations which dominate a subject field). These organizational abstractions are at the highest levels of abstraction and complexity and include two subcategories:

1. Knowledge of Principles and Generalizations, which includes knowledge of particular abstractions, which summarize observations of phenomena. These abstractions are of value in explaining, describing, predicting, or in determining the most appropriate and relevant action or direction to be taken. Illustrative instructional objectives are:

- o Knowledge of the important principles by which our experience with biological phenomena is summarized.
- o The recall of major generalizations about particular cultures.

2. *Knowledge of Theories and Structures* is knowledge of the body of principles and generalizations together with their interrelations, which present a clear, rounded, and systematic view of a complex phenomenon, problem, or field. These are the most abstract formulations, and they can be used to show the interrelation and organization of a great range of specifics. Illustrative instructional objectives are:

- o The recall of major theories about particular cultures.
- o Knowledge of a relatively complete formulation of the theory of evolution.

Intellectual Abilities and Skills

The remaining areas of the cognitive domain involve intellectual abilities and skills. These refer to organized modes of operation and generalized techniques for dealing with materials and problems. The abilities and skills objectives emphasize the mental processes of organizing and reorganizing material to achieve a particular purpose. The materials may be given or remembered and may include metacognitive abilities and skills that help the learner monitor and adjust his or her learning. Instructors apply theses types of intellectual abilities and skills to the design and delivery of instruction.

Comprehension. Comprehension represents *the lowest level of understanding*. Here, the individual knows what is being communicated and can make use of the material or idea being communicated without necessarily relating it to other material or seeing its fullest implications. It should be remembered that all instruction is a form of communication, but in the following discussions of comprehension and some of the other cognitive areas "communication" is used more narrowly.. Comprehension includes three subcategories:

1. Translation is comprehension as evidenced by the care and accuracy with which the communication is paraphrased or rendered from one language or form of communication to another. It is *judged on the basis of faithfulness and accuracy* (i.e., the extent to which the material in the original communication is preserved although the form of the communication has been altered). Two illustrative instructional objectives are:

o The ability to understand non-literal statements (metaphor, symbolism, irony, exaggeration).
o Skill in translating mathematical verbal material into symbolic statements and vice versa.

2. Interpretation is the explanation or summarization of a communication. It differs from translation by *requiring a reordering, rearrangement, or a new view* of the material. Illustrative instructional objectives include:

o The ability to grasp the thought of the work as a whole at any desired level of generality.
o The ability to interpret various types of social data.

3. Extrapolation is the extension of trends or tendencies beyond the given data to determine implications, consequences, corollaries, or effects, which are in accordance with the conditions described in the original material. Two illustrative instructional objectives are:

o The ability to deal with the conclusions of a work in terms of the immediate inference made from the explicit statements.
o Skill in predicting continuation of trends.

Application. Application is the *use of abstractions in particular and concrete situations* and may include general ideas, rules of procedures, or generalized methods. The abstractions may also be technical principles, ideas, and theories, which must be remembered and applied. Two instructional objectives are:

o Application to the phenomena discussed in one paper of the scientific terms or concepts used in other papers.
o The ability to predict the probable effect of a change in a factor on a biological situation previously at equilibrium.

<u>Analysis</u>. Analysis is the *breakdown of a communication into its constituent elements* or parts such that the relative hierarchy of ideas is made clear and/or the relations between the ideas expressed are made explicit. They are intended to clarify the communication, to indicate how the communication is organized, and the way in which it manages to convey its effects, as well as its basis and arrangement. Analysis includes three subcategories:

1. *Analysis of Elements.* Two illustrative instructional objectives for analysis of the elements included in a communication are:
   o The ability to recognize unstated assumptions.
   o Skill in distinguishing facts from hypotheses.

2. *Analysis of Relationships.* This involves analyzing the connections and interactions between elements and parts of a communication. Illustrative instructional objectives include:
   o Ability to check the consistency of hypotheses with given information and assumptions.
   o Skill in comprehending the interrelationships among the ideas in a passage.

3. *Analysis of Organizational Principles.* This is an analysis of the organization, systematic arrangement, and structure, which hold the communication together. This includes the "explicit" as well as "implicit" structure. It includes the bases, necessary arrangement, and the mechanics, which make the communication a unit. Here are two illustrative instructional objectives:
   o The ability to recognize form and pattern in literacy or artistic works as a means of understanding their meaning.
   o Ability to recognize the general techniques used in persuasive materials, such as advertising, propaganda, etc.

<u>Synthesis</u>. Synthesis is the putting together of elements and parts so as to form a whole. It involves the process of *arranging and combining pieces, parts, or elements in such a way as to constitute a pattern or structure not clearly there before.* Synthesis includes three subcategories:

1. *Production of a Unique Communication.* This is the development of a communication in which the writer or

speaker attempts to convey ideas, feelings, and/or experiences to others. Two illustrative instructional objectives are:
- o Skill in writing, using an excellent organization of ideas and statements.
- o Ability to describe a personal experience clearly and logically.

2. Production of a Plan, or Proposed Set of Operations. This is the development of a plan of work or the proposal of a plan of operations. It should satisfy requirements of the task, which may be given to the learner or which he or she may develop on their own. Illustrative instructional objectives include:
- o Ability to propose ways of testing hypotheses.
- o Ability to plan a unit of instruction for a particular teaching situation.

3. Derivation of a Set of Abstract Relations. This is the development of a set of abstractions relations either to classify or explain particular data or phenomena, or the deduction of propositions and relations from a set of basic propositions or symbolic representations. Two illustrative instructional objectives are:
- o Ability to formulate appropriate hypotheses based upon an analysis of the variables involved, and to modify such hypotheses in the light of new data and considerations.
- o Ability to make mathematical discoveries and generalizations.

Evaluation. Evaluation consists of *judgments about the value of material and methods* for given purposes. It can include either quantitative or qualitative judgments about the extent to which material and methods satisfy criteria (or combinations of both). Evaluation includes two subcategories:
1. *Judgments in Terms of Internal Evidence.* This is evaluation of the accuracy of a communication from such evidence as logical accuracy, consistency, and other internal criteria. Here are two illustrative instructional objectives:
- o Judging by internal standards, the ability to assess general probability of accuracy in reporting facts from the care given to exactness of statement, documentation, proof, etc.

203

o The ability to indicate logical fallacies in arguments.

2. *Judgments in Terms of External Criteria.* This involves evaluation of material with reference to selected or remembered criteria. Illustrative instructional objectives include:

- o The comparison of major theories, generalizations, and facts about particular cultures.
- o Judging by external standards, the ability to compare a work with the highest known standards in its field—especially with other works of recognized excellence.

The Motor (Psychomotor) Domain

The *motor domain* involves learning tasks that require movements. Whereas the cognitive domain is concerned with knowledge, skills, and abilities (KSAs), the motor domain usually focuses on the learning of skills. However, as was discussed in Chapter 6, motor skills also include cognitive components. Acknowledging these mental or cognitive components, this domain is sometimes referred to as the psychomotor domain. To further understand the unique requirements needed to learn motor skills, Simpson (1972) developed a taxonomy of the motor domain that parallels the organization Bloom's taxonomy approach for the cognitive domain.

Perception. Perception is the essential first step in performing a motor act. It involves *becoming aware of objects, qualities, or relations by way of the sense organs* (i.e., opening the input screen). It is a necessary but not sufficient condition for motor activity. It is fundamental in the situation-interpretation-action chain leading to motor activity. Perception includes three subcategories corresponding to three different levels of the perception process.

1. *Sensory Stimulation* is the impingement of a stimulus upon one or more of the sense organs. The following sensory systems can be stimulated separately or in combination.

- o *Auditory:* Hearing or the sense organs of hearing

o *Visual*: Concerned with the mental pictures or images obtained through the eyes
o *Tactile:* Pertaining to the sense of touch.
o *Taste*: Determine the relish or flavor of by taking a portion into the mouth.
o *Smell:* To perceive by excitation of the olfactory nerves.
o *Kinesthetic:* The muscle sense; pertaining to sensitivity from activation of receptors in the muscles, tendons, and joints.

Illustrative instructional objectives include:
o Sensitivity to auditory cues in playing a musical instrument as a member of a group.
o Awareness of differences in the "hand" (feel) of various fabrics.
o Sensitivity to flavors in seasoning food.

2. Cue Selection. This involves deciding to what cues one must respond in order to satisfy the particular requirements of task performance. It also involves identifying the cue or cues and associating them with the task to be performed. It may involve grouping the cues in terms of past experience and knowledge (i.e., interactions among the input screen, associator, and memory). The cues that are relevant to the situation are selected as a guide to action and irrelevant cues are ignored or discarded. Illustrative instructional objectives include:
o Recognition of operating difficulties with machinery through the sound of the machine in operation.
o Sensing where the needle should be set in beginning machine stitching.
o Recognizing factors to take into account in hitting a softball.

3. Translation. This is relating perception to action in performing a motor act. It is the mental process of determining the meaning of the cues received for action. It involves having an image reminding one of something or "having an idea," as a result of cues received (symbolic translation). It may also involve insight, which is essential in solving a problem through perceiving the relationships essential to solution. Sensory translation requires "feedback" (i.e., knowledge of the

205

effects of the process). Translation is a continuous part of any motor act being performed. Illustrative instructional objectives include:

o Ability to relate music to dance form.
o Ability to follow a recipe in preparing food.
o Knowledge of the "feel" of operating a sewing machine successfully and use of this knowledge as a guide in stitching.

Set. Set is *a preparatory adjustment or readiness* for a particular kind of action or experience. There are three subcategories of set:

1. *Mental Set.* This is readiness, in the mental sense, to perform a certain motor act. It involves, as prerequisite, the level of perception and its subcategories. Discrimination (using judgment in making distinctions) is also an aspect of mental set. Illustrative instructional objectives include:

o Knowledge of steps in setting the table.
o Knowledge of tools appropriate to performance of various sewing operations.

2. *Physical Set.* This is physical readiness (having made the anatomical adjustments necessary for a motor act to be performed). It involves sensory attending, or focusing the attention of the needed sensory organs and postural set, or positioning of the body (i.e., interactions among memory and motor). Illustrative instructional objectives include:

o Achievement of bodily stance preparatory to bowling.
o Positioning of hands preparatory to typing.

3. *Emotional Set.* This is readiness in terms of attitudes favorable to the motor acts taking place. It implies a willingness to respond. This subcategory is very similar to the second subcategory of affective responding discussed below. Illustrative instructional objectives include:

o Disposition to perform sewing machine operation to best of ability.
o Desire to operate a production drill press with skill.

Guided Response. Guided response is an early step in the development of skill. The emphasis here is upon the abilities, which are components of the more complex skill. Guided response is the *overt behavioral act of an individual under the guidance of the instructor* or in response to self-evaluation where the learner has a model or criteria against which he or she can judge their performance. This requires a readiness to respond, in terms of set to produce the overt behavioral act and selection of the appropriate response. Guided response includes two major subcategories:

1. *Imitation* is the execution of an act as a direct response to the perception of another person performing the act. Illustrative instructional objectives:
   o Imitation of the process of stay-stitching the curved neck edge of a bodice.
   o Performing a dance step as demonstrated.
   o Debeaking a chick in the manner demonstrated.

2. *Trial and Error.* This is trying various responses, usually with some rationale for each response, until an appropriate response is achieved. The appropriate response is the one, which meets the requirements of task performance (i.e., it "gets the job done" or does it more efficiently). This may require multiple-response learning where the proper response is selected out of varied behavior, possibly through the influence of reward and punishment. Illustrative instructional objectives include:
   o Discovering the most efficient method or ironing a blouse through trial of various procedures.
   o Determining the sequence for cleaning a room through trial of several patterns.

Mechanism. Mechanism is when *the learned response has become habitual.* The learner has achieved a certain confidence and degree of proficiency in the performance of the act (sometimes referred to as autonomous behavior). The act has become a part of his or her repertoire of possible responses to stimuli and the demands of situations where the response is an appropriate one. The response may be more complex than at the preceding level. Illustrative instructional objectives include:
   o Ability to perform a hand-hemming operation.
   o Ability to mix ingredients for butter cake.
   o Ability to pollinate an oat flower.

Complex Overt Response. At this level, *the individual can perform a complete, complex motor skill.* It is considered complex because of the movement pattern required. The act can be carried out smoothly and efficiently (i.e., with minimum expenditure of time and energy). There are two subcategories of complex overt responses:

1. *Resolution of Uncertainty.* The performer knows the sequence or action required and so proceeds with confidence. The act is performed without hesitation to obtain a mental picture of task sequence. Illustrative instructional objectives include:

o   Skill in operating a milling machine.
o   Skill in setting up and operating a production band saw.

2. *Automatic Performance.* Here, the individual can perform a finely coordinated motor skill with a great deal of ease and muscle control. Illustrative instructional objectives include:

o   Skill in performing basic steps of national folk dances.
o   Skill in tailoring a suit.
o   Skill in performing on the violin.

Adaptation. Adaptation is *altering motor activities to meet the demands of new problematic situations* requiring a physical response. An illustrative instructional objective is:

o   Developing a modern dance composition through adapting known abilities and skills in dance.

Origination. This is *creating new motor acts* or ways of manipulating materials out of understandings, abilities, and skills developed in the motor area. Illustrative instructional objectives include:

o   Creation of a modern dance.
o   Creation of a new game requiring a motor response.

The Affective Domain

The *affective domain* refers to how humans deal with things emotionally, such as feelings, motivations, and attitudes. Affective behaviors influence how a learner approaches instruction, no matter which type of material (cognitive or motor) needs to be learned. Affective behaviors primarily influence interactions among the learner's decider subsystem, input transducer, associator, and memory to open the input screen to the material to be learned. Behaviors in this domain have been classified into 5 general categories: receiving (or attending), responding, valuing, organizing, and characterizing by a value or value complex (Krathwohl, et al., 1964).

Receiving (Attending)

Receiving *involves an awareness of other's feelings, willingness to receive information, and selected attention.* Is the receiver (learner) aware of the existence of certain phenomena and stimuli and is he or she willing to receive or to attend to them? This is the first, crucial step if the learner is to be properly oriented to learn what the instructor wishes to teach. As the result of previous experience (formal or informal), the learner brings to each situation a point of view (set), which may facilitate or hinder attention to the phenomena to be learned. Receiving has been divided into three subcategories that indicate three different levels of attending to phenomena.

1. *Awareness.* This is almost a cognitive behavior. However, unlike knowledge, the lowest level of the cognitive domain, it is not so much concerned with a memory of, or ability to recall, an item or fact. Rather, it requires that *the learner be merely conscious of something*—that he or she takes into account a situation, phenomenon, object, or stage of affairs. It does not imply an assessment of the qualities or nature of the stimulus and does not necessarily imply attention. There can be simple awareness without specific recognition of the characteristics of the object. The learner may not be able to verbalize the aspects of the stimulus, which cause the awareness. Illustrative instructional objectives include:
   o Develops awareness of aesthetic factors in dress, furnishings, architecture, city design, good art, and the like.
   o Develops some consciousness of color, form, arrangement, and design in the objects and structures around him and in descriptive or symbolic representations of people, things, and situations.

2. *Willingness to Receive.* This is a step up the ladder but we are still dealing with what appears to be cognitive behavior. It is the behavior of *being willing to tolerate a given stimulus, not to avoid it.* Like awareness, it involves a neutrality or suspended judgment toward the stimulus. At worst, the learner

is not actively seeking to avoid the stimulus. At best, he or she is willing to take notice of the phenomenon and give it attention. Illustrative instructional objectives include:

- o Attends (carefully) when others speak—in direct conversation, on the telephone, in audiences, or other instructional situations.
- o Appreciation (tolerance) of cultural patterns exhibited by individuals from other groups—religious, social, political, economic, national, etc.
- o Increase in sensitivity to human need and pressing social problems.

3. Controlled or Selected Attention. This is a somewhat higher level that includes a new phenomenon, *the differentiation of aspects of a stimulus which is perceived as clearly marked off from adjacent impressions* (e.g., the differentiation of a given stimulus into figure and ground). The perception is still without tension or assessment, and the learner may not know the technical terms or symbols with which to describe it correctly or precisely to others. In some instances it may refer not so much to the selectivity of attention as to the control of attention, so that when certain stimuli are present they will be attended to. There is an element of the learner's controlling his or her attention so that the favored stimulus is selected and attended to despite competing and distracting stimuli. Illustrative instructional objectives include:

- o Listens to music with some discrimination as to its mood and meaning and with some recognition of the contributions of various musical elements and instruments to the total effect.
- o Alertness toward human values and judgments on life as they are recorded in literature.

Responding

Responding involves responses, which go beyond merely attending to the phenomenon. The learner is sufficiently motivated that he or she is *not just willing to attend, but he or she is actively attending.* As a first stage in a "learning by doing" process the learner is committed in some small measure to the phenomena involved. This is a very low level of commitment, but he or she is doing something with or about the phenomenon besides merely perceiving it, as would be true at the previous level below this (controlled or selected attention). Responding includes three subcategories.

1. *Acquiescence in Responding.* This behavior could be described with the words "obedience" or "compliance." Both of theses terms indicate that there is a passiveness so far as the initiation of the behavior is concerned, and the stimulus calling for this behavior is not subtle. *Compliance* is perhaps a better term than obedience, since there is more of the element of reaction to a suggestion and less of the implication of resistance or yielding unwillingly. *The learner makes the response, but has not fully accepted the necessity for doing so.* Illustrative instructional objectives include:

   o   Willingness to comply with health regulations.
   o   Obeys the playground regulations.

2. *Willingness to Respond.* The key to this level is in the term "willingness." It implies *the capacity for voluntary activity.* The learner is sufficiently committed to exhibiting the behavior that he or she does so not just because of a fear of punishment, but voluntarily. The element of resistance or of yielding unwillingly, which is possibly present at the previous level, is here replaced with consent based on the learner's own choice. Illustrative instructional objectives include:

   o   Becomes acquainted with significant current issues in international, political, social, and economic affairs through voluntary reading and discussion.
   o   Acceptance of responsibility for his or her own health and for the protection of the health of others.

3. *Satisfaction in Response.* The level includes an additional element beyond the willingness to respond. *The behavior is accompanied by a feeling of satisfaction,* an emotional response, generally of pleasure, zest, or enjoyment. This emotional component is found in other higher levels, but is placed here to maintain the hierarchy of increasing complexity of responses. It should not be conceived as appearing or occurring at only this level. Illustrative instructional objectives include:

   o   Enjoyment of self-expression in music and in arts and crafts as another means of personal enrichment.

- ○ Finds pleasure in reading for recreation.
- ○ Takes pleasure in conversing with many different kinds of people.

Valuing

The term valuing refers to *the belief or feeling that a thing, phenomenon, or behavior has worth*. Behavior categorized at this level is sufficiently consistent and stable to have taken on the characteristics of a belief or an attitude. The objectives classified here are the elements from which the consciousness of the individual is transformed into active control of behavior. An important element of behavior characterized by valuing is that it is motivated, not by the desire to comply or obey, but by the individual's commitment to the underlying value guiding the behavior. Valuing includes three subcategories of behavior.

1. *Acceptance of a Value*. At this level the learner *ascribes worth to a phenomenon, behavior, or object*. The term "belief," which is defined as "conviction of the truth of some statement or the reality of some being or phenomenon when based on examination of evidence" (Webster's New Collegiate Dictionary, 1977, p. 101), describes quite well what may be thought of as the dominant characteristic here. Beliefs have varying degrees of certitude. This lowest level of valuing is concerned with the lowest levels of certainty; that is, there is more of a readiness to re-evaluate one's position than at the higher levels. It is a position that is somewhat tentative. Illustrative instructional objectives include:

- ○ Continuing desire to develop the ability to speak and write effectively.
- ○ Grows in one's sense of kinship with human beings of all nations.

2. *Preference for a Value*. Behavior at this level implies not just the acceptance of a value to the point of being willing to be identified with it, but *the individual is sufficiently committed to the value to pursue it, to seek it our, to want it*. Illustrative instructional objectives include:

- ○ Assumes responsibility for drawing reticent members of a group into conversation.

212

o Deliberately examines a variety of viewpoints on controversial issues with a view to forming opinions about them.

o Actively participates in arranging for the showing of contemporary artistic efforts.

3. Commitment. At this level, belief involves a high degree of certainty. The ideas of "conviction" and "certainty beyond a shadow of a doubt" help to define this level of behavior. In some instances this may border on faith, in the sense of it being *a firm emotional acceptance of a belief upon admittedly nonrational grounds.* Loyalty to a position, group, or cause would also be classified here. The person who displays behavior at this level is clearly perceived as holding the value and may act to further the thing valued in some way. Illustrative instructional objectives include:

o Devotion to those ideas and ideals, which are the foundation of democracy.

o Faith in the power of reason and in methods of experiment and discussion.

<u>Organizing</u>

As the learner successively internalizes values, he or she encounters situations for which more than one value is relevant. Thus it becomes necessary to (1) organize the values into a system, (2) determine the interrelationships among them, and (3) establish the dominant and pervasive ones. Such a system is built gradually, subject to change as new values are incorporated. This category is subdivided into two levels, since a prerequisite to interrelating is the conceptualization of the value in a form, which permits organization. Conceptualization forms the first subdivision in the organization process and organization of a value system is the second.

1. *Conceptualization of a Value.* In the previous category (valuing), it was noted that consistency and stability are integral characteristics of the particular value or belief. At this level the quality of abstraction or conceptualization is added. This *permits the learner to see how the value relates to those that he or she already holds or to new ones that he or she is coming to hold.* Illustrative instructional objectives include:

213

o Attempts to identify the characteristics of an admired art object.

o Forms judgments as to the responsibility of society for conserving human and material resources.

2. *Organization of a Value System.* Here, the learner is required to bring together a complex of values, possibly disparate values, and to *bring these into an ordered relationship with one another.* Ideally, the ordered relationship will be one, which is harmonious and internally consistent. In many instances the organization of values may result in their synthesis into a new value or value complex of a higher order. Here are two illustrative instructional objectives:

o Weighs alternative social policies and practices against the standards of the public welfare rather than the advantage of specialized and narrow interest groups.

o Develops a plan for regulating rest periods in accordance with the demands of his or her activities.

Characterizing by a Value or Value Complex

At this level of internalization the values already have a place in the learner's value hierarchy, are organized into some kind of internally consistent system, have controlled the behavior of the learner for a sufficient time that *he or she has adapted to behaving this way.* An evocation of the behavior no longer arouses emotion or affect except when the learner is threatened or challenged. The learner acts consistently in accordance with the values he or she has internalized at this level. This level contains two subcategories.

1. *Generalized Set.* The generalized set *gives an internal consistency to the system of attitudes and values at any particular moment.* It is selective responding at a very high level. It can be viewed as a determining tendency, an orientation toward phenomena, or a predisposition to act in a certain way. It is a persistent and consistent response to a family of related situations or objects. It may often be an unconscious set, which guides action without conscious forethought. A generalized set is a basic orientation, which enables the individual to reduce and order the complex world

about him and to act consistently and effectively in it. Illustrative instructional objectives include:

o Readiness to revise judgments and to change behavior in the light of evidence.

o Judges problems and issues in terms of situations, issues, purposes, and consequences involved rather than in terms of fixed, dogmatic precepts or emotionally wishful thinking.

2. Characterization. This is the peak of the internalization process. It includes those objectives, which are broadest with respect both to the phenomena covered and to the range of behavior, which they comprise. Thus, here are found those objectives which concern one's view of the universe and one's philosophy of life. Instructional objectives categorized here are more than generalized sets in the sense that they involve a greater inclusiveness and, within the group of attitudes, behaviors, beliefs, or ideas, an emphasis on internal consistency. As the title of the category implies, these objectives are so encompassing that they tend to characterize the individual almost completely.

o Develops a code of behavior for regulation of one's personal and civic life based on ethical principles consistent with democratic ideals.

o Develops a consistent philosophy of life.

Combinations of Knowledge, Skills, and Abilities

The taxonomies discussed above may give the impression that instruction focuses on separate knowledge, skills, and abilities (KSAs). This could not be further from the truth. Almost everything that must be learned requires combinations of knowledge, skills, and abilities. Furthermore, this learning is influenced by the learner's affect (emotions or attitudes). This influence sometimes leads to a substitution of the term "attitudes" for "abilities" when persons use the acronym KSAs (e.g., Department of Defense, 2001, p. 50-52).

The taxonomies help us focus on important components of instruction for particular tasks, but the components should not be viewed in isolation. The determination of specific learning objectives and the sequencing of instruction should be based on a thorough analysis of task requirements from the perspective or all three domains. The instructional objectives should influence the choices of instructional approach and the use of instructional aids to enhance the effectiveness of instructional communication. Section III examines the use of instructional media as aids in this process.

Section III
Research on the Use of
Instructional Media

In the previous chapter, instruction was characterized as a communication process. Much of the data summarized in Section II were generated in laboratory settings and focused primarily on processes occurring within the learner. Fewer research efforts have examined the instructional process itself (e.g., teaching behaviors, learner apprehension). This section provides a closer examination of instructional communication by summarizing research that has examined the effectiveness of various instructional media (aids). Some of this research has also been conducted in the laboratory, but the majority of the data were collected in applied settings. Chapter 9 begins the section with a brief summary of the history of instructional media followed by a discussion of some of the issues that are involved in the use of instructional media and concludes with an overview of the results of research on the general effectiveness of instructional media. The following two chapters take a closer look at two specific types of instructional media: simulations and instructional games. Chapter 10 discusses issues that are important in the uses of instructional simulations and summarizes research on the effectiveness of instructional simulations. Chapter 11 provides a discussion of instructional games and a summary of research on their effectiveness.

Chapter 9
Instructional Media: Issues and Research

In recent years, the use of instructional media (often called instructional technologies) has rapidly increased. The media were developed to assist instructors to more effectively communicate instructional information. Various instructional media were used for centuries (e.g., drawings, figurines, wooden swords), but in the 1950s and 1960s computers began to be used as instructional aids. There was a proliferation of computer-assisted instruction (CAI) that used learning principles, such as those of Skinner (1954) and others. As computers became more powerful and versatile, a variety of instructional media, such as graphics, animations, and simulations were designed and applied in a variety of instructional contexts. The use of increasingly sophisticated media has led to a debate between those that believe that the choice of medium is the most important decision in instructional design and those that believe that instructional media are only vehicles for delivery of instruction. This chapter begins with a brief summary of the history of the use of instructional media and then examines some of the research that has assessed the effectiveness of these media.

The Use of Instructional Media:
A Brief Historical Summary

Robert Reiser (2001a) provided a detailed history of the use of instructional media. This summary is based on his article. Reiser observed that instructional media have been used in the United States since the first decade of the 20th century. Thomas Edison forecast that the use of motion pictures would make books obsolete in schools (p. 55). The potential of motion pictures was almost universally recognized as evidenced by the inclusion of the Department of Visual Instruction as part of the National Education Association in 1932. Even though this type of optimistic forecast has accompanied the introduction of many new instructional media, their effectiveness almost never matched these initial forecasts.

219

The need to train large numbers of troops during World War II stimulated the development and use of training films and filmstrips. After the war, several research programs began to examine the features of audiovisual materials that affected learning. Unfortunately, "educational practices were not greatly affected by these research programs in that many practitioners either ignored or were not made aware of the research findings" (Reiser, 2001a, p. 57).

In the early 1950s researchers began to focus on how media affect the communication process "involving a sender and a receiver of a message, and a channel, or medium, through which the message was sent" (Reiser, 2001a, p. 58). Specifically, the growth of television during the 1950s stimulated research on "educational" TV.

During the 1970s, "the terms *educational technology* and *instructional technology* began to replace audiovisual instruction to describe media for instructional purposes" (Reiser, 2001a, p. 59, authors emphasis). The growth of computers also began to have an influence on instruction through the introduction of computer-assisted instruction (CAI) programs such as PLATO and TICCIT. Despite their promise, "by the end of the 1970s, CAI had had very little impact on education" (p. 59).

New computer applications such as CD-ROMs and the Internet have renewed interest in instructional media. Reiser believes that these digital media will bring about great changes in instructional practices. However, he also believes that "such changes, both in schools and in other instructional settings, are likely to come about more slowly and be less extensive than most media enthusiasts currently predict" (Reiser, 2001a, p. 62). One of the reasons for this cautious forecast is Reiser's observation that "most of the practices related to instructional media have occurred independent of developments associated with instructional design" (2001b, p. 58). This observation is at the heart of the media debate discussed in the next section.

The Media Debate

One of the earliest studies that compared the effectiveness of different media was conducted for the U.S. Army (Hall & Cushing, 1947). The researchers presented a lesson on micrometer calibration using three different media: film, classroom instructor, or self-studying with a workbook. All three lessons contained the same words and used the same visuals except the film used moving pictures. All learners were tested at the end of the lessons, but no differences in learning were found among the three groups. Many media comparison studies since this time have also yielded similar results. For example, a recent review of the learning effects of hypermedia delivered over the Internet (Dillion & Gabbard, 1998) found only limited benefits from using this technology.

The lack of media effects led to the following conclusion: "There is no compelling evidence in the past 70 years of published and unpublished research that media cause learning increases under any condition" (Clark, R. E., 1994, p. 25). This statement eloquently summarizes the view of individuals who believe that the focus of instructional design should be on instructional methods, not on the media that deliver instruction (e.g., Clark, R. E., & Solomon, 1986; Levie & Dickie, 1973; Lumsdaine, 1963; Mielke, 1968; Schramm, 1977). We shall refer to this group as the *instructional methods camp*. An alternative view, which can be called the *instructional media camp*, believe that specific media have critical attributes that recommend them as the choice for teaching specific types of tasks (e.g., Kozma, 1991; Koumi, 1994; Reiser, 1994)

R. E. Clark (1983, 1994) has been a leader in the instructional methods camp. He stated the view that "media are mere vehicles that deliver instruction but do not influence student achievement any more than the truck that delivers our groceries causes changes in our nutrition" (Clark, R. E., 1983, p. 445). In other words, it is instructional methods that are the critical factor in any successful learning system. He defined an *instructional method* as "any way to shape information that activates, supplements or compensates for the cognitive processes necessary for achievement or motivation" (Clark, R. E., 1994, p. 23).

Although he recognized the value of instructional media and believed that some form of instructional delivery is necessary, he did not believe that the use of any given instructional medium is sufficient to promote learning. "If any learning occurs as a result of exposure to any media, the learning is caused by the instructional method embedded in the media presentation" (Clark, R. E., 1994, p. 26). He questioned studies that showed media could influence student learning by asking if they were comparing apples and oranges. To demonstrate a media effect on learning, "all other aspects, including subject matter content and method of instruction must be identical" (Clark, R. E., 1983, p. 448). He did not believe that this was the case in most studies and issued the "replaceability challenge" to the media camp. "We need to ask whether there are other media or another set of media attributes that would yield similar learning gains" (p. 22). If the answer to this challenge was yes, Clark reasoned that the instructional media did not cause the observed learning effects. Clark's conclusion was that "media and their attributes have important influences on the cost or speed of learning but only the use of adequate instructional methods will influence learning" (Clark, R. E., 1994, p. 27).

On the other hand, the instructional media camp maintains that instructional media and methods are inseparable. Kozma (1991) argued that the learner strategically manages the available cognitive resources by extracting information from the environment and integrating it. He further argued that instructional media are an integral part of the instructional design process and careful use of media will enable learners to take advantages of its strengths to construct knowledge.

Some in the media camp believe that there is more to an instructional medium than just a delivery vehicle. Reiser (1994) stated that there is evidence "that learners preconceptions about the effort required to learn from a medium will influence the mental effort they expend...and that the amount of effort spent will, in some cases, influence learning" (p. 47). He also felt that "certain media attributes make certain methods possible" (p. 45).

In answer to Clark's observation that many media studies are flawed, Koumi (1994) observed that it is no wonder that poorly produced multi-media materials show no advantage. This seems like a "back-door" agreement with Clark. For media to be effective, they must use well-designed instructional methods that take advantage of the medium's instructional strengths. Koumi echoed Reiser in the belief that we should try to develop and refine criteria for employing media to the best effect.

Media Selection

Choosing the appropriate instructional medium can be very difficult. However, researchers have developed media selection methods that help the instructional designer make this selection. Gagné, Reiser, and Larsen (1981) and Reiser, Gagné, Wager, Larsen, Hewlett, Noel, Winner, and Fagan (1981) developed a media selection approach that used "successive exclusion" to help select an instructional medium. This approach provided "a procedure for narrowing the range of media possibilities" (p. 3). Once this range was narrowed to a small set of possible media, "practical factors," such as cost, availability, speed, etc. could be used to make the final media selection decision. Higgins and Reiser (1985) compared an "intuitive" approach to such a formal media selection procedure. They found that "more than twice as many subjects made the 'correct' media selection decision when they used the formal selection procedures" (p. 6).

A Taxonomy of Media Attributes

Levie and Dickie (1973) developed a taxonomy of media attributes to organize their summary of media research. Their taxonomy included three major divisions: sign type, sensory modality used, and level of realism provided. Media were characterized by describing their attributes in each of these areas or as combinations of attributes from all categories.

Sign type referred to the type of information presented by the medium (e.g., text, image, or sound). They defined a sign as "a stimulus intentionally produced by a communicator for the purpose of making reference to some other object, event or concept" (p. 861). Signs can be either iconic or digital. An *iconic sign* is "one which in some way resembles the thing is stands for" (p. 861). Examples of iconic signs include photographs, drawings, sculptures, and maps. An iconic sign must be enough like its referent so that the viewer can make the connection. A *digital sign* "in no way resembles its referent; it is arbitrary" (p. 861). Examples of digital signs include words, numbers, Morse code, and semaphore. The receiver of a digital sign must "know the code" to interpret the sign.

Levie and Dickie's (1973) second category is the *type of sensory modality* activated by the medium (e.g., vision or audition) or how the medium combines sensory modalities (e.g., text with narration). From their review, Levie and Dickie concluded that studies "have usually shown a superiority of reading over listening" (p. 868). An instructional advantage of sound plus picture combinations has been shown in some cases. They explained these cases by stating that the "nonverbal stimuli may act as reinforcers of responses elicited by words, thereby increasing learning" (p. 871).

Levie and Dickie's (1973) third media category is *level of realism*. This category includes three dimensions: amount of detail (e.g., line drawings versus photographs), chroma (e.g., color versus black and white), and presence or absence of motion cues.

Levie and Dickie's taxonomy focused on the media types available in the early 1970s. However, it is still useful as a means to categorize some of the important characteristics of today's instructional media. By detailing the similarities and differences among media types it is easier to compare and evaluate them.

Media Principles

Although we still have much to learn about the effectiveness of instructional media, some principles for the effective use of instructional media have been developed. In addition to the work of Levie and Dickie (1973), Bishop and Cates (2001) used a synthesis of information processing theory and communication theory as a foundation for the use of sound in multimedia instruction. Aarntzen (1993) focused on the use of audio in courseware. Najjar (1998) summarized principles of user interface design that maximize the learning effectiveness of multimedia instruction. Mayer and his colleges (e.g., Mayer, 2001b; Mayer, 2003; Moreno & Mayer, 1999) focused on both the audio/verbal channel and the visual/pictorial channel in their research on the use of media. Mayer's work is based on *cognitive load theory* (Chandler & Sweller, 1991; Sweller, Chandler, Tierney, & Cooper, 1990; Sweller & Chandler, 1994), *dual-coding theory* (Clark, J. M. & Paivio, 1991), and Baddeley's *working memory model* (1986, 1992, and 1999). Below are some instructional design principles that have resulted from these and related efforts.

- *Media Choice Principle*: Choose the medium that best communicates the information to be learned (Najjar, 1998). For example:
  - o For a small amount of information to be remembered for a short time, audio is better than text.
  - o Text is better than sound for longer retention.
  - o Pictures are useful for presenting spatial information, especially for complex tasks (Marcus, Cooper, & Sweller, 1996).
  - o Simple illustrations with captions are more effective than text for summarizing information (Mayer, Bove, Bryman, Mars, & Tapangco, 1996).
- *Multimedia Principle*: Students learn better from words and pictures than from words alone (Mayer, 2003, p. 37; also, Carney & Levin, 2002; Mayer, 1989; Mayer & Anderson, R. B., 1991; Mayer & Moreno, 2003).
- *Spatial Contiguity Principle*: Students learn better when corresponding words and pictures are presented near rather than far from each other on the page or screen (Mayer, 2003, p. 49). This principle can also be interpreted to mean that instructional information should be integrated as much as possible. For example, Sweller, and his colleagues (1990) compared examples of a geometry problem with related text underneath the diagram with an integrated (contiguous) example that placed related text in the diagram. Their results showed that the integrated version reduced divided attention and cognitive load in the learners.
- *Temporal Contiguity Principle*: Students learn better when corresponding words and pictures are presented so they coincide meaningfully (Mayer, 2003, p. 51; Mayer & Anderson, R. B., 1992; Mayer & Sims, 1994).
- *Irrelevancy Principle*: Analyses of illustrations in instructional texts have found that only a few of the illustrations serve important instructional purposes (Mayer, Sims, & Tajika, 1995; Woodword, 1993). This is unfortunate because students learn better when extraneous words, pictures, and sounds are excluded rather than included (Mayer, 2003, p. 33; Harp & Mayer, 1998; Moreno & Mayer,

2000). Gratuitous use of media can detract from learning. As Levie and Dickie (1973) put it, "Realism cues which are not relevant to the learning task may produce divergent responses especially under conditions of high information loads" (p. 875). Unrelated illustrations "may actually decrease learning" (Najjar, 1998, p. 313).

• *Modality Principle*: Students learn better from animation and narration than from animation and on-screen text (Mayer, 2003, p. 35). This has been called the "split attention effect" (Mayer & Moreno, 1998; Mousavi, Low, & Sweller, 1995). However, this general principle must be tempered by specific guidance on the type of material to be learned and the conditions in which a given modality is applied. For example, Rieber (1990) found that fourth- and fifth-grade students learned science principles better from animated presentations only if practice was provided. Thus, the specific conditions that improve the learning of specific material must be understood before decisions are made to use one modality over another. Another important issue when delivering instructional information using multiple modalities is the timing of delivery. Kalyuga (2000) found that combining a diagram, text, and narration can result in cognitive overload and reductions in learning if the text and narration is presented simultaneously. When it is necessary for narration to be redundant with text, Kalyuga recommended that written materials be delayed and presented after the auditory narration has been fully articulated.

• *Redundancy Principle*: "Learning is facilitated by increasing the redundancy of relevant cues and reducing the number of cues that are irrelevant to the learning task" (Levie and Dickie, 1973, p. 875; Mayer, 2003, p. 45). Media should elaborate the instructional information (Najjar, 1998, p. 313; Kalyuga, Chandler, & Sweller, 1999; Clark, R. C. & Mayer, 2003; Moreno & Mayer, 2002), but should not include features that are interesting but not relevant (Harp & Mayer, 1997; Mayer, Heiser, & Lonn, 2001). Fox (2004) found additional support for this principle. Using signal detection methods, she found that subjects were better able to discriminate information from video news stories with redundant visuals than from news stories with dissonant visuals.

• *Interaction Principle*: A cognitively engaging, interactive user interface "appears to have a significant positive effect on learning from multimedia" (Najjar, 1998, p. 314).

• *Prior Knowledge Principle*: Media design effects are stronger for learners with low-knowledge of the subject area (inexperienced learners) (Mayer, & Gallini, 1990). High knowledge and high aptitude learners can adjust to and benefit from almost any media design (Mayer, 2003, p. 43). However, some data indicate that if an instructional presentation forces an experienced learner to "attend to the audio explanations continuously without the possibility of skipping or ignoring them, learning might be inhibited" (Kalyuga, Chandler, & Sweller, 2000, p. 135).

• *Voice Principle*: People learn better from narration when the voice is human (rather than a machine voice) and speaks with a standard accent (Mayer, 2003, p. 53).

• *Personalization Principle*: Learning is facilitated in multimedia lessons when the words are in conversational style rather than formal style (Mayer, 2003, p. 39).

• *Pretraining Principle*: People learn better from multimedia when they already know something about the topic (e.g., names and functions of components) (Mayer, 2003, p. 41; Mayer, Mathias, & Wetzell, 2002).

• *Signaling Principle*: Multimedia explanations using narrated animations should include highlights of the key steps, sections headings that correspond to the key steps, and/or other techniques to signal the importance of the information (Mayer, 2003, p. 47; Loman & Mayer, 1983; Mautone & Mayer, 2001).

• *Pacing Control Principle*: The cognitive load imposed on the learner can be reduced and deeper learning can be achieved by allowing the learner to control the rate of presentation (Mayer & Chandler, 2001).

• *Appropriate Instructional Cues Principle*: The instructional medium or mix of media should be chosen on the basis of the media attributes that will facilitate the learning of specific tasks. Levie and Dickie (1973) summarized the need for additional research on which specific media attributes should be used for instruction on specific tasks. "No single level of independent variable is consistently superior" (p. 877). They recommended that instructional researchers should direct their efforts toward "discovering the conditions under which different levels of attributes are differentially effective. What media attributes will facilitate learning for what kinds of tasks?" (p. 877).

The choice of which instructional medium to use is made more complex by the desire to combine media in a given instructional program. *Multimedia* is the term often applied to this combination. Tessmer (1995) defined multimedia as "a computer-driven interactive communication system for various types of textual, graphic, video, and auditory information" (p. 128). Such combinations of media make it even more important to choose the mix of media that will most effectively support learning.

Effectiveness Assessments of Multimedia Programs

The effectiveness of whole multimedia programs is sometimes assessed without targeting specific characteristics of the programs. For example, Hansen, Resnick, and Galea (2002) evaluated the effectiveness of a multimedia communications skills training CD-ROM for social work students. They found that learners' improved their scores from a pretest to a posttest and also rated the course as "helpful." Unfortunately, there was no comparison with alternate forms of instruction nor was there an assessment of specific media approaches within the course. This type of evaluation is useful for the developers and sponsors of a new course or instructional approach. However, it is of little help for individuals seeking general guidance or wishing to understand how to make tradeoffs among different media combinations or instructional approaches.

Learning Agents

A new media technology that shows promise is the use of on-screen learning agents. Sometimes called *pedagogical agents* or *avatars*, these agents are on-screen characters that assist the learner. They may provide learning advice or hints during a lesson

228

or may serve as the interface to help a learner interact with the course. In computer-based or internet-delivered courses, these agents may be able to assume many of the motivational and instructional roles of a live instructor.

Although still very new, some research has already shown that these agents can enhance learner performance. Moreno, Mayer, Spires and Lester (2001) demonstrated that on-screen agents can lead to better learning when compared to lessons with the same content but without the agent. However, instructional designers should be cautious in the use of these agents to avoid frustrating the learner with triviality or boredom.

Atkinson (2002) examined whether using agents would help learners understand examples. He found that learners who were given vocal explanation of examples by animated pedagogical agents outperformed learners who only received textual explanations of the same examples.

Baylor and Ryu (2003) found that animated agents were perceived as more "engaging" than static agents. However the perceived credibility of the agent was the same regardless of whether the agent was static or animated.

Moreno and Mayer (2004) examined the role of personalized agent messages in a computer-based simulation used to teach college students about the characteristics of plants. They found that the learners who received personalized agent messages performed better than those who received non-personalized messages on both retention and problem-solving transfer tests.

One-on-one tutoring has long been recognized as superior to group classroom instruction (Bloom, 1984). Agents may serve as tutors if they can be designed to perform the same roles as a human tutor. Chi, Siler, Jeong, Yamauci, and Housmann (2001) studied the instructional effectiveness of human tutors. They found that the learning advantage of tutoring is the result of multiple factors. Foremost among these is the opportunity afforded by tutoring for the learners to engage in more interactions with the tutor (as compared to a classroom instructor). Human tutors also provide the opportunity for the learners to more deeply interact with the instructional content by engaging in constructive activities such as asking questions and trying out self-explanations. They conclude that intelligent tutoring systems should be designed to elicit learners' constructive responses, perhaps through the use of natural language recognition to understand and respond to learner questions.

The next chapter examines research on instructional simulations that often include combinations of media attributes. Simulations offer the opportunity for learners to receive instructional information and experience phenomena in a more realistic environment than a classroom.

Chapter 10
Research on Instructional Simulations

Instructional simulations are usually created by combining a variety of media attributes (e.g., sound, motion, and text) to instantiate a simplified model of some process or entity. The following sections include definitions of important terms in the simulation field, a brief history of the use of instructional simulations, a summary of research on the effectiveness of instructional simulations, and a discussion of how to choose the appropriate simulation attributes for teaching specific tasks and skills.

Definitions of Important Terms in Instructional Simulation

The field of instructional simulation is filled with somewhat esoteric terms. Some of the most important terms are defined below to help the reader understand this complex instructional area. This discussion begins by distinguishing between the terms model and simulation. People often confuse the terms model and simulation and mistakenly use the terms interchangeably. There are important differences between a model and a simulation although they are closely related to each other.

A *model* is "a physical, mathematical, or otherwise logical representation of a system, entity, phenomenon, or process" (Department of Defense, 1997, p. 138). There are several reasons why models are important:

1. Models aid us in understanding complex concepts and processes because they can help simplify and explain them.
2. Models provide a means to test our understanding of these concepts and processes.
3. Models are the foundation for developing dynamic simulations by providing the rules and the data that allow a simulation to function in a specific way to meet a specific purpose.

A *simulation* is "a method for implementing a model over time" (Department of Defense, 1997, p. 160). The Department of

Defense identifies three types of simulations: live, virtual, and constructive.

Live Simulations involve real people operating real systems. An example is the Multiple Integrated Laser Engagement Simulation (MILES). This system, the precursor of the laser tag game, attaches laser emitters and receivers to weapons so troops can practice in simulated, but realistic conditions.

Virtual Simulations involve real people operating simulated systems. A flight simulator and a driving simulator are examples of virtual simulations.

Constructive Simulations involve simulated people operating simulated systems. Real people make inputs into the simulation and the simulation determines the outcomes of the exercise. Two examples are: 1) a computer-controlled war game and 2) a simulation of the activities of a team dealing with an oil spill.

Live, virtual, and constructive simulations are not mutually exclusive and are often combined in a given instructional exercise.

When used as an instructional medium, simulations can provide important instructional advantages over other instructional approaches:

1. Instructional simulations are available almost any time when compared to using actual equipment that may be unavailable due to other commitments.

2. Simulations can be run faster than actual equipment because simulated exercises can be reset and rerun very quickly (e.g., when training air traffic controllers, simulated aircraft or other simulated entities can be quickly added or removed from instructional scenarios).

3. Simulation scenarios are reproducible, so they can be used to teach lessons that require repetition.

4. Simulations can provide the learner with more trials in a given amount of time by eliminating tasks that are not central to the instructional objective. For example, if the objective is to train in-flight refueling the simulation can omit takeoff or landing tasks.

5. Simulations can provide the learner with cause-and-effect feedback almost immediately, when it is most effective.

The term *simulation* should not be confused with *simulator*. A simulator is a type of device, which "(a) attempts to duplicate the essential features of a task situation and (b) provides for direct practice" (Kinkade & Wheaton, 1972, p. 671). A simulation, on the other hand, does not have to be any type of equipment (although it may involve the use of equipment). Morris and Thomas (1976) defined a simulation as "the ongoing representation of certain features of a real situation to achieve some specific training objective" (p. 66). They went on to define a simulator as "the media through which a trainee may experience the simulation" (p. 66).

One often encounters the term training device in the simulation research literature. Kinkade and Wheaton (1972) defined a *training device* is "any arrangement of equipment, components, apparatus, or materials which provides conditions that help trainees learn a task" (p. 670). In the following discussions, the terms simulator and training device will be used interchangeably unless a specific distinction needs to be made.

A History of Instructional Simulation

Instructional simulation, while often perceived as a new field, actually has a rich history. A brief review of the history of instructional simulations includes the following:

- Ancient civilizations used rudimentary forms of instructional simulations like practice with wooden swords. The Egyptians and Sumerians (2500 B.C.), used figurine warriors to represent different warring factions.
- The Chinese (500 B.C.) created one of the earliest "war games" (a type of simulation), called Wei Hai or "encirclement."
- The Olympics (200 B.C.) were originally founded with events that primarily simulated warfare.
- The Romans (300 B.C. – 100 A.D.) are credited with creating the first "professional" army. A large part of daily life for the Roman Legions was to practice their battlefield skills, learning complex formations and complex battlefield strategies. Soldiers would engage in this combat training with wooden swords, called Rudis.
- Around 700 A.D. in India, Chaturanga was created. This was a popular game with a sectioned board that led to the game we now know as chess. The game was originally

created for entertainment, but was later used to depict armed combat.

• German, Christopher Weikman created a war game called military chess or "Koenigspiel" (1644 A.D.). As German war games evolved, they introduced scenario-based exercises, detailed terrain maps on sand tables, time and distance considerations, and the use of probability to determine the effects of combat. Many of these fundamental elements of military instructional simulation are still in use today.

• U.S. Army Major Lawrence Livermore brought a modified version of the German war game to the United States in 1879. Livermore added increasingly complex elements to the war game including the tracking of supplies, the use of more sophisticated symbology to represent troops and equipment, and the creation of indices for fire control (e.g. the distance that a bullet will travel) and troop movement (e.g., speed over various types of terrain). Most importantly, Major Livermore introduced consideration of the human element into the simulation by including the impact of time and its effect on fatigue.

• The start of the 20th Century heralded a new era for the field of instructional simulation. The increasing cost of military equipment and supplies led to the development of training exercises that utilized simulated equipment to allows soldiers to practice.

• During WWI, the US Army used wooden simulations for artillery practice.

• After World War I, an American, Ed Link, built the first aircraft simulator. This unit was used in 1936 by the US Army Air Corps to train airmail pilots.

• In the 1930s, the Japanese used war gaming to simulate their war plans.

• At the beginning of WWII, with all available resources committed to the war effort, new pilots had no way to train before climbing into a real plane for the first time. Ed Link improved on his earlier aircraft simulator with the invention of the first modern flight simulator, the Blue Box trainer. Thousands of pilots were trained in hundreds of these simulators.

- After WWII, the development of computers accelerated the use of instructional simulations. For example, the first electronic flight simulator was created by Link Systems in 1950.
- NASA used simulations to train astronauts during the 1960s. Apollo 11 commander Armstrong described the moon landing as "just like the simulator." Testing various procedures on a simulator was critical in the Apollo 13 rescue.
- During the 1970s and 1980s, personal computers made simulations available in business and education.
- During the 1990s the growth of the Internet offered the promise of web-based instruction.
- Today, data storage devices (e.g., CD-ROMs, DVDs) and broadband Internet increase the capabilities and potential of computer-based instruction.

The Design and Use of Instructional Simulations

Greenblat and Uretsky (1977) discussed the steps required in developing computer simulations.

- *Develop a mathematical model.* The first step is to develop a mathematical model of the system being simulated. This model must represent the system with clear identification of the exogenous variables (those whose values must be determined outside of the model), the endogenous variables (those whose values are developed by the model), and initial conditions that must be supplied by the investigator.
- *Supply data values.* Data values must be supplied for all exogenous variables and initial conditions.
- *Identify probabilistic variables.* All variables whose values change based on probabilistic functions must be identified and represented within the model and the mathematical representations of the functions must be determined.
- *Formulate equations.* All equations that are to be used in the model must be formulated in such a way that their solutions may be derived by the computer. This may require iterative execution of the model on the computer.

- *Validate the model.* Once the model is executed on the computer the results must be analyzed for validity and reliability.

Once these steps have been completed, the model may be used as the basis for a dynamic simulation. A variety of such simulations have been developed as instructional tools.

Gagné (1954) provided one of the earliest systematic statements of the important research issues in the design and use of instructional simulations. At least two of these research issues are still relevant today:

1. How will the effectiveness of the instructional simulation be determined?
2. How does the purpose of the instructional simulation specify its design characteristics?

The next section summarizes some of the research on the effectiveness of instructional simulations used in a variety of task areas. A section that discusses how the conceptual metaphor, simulation fidelity, can be used to relate the purpose of the instructional simulation to its design characteristics follows this.

The Effectiveness of Simulations

As is clear from the brief historical summary above, instructional simulations have been effectively used in many different contexts. However, in most cases, no formal evaluation of their effectiveness was conducted. This is sometimes due to lack of resources, but more often because the simulation is viewed by users as "better than what we had." Nevertheless, over the years there have been quite a few instructional effectiveness evaluations of simulations. For example, Lee (1999) conducted a meta-analysis on instructional simulations (his term). Nineteen studies met the criteria for inclusion in the analysis. Three modes of simulations were identified:

1. *Presentations*: simulations used to supplement expository instruction.
2. *Practice*: used to provide learners with a large number of examples and guidance for interaction with the material to be learned.
3. *Hybrids*: combinations of the other two modes

Lee (1999) found many methodological problems and confounding variables that make it difficult to draw firm conclusions about the effectiveness of the instructional simulations. Nevertheless, several initial conclusions can be regarded as first steps toward a better understanding of instructional simulations in the future. First, when used for presentations, hybrid simulations appeared to be more effective than pure simulations. Second, hybrid simulations seem to be equally effective for both presentation and practice. Third, learners seem to perform better when provided with specific guidance on how to use the simulation.

Dekkers and Donati (1981) identified over 93 studies of computer and motion simulations that were suitable for a meta-analysis. Using a series of *t* tests, they found no significant differences at the .05 level between the use of simulations and other instructional treatments. This approach yielded some information on the general effectiveness of simulations. However, more useful information can be gained by examining research efforts that have evaluated specific types of simulations in various task areas.

Aviation Simulation Research

Aviation simulations have been used as instructional aids since Ed Link's primitive airplane trainers. Several reviews of aviation simulation research have been conducted (e.g., Koonce, 1984; Valverde, 1973; Waag, 1981; Hays & Singer, 1989). This section summarizes a few of the most influential evaluations of aviation simulation in three research areas: visual systems, motion systems, and whole device evaluations.

Visual Systems

The earliest fight simulators did not have visual systems. They were primarily used for equipment familiarization, communications training, and instruction on emergency procedures. During the 1960s computer-based visual systems began to be used in flight simulators and some evaluations of their effectiveness were conducted. Two research programs sought to determine how much realism or fidelity was required in a visual system (e.g., Demaree, Norman, & Matheney 1965; Ellis, Lowes, Matheny, & Norman, 1968). These researchers found that learners could achieve criterion levels of performance even if the instructional simulation used a degraded visual system. However, neither effort measured transfer to actual aircraft, so their results were tentative.

As computer graphics improved, the visual systems for aviation simulators became more and more sophisticated. Various studies showed the positive instructional value for these high fidelity visual systems (e.g., Browning, Ryan, Scott, & Smode, 1977; Lintern, 1980). However, positive support for visual systems was not universal. Hagan, Durall, and Prophet (1979) found that the addition of a visual system only enhanced the instructional effectiveness of the simulator for certain tasks. The visual system was effective for training weapons delivery tasks, but did not enhance performance on equipment familiarization or carrier qualifications.

If the task requires detailed visual cues, it is likely that the addition of a high-fidelity visual system will improve instructional effectiveness. This is true for aviation tasks and is probably true for tasks in other areas, such as learning to drive an automobile or operate heavy equipment.

<u>Motion Systems</u>

Until fairly recently, a major cost driver in aviation simulators was the addition of a motion system. Early motion systems were very complex, using huge hydraulic pistons to provide movement in all direction (roll, pitch, and yaw). Modern motion systems are much less costly because they use electromechanical or other types of motion generators. Nevertheless, the results of research on motion systems can help us identify when it is important to include this feature in aviation simulators.

Several studies supported the general use of motion systems (e.g., Jacobs, Williges, & Roscoe, 1973; Roscoe & Williges, 1975). Another study (Ricard, Parrish, Ashworth, & Wells, 1981) found that motion was especially important for learning tasks on marginally stable vehicles such as helicopter hovering. Other studies have found that the presence of motion did not appreciable add to the effectiveness of the simulator (e.g., Ryan, Scott, & Browning, 1978; Pohlman & Reed, 1978; Martin & Waag, 1978).

Whether to include motion in a simulator should be determined by the requirements of the task. Motion appears to have the most potential for enhancing simulator instruction on tasks requiring control in a marginally stable condition (Martin, 1981). The decision of whether to include motion cues in the simulations should be determined by analyzing the requirements of motion cues as they relate to the requirements of the task and the learning objectives of the instructional program (Caro, 1979).

Whole Device Evaluations

Most aviation simulation training for pilots in the military is combined with additional training in the aircraft. Many studies have compared this combined training to training in the aircraft alone. Hays and his colleagues (Jacobs, Prince, Hays, & Salas, 1990; Hays, Jacobs, Prince, & Salas, 1992) conducted a meta-analysis of research on the use of simulations for aircraft training. They reviewed 247 journal articles, book chapters, and technical reports on the training effectiveness of aviation simulation published between 1957 and 1986. More than 90% of the experiments favored the use of simulators combined with aircraft training when compared to aircraft training alone.

Gray (1979) conducted an evaluation of a part-task training simulator for in-flight refueling operations. Instruction in the simulator was found to be more effective than training in the aircraft for inexperienced learners and equally as effective for experienced learners.

Holman (1979) conducted a 2-group transfer of training experiment to determine the effectiveness of training for the CH-47 helicopter. Twenty-four maneuvers were taught either in the simulator or in the aircraft and then performance was measured in the aircraft. Simulator training was found to be superior for all maneuvers except those that required extensive visual ground referencing at low altitudes, such as hovering, or night operations. This demonstrated that, to be effective, simulators must be designed to train specific tasks.

Aviation cockpit procedures have also been trained with instructional simulations. One study found that a simple, low-cost

239

procedures simulator resulted in performance that was equivalent to the performance of the control group trained in a much more expensive cockpit procedures trainer (Caro, Corley, Spears, & Blaiwes, 1982).

After reviewing numerous aircraft simulation training effectiveness studies, Caro (1973) concluded that the characteristics of the simulator is not as important as the design of the training program that uses the simulator. This conclusion is probably true for a wide variety of instructional media.

Research on Simulations for Equipment Operation and Maintenance

Instructional simulations are often used to train the operators of many kinds of equipment besides aircraft. Driving simulators have been shown to be more cost-effective than using actual equipment (Puig, 1972) and to be more sensitive to differences between levels of driving experience than an instrumented car on the road (Blaauw, 1982).

Ship handling is a demanding operator task, especially when large tankers or submarines must be operated in restricted waters. Williams, Goldberg, and Gilder (1982) demonstrated that simulated ship handling exercises were as effective in improving performance as was real-world experience.

A within-simulator effectiveness evaluation of a virtual reality-based submarine ship handling simulator was conducted at two Navy training facilities (Hays, Vincenzi, Seamon, & Bradley, 1998; Hays & Vincenzi, 2000). Data were collected on fifteen ship handling variables grouped into seven skill categories. Significant learning (skill improvements) for all experience levels (0 to 14 years) was found on eleven of the fifteen variables. For example, learners improved: 39% in checking navigation aids and 57% in managing contacts with other vessels. No major simulator side effects problems were found during the evaluation, even though trainees averaged almost two hours in the head-mounted display. Details on the development and evaluation of this simulator are provided in Chapter 13.

Instructional simulations have also been used to teach equipment maintenance. One of the most complicated maintenance tasks is troubleshooting. It involves knowledge and skills that cover both the operation of the equipment and its underlying functionality. It also can involve the use of test equipment, which is another operation task. Most importantly, troubleshooting requires such in-depth knowledge that the maintainer can reason from anomalous system performance to the root cause(s) of the malfunction.

The performance of maintainers trained on a three dimensional maintenance simulator was found to be the same as the performance of maintainers trained on the actual equipment (Cicchinelli, Harmon, Keller, & Kottenstette, 1980). However a life-cycle cost analysis showed that training on the simulator was half as expensive as training on the actual equipment as was the current practice. Similar results were found when the performance of learners trained on an actual test station was compared to the performance of those trained on either a three-dimensional simulator, or a two-dimensional "flat panel" simulator (Cicchinelli, Harmon, & Keller, 1982).

Many operations and maintenance tasks require individuals to follow procedures. Johnson (1981) compared the effectiveness of training on two simulators to training on the actual equipment for an 87-step procedure. This procedure involved using a control panel to set up a conveyor line. The two simulators differed in their level of fidelity (realism). One simulator was interactive, reproducing the operations of the controls and displays of the operational equipment. The other was a photographic mock-up of the actual equipment on which the trainees used a marker to indicate control actions and display changes. They found that both simulators provided training that was as effective as the actual equipment as long as the trainees were able to obtain all of the necessary cues and feedback required to perform the procedures.

Many training developers have resisted the use of low fidelity simulations for maintenance training because they believed that the reduced physical similarity to the actual equipment (e.g., the number of test points available on the simulation) would reduce its effectiveness. McDonald, Waldrop, and White (1983) tested this assumption. Their experiment used two different versions of circuit boards (3 dimensional and 2 dimensional pictures mounted over the circuit boards with test point wires projecting through the pictures) and three levels of test point accessibility (100%, 67%, and 33%). Their results found no differences between any of these training conditions.

Simulations to Train the Use of Force

Police officers and military personnel are regularly confronted with situations that require them to use force. The split-second decision whether to use or not to use force and the level of force to use can have life changing implications for these individuals. Simulations which train people when and how to use force have become a widely accepted instructional tool. This is true for both police officers and soldiers and marines who must engage in urban warfare.

There have been few empirical studies that investigated the effectiveness of these types of simulations. Bennell and Jones (2004) found only 4 studies that assessed the effectiveness of use of force simulator systems (Boyd, 1992; Helsen & Starkes, 1999; Justice and Safety Center, 2002; and Scharr, 2001). Each of the studies used subjective assessments of training effectiveness, such as trainee ratings of perceived effectiveness (Boyd, 1992; Scharr, 2001) or expert ratings of trainee performance (Helsen & Starkes, 1999; Justice and Safety Center, 2002). The Justice and Safety Center used instructor assessments of shooting accuracy, use of cover, appropriate use of force, and safety issues (e.g., keeping the weapon operational). Only the Helsen and Starkes (1999) study supplemented subjective measures with objective performance measures (i.e., the trainees' shooting accuracy). In addition, they also rated the trainees' number and length of visual fixations on relevant stimuli and number of preventative actions they took during simulation scenarios.

Although the data are sparse, Bennell and Jones (2004) cited the Arnspiger and Bowers (1996) article in the *FBI Law Enforcement Bulletin* stating that simulations are beneficial for use of force training because they permit multiple practice trials in the parallel performance of motor and cognitive skills. Such a view may be correct. However, additional research is needed to specify the optimal ways to use simulations for this important area of training.

Instructional Simulations for Business Tasks

Simulations have been used for many years to train personnel in business situations. The "in-basket technique" is often used to provide instruction and practice in these situations. This technique is essentially a role-playing simulation where learners are given a variety of realistic problems that they might face on the job as if the problems appeared in their in-basket. Fredericksen (1974) identified 6 factors, which described these executive paper-work problems and constituted the domain for in-basket simulations.

1. Items requiring evaluations of procedures for accomplishing organizational goals.
2. Items permitting a routine solution.
3. Items requiring solutions of interorganizational problems.
4. Items requiring solution of personnel problems.
5. Items recommending a change in policy.
6. Items presenting conflicting demands on staff time.

The assumption behind the use of these simulations is that management trainees can learn the necessary skills and knowledge in a non-threatening role-playing simulation. It is hoped that they can later transfer theses skills and knowledge to similar situations on the job.

Rubin (1978) described another form of management simulation. This large-scale computer simulation, called PARADIGM, dealt with the flow of competing ideas through evolving groups. It was used to help managers learn the skills that they required to develop and nurture ideas in a large organization. The simulation focused on the ways messages are transmitted and how the information is used in developing ideas within groups. Persons participating in the simulation were able to text various methods of persuasion under a variety of external constraints. The effectiveness of the simulation was not reported.

Simulating the Environment

Simulations of the environment have been used to study and teach urban planning and develop greater understanding of the cognitive and personality processes involved in human-environment interactions. These simulations "emphasize the functional, operational properties of the man-environment

243

interaction under investigation" (McKechnie, 1977, p. 172). An example of this type of simulation was developed at the University of California at Berkley (Appleyard & Craik, 1974). This simulation allowed an operator to create a movie or videotape "tour" through a scale model the presents an eye-level drive or walk through a scene. Subsequent simulations have built on this early work and now often use computer graphics to represent the environment (e.g., the VESUB project, Hays & Vincenzi, 2000).

Discovery Simulations

Discovery simulations are used to help learners "discover relationships between variables of the simulated domain" (Swaak & deJong, 2001, p. 285). According to these authors, discovery simulations can be effective instructional approaches because they have three general characteristics. They are *rich* in the sense that the can contain a large amount of information that can be accessed in several dynamic ways. They also have *low transparency* as compared to text books by providing the learner a "direct view" of the variables and relationships among variables in the simulated domain. Thirdly, they provide a mechanism for *active interaction* by requiring the learner to perform "experiments" to make up their own "meaningful" learning.

Swaak and deJong (2001) conducted a series of five studies to determine the instructional effectiveness of discovery simulations for teaching principles of physics. Unlike pure, unstructured exploratory discovery, their simulations were structured. They included explanations and descriptions of the variables of interest, small sequential steps that each added a new variable, and structured activities (exercise) that pointed the learner to important phenomena that needed to be learned. They found that the simulations led to improved learning and they concluded that the structured activities contributed most clearly to the instructional effectiveness of the simulations. This conclusion supports similar views that the way a simulator is used is as important as how it is designed (e.g., Caro, 1973).

The efforts summarized above are only a small sample of the instructional uses of simulations. Looking at these and other research efforts, one principle clearly emerges. Instructional simulations can be effective if they are designed to support the instructional requirements of the task. Gagné's (1954) second research question asked how the purpose of the instructional simulation determines its design characteristics. This question is discussed in the next section.

Determining the Characteristics of Simulations

No instructional simulation can capture all of the characteristics of a real situation. If it did, it would be the real situation, not a simulation. Each of the possible characteristics that can be simulated adds to the cost of the simulation and increases its development time. Furthermore, for instructional purposes, it is often desired to omit certain characteristics of the real situation so the instruction can focus on specific tasks. Thus, it is of vital importance to determine which characteristics of the real situation can and should be simulated. A conceptual metaphor that often helps simulation designers make these important choices is simulation fidelity.

Simulation Fidelity

Simulation fidelity is the degree of similarity between the simulated situation and the operational situation that is simulated. This degree of similarity can be conceptualized under two major dimensions: (1) the physical characteristics of the simulation (e.g., visual, spatial, and kinesthetic); and (2) the functional characteristics of the simulation (e.g., the informational (stimulus) and action (response) options provided by the simulation).

Baum, Reidel, Hays, and Mirabella (1982) confirmed the separate and interactive effects of the physical and functional dimensions of fidelity in a perceptual-motor task. They concluded that in fidelity research, it is not sufficient to study general levels of fidelity. Rather, fidelity must be operationalized in terms of at least two dimensions: physical and functional similarity.

Physical fidelity is how the simulation looks; the physical characteristics of the simulation. *Functional fidelity* is how the simulation works or provides the necessary information to support the task. These two fidelity dimensions are related (e.g., if the physical characteristics of the simulation are changed, its functional fidelity will also change). In general, the functional requirements of the simulation should dictate its physical characteristics.

The simulation's functional fidelity (the information or stimulus and response options) is how the simulation provides required information so the student can learn the task. Depending upon the task, the information can come through any of the senses. For example, if a trainee is learning to fly a plane in a simulated cockpit, and the task is to fly at a specific altitude, then the simulated altimeter must be represented in enough detail that the learner can read the altitude. On the other hand, if the training task is only to locate the display next to the altitude indicator, then the simulation does not need to include a functioning altimeter.

In order to respond to the information (act appropriately), the learner must have the ability to make input to the simulation. For example, if the student needs to learn how to change altitude, a simulated control device must actually move and this movement must result in a change in the simulated altitude.

The instructional developer and simulation designer must ask questions like:

1. "What information does one need to accomplish the task?"
2. "How does one obtain this information?"
3. "What actions must one take to accomplish the task?"
4. How does one perform these actions and what feedback information informs one that the task has been accomplished correctly?"

Answers to these types of questions help determine the functional requirements of the simulation. These functional requirements then drive the decisions about how to design the physical characteristics of the simulation.

Aspects of Fidelity

It is not possible to simulate everything, so designers must choose the level of fidelity for each of the major characteristics (aspects) of the simulation that will support the instructional objectives. Simulations can be very complex with many different subsystems, each with their own characteristics. Fidelity tradeoffs must be made for all of these characteristics in each subsystem of a simulation. Three example "aspects" of fidelity will be used to explain some of these tradeoff issues.

1. *Audio fidelity.* This is the aspect of simulation fidelity that is familiar to most persons. Most people have all heard the term "hi-fidelity" in the context of stereo systems. Audio fidelity is especially important in simulations that require the delivery of sound information (e.g., communications, equipment sounds that may indicate problems, other important sounds).

2. *Visual fidelity.* This aspect of fidelity is especially important in simulations with visual displays. The fidelity of the visual display is usually determined by three characteristics: its resolution, number of pixels, and number of polygons.

   o *Resolution* is "the degree of detail and precision used in the representation of real world aspects in a model or simulation" (Department of Defense, 1997, p. 130).

   o *Pixel (picture element)* "refers to the smallest visual unit in an image on a computer display" (p. 123).

   o *Polygon*: "a flat plane figure with multiple sides, the basic building block of virtual worlds. The more polygons a computer can display and manipulate per second, the more realistic the virtual world will appear" (p. 123).

   Another important consideration when determining level of visual fidelity is visual latency. In general terms, *latency* is defined as: "The time required for a device to begin physical output of a desired piece of data once processing is complete" (p. 110). Thus, visual latency is the time between an input to the simulation and a change in the visual display. Higher the visual fidelity usually results in longer the visual latency because more computational time is required.

3. *Motion (movement) fidelity.* This aspect of fidelity is concerned with how the motion of simulation compares to the motion of the operational system. Similar to latency in visual systems, there is also *motion latency*. Reducing the time between an action and its response in the motion system requires faster, more expensive computers. The type or degrees of motion also need to be determined. Some simulations only require up and down motion (2 degrees) while others may need motion in all directions (6

degrees). The more degrees of motion, the more expensive the motion system.

Variables that Interact with Fidelity. In is not sufficient to focus exclusively on the physical and functional characteristics of the simulation. It is also necessary to determine how the fidelity of a simulation interacts with several variables, including: those related to the task, those related to the instructional environment and learners, and variables related to how the simulation will be used.

At least eight *task-related variables* are believed to have a direct impact on training effectiveness (Hays & Singer, 1989).

1. *Task Domain.* Different fidelity configurations may be necessary depending on whether it is an equipment operation or maintenance task. Operation tasks may also involve either moving equipment (e.g., driver training) or stationary equipment (e.g., operation of radar displays). Maintenance tasks may require access to test points and use of test equipment.

2. *Task Type.* A match must be found between the type of task and the characteristics of the simulation. For example, cognitive tasks probably require high levels of functional fidelity while motor tasks probably require higher levels of physical fidelity. Fleishman and his associates (Fleishman, 1967; Fleishman & Quaintance, 1984) developed one of the most often used taxonomies of tasks.

3. *Task Difficulty.* This variable involves both the complexity of the task (e.g., number of actions per unit of time) and the constraints placed upon it by the environment in which the task is performed (e.g., high noise levels).

4. *Task Frequency.* How often a task is performed may have a paradoxical effect on the design of the simulator. Frequently performed tasks may not require a highly complex training simulator because they are performed so often on the job. Infrequently performed tasks may require a complex simulator simply because it is the only way to obtain practice.

5. *Task Criticality.* This variable has two major components: delay tolerance and the consequences of inadequate performance. Delay tolerance refers to the amount of delay that can be tolerated between the time the need for task performance becomes apparent and the time actual

performance must begin. The consequences of inadequate performance, refers to the impact of human error on the system.

6. *Task Learning Difficulty.* Tasks that are difficult to learn may require special instructional features (e.g., ability to redo or replay a task sequence). This variable is influenced by the level of proficiency necessary for task performance and the difficulty of acquiring the required skills or knowledge. Swezey and Evans (1980) defined four levels of task difficulty: easy (the learner can accomplish the task one he or she is informed that action is needed; virtually no practice or study is required); modestly difficult (the learner can accomplish most of the activity subsequent to instruction with little practice or study, but some of the activity does require minimal practice or study to sustain competent performance at the desired level of proficiency); difficult (the learner can accomplish the activity following instruction, but only with consistent practice or study); and highly difficult (the learner requires extensive instruction, practice or study to accomplish the activity; the requirement borders on expert performance standards).

7. *Task Practice Requirements.* This refers to the extent to which initial practice and/or sustainment training are required to establish and maintain acceptable proficiency on the task.

8. *Task Skills and Knowledge.* The specific skills and knowledge required by the task have a strong influence on the design of the simulation. For example, procedural skills will initially transfer, but often require regular practice to be sustained.

Variables related to the *instructional environment and personnel* include: instructional program constraints (e.g., funding, time available, safety concerns); the purpose of the instruction (e.g., initial or refresher learning); the learner population (e.g., age, experience, motivation); the instructor population (e.g., job experts, educators; and the instructional principles used (e.g., scenario based, structured practice). Each or these variables must be considered to ensure that the fidelity characteristics of the simulation support these needs.

Simulation utilization variables include user acceptance and motivation and whether or not the simulation is used as it was designed. Learners may not be motivated if the simulation does not closely resemble the actual equipment even if this similarity is not required for instructional purposes. An instructor can affect the motivation of learners by how he or she refers to the simulation. If the instructor espouses its usefulness, the simulation is more likely to motivate the learner. Sometimes, simulators are not used the way they were designed. For example, a simulation designer may have provided capabilities to track certain learner activities or actions, but the on-site instructor never requires or allows the learners to practice these actions.

Chapter 11
Research on the Effectiveness of
Instructional Games

Recently there has been increased interest in the use of instructional games. It has been argued that young people, raised playing video games, have changed in ways that turn them off to conventional instruction (Prensky, 2001, p. 01-6). It has also been suggested that instructional games, because of their applied and dynamic nature, can heighten the learner's motivation and interest more effectively than classroom lectures (Greenblat, 1981, p. 147). Another suggested benefit of instructional games is that they may improve the retention of learned skills and knowledge. In an early review of gaming research, Pierfy (1977) reported that 8 of 11 studies that used posttests to measure learning found significantly better retention when gaming techniques were used.

Certainly, it can be argued that games can attract and hold an individual's attention. It is less certain that they always provide instructional value. Before discussing the research on instructional games, it is important to distinguish games from other instructional activities.

Confusion in Terms

In the literature on instructional games, we often find the terms simulations, games, simulation-games, and computer games used interchangeably (e.g., Greenblat & Duke, 1981; Reiber, 1996; Thomas, Cahill & Santilli, 1997). Greenblat (1981) observed that "in many studies, 'games' and 'simulations' are at least implicitly treated as homogeneous" (p. 181). Although aware of the problem, even Greenblat used the term simulation in one sentence and the term game in the next sentence to describe the same thing (p. 144).

All simulations are based on models of reality. A *model* can be defined as "a physical, mathematical, or otherwise logical representation of a system, entity, phenomenon, or process (Department of Defense, 1997, p. 138). A *simulation* is "a method for implementing a model over time" (p. 160). Thus, a model provides the rules and data that are used to represent some portion of reality. Then, a simulation uses these rules and data to dynamically represent these aspects of reality for some purpose. A specific type of simulation is sometimes called a *microworld* (e.g., Miller, Lehman, & Koedinger, 1999). Microworlds are simulations that attempt to capture the relevant aspects of some topic or phenomena so learners can interact within it to observe the effects of their interactions. For our purposes, microworlds will be referred to as simulations unless there is a reason to make a distinction between the two terms. Simulations can incorporate aspects of games (e.g., goals, rules, rewards, etc.) or be used as games, but only if the simulation includes these game aspects, should it be called a simulation game.

One of the purposes of simulations can be to provide instruction, but only if they are designed to do so. For example, Simons (1993) believes that "the educational value of a simulation comes with repeated simulation of a model" (p. 137). In this type of application, the learner is able to try various policies or parameters and observe the results. Through this closed-loop process, the learner gradually builds an understanding of the simulated system. This is a powerful instructional benefit of simulation games. Unfortunately, most of these games do not meet their potential. Simons explains that simulation games are ineffective because they do not "directly communicate their underlying models and the reasons for those models' behaviors" (p. 148). As discussed in later section, empirical data indicate that games are more instructionally effective if they include instructional support and are designed to support specific instructional objectives. With this in mind, Simons' quote might be rephrased in instructional terms—*a simulation game is ineffective if it does not directly link game events to instructional objectives and does not ensure that the learner understands whether he or she has met those objectives.*

Not every game is intended to for instruction. Most games are intended for enjoyment. Just putting a game in a course does not ensure that it will aid the learning of the intended knowledge or skill. Games can be designed for instruction, but only if they are designed to support specific instructional objectives and are incorporated logically into an instructional program. Before elaborating on this point, it is useful to discuss the various types of games and the characteristics that make them games.

Descriptions and Classifications of Games

Some authors (e.g., de Felix & Johnson, 1993) described games by listing their structural components, such as dynamic visuals, interaction, rules, and goals. Others (e.g., Gredler, 1996) stated that the essential elements of a game are the task, the player's role, the multiple paths to the goal, and the degree of player control. Baranauskas, Neto, and Borges (1999) stated that the essence of gaming is challenge and risk.

Csikszentmihalyi (1990) discussed how Roger Caillois (1958/2001), the French psychological anthropologist, classified games into four broad classes based on the kind of experiences they provide.

1. *Agnostic games* are those that have competition as their main feature (e.g., sports and athletic events). These types of games stretch the player's skills to meet the challenge provided by the skills of their opponents.

2. *Aleatory games* involve the element of chance (e.g., dice or bingo). These games give the illusion that the player somehow controls the inscrutable future.

3. *Vertigo or Ilinix games* are activities that alter one's consciousness by scrambling ordinary perception. Examples are riding a merry-go-round, skydiving, or young children turning around in circles until they are dizzy.

4. *Mimicry games* allow the player to create alternative realities (e.g., dance, theater, and the arts in general). These games make one feel as though they are more than they actually are through fantasy, pretence, and disguise. Caillois (1958/2001) uses the term simulation as a synonym for mimicry (p. 36).

Any given game may include some or all of these experiences, but it is usually designed to only provide a subset of these experiences. Furthermore, games are played with a variety of media, from game boards to networked computers. It is not the medium on which the game is played, but its characteristics that make it a game. One of the most important of these characteristics is the specificity of the game's rules. Caillois (1958/2001) discussed the issue of rules by defining a continuum anchored by the terms *paidia* and *ludus*. He defined *paidia* as "the spontaneous manifestations of the play instinct" (pp. 27-28). Games at the *paidia* end of the continuum have few or no rules and are played for shear joy. At the other end of the continuum we find *ludus*, which "is complementary to and a refinement of *paidia*, which it disciplines and enriches" (p. 29). *Ludus* refers to games with rules and requirements for play. The more a game is bounded by specific rules, the closer it falls toward the *ludus* end of the continuum. For example the *paidia* feelings found in *illinix* (vertigo) games are challenged and constrained by the rules and skills required in mountain climbing or tightrope walking.

The "Folk Model" divides games into 4 (non-exclusive) categories: games of skill, games of chance, games of strategy, and simulation games (Wikipedia, 2005).

1. *Games of skill* include: board games, card games, letter games, mathematical games, puzzle games, guessing games, word games, games of physical skill, and instructional games.
2. *Games of chance* include: dice games, card games, casino games, lottery-type games, Bingo, and Piñata.
3. *Games of strategy* include: Checkers, Chess, Go, and Mastermind.
4. *Simulation games* include: role-playing games, board games like Monopoly, and computer and video games.

Björk and Holopainen (2003) described games in terms of four overlapping conceptual groups.

1. The *overall activity of the game*. This is how the players understand the meaning of the activity and how the activity unfolds. Sub components of activities include:
   - The *game instance*, which is the specific players, their experience, and the location and requirements of a single completion of a game.
   - The *game session*, which is the activity defined by the time spent on playing a game instance.
2. The *boundary components of the game*. These include the rules, modes of play, and goals of the game.
3. The *temporal components of the game*. These are used to record the activity of playing the game. They include

discrete actions (e.g., moving a chess piece) or continuous actions (e.g., driving a racing car). Temporal components include:

- *Events*, which are discrete points in the game where the game state changes. Events usually occur as the result of player actions, but can also be the result of trigger events such as elapsed time.
- *Closures* are a change of game state resulting from completion of a goal or subgoal.
- *End conditions*, which specify when a closure occurs.
- *Evaluation functions*, which determine the outcome of an event.

4. The *objective components of the game*, such as the types of players, the game interface, and the physical and logical components that inform players about the current game state (e.g., tokens that represent which player is currently in control or physical elements that describe the game space like chess squares).

Leemkvil, de Jong, and Ootes (2000) and Bright and Harvey (1984) discussed several characteristics of games. According to these authors, all games include:

- *Voluntary Play*. A game is freely engaged in. Persons normally play games because they want to, not because it is required.
- *Some goal state that must be reached*. The goal state may be the same each time a game is played or it can change over time. The goal may also consist of subgoals that may change during play (e.g., when a player reaches a certain proficiency and moves to a higher difficulty level). Players can sometimes set their own goals.
- *Constraints and rules*. These define which actions are allowed and which are not. They also define the setting and goals of the game. Certain actions may introduce additional constraints, often defined by if-then statements (e.g., *If* a player misses a target three times, *then* he or she must complete a practice session and achieve a criterion score before the game can continue). Time limits on certain actions are sometimes used to induce constraints.

- *Competition.* Players can compete in several ways:
  - With other players or teams by beating them to a goal or outperforming them by achieving a higher score.
  - With the system (e.g., by moving to higher difficulty levels).
  - With themselves (e.g., by improving their performance).
- *A specific context.* A game is always situated in a specific context that makes it more or less realistic, appealing, or motivating to the players. This context is *separate from real life* in terms of time and space. Leemkvil et al. quote Graham and Grey concerning how game players must place themselves into the situated game context. "In one sense all gaming involves role playing since the individual participants are asked to assume the situation assigned" (Leemkvil, et al., 2000, p. 15 citing Graham and Grey).

Dorn (1989) defined a game as "any contest or play among adversaries or players operating under constraints or rules for an objective goal" (p. 2). He defined a simulation as "an operating representation of central features of reality" (p. 2). He then defined a simulation game as "activities undertaken by players whose actions are constrained by a set of explicit rules particular to that game and by a predetermined end point. The elements of the game constitute a more or less accurate representation or model of some external reality with which players interact by playing roles in much the same way as they would interact with reality itself" (p. 3).

A Game Designer's Definition of a Game. Greg Costikyan is a game designer and commentator on gaming. He defined a game as "an interactive structure of endogenous meaning that requires players to struggle toward a goal" (Costikyan, 2002, p. 22). Let us look at each of these components in greater detail. Costikyan maintained that a game's structure is the rules, components, and other characteristics (e.g., delivery medium) that define the way people play the game. He stated that this structure is interactive because the game changes based upon the actions of the players. This structure also provides the meaning of the game. Thus, a game's meaning is endogenous—it is created by the internal structure of the game and has no meaning outside of the game.

Furthermore, the game's endogenous meaning defines the goals which game players attempt to achieve. Finally, players must struggle to achieve the goals of a game. In this sense, struggle means that the players must work to achieve the goals. A good game challenges the players, often allowing them to move to greater levels of difficulty as they become more skilled at the game.

Hybrid Games

As discussed above, the terms game and simulation are often confused. As defined above, a simulation is "a method for implementing a model over time" (Department of Defense, 1997, p. 138). A *case study* is an actual or hypothetical problem situation taken from the real world. Leemkvil, et al. (2000) discussed the relationships among games, simulations, and case studies using a diagram like the one shown in Figure 11.1. As shown in the figure,

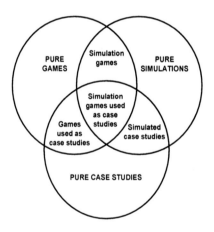

Figure 11.1:
Relationship among Games, Simulations and Case Studies

games, simulations, or case studies can be found in a pure form or as hybrids with the other types. In the literature on games, the simulation game is the most often encountered hybrid.

Elements of Enjoyment

One of the aspects that attract people to games is that they are enjoyable. Csikszentmihalyi (1990) studied many enjoyable activities, including games. He argued that there are several elements (components) that make an activity enjoyable.

- *A challenging activity that requires skills.* Individuals report that they enjoy activities that challenge their skills. "...the overwhelming proportion of optimal experiences are reported to occur within sequences of activities that are goal-directed and bounded by rules—activities that require the investment of psychic energy, and that could not be done without the appropriate skills" (p. 49). Csikszentmihalyi explained that "an 'activity' need not be active in the physical sense and the 'skill' necessary to engage in it need not be a physical skill" (p. 49). What is necessary is that the individual directs his or her attention (psychic energy) to the task and applies skills to accomplish it. One of the aspects of games that offer challenge is competition. However, "competition is enjoyable when it is a means to perfect one's skills; when it becomes an end in itself, it ceases to be fun" (p. 50).
- *The merging of action and awareness.* Another element of enjoyment is when one "loses" oneself in the activity. "People become so involved in what they are doing that the activity becomes spontaneous, almost automatic; they stop being aware of themselves as separate from the actions they are performing" (p. 53). This merging of an individual's action and activity is why Csikszentmihalyi called an optimal experience "flow." "The short and simple word describes well the sense of seemingly effortless movement" (p. 54).
- *Clear goals and feedback.* "The reason it is possible to achieve such complete involvement in a flow experience is that goals are usually clear, and feedback immediate" (p. 54). This is another important feature of games. It is

usually clear if a goal has been made or a target hit. One does not have to wonder if they performed correctly, the game provides immediate feedback.

- *Paradox of control.* Enjoyable experiences involve a sense of control—or, "more precisely, as lacking the sense of worry about losing control that is typical in many situations of normal life" (p. 59). "What people enjoy is not the sense of *being* in control, but the sense of *exercising* control in difficult situations...Only when a doubtful outcome is at stake, and one is able to influence that outcome, can a person really know whether she is in control" (p. 61, author's emphasis).

- *The loss of self-consciousness.* Because attention is so focused, because the activity is so engrossing, "there is not enough attention left over to allow a person to consider either the past or the future, or any other temporarily irrelevant stimuli" (p. 62). When enjoying an activity, like a game, one of the items that disappears from awareness is our thinking about our own self. Loss of self-consciousness "does not involve a loss *of* self, and certainly not a loss of consciousness, but rather, only a loss of consciousness of the self" (p. 64, author's emphasis).

- *The transformation of time.* In an enjoyable activity, "time no longer seems to pass the way it ordinarily does" (p. 66). One second can seem to stretch out for minutes or conversely an hour can seem like only a few minutes.

- *The Autelic (intrinsically rewarding) experience.* An enjoyable activity is intrinsically rewarding. The word autelic derives from two Greek words, *auto* meaning self and *telos* meaning goal. "It refers to a self-contained activity, one that is done not with the expectation of some future benefit, but simply because the doing itself is the reward" (p. 67).

Working Definition of a Game

Based on the above definitions and for the purposes of this chapter, the following is a working definition of a game.

259

The Science of Learning

A game is an artificially constructed, competitive activity with a specific goal, a set of rules and constraints that is located in a specific context.

A game is not reality. It is a constructed activity that resembles portions of reality. It provides a competitive environment for a player by challenging him or her to reach a goal. The purpose of the game (e.g., enjoyment, information, instruction, etc.) helps define the goals, rules, and context of the game.

Instructional Uses of Games

Most definitions of games, including the working definition above do not include any reference to instruction. Most games are played because they provide enjoyment, not because the player wants to learn something. However, *instruction is a specific type of interaction*. It is an interactive dialogue between the learner and the instructional material (Jacobs & Dempsey, J. V., 1993). The control of the learning experience is an essential feature of instruction. Without this control, we cannot be sure that the student learned what is required from a given instructional product. Instruction, as a minimum, must include the following four elements. First, instruction must be designed to support specific instructional objectives, which are determined by job requirements. Second, instruction must include the opportunity for a learner to interact with the instructional content in a meaningful way. Third, the student's performance must be assessed to determine if he or she has learned what was intended. Finally, the results of the assessment must be presented to the learner in a relevant and timely manner to either reinforce correct actions or to provide remediation for incorrect actions. If these four elements are not present, we are not dealing with instruction.

Games can be used as instructional activities or some of the aspects of games can be incorporated into other instructional activities to make them more enjoyable for the learner (Garris, Ahlers, & Driskell, 2002). For example, Parker and Lepper (1992) found that learners preferred educational programs that included fantasy elements. They also found that learners showed greater learning and retention in the fantasy conditions when compared to activities without fantasy elements.

Hays and Singer (1989) discussed several ways that games *could* be used for instruction. They observed that *potentially*, games can:

- Be used to assess entry level performance
- Measure criterion performance
- Aid in formative and summative evaluations of instructional approaches and programs
- Provide instructional information on specific knowledge and skills
- Help change attitudes
- Serve as advance organizers prior to other forms of instruction
- Replace alternate forms of instruction to transmit facts, teach skills, and provide insights
- Serve as a means for drill and practice
- Help integrate and maintain skills
- Illustrate the dynamics or abstract principles of a task

Based on their review of several studies of motivating computer games, Malone (1981) and Malone and Lepper (1987) provided a framework for designing intrinsically motivating instructional environments. Many of these design heuristics can be used to help design motivational instructional activities other than games. However, they are most relevant for the design of instructional games. Table 11.1 provides brief descriptions of these motivational heuristics. The reader should consult the original articles for additional details.

As should be apparent from the above discussions, it is difficult to distinguish games from other instructional activities that incorporate game elements. Nevertheless, there have been many efforts that have tried to evaluate the effectiveness of instructional games. The next sections summarize some of the research on the instructional effectiveness of games.

Table 11.1:
Design Heuristics for Motivating Inᵣtructional Environments

INDIVIDUAL MOTIVATIONS	Challenge	Goals: (a) clear, fixed goals; or (b) ability for learners to generate goals for themselves
		Uncertain Outcomes: (a) variable difficulty; (b) multiple levels of goals; (c) hidden information, selectively revealed; and (d) randomness
		Performance Feedback: frequent, clear, constructive, and encouraging
		Self-Esteem: (a) gradually increasing difficulty levels to promote feelings of competence; (b) goals that are meaningful to the learner
	Curiosity	Sensory Curiosity: may be promoted using variable audio & visual effects
		Cognitive Curiosity: may be promoted by: (a) using surprise, paradoxes, incompleteness; and (b) using activities that contain topics in which the learner is already interested
	Control	Contingency: learning environment should be responsive to learner actions
		Choice: activities should provide learner with choice over various aspects of the learning environment (e.g., narration or full text)
		Power: activity should allow learner to produce powerful effects

Table 11.1:
(continued)

INDIVIDUAL MOTIVATIONS (continued)	**Fantasy**	<u>Emotional aspects</u>: appeal to the emotional needs of learners
		<u>Cognitive Aspects</u>: use appropriate metaphors or analogies for the material to be learned
		<u>Endogeneity</u>: fantasies should have an integral (endogenous) relationship to the material to be learned
INTER-PERSONAL MOTIVATIONS	<u>Cooperation</u>: design some activities to promote cooperation among learners	
	<u>Competition</u>: design some activities to require learners to compete with one another (e.g., actions affect each other)	
	<u>Recognition</u>: learners' efforts should receive social recognition so they are appreciated by others	

Research on Instructional Games

There have been many articles written and published on the use of instructional games. Most of this literature is based on the writers' opinions about the *potential* of instructional games (e.g., Driskell & Dwyer, 1984; Rieber, Smith, & Noah, 1998) and the questions that must be answered about how games will be developed to make them instructionally sound (e.g., Oblinger, 2004). Far fewer articles have documented the empirical data on the effectiveness of instructional games. The following sections provide summaries of the results of some of these empirical research efforts. The first section summarizes the results of review articles, which attempted to draw general conclusions about the effectiveness of instructional games from collections of research efforts. Other review articles are not summarized, but were used to locate original articles on research efforts (e.g., Dempsey, J. V., Rasmussen, & Lucassen, 1996; Hogle, 1996; Leemkuil, do Jong, & Ootes, 2000). Subsequent sections provide summaries of individual research efforts that have evaluated specific instructional games for different types of learners (e.g., school children, college students, or military trainees) and for different types of learning tasks (e.g., factual information, technical skills, etc.). These summaries focus on the effects of each game on learner performance and also, where possible, describe the characteristics of the games used in the studies. Where the information is available, the summaries include how the game was used in a given instructional program.

Review Articles on the Effectiveness of Instructional Games

Simulation games have been used extensively in sociology and social science courses. Pierfy (1977) concluded from a review of 22 research studies that "in terms of fostering student learning, simulation games are no more effective than conventional classroom instruction" (p. 266). However, he did find that some research indicated that the use of games might improve the retention of learned information. Dorn (1989) also reviewed the use of simulation games in this area. He maintained that simulation games are based on the model of *experiential learning*. In this model, learners first act in a particular instance of application. In the second stage, they attempt to understand the effects of their behaviors and decisions in the particular instance. Thirdly, they seek to understand the general principles under which that instance falls. Finally, they apply the principles to new circumstances so that the learning is useful to their future behavior.

Dorn (1989) found mixed results from his review. He observed that there are consistent results that show that games generate interest and motivation in learners. This does not automatically produce greater interest in the subject matter or in learning in general. He cited some research that showed that simulation games did not increase learners' interest in comparison to other active learning techniques like case studies. However, in general, he found that games appear to be as effective as other techniques for teaching factual information, principles, and concepts.

Dorn observed that the results of research that evaluated the ability of simulation games to affect attitudes are confusing and contradictory. Although games appear to change attitudes, this does not occur every time a game is played. Furthermore, some games have been shown to increase positive attitudes and others resulted in an increase in negative attitudes.

To meet instructional goals, Dorn maintained that simulation games must be designed and used properly. Instructional games should:

1. Be selected to accomplish particular goals and should be supplemented with discussions, lectures, and other instructional methods.

2. Not be inserted into a course as random events. Rather they should be designed to meet specific instructional purposes.

3. Include debriefing after the game. Debriefing is crucial and should be more than a simple recounting of the game. It should be a structured, guided, activity that brings meaning to the experience and fosters learning from that meaning.

In 1981, after reviewing books, articles, newsletters, and advertisements about simulation games, Cathy Stein Greenblat listed the claims made in support of their use. These claims were divided into 6 categories: (1) motivation and interest, (2) cognitive learning, (3) changes in later course work, (4) affective learning concerning the subject matter, (5) general affective learning, and (6) changes in the classroom structure and relations. She then summarized the available data in support of these claims.

The strongest empirical support was for the claims that games improve learner motivation and interest (category 1). However, Greenblat observed that most of the discussions concerning the heightened motivation provided by games were supported by anecdotal evidence. There were some data to support the claims in category 2 (cognitive learning), but these data were weak. She found no evidence to support the claims in category 3 (changes in later course work) and little data on the claims in category 6 (changes in the classroom). Some evidence indicated that learners' attitudes about the subject matter (category 4) could be changed through the use of games. However, sometimes these attitudes changed in the *opposite* direction to that which was desired by the game designers. There was even less evidence in support of general affective changes (category 5). Her conclusion was that "there is, at the moment, little hard data to show that such participation leads to greater interest in the subject matter, the course, or learning in general" (Greenblat, 1981, p. 149).

Bredemeir and Greenblat (1981) attempted to synthesize the findings on the educational effectiveness of simulation games available at that time. They found *little hard evidence* on the effectiveness of these games except for some support that games result in increased retention of material. However, like many other reviewers, they concluded that simulation games "are at least as effective as other methods in facilitating subject matter learning" (p. 165). However, their overall conclusions were that "we do not yet have (1) a theoretically based taxonomy of games with (2) clear theories about (a) what aspects of them are expected to have (b) what sorts of distinct effects (c) on what sorts of students (d) for what reasons" (p. 169). As we shall see in subsequent discussions and summaries of more recent research, we are still struggling with the same basic questions.

VanSickle (1986) conducted a quantitative analysis of simulation gaming compared to other instructional procedures. He concluded that there was *weak support* for simulation gaming over other approaches (primarily classroom lecture). This conclusion is suspect for several reasons. First, he did not describe the characteristics of the simulation games used in his analysis. Furthermore, 6 of the 22 studies (27%) did not compare learners who participated in simulation games with other forms of instruction. Finally, he applied several mathematical transformations to the data prior to drawing his conclusions (e.g., he converted means and standard deviations to effect sizes, then averaged these). These transformations may have introduced errors into his results. Even without these cautions, his results only showed a moderate advantage of simulation games. When looking at the specific studies in terms of learner performance:

- only 5 findings (23%) favored simulation gaming and 13 findings (59%) showed no differential impact on immediate recall of knowledge; and
- only 2 findings (9%) favored simulation gaming and 15 findings (68%) showed no significant differences on retention of knowledge.

Thus, from this review, it is *not possible* to conclude that simulation gaming is the *preferred* instructional approach.

Randel, Morris, Wetzel, and Whitehill (1992) reviewed 68 studies that compared the instructional effectiveness of games to conventional classroom instruction. These studies covered a 28-year span of time. Of the 68 studies, 38 (56%) showed no differences between games and conventional instruction; 22 (32%) favored games (5 additional studies favored games, but their controls were questionable); and 3 studies (4%) favored classroom instruction. The games were used to provide instruction in social sciences, math, language arts, logic, physics, and biology. Math was the subject area with the greatest percentage of results favoring games. The review also indicated that games resulted in greater retention of the learned information. The authors reached several conclusions based upon their review:

1. "That only 68 studies were reported in 28 years reflects a trend to use descriptive reports rather than empirical studies comparing games with classroom instruction" (Randel, et al., 1992, p. 269).

2. A consistent finding was that games were rated as more interesting than conventional instruction.

3. Careful consideration should be given to the measures used to demonstrate the effects of games. "If the test for effectiveness does not match what the game is teaching, negative results will occur" (p. 271).

4. The experimental designs used to evaluate games need to be more rigorous. Reliability and validity are often not reported. Random sampling is often not used. Experimental designs need to reduce confounding variables such as, Hawthorne effect, teacher bias, selection effects, and time differences for treatments.

Dempsey, J. V., Lucassen, Gilley, and Rasmussen (1993-1994) conducted a review of the gaming literature. They collected 51 journal articles based on the results of electronic searches (e.g., ERIC, PSYCHLIT). Most of the articles were discussions (n = 28). A smaller number summarized research efforts (n = 16). The rest were theoretical discussions and reviews (n = 4) or descriptions of how a given game was designed or developed (n = 3). In terms of the types of games described, simulation games accounted for the largest number of articles (n = 30). Puzzle and adventure games were described in only 3 articles. They also tallied the types of learning outcomes and the functions of the games described in the articles. Table 11.2 shows the frequency of articles for each type of game function reported. Table 11.3 shows the frequency of articles by type of the learning outcome sought through using the game.

Table 11.2:
Percentage of Articles by Game Function from
Dempsey, J. V., et al. (1993-1994)

Function of Game	Percentage of Articles
Learn New Skills	23%
Practice Existing Skills	21%
Not Able to Determine	14%
Change Attitudes	11%
Other	11%
Drill Existing Skills	9%
Tutor	6%
Promote Self-Esteem	3%
Amuse	2%

Table 11.3:
Percentage of Articles by Learning Outcomes from
Dempsey, J. V., et al. (1993-1994)

Learning Outcomes	Percentage of Articles
Problem Solving	23%
Not Able to Determine	21%
Attitude	13%
Verbal Information	10%
Cognitive Strategy	9%
Concrete Concept	9%
Rules	7%
Other	4%
Defined Concept	3%

A few interesting observations can be made from looking at these frequency data (Table 11.2). Most games were used to teach new skills or to practice existing skills. The next highest percentage of game functions was "not able to determine." This is a problem with the way gaming research is presented. In the opinion of this author, if one wishes to publish the results of research, he or she should ensure that enough information is provided so the reader can fully understand the intent and results of the research. The function of the instructional game is certainly an important item of information if we wish to base future decisions on the results of the research.

In terms of the learning outcome of the games (Table 11.3) they found that the largest number sought to help learners in problem solving (23%), followed by attitudes (13%) and verbal information (10%). Again, an unfortunate result is that like game functions, a similar informational gap was found in the literature on learning outcomes. The second most frequent percentage that Dempsey, J. V., et al. (1993-1994) found when looking for learning outcomes is "not able to determine" (21%). If future instructional game designers and developers are to benefit from previous research, the research must be documented in a manner that will provide all the necessary information.

Egenfeldt-Nielsen (2003) conducted a review of the educational usage of games by surveying both single studies and other review articles. The review focused on non-electronic games, but did not distinguish between simulations and games. He concluded that there is "currently no evidence for a better or worse learning outcome, when games are used" (p. 1).

Maria Klawe, a senior game developer stated in a public lecture on "The Effective Design and Use of Educational Computer Games" that the "most common problem with educational software is that students don't pay attention to or learn the way that designers intended" (quoted in Jenson & de Castell, 2002, p. 6 of 15). Caftori (1994) supported this view by providing several examples of how educational software games do not always play an educational role, at least not the role they were intended to play. One history simulation game (*The Oregon Trail Game*) was intended to introduce children to the life of covered-wagon travelers on their way to Oregon in 1848. It contained a number of problem-solving situations like crossing a river, managing food, or dealing with disease outbreaks. It also provided opportunities for the children to shoot at dangerous animals and other targets. Unfortunately, the children concentrated on reaching the end of the trail as fast as possible and shooting animals for the sake of shooting. The critical information about the type of terrain and the animals associated with it were not noticed and/or learned by the children. Similar problems were encountered with other games. Even though the children interacted with the games, "they were able to do it in such a way that at least some (if not all) of the specified educational objectives have been missed" (Caftori & Paprzycki, 1997, p. 1 of 8). This is a conclusion that we will encounter throughout our review of the literature: *an instructional game will only be effective if it is designed to meet specific instructional objectives.*

Summaries of Research on Specific Instructional Games

The following sections contain summaries of research on the instructional effects of specific games. The organization of the summaries is based on the type of learner and/or the type of task that was targeted by the game. The first section summarizes the effectiveness of games used to teach school children in pre-kindergarten through the 12th grade. This is followed by summaries of instructional games used with college students. Games used to provide instruction in the workplace are summarized in the final section.

Games Used in Schools (Pre-K-12)

Many different games have been used to teach a variety of topics to schoolchildren in pre-kindergarten through 12th grade. The following are summaries of the results of some of this research. The summaries are organized by topic area.

Games Used to Teach Math. Koran and McLaughlin (1990) compared the effectiveness of a drill and practice math game for teaching basic multiplication facts. Twenty-eight fifth grade students participated in ten days of instruction. Their performance was measured using daily tests and a test at the end of the program. Both the game and the drill and practice conditions were found to be equally effective, but the students preferred the game.

Two different card games were evaluated in an elementary school classroom environment to help teach fractions, decimals, and percentages (Rowe, 2001). The students played both games and were then tested on standard questions about the math topics. Only one of the games, *Percent Rummy*, was found to improve the learners' performance. The other game, *Find the Missing Number*, was difficult to use, did not stimulate the learners and did not result in improved performance. These results indicate that every game is not useful instructionally. The instructional effectiveness of a game depends on its characteristics and how it is used.

Van Eck and Dempsey, J. (2002) evaluated the effects of different ways of using an instructional game. They measured the math problem-solving skills of 7th and 8th grade students after they had been given instruction using a computer simulation game using competition and contextual advisement. Some of the students experienced the game in a "competitive" context and others experienced it in a "non-competitive" context. The competition group was told that they were competing with a computer character. A face icon, representing the character, was continuously shown on the computer screen. The non-competition group was only encouraged to work quickly and accurately. Some students were able to access contextual advisement by watching videos of computer characters that provided hints and encouragement. Other students did not have access to contextual advisement. These conditions resulted in a 2x2 design. The performance of these groups was compared to an outside control group who solved identical word problems outside of a game context.

The math problems in both game and control conditions involved determining how much paint, wallpaper, and other materials were necessary to fix up a room. The performance of the students was assessed on a transfer task requiring them to apply the same skills to determine how much paint and other materials were required to fix up a different room. The researchers found an interesting interaction between competition and contextual advisement. The non-competition group had higher transfer when they had access to contextual advisement, but the competition group had higher transfer when they did not access contextual advisement. Unfortunately, these results may be moot because the control group performed as well as the game groups.

An Internet game was used in conjunction with other classroom activities to teach probabilities and statistics to 4- and 5-year old children (Pange, 2003). After a number of activities such as throwing dice and coins, the children played the game to improve their understanding of probabilities. The game required the children to pick one of three doors to find a hidden car, demonstrating a one-in-three chance. After the game, the teacher discussed all of the activities. The children showed improvement in their understanding of probability. The teachers liked using the game and reported that it excited the students' curiosity and made the teaching more interesting. No determination can be made about the separate instructional effectiveness of the game.

Laffey, Espinosa, Moore, and Lodree (2003) attempted to evaluate the potential of interactive computer technology (ICT) for teaching math skills to young, low income, urban children. The ICT environment included several commercially available math games, such as *Mighty Math* and *Millie's Math House*. The 61 study participants were all Pre-K, Kindergarten, or first-graders. The children were randomly assigned to treatment (ICT) or control groups and took a math pretest. Some of the children were also identified as "at-risk," because of previous behavior problems. Both groups received the same math instruction in their classroom. The ICT group participated in two 20-25-minute ICT sessions per week over an eight week period. Both groups later answered posttest questions. Results were based on the difference between pre- and posttest scores. The ICT group had significantly higher gain scores than the comparison group. Within the treatment group, the not-at-risk children gained more than the at-risk children. From this study, it is not possible to draw conclusions about the effectiveness of the games because no details are provided. The results are also confounded because the ICT group received more math instruction than the control group. The authors conclude that their study demonstrates the "potential" of ICT environments. Like many other studies that demonstrate "potential," this research does not provide guidance on how to design and implement instructional games.

A video-game approach was evaluated for teaching basic math and reading comprehension skills to first- and second-graders in economically disadvantaged schools in Chile (Rosas, Nussbaum, Cumsille, Marianov, Correa, Flores, Grau, Lagos, López, López, Rodriguez, & Salinas, 2003). The games were designed to play on a device that looked almost identical to the popular *Gameboy* system. The performance of an experimental group, who used the videogames, was compared to a group from the same school, who did not use the games, and a group from another school. Although both groups from the target school outperformed the external group, there was no difference in their performance. Thus, there is no support for the effectiveness of the game approach over traditional instruction on these basic learning tasks.

Teaching Vocabulary. Malouf (1987-1988) investigated the motivational effect of computer games for special education students. He compared the performance of sixth-, seventh-, and eighth-grade learning-disabled students who were learning vocabulary skills. His results showed no difference between a computer program with game features and the same program without the game features. However, the game condition resulted in significantly higher levels of continuing motivation than the non-game condition.

Teaching Pedestrian Safety. Renaud and Stolovitch (1988) investigated if a game could be used to help five-year-old children improve their pedestrian safety. One hundred and thirty-six 5-year olds were assigned to 4 groups: 3 experimental groups and 1 control group (who received no instruction). The experimental groups included 3 variations of a simulation game. The first version of the game included role playing and interactions among players. The second version of the game included behavior modeling and specific instruction from the experimenter. The third game included all the elements of the other games. The childrens' learning was measured using pictures of a road, to which the children added stickers to answer a series of questions. All of the experimental groups outperformed the control group. The group that engaged in role playing and player interactions performed slightly better than the groups that experienced behavior modeling.

Using Games to Study Motivation. Motivation can be assessed by the amount of involvement players demonstrate in a game. Wishart (1990) examined three game characteristics (control, challenge, and complexity) to determine their effects on learner involvement. She developed three versions of a role-playing game to teach children fire safety knowledge. Three hundred children (ranging in age from 5 years 9 months to 12 years 3 months with a mean age of 8 years 11 months) participated in the study. Six versions of the game were developed, each with a different combination of player control, game challenge, and game complexity. All the subjects took a pretest on fire safety knowledge before playing one of the versions of the game. In the game, a player was presented with a fire safety situation and given a choice of actions. After making the choice, the player advanced to another situation. At the end of the game, the players answered posttest questions about fire safety. She found that learner involvement was increased the most when the players had more control of the game. The separate addition of complexity and challenge to control did not increase learner involvement, but together they did. Furthermore, increased learner involvement was shown to increase the improvement of posttest scores. This research demonstrates that specific game designs can positively affect learning outcomes. Thus, it is important to design instructional games to increase learner involvement.

Costable, De Angeli, Roselli, Lanzilotti, and Plantamura (2003) also investigated motivation. However, they did not look at how a game motivated learners. Rather, they investigated the relationship between learner motivation and the effectiveness of the game. They conducted two experiments with an educational software product called *Logiocando*. It was developed to teach 9-10 year-olds the basic concepts of logic. The product contained Explanation Sections, Logic Games Sections, and Test Sections. The games increased in complexity as the learners successfully completed the simpler exercises. Costable, et al. compared the performance of learners in a lecture group to that of a group of learners who used *Logiocando*. In their first experiment, they found that the lecture group outperformed the game group. However, in their second experiment, they specifically motivated the learners prior to their interactions with the games. They explained that the learners' performance would be carefully monitored by their teachers and would be considered as part of their class work. This time, the learners who used *Logiocando* performed as well as the learners who received lectures. The researchers concluded that with proper motivation, these types of gaming exercises were as effective as traditional lecture methods in helping children improve their knowledge of logic.

The Costable, et al. study introduced an interesting issue about how to use instructional games. Many people believe that the game itself will motivate learners. However, this research indicates that other sources of motivation may also be necessary if a game is to be instructionally effective. Thus, for games, as with other types of instructional activities, how the activity is used is as important as the design of the activity itself.

As discussed earlier, Malouf (1987-1988) investigated whether playing a vocabulary skill game would increase children's motivation to continue studying the topic. He compared two groups of sixth-, seventh-, and eighth-grade learning disabled students who played either the game or used a computer program without game features. He found that the game and nongame programs produced equal gains in vocabulary skill. In addition, the learners who played the game demonstrated significantly higher levels of continuing motivation than the learners who used the nongame program. This indicates that instructional games can have motivational advantages beyond immediate learning gains.

Games Used to Teach Geography. Wiebe and Martin (1994) investigated the effectiveness of a commercial game for teaching geography facts. The game, *Where in the World is Carmen Sandiego*, was compared to map drawing and non-computer games (e.g., "Concentration") with two groups of fifth- and sixth-grade students. Posttests revealed no significant differences between the two groups in their recall of geography facts or their attitudes towards studying geography. The authors concluded that non-computer games and activities can be just as beneficial as computer-based games. Unfortunately, it is not possible to determine if the non-computer games or the map drawing exercises had separate effects on learning or if it was a combination of these activities that was as effective as the computer game.

A tutoring software system that used an adventure game interface and adventure-type scenarios was compared to a tutoring system that did not use these game aspects for teaching geography to fourth graders (Virvou, Katsionis, & Manos, 2005). Based on the number of errors on a posttest, it was found that the learners who used the adventure game interface improved their performance over the learners who used the other system. It was also found that learners who had the poorest performance in geography before using the game received the most benefit. The success of the game can be attributed to the instructional support (e.g., advice, suggestions) that was incorporated into the game. Similar instructional support was not as effective in the non-game condition. Thus, the combination of instruction support with game characteristics appears to be an effective method for teaching geography principles to children.

Teaching Electronic Circuits. Although not specifically called a game, the following study provides useful information that can apply to instructional games. A simulation was used as a supplement to laboratory instruction and exercises to teach two-person teams of 15 year-olds tasks involving electronic circuits (Ronen & Eliahu, 2000). The learners in the experimental condition were given the option to use the simulation to help complete two exercises. The learners in the control group only used existing materials (e.g., workbooks). Although some indications of higher achievement were shown in the group that used the simulation, the authors' observations about learners who did not benefit from the simulation may be more interesting. They observed that the simulation was not effective for three groups:

1. Learners who did not need additional assistance (about 10% of the total) and did not use the simulation. Some did use it in later more advanced tasks.

2. Learners with insufficient understanding of the domain (about 10-15%), who only performed random trials on the simulation rather that actions that would help them on their specific tasks.

3. A few students would not use the computer (about 5%) because they "hated computers."

Teaching Physics. White (1984) used a series of simple force and motion video games to teach high-school students the principles of Newtonian physics. The games all used a representation of a space ship to illustrate the effects of force on motion in a frictionless environment. The games required the students to move the space ship to various targets by applying different amounts and directions of force. The performance of the students on a series of posttest force and motion problems was compared to a group that received no instruction (both groups scored similarly on a pretest). The students who played the games improved their answering of the force and motion problems more than those who did not play the games. This study does show that these games can provide effective instruction on Newtonian force and motion principles. However, there was no comparison to other instructional approaches, so it is not possible to conclude that games are the most effective way to teach these principles. Use of Games for Health Care Education. Games have been used to help teach people about health care issues and the health care system. Sleet and Stadskley (1977) provided an annotated bibliography of 66 simulation games used in health education. These games were used in a variety of health care areas including: disease management; drug use and abuse; ecology; family planning and human sexuality; nursing; nutrition; physical fitness; and safety. The games allowed individuals to experience various roles and requirements of both health care personnel and their patients. These authors provided no information on the instructional effectiveness of the games.

Thomas, et al. (1997) used an interactive computer game, *Life Challenge*, as a tool to enhance adolescents' sense of self-efficacy in HIV/AIDS prevention. The game allowed learners to travel to different times and role play with imaginary partners, then to hear their recorded statements and decide to "try again" or stay with their original statements. There was also a game show segment where the learners picked the contestant they felt gave the best line in each situation. A pretest, posttest comparison of true-false questions was used to determine if there were learning gains on 7 knowledge items. Learning gains were found on 3 of the 7 items. Learners also showed improved self-efficacy when their pre-test and posttest scores were compared on several self-efficacy items. All learners showed increased self-efficacy with the strongest gains shown by those who began with the lowest self-efficacy scores. Unfortunately, it is not possible to attribute these effects to the game alone since there were no comparisons to other instructional methods.

Brown, Lieberman, Gemeny, Fan, Wilson, and Pasta (1997) assessed the effectiveness of a role-playing video game to teach young diabetic patients about diabetes. They compared two groups of young diabetics (ages 8 to 16). One group played an interactive adventure video game (Packy & Marlon), in which they played the role of a character that had diabetes. The other group played a video game containing no diabetes-related content. The two groups played their games at home as often as they wished. They were interviewed and their parents filled out a questionnaire at the beginning of the study, after three months, and after six months.

After six months, the group that played the diabetes game showed higher perceived self-efficacy for diabetes self-management, increased their communication with their parents about diabetes, and improved their daily diabetes self-management behaviors (e.g., monitoring the blood glucose levels and taking insulin as needed). The control group did not change their behaviors. Although the game shows promise, the study did not compare game use with other instructional approaches.

Similar conclusions can be drawn about the evaluation of a game to teach bilingual children about the food pyramid and better eating habits. Serrano and Anderson, J. E. (2004) found that fifth graders had better knowledge about nutrition and the food pyramid after playing a game when compared to a group that had no instruction. This shows that a game can be better than nothing, but does not help us decide whether using a game is the most effective instructional approach.

Games Used in College

Teaching Social Science. Szafran and Mandolini (1980) examined the effectiveness of a simulation game called *SIMSOC: Simulated Society* for teaching undergraduates in an introductory sociology course. The non-computer game was intended to create a situation where the student examined the processes of social conflict and social control in a simulated society. The results of the game were compared to the performance of students who received conventional classroom instruction. Performance was evaluated in terms of improvements in the students' test scores and their ability to recognize sociological concepts in nonsociological writings (e.g., excerpts from a novel, a magazine story, and a newspaper article). No statistically significant differences were found in the performance of the two groups. They concluded that "there continues to be no evidence that simulation games substantially increase cognitive knowledge" (p. 334).

Teaching Abnormal Psychology. Brewster (1996) used games in both an interactive multimedia computer environment and in a more traditional classroom environment to teach undergraduates the principles of abnormal psychology. The games were modifications of *Concentration* and *Jeopardy*. She found no differences among the groups on any measure of performance. It appears that multimedia is not necessary for games to provide an effective instructional approach. However, this study does not tell us when to use the games rather than other instructional methods. Teaching Economics. Fraas (1982) compared a simulation gaming approach to the lecture-discussion method for teaching college-level economics principles. The game condition consisted of seven commercial simulation games used in succession. Unfortunately, detailed descriptions of the games were not provided in this publication. He found that neither method was superior to the other in overall effectiveness. However, he also found that learners with less previous knowledge of economics showed better improvement with the simulation game approach. This was also true of students with lower SAT scores. The reverse was also found. Students with higher SAT scores and/or more previous economic knowledge appeared to learn better from the lecture-discussion. This study indicates that games may be differentially effective for learners with different abilities or experiences.

Gremmen and Potters (1995) evaluated whether lectures supplemented with a game were more effective for teaching economics principles than lectures alone. They compared the performance of two groups on a multiple-choice economics test. The group who received a lectures supplemented with the game outperformed the group that only received the lectures.

Reasoning Skills. Wood and Stewart (1987) tried to determine if use of a computerized version of the game *Mastermind* would help college students improve their skills in practical reasoning. Thirty students were divided into two groups. Both groups took a pre and posttest on the *Watson-Galser Thinking Appraisal*. The experimental group played the game between test administrations, but the control group received no treatment. The experimental group reduced their errors on the posttest relative to the control group and indicated that they enjoyed the experience. However, it is not clear whether the game directly affected these results or if they were changed due to repetition of the test and/or more time on the task. If the game did influence the results, it is still not clear what game characteristics might have affected the learners' performance.

Teaching About Learning. Klein and Freitag (1991) compared the instructional effectiveness of using a board game to the use of a worksheet for teaching the principles of the information-processing model of learning to undergraduate education majors. The game and worksheet were designed to supplement and provide practice on material from assigned textbook reading. The board game included a set of 25 game cards with practice questions about the topic. The rules of the game "were developed to encourage cooperation, competition, and active participation" (p. 304). The worksheet included the same 25 questions that appeared on the game cards. No performance differences were found as a result of the two methods of instruction. However, the learners who reported that they had read the textbook assignment performed better than those who did not complete the assignment.

Games Used to Change Attitudes. Williams (1980) evaluated the effectiveness of a simulation game to change the attitudes of college students toward a negatively-presented historical character. The students first read a fictional history of a struggle among four noblemen. One nobleman was presented as a "villain." After the reading, they all filled out an attitude questionnaire about the characters. Then they were separated into two experimental groups and one control group. The control group engaged in a non-related activity while the two experimental groups engaged in a simulation game in which they had to "play" the role of the negative character. One experimental group (dissonance) was not given praise or reward for playing the character. The other experimental group (incentive) was given praise and a monetary reward for their role play. It was assumed that cognitive dissonance would increase in the group that had to play the negative character with no outside incentives. Both of the experimental groups changed their attitudes toward the negative character to a significantly greater degree than the students in the control group. No differences were found in the attitude change between the two experimental groups.

Another study (Bredemeier, Bernstein, & Oxman, 1982) found that a game designed to change college students' attitudes on dogmatism and ethnocentrism was effective when used in an anthropology class compared to another anthropology class that did not use the game. However, the same game, used in a different course (philosophy) did not result in the same degree of attitude change. These results indicate the importance of placing instructional games in the appropriate instructional context.

Teaching Empathic Understanding. A role-playing game was compared to classroom lectures for improving the empathic understanding of first-year university students (Barak, Engle, Katzir, & Fisher, 1987). The game was designed to improve the communication skills involved in empathy (understanding another person and communicating this understanding to him or her). It involved analysis, diagnosis, and understanding a target "client." Learners in the game group took turns playing the role of the "client" while other players listened to the "client" describing his or her situation. The control group participated in a lecture and group discussion about listening and understanding others feelings. The performance of the experimental group significantly improved, but the performance of the control group did not change. The authors concluded that the game was an effective method for improving empathic skills.

Teaching Physics, Electronics, and Engineering Principles. Rieber and Noah (1997) used a game to teach university students the relationships between acceleration and velocity. When compared to participants who were taught these topics without a gaming context, it was found that *the game actually interfered* with the participants' learning of these principles. The authors examined several patterns of interaction with the game that may have led to this outcome. The participants who were given assistance by an outside agent were better able to consider the relevancy of the game for learning the science principles. "When left on their own, participants had much difficulty in focusing their attention on how to manipulate the task in order to learn more about the content" (p. 8). Without assistance, "participants focused far too much on the competitive nature of the game and, as a result their ability to monitor their own comprehension was inhibited" (p. 8). This study, although exploratory in nature, illustrates the important issue of the instructional support that surrounds a game and how the game is used to support instruction. Without instructional support, a game may be not only ineffective, but it may be detrimental to learning.

Miller, et al. (1999) examined three versions of an instructional simulation game (Electronic Field Hockey) to determine which was most effective in helping undergraduate students develop a better understanding of the physics of electrical interactions. The simulation allowed learners to observe how obstacles with various electrical charges influenced the trajectory of a "puck" with an electrical charge. The three versions of the simulation were:

1. A *no-goal condition*, which included no obstacles, no net, and no specific task.
2. A *standard-goal condition*, in which the learners' task was to try to position the obstacles so that their charges would cause the "puck" to avoid them and go into the hockey net.
3. A *specific path condition*, which showed the learners an ideal trajectory, which they attempted to duplicate. It also showed the difference between the ideal trajectory and their actual trajectory that was obtained by their placement of the obstacles.

Both the no-goal and specific-path conditions produced higher learner scores than the standard-goal condition. The authors concluded that these two conditions required learners to engage in broader exploration and to be more selective in interpreting the evidence than the standard-goal condition. The study highlights the importance of carefully selecting and analyzing the intended goals of an instructional game before it is implemented.

Crown (2001) conducted a study to determine the effect of web-based games on the visualization skills of engineering graphics students. However, it is difficult to determine the effect of his instructional games because the game pages were only part of an instructional CD. Although learners who used the instructional CD showed positive performance on exams, it is not possible to separate the effect of the game pages from the effect of other instructional material presented on the CD.

Teaching Principles of Underwater Sound Propagation. Shrestha (1990) compared a simple game to more traditional lecture-type instruction on the principles of underwater sound propagation. She found no learning differences between two groups of college students. However, she did find that the learners in the game condition spent more time interacting with the game. She concluded that games may have motivational benefits over the traditional instruction.

Games to Teach Health Care Decisions. Westbrook and Braithwaite (2001) evaluated a web-based educational game to help college undergraduates make better health care decisions. The game presented four families in a series of health care events. It then generated problems that required the learners to seek out information to assist the families in making decisions like which type of care to seek and how much it would cost. The participants were 55 students from Australia and South-East Asia. They worked in competing teams of six persons. Each team member contributed to a common discussion log over a four week period.

The evaluation consisted of a pre- and post-questionnaire that assessed: (1) the participants' interest in and knowledge of the health care system, (2) their experience with computers, (3) their views on team work, and (4) their demographics. Only two questions assessed the learners' factual knowledge.

Although a higher percentage of the participants correctly answered the factual questions on the posttest, these results were highly confounded. Prior to the game, the participants had already received 9 weeks of lectures, which included the topics covered in the game. The authors concluded that the improvement on the factual questions indicated the effectiveness of the game. However, other events during the 13-week period (9 weeks of lectures and 4 weeks of game participation) could have influenced their answers.

The Westbrook and Braithwaite (2001) study illustrates many of the problems that make it difficult to reach conclusions about either the effectiveness of a specific instructional game or the effectiveness of games in general. Some of these problems include:

1. The evaluators' interest in "proving" the effectiveness of their game (i.e., they developed the game and wanted it to work).
2. No control group who experienced an alternate form of instruction to compare to the game.
3. No clear and detailed description of the game itself (e.g., what characteristics made it a "game").
4. Lack of control of possible confounding variables (e.g., events prior to and during the evaluation).

Teaching Marketing, Business, and Management Principles. Fritzsche (1981) compared the use of a marketing simulation game, *Marketing in Action*, as either the central delivery vehicle for instructional information or as a supplement to the standard lecture on the same material. No differences were found between the two conditions on college students' midterm and final examination grades. Thus, Fritzsche concluded that the game alone was as effective as the lecture with the game as a supplement. The equivalence in effectiveness may be because the game (Day, 1962) included detailed instructions on how and why to fill out the simulated management decision forms. These may have had as much effect on later performance as playing the game itself.

Wellington and Faria (1996) studied the effect of team cohesion, player attitudes, and performance expectations on the instructional effectiveness of a simulation game. Although they do not specifically describe the simulation games, it appears to be a marketing simulation specifically developed for an introductory marketing course. The game was played by 389 students from two sections of a *Principles of Marketing* course. They were divided into 108 teams of three or four players. The teams competed with one another and each team had to make six decisions during the competition. The teams that were more cohesive at the start of the competitions outperformed the teams that were less cohesive. The game did not appear to change the cohesiveness of the teams over the course of the competition. Furthermore, learner attitudes were not found to be statistically related to final game performance although learner expectations were positively related to performance. Unfortunately, this research tells us very little about the specific characteristics of the game. It also does not compare the use of the game with other instructional approaches.

Rowland and Gardner (1973) did not find positive support for the instructional value of a business and management game. In their study of 200 college students who played the *Marksim* business game as seven-person teams, there was no positive relationship between playing the game and grades in a marketing course. They concluded that business games were not the educational panacea envisaged by many advocates.

Using Games in the Workplace

Teaching Attention Allocation Skills. Gopher, Weil, and Barebet (1994) found positive learning effects from a video game called *Space Fortress*. They found that attention allocation skills could be trained using the game. These attention allocation skills were found to transfer to piloting skills in complex fighter aircraft.

However, these results are ambiguous because other training (e.g., verbal tips and other part-task training sessions) may also have affected the outcomes.

Teaching Periscope Skills. Garris, et al. (2002) described an initial evaluation of a gamed called *BOTTOM GUN*. It was developed to help Navy personnel learn periscope skills such as distance estimation and angle-on-the-bow (i.e., the angle at which an observed ship is visually presented to the periscope observer). The game was designed to incorporate game characteristics such as curiosity, competition and control, as well as, visual and sound effects. Although an initial evaluation, their results indicated that learners using the game showed more improved performance than those using a trainer without game elements.

Teaching Principles of Chemical, Biological, and Radiological Defense. Ricci, Salas, and Cannon-Bowers (1996) investigated the learning effects of a very simple game. They compared three groups of Navy trainees (mean age = 20 yrs.) who were taught the basic principles of chemical, biological, and radiological defense. One group (text group) studied a printed text (a 63-page pocket handbook). The second group (test group) was given a printed copy of 88 multiple-choice questions with answers. The third group (game group) interacted with a computer program that presented the 88 questions in random fashion in boxes that resembled a slot machine. This group was given 3 minutes to answer each question and received points for correct answers. Both the test and game groups performed better than the text group on a posttest. However, no performance differences were shown between the test and game groups although the game group scored higher on a retention test given four weeks later. The results of this study are questionable because the game condition was basically a way to randomize the presentation of the questions and may not have been a true game.

Teaching Technical Skills. Oxford, Harman, and Holland (1987) reported the initial evaluations of two hand-held computerized game-based training aids for Army trainees. The two training aids, called *Tutor* and *CHIP*, used simple games (e.g., matching pictures to verbal or visual stimuli to send a projectile against an "enemy" target) to teach technical terminology and basic technical skills. Learners who used the aids completed more instructional units than a group who used a workbook containing the same content. The training aid group also outperformed the workbook group. Although these data were very tentative and the games were simplistic, they did show the instructional potential of gaming activities.

Whitehill and McDonald (1993) compared the effects of the presentation of circuit repair problems in a drill format to presentation of the same problems in a game context. The drill context simply presented the circuit problems one at a time. However, the game context required learners to simulate the role of an electrician repairing the circuits. They used a computer to move a cursor around a Navy ship's floor plan to locate and solve the problems. Video game sound effects accompanied the movement of the cursor through the ship. The payoff for solving the problems was either fixed or variable based on problem difficulty. Although they found no performance differences between learners in either the drill or game conditions, they did find that combining the game with variable payoff resulted in increased learner persistence.

Parchman, Ellis, Christinaz, and Vogel (2000) evaluated four different instructional conditions, including a game, to train basic electricity and electronics fundamentals to beginning Navy electronic technicians. They compared conventional classroom instruction (CI) with computer-based drill and practice (CBDR), enhanced computer-based instruction (ECBI) that added compelling graphics, animations, and simulations to the CBDR, and a role-playing adventure game. The trainees in the CBDR and ECBI conditions outperformed those trained in either the conventional instruction or the game. The CBDR and ECBI conditions were equally effective in teaching symbols and definitions. However, cause-and-effect relationships were learned better by trainees in the ECBI condition. This is probably because of the enhanced visualizations provided by the ECBI program. The ECBI-trained learners were also more confident than those in the other groups that they had learned the required material.

These researchers concluded that instructional developers should to be cautious and not rush into exclusively using games until additional data are available on their effectiveness. Other computer-based instructional approaches may be more effective than games for certain types of instruction. They also recommended that instructional developers not overdevelop computer-based instruction. Simple computer-based instruction may be sufficient when the objective is to teach definitions and symbols. When more complex material needs to be learned (e.g., cause-and-effect relationships), enhanced computer-based instruction may be required.

Business and Management Games. Gaming has been used to teach business and management skills for many years. Faria (1989) observed that business games are direct descendents of war games, dating back at least to the German Kriegspiel of the mid-19th century. He also observed that the RAND Corporation developed an instructional simulation game in 1955. Called *Monopologs*, it was intended to allow U. S. Air Force logistics personnel to make logistics decisions in a "risk-free" environment. No data could be located on the effectiveness of the game.

The first widely known business game was developed by the American management Association in 1956. Called *AMA's Top Management Decision Simulation*, it provided an environment in which two teams of players could represent officers of firms and make business decisions (Cohen & Rhenman, 1961). Five teams with three to five persons each produced a single product, which they sold in competition with other teams. Many varieties of this game were developed in subsequent years, although no data on its effectiveness were found.

In the early 1960s, a game was used to teach diplomats international relations skills (Benson, 1961). The *Simple Diplomatic Game* reproduced, in simplified form, features of the international political arena and allowed learners to see the effects of their actions in a larger action-counteraction cycle. No data were found on its effectiveness.

Faria (1989) conducted surveys of training managers, businesses, and business schools on their use of games. Of the 223 training managers who responded, 54.7% indicated that their companies used simulation games in their training programs. Results also indicated that at least 5000 firms were using business games and 1,700 four-year business schools used games in their programs. Wolfe (1997) observed that by 1974 hundreds of articles on business gaming had appeared in the business and professional press.

Cohen and Rhenman (1961) and Morris (1976) maintained that all management games share several common features.

287

1. They allow the presentation of feedback based on the results of players' actions.
2. They represent the environment in logical or mathematical relations. Some of these relations are known to the players as "rules" while others are only vaguely qualified and become known during play.
3. They allow interaction between players and the environment. Sometimes players can assume the roles of managers in different functional areas within a company to learn how these areas differ from their own.
4. They provide a simplified view of reality so players can focus on single issues or areas as they learn.

Citing Cohen and Rhenman (1961) and Morris (1976), Hays and Singer (1989, pp. 198-200) mentioned several educational properties of business and management games:

1. They can provide training on the interactions of functional specialties within companies. The players can learn how their specialty is dependent on others, and how to interact more effectively to reach common goals.
2. Playing the game may sensitize learners to the fact that in the real world they must take particular actions solely for the sake of information gathering.
3. Games can offer the trainee the opportunity to learn and refine a variety of analytic tools.
4. Games may allow learners to become aware of the psychological and organizational interactions and interdependencies in business.
5. Players may learn that most decisions are made by teams of several persons and that these decisions are constrained by a variety of variables, such as time, complexity of the decision, and personality factors of the players.
6. Games can teach institutional facts about the learners' company (e.g., standard operating procedures).

These properties and many of those mentioned by other authors also apply to games outside of business and management.

Thornton and Cleveland (1990) described management gaming simulations as a hierarchy of increasing complexity. Their hierarchy included:

1. *One-on-one interview simulations* that are "short, yet powerful, simulations of specific interpersonal

interactions" (p. 192). The authors list several studies that indicated that these were effective in enhancing supervisory skills. However they also cited contradictory evidence that showed no behavior change as a result of participating in this type of gaming simulations.

2. *Leaderless group discussions* simulate "numerous ad hoc committee situations in organizations in which problem analysis and decision making take place" (p. 192). The authors cited no specific data on the instructional effectiveness of these discussion simulations.

3. *In-basket technique.* A type of simulation named after the in-tray on a manager's desk has been used to practice administrative skills. Although the technique has been shown to have predictive validity and is used in "virtually all assessment centers" (p. 193) for managerial selection, Thornton and Cleveland cited no data on their instructional effectiveness.

4. *Complex decision-making simulations* have been used to study the components of managerial decision-making (Streufert, 1986). However, Thornton and Cleveland found no evaluations of their instructional effectiveness.

5. *Large-scale behavioral simulations* involve "multiple business problems and opportunities, intensive and extensive interaction among managers, and observation by trained staff" (p. 193-194). Little published empirical information was available on these simulations.

Morris and Holman (1976) reported the successful application of business gaming at a large pharmaceutical company. A business management competition was held with 638 people divided into 192 teams. These teams, from various divisions, learned an appreciation of business, as a whole, rather than just their work functions. Some of the lessons learned included: methods of increasing profits by either increasing income or decreasing expenditures; team work skills; methods to get along with the competition; and marketing techniques.

Carlson and Hill (1982) examined the effectiveness of a gaming approach to reducing absenteeism and tardiness at a small manufacturing firm. They found that the impact of gaming was minimal on these two areas. However, they did find that when gaming was used as a vehicle for employee communication, it resulted in statistically significant improvement in employee attitudes and cooperation.

Wolfe (1997) conducted a review of business games used to teach strategic management skills. He reviewed seven studies conducted between 1966 and 1988 that: 1) compared game use with at least one other instructional approach, 2) had predefined, objectively measured learning objectives, and 3) objectively measured learning outcomes. He divided the studies into those that concentrated on results (substantive evaluations) and those that examined the effects of how the game was used (procedural studies).

From his review, Wolfe concluded that there is evidence that computer-based general management games are effective in producing knowledge gains. He found that the only alternative instructional approach that was compared to games was case studies. Both methods produced learning, but games appeared to be superior. It should be remembered, as discussed above, games can be designed as hybrids, incorporating the characteristics of case studies. Although he reported no data on these game-case study hybrids, in future studies, this approach may be found to be effective.

Wolfe found less clear data on the way games are used. Some studies found less complex games as effective as more complex games while others found that more complex games provided better learning outcomes. However, this result is confounded in at least one study because the more complex game included more relevant topics than the less complex games. Wolfe found little data on the role of the instructor in influencing the learning outcomes of games other than that some type of instructor involvement (instructional support) appeared to be required. Instructional support is one of the topics discussed in the next section.

Other Issues in Instructional Gaming

<u>Types of Competition in a Game</u>

As noted above, competition (challenge) is one of the most important characteristics that make games enjoyable (Csikszentmihalyi, 1990) and motivating (Malone, 1981; Malone

& Lepper, 1987). Fisher (1976) examined three different types of motivation in a vocabulary skills game (*The Dictionary Game*). Three groups of college students played the game under different types of competition conditions and their performance was compared with each other and with a control group that did not play the game. The first treatment group played the game with 1-to-1 person interpersonal competition. The second treatment group played with 1-to-2 person interpersonal competition. The third treatment group played as three-person groups with 1-to-1 intergroup competition. Post-game performance was measured on a ten-item multiple-choice test. Results showed that learners in all three game conditions performed better than the non-game group. The 1-to-2 interpersonal competition group had the highest score, followed by the 1-to-1 interpersonal competition group and the 1-to-1 intergroup competition group. These results show that specific types of competition can affect the instructional effectiveness of a game. However, since the game was not compared to any alternate types of instruction, it is not possible to say that gaming is the preferred approach to teach vocabulary skills.

Adding Instructional Support to a Game

Leutner (1993) investigated the effectiveness of two varieties of instructional support in a computer-based simulation game to teach economic concepts to seventh-graders and later to university students. The game, *Hunger in the Sahel*, is a role-playing simulation where learners run a small farm and must deal with issues such as rainfall and temperature extremes. The two varieties of instructional support were system-initiated advice and learner-requested background information. He found that learners without any instructional support learned to play the game, but only learned a minimal amount about domain-specific concepts. The opposite occurred with the learners given advice. They learned more domain-specific concepts, but only learned to play the game to a limited degree. Leutner (1993) stated that it is "very useful to make pieces of information, which are implicitly available in the system, explicit through appropriate instructional support during system exploration" (p. 219).

The importance of instructional support was also discussed by de Jong and van Joolingen (1998). These authors reviewed the effectiveness of discovery learning in simulated environments. Discovery learning is often cited as one of the strengths of instructional simulations and games. The assumption is that learners gain a deeper understanding of a topic if they are allowed to freely explore a domain and "discover" important information and interactions among phenomena. However, after reviewing many studies on discovery learning in simulations, these authors stated: "The general conclusion that emerges from these studies is that there is no clear and univocal outcome in favor of simulations" (de Jong and van Joolingen, 1998, p. 181). They explained these results by highlighting several intrinsic problems with discovery learning. These problems center on difficulties that learners have with forming and testing hypotheses in these discovery environments. The reader is encouraged to consult the original source for details on these problems. The authors concluded that the crucial aspects of successful discovery learning are well-designed instructional goals and instructional support for the learner.

Mayer, Mautone, and Prothero (2002) investigated the effect of adding prior pictorial representations of possible features that would be encountered in a game to teach geology principles. These researchers reported the results of 4 experiments with college students. A game called *The Profile Game* was designed to help learners determine which geological features were present on a certain portion of the planet's surface. Prior to playing the game in each experiment, the students either received prior pictorial support or did not. The specifics of how the support was used differed across the experiments. In the first two experiments, no differences were found due to the pictorial support. However, in the second two experiments, the pictorial support groups outperformed the no-support groups. The support given in the second two experiments was accompanied with more detailed instructions on how to use the support. Thus, it appears that instructional support can enhance the instructional effectiveness of games if it supports "guided discovery" rather than just providing information.

What is Learned in an Adventure Game?

Adventure games are very popular and many have advocated their use for instructional purposes. To determine what is learned in this type of game, Ju and Wagner (1997) had 12 college students play *Indiana Jones and the Fate of Atlantis* in which they had to find their way through a South American jungle. The students played the game individually. After an hour of play, they stopped the game and asked the players to answer a set of questions, referring to the material encountered during previous play. No player answered all questions correctly. When the responses were analyzed by question type, they found that more correct answers were given to the questions that asked about physical objects in the game or attributes about the game (mean correct responses of .83 and .84 respectively). Questions about concepts and cause-effect thinking only produced mean correct responses of .55 and .50. The least successful answers (.38 correct) were on questions that required the user to respond with a "plan" or procedure. These results demonstrated that different types of learning can result from an adventure game. This is another indication of the importance of designing instructional games to contain events that meet specific instructional objectives.

The Danger of Evaluator Interest

An area of game research that indicates how the evaluator's "interests" may influence the results is the investigation of chess playing as a way to develop children's cognitive skills and scholastic achievement. Dauvergn (2000) summarized several studies that he claimed show that "chess is one of the most powerful educational tools available to strengthen a child's mind" (p. 2 of 6). However, as Thompson (2003) pointed out, most of these studies were quasi-experimental in nature and were conducted by chess enthusiasts (some from the U. S. Chess Federation). Thompson (2003) conducted a controlled study that compared the scholastic performance of chess players and non-chess players. When he controlled for grade level and IQ, he found no significant effect of chess playing on scholastic performance. He concluded that the chess enthusiasts want to see a positive effect from playing chess and therefore do not control for other factors like general intelligence. His belief is that children who are interested in chess also tend to be more capable in general scholastic skills. Whichever view is correct, it is important that the interests and goals of researchers be accounted for when interpreting the results of their investigations.

The Instructional Value of a Game Developed for Another Purpose

Recently, a game developed for Army recruiting was evaluated to determine its instructional effectiveness. The Office of Economic and Manpower Analysis at the United States Military Academy developed the game, *America's Army*, as a *recruiting tool*. It was intended to inform the "recruiting age" public about the U. S. Army. Because it was so popular (over 2 million players registered on the web site), some believed it could be assessed to identify features that motivated players and provided instruction.

Belanich, Sibley, and Orvis (2004) assessed the knowledge that 21 players gained from the game using a 35-question posttest. The questions were designed to assess procedural, episodic, and factual knowledge that was either relevant to game play or that did not impact game play. They found that players correctly answered a higher percentage of procedural questions, followed by episodic and factual questions in descending order. They also found that the realism, challenge, exploration, and control afforded by the game were the factors that influenced player motivation.

On the surface, these results seem to indicate that the game provided effective instruction. However, when one examines the study more closely, it becomes apparent that the players only learned procedures, experiences, and facts *about the game*. There is no indication that any of the learned information is relevant to real-world Army requirements. For example, one of the procedural questions asks *how to select* a "Flash/Bang" grenade. The possible answers involve pressing a number key or clicking the mouse. These procedures are irrelevant in the real world. From reading the report, it does not seem that the game provided real-world relevant instruction, such as *when to choose* this type of grenade.

This study illustrates one of the greatest dangers of using games for instruction. Yes, they may be motivational and they may help learners retain information. However, if the game is not designed to directly support specific instructional objectives related to actual job requirements, much of the learning may be irrelevant. This is also what was found in the evaluation of *The Oregon Trail Game* (Caftori, 1994). As discussed earlier, children only learned "shoot-em-up" skills rather than the historical information that game designers hoped the game would provide.

This study (Belanich, et al., 2004), like many others, indicates the *potential* of games for instruction. However, it also highlights the need to carefully design and develop games that will support specific instructional objectives and that will fit into larger programs of instruction.

The Importance of Debriefing

After participation in an instructional game, it is very important to conduct a debriefing session with the participants (Crookall, 1992; Garris, et al., 2002). Debriefing gives the learners the opportunity to reflect on their experience with the game and understand how this experience supported the instructional objectives of the course or program of instruction. Lederman (1992) reviewed the literature on debriefing and presented a model of the debriefing process. According to her model, debriefing should consist of three phases:

- *Phase 1: Systematic reflection and analysis.* This phase introduces the learners to a systematic self-reflective process about their game experience. It should include a summary of the game experience as it supports the instructional objectives.
- *Phase 2: Intensification and personalization.* The second phase is a deeper examination of the learners' game experiences. Each learner should be guided through reflections on their own individual experiences and the meanings these experiences have for them. It is the job of the debriefing facilitator (e.g., instructor) to help ensure that the meaning of the experiences tie into the instructional objectives.
- *Phase 3: Generalization and application.* Here, the learners are led beyond their own individual experiences to the broader applications of the experiences. For example, they might engage in discussions of how their experiences can contribute to their success on the job or in additional learning situations.

The key point is that *no instructional game should be conceived as a stand-alone activity*. It should be designed and implemented as part of a larger instructional program that meets the specific instructional requirements of the task and the learners. As Lederman puts it, "The process of debriefing is not ancillary to the educational experience to which it is tied. Debriefing is an integral part of any learning experience that is designed to be experience based" (Lederman, 1992, p. 158). As mentioned above, when instruction is designed to be delivered without an instructor (e.g., stand-alone CBI), debriefing should be included with other instructional support as part of the instructional software.

Summary of Empirical Evidence on Instructional Games

Instructional games have been used for a wide variety of tasks with learners of different ages. Past reviews have found that the majority of articles on instructional games are opinions about whether to use games and about the potential of games to provide effective instruction (e.g., Dempsey, J. V., et al., 1993-1994). Far fewer articles provided empirical data on research that has investigated the instructional effectiveness of games. This was also found in the present review. Over 270 documents were obtained from the literature on games. Of these, only 48 provided empirical data on the instructional effectiveness of games. This chapter included discussions the results of other review articles and also articles on the effectiveness of specific games. Table 11.4 provides a summary of the 48 empirical articles discussed in earlier sections.

Several observations can be derived from an examination of Table 11.4. First, the empirical research on instructional games examined their effects for a *wide range of age groups*. Twelve of the studies examined the learning effects of games with elementary school children and two with high school students. Twenty-one studies used instructional games with college students. Six studies examined game effects with military trainees and the remainder of the studies evaluated games for adults working in various industries. *The results of any given study must be evaluated in a restricted manner*. We cannot generalize the

Table 11.4:
Summary of Empirical Effectiveness Studies Reviewed

Study	Learning Task	Age/Grade	Results
Koran & McLaughlin (1990)	Math Facts	5th Gr.	No Differences
Rowe (2001)	Math	Elementary School	Only **one of two** games provided learning. No comparison to other approaches.
VanEck & Dempsey, J. (2002)	Math Problem Solving	7-8th Gr.	No Differences
Pange (2003)	Probability	4-5 yrs.	Can't Determine
Laffey, et al. (2003)	Math Skills	Pre-K-1st Gr.	Can't Determine
Rosas, et al. (2003)	Basic Math & Reading	1st & 2nd Gr.	No Differences
Malouf (1987-88)	Vocabulary	6-8th Gr.	No Differences
Renaud & Stolovitch (1988)	Pedestrian Safety	5 yrs.	**Learning**, but no comparison
Wishart (1990)	Motivation	5 – 12 yrs.	**Learning**, but no comparison
Costable, et al. (2003)	Basic Logic	9-10 yrs.	No Differences
Wiebe & Martin (1994)	Geography Facts	5th-6th Gr.	No Differences
Virvou, et al. (2005)	Geography	4th Gr.	**Game** favored over non-game software
Ronen & Eliahu (2000)	Electronics	15 yrs.	**Slight**, but not effective for certain groups
White (1984)	Physics	H.School	**Learning**, but no comparison
Thomas, et al. (1997)	Self-efficacy in HIV/AIDS prevention	Adolescents	Can't Determine
Brown, et al. (1997)	Diabetes Facts	8-16 yrs.	Can't Determine
Serrano & Anderson , J. E.. (2004)	Nutrition Facts	5th Gr.	**Learning**, but no comparison

Table 11.4:
(continued)

Study	Learning Task	Age/Grade	Results
Szafron & Mandolini (1980)	Sociology	College	**Learning,** but <u>no comparison</u>
Brewster (1996)	Psychology	College	No Differences
Fraas (1982)	Economics	College	No Differences (game better for learners with less previous knowledge)
Gremmen & Potters (1995)	Economics	College	**Game supplementing lecture favored** over lecture alone
Wood & Stewart (1987)	Practical Reasoning	College	**Learning,** but only compared to no instruction.
Klein & Freitag (1991)	Principles of Learning	College	No Differences
Williams (1980)	Attitudes toward subject matter	College	**Favored Game** over non-related activity
Bredemeier, et al. (1982)	Attitudes toward subject matter	College	**Game successful** in appropriate context
Barak, et al. (1987)	Empathy	College	**Favored Game** over lecture & discussion.
Rieber & Noah (1997)	Physics Principles	College	**Game <u>interfered</u> with learning**
Miller, et al. (1999)	Electrical Interactions	College	No comparison to alternate instruction. Different versions of game were compared.
Crown (2001)	Engineering Visualization	College	Can't Determine
Shrestha (1990)	Underwater Sound Propagation	College	No Differences
Westbrook & Braithwaite (2001)	Health Care Decisions	College	Can't Determine

Table 11.4:
(continued)

Study	Learning Task	Age/Grade	Results
Frizsche (1981)	Marketing	College	Game alone as good as game and lecture
Wellington & Faria (1996)	Team Cohesion & Attitudes	College	No Comparison
Rowland & Gardner (1973)	Marketing	College	No support for game
Gopher, et al. (1994)	Attention Allocation Skills	Pilot Trainees	**Learning**, but no comparison
Garris, et al. (2002)	Periscope Skills	Navy Trainees	**Favored Game** (over trainer without game elements)
Ricci, et al. (1996)	CBRD Defense Principles	Navy Trainees (Mean age = 20yrs.)	No Differences ("game" slightly better for retention)
Oxford, et al. (1987)	Technical Skills & Terminology	Army Trainees	**Favored Game** (over workbook)
Whitehill & McDonald (1993)	Electrical Repairs	Navy Trainees	No Differences
Parchman, et al. (2000)	Electronics Fundamentals	Navy Trainees	Drill & Practice favored over game
Morris & Holman (1976)	Business Issues	Adults	No Comparison
Carlson & Hill (1982)	Attendance Attitudes	Adults	No effect
Fisher (1976)	Different types of Competition	College	No Comparison
Leutner (1993)	Economics Concepts	7th Gr. & College	Without instructional support, **Only Learned Game**
Mayer, et al. (2002)	Geology	College	Instructional support enhanced value of game

Table 11.4:
(continued)

Study	Learning Task	Age/Grade	Results
Mayer, et al. (2002)	Geology	College	Instructional support enhanced value of game
Ju & Wagner (1997)	Playing an adventure game	College	Learned more about physical objects in game than concepts
Thompson (2003)	Effect of playing chess on scholastic performance	Elementary school children	No effect
Belanich, et al. (2004)	What is learned in a game?		Learned only game-relevant skills not real-world skills

results of a study conducted with one age group to another age group.

The empirical research also includes studies that examined the instructional effectiveness of games for *many different tasks*. These tasks range from basic mathematics principles to complex business and marketing decision-making. They include general reasoning skills and specific electronics repair tasks. Care should also be taken when generalizing from one instructional task to tasks in another domain.

The empirical research *does not make a compelling case for games as the preferred instructional method*. In most cases, the research shows no instructional advantage of games over other instructional approaches (such as lectures). In several cases, games were shown to provide effective learning, but were not compared to other instructional methods. The research does not allow us to conclude that games are more effective than other well-designed instructional activities.

Too much of the empirical research on instructional games contains methodological problems (e.g., experimental confounds) that make it difficult to draw valid conclusions about the effectiveness of the games. Researchers need to ensure that they understand experimental design and apply sound decisions when designing and reporting their research. In addition, editors of educationally oriented journals need to filter out studies that do not follow sound experimental design procedures.

A Reexamination of the "Claims"

As discussed earlier, Greenblat (1981) summarized evidence in support of six categories of "claims" about the efficacy of games used for instructional purposes. We can use the same categories of claims to help us summarize the research on the instructional uses of games since that time. By comparing the evidence presented by Greenblat in 1981 to the results of later research we can draw some conclusions about the progress that has been made over the last 25 years in our understanding of the effectiveness of games for instructional purposes. Table 11.5 summarizes the evidence, then and now.

Comparing the evidence on the instructional effectiveness of games that was available in 1981 to the results of more recent research shows that there are still many questions that need to be answered about when and how to use games. The first "claim," that games improve the motivation and interest of learners, is still weakly supported. There has been little additional evidence beyond a few studies that use self-reports or time-on-task to show that games are motivational. Unfortunately, there is little evidence that these measures of motivation are related to improved task performance. Games do motivate. They motivate players to play the game. This can be beneficial if the game is designed to target and meet instructional objectives. Otherwise, learners may spend their time learning to be successful at the game without receiving instructional benefits from these experiences.

The second "claim," that games enhance cognitive learning, continues to be supported. The research shows that people can learn from games. However, the research *does not indicate* that games are superior to other instructional methods in all cases. Like any instructional activity, games should be chosen because they provide learners with interactive experiences that help them meet instructional objectives.

Table 11.5:
Evidence in Support of the "Claims":
Then and Now

Categories of Claims	Original Evidence (prior to 1981)	Later Evidence (1981 - 2005)
1. Motivation & Interest	Strongest support. A great deal of anecdotal reports. Only one study (Robinson et al., 1966) used several indicators of motivation to show simulation-games generated greater interest than other modes of teaching.	Little additional evidence. A few studies found that learners indicated that they enjoyed games and spent more time playing. However, only weak connection between this and improved performance.
2. Cognitive Learning	Some weak empirical evidence favoring games. Some showing no differences.	Similar pattern. Some studies show that games are effective for some learning tasks, but do not show them superior to other instructional approaches. Some evidence shows that games can be detrimental to learning if they do not include instructional support. Some games are more effective if they are followed by a debriefing session that highlights the importance of the game experiences in terms of instructional objectives.
3. Changes in Later Course Work	None	None Found
4. Affective Learning (re: Subject Matter)	Mixed results. Some anecdotal evidence. Empirical evidence shows increases in both positive and in negative attitudes.	Two studies provide some additional support. There are indications that a game is more effective if used in the appropriate context.
5. General Affective Learning	Almost none	None Found
6. Changes in Classroom Structure & Relations	None	None Found

The third and sixth "claims" were not supported. No additional evidence was found that games change later course work. This effect may occur, but no research was found to support this "claim." This may be because it is difficult to track learners from one class to another and document this effect. Likewise, no evidence was found for the sixth "claim," that the use of games changes the classroom structure and relations. This does not mean that instructors who use games in their courses do not change their classroom structure or that game players do not change how they relate to other learners. Some anecdotal evidence indicates that these changes do occur, but no empirical evidence was found.

Finally, the fourth and fifth "claims," that games change learners' feelings (affect) about the learning domain and learning in general has mixed support. Two studies (Williams, 1980; and Bredemeier, et al., 1982) provide some support for the utility of games to change learners' attitudes toward subject matter (claim 4). No empirical research was found that supports the claim that games can change learners' attitudes about learning in general (claim 5).

In summary, this review identified several general problems with instructional game research that make it difficult to draw firm conclusions. These problems include:

1. There are many published articles, but most are opinions about the "potential" of games. There are few empirical studies.

2. There is considerable confusion in the use of terms. It is often difficult to determine if the instructional activity was actually a game. When is a simulation a game? Are all competitive activities games?

3. There are many methodological flaws in the empirical game research, such as poor experimental designs that lack the control of possible confounding variables (e.g., events prior to and during the evaluation).

4. Some of the research appears to be biased by the evaluators' interest in "proving" the effectiveness of their game (i.e., they developed the game and wanted it to work).

5. Too much research fails to use control groups who experienced an alternate form of instruction to compare to the game.
6. Most published articles provide no clear and detailed description of the game itself (e.g., what characteristics made it a "game").

To Game or Not to Game?

As can be seen from the above discussions, the research on the use of instructional games is mixed. It appears that games can be of instructional value if they are well designed and targeted to meet specific instructional objectives. Unfortunately, many program managers and game developers do not appreciate the importance of instructional design. They often assume that the game is sufficient, in itself, to provide the necessary instruction. Squire (2005) conducted case studies of three companies that develop game-based learning products. "It is worth noting that *none* of the featured companies *started in instructional design*...they come from business strategy, marketing, and the games industry" (p. 13, my emphasis). Although each company used interdisciplinary design teams to create their instructional games, none of the teams included instructional developers. The teams usually consisted of: 1) graphic artists, 2) program managers, and 3) programmers. Commenting on the avoidance of instructional designers, Squire stated, "Most game-based learning approaches do not employ that particular category of expert whatsoever" (p. 35). In most cases, the game designers fulfilled the role of instructional developer. It appears that the "instructional gaming" industry does not value the skills of instructional developers.

This is not a new phenomenon. In the late 1980s, Greenblat (1987) observed that the teaching enterprise was undervalued in our society. Technological issues involved in game development seem better able to catch people's interest, while the development of instructional objectives and logical programs of instruction seems to be boring. The data on instructional effectiveness of games (e.g., Randel, et al., 1992; Parchman, et al., 2000; Wolfe, 1997) indicate that the role of the instructor and the way a game is incorporated into an instructional program are major factors in whether a game will contribute to successful learning. Nevertheless, it is not clear that current game-development teams understand the principles of instructional development. It may be up to the program managers and other individuals who procure instructional games to demand that they support instructional objectives and that this support be demonstrated. This will then probably require that game companies begin to include individuals who understand learning and instruction on their development teams. As illustrated in Figure 11.2, it is more likely that games will be instructionally effective if the specific characteristics of the game (e.g., setting, player roles and activities, rules, etc.) overlap with specific instructional objectives. This overlap must be consciously structured on the basis of a thorough analysis of the reasons for the instruction and the instructional objectives to be met.

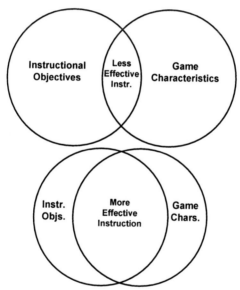

Figure 11.2:
Instructional Effectiveness as Degree of Overlap among Instructional Objectives and Game Characteristics

Rieber (1996) advocated a mixing of simulations and games in a hybrid-learning environment. This approach would use the strengths of simulations (e.g., dynamic and interactive representations of real-world systems or phenomena) and the strengths of games (e.g., challenge and fantasy) to create instructionally sound, realistic learning activities. Additional research needs to be conducted to provide guidance about how to create effective hybrid learning environments (e.g., how to determine if the specific features of specific hybrid games will support instructional objectives).

Much of the empirical research indicates that instructional games are only effective if they are designed to support instructional objectives. This is more likely if the design of the instructional game is the result of a systematic analysis process. Atkinson (1977) advocated that the design and development of instructional games should follow the same basic systems approach that is required for the design of any instructional activity. The basic steps in this approach are shown in Figure 11.3 as applied to the design and use of instructional games. The first section of the approach includes steps that are exactly the same, no matter what the outcome (e.g., choosing a game or another instructional activity). The first two steps are to identify the instructional problem and the instructional objectives. A problem statement is a general statement of the overall instructional problem (e.g., improve students overall understanding of and competence in a topic area). Next, specific instructional objectives must be determined. These objectives should be stated in terms of observable learner behaviors, under specific conditions that help the learners reach an acceptable level of performance. These foundational requirements are next used to help determine the possible alternative instructional strategies and/or approaches that can be selected. The choice of a specific instructional strategy is then determined on the basis of the constraints of each instructional situation (e.g., numbers of students, available facilities, budget, etc.). Only when a gaming approach has been selected from the alternative instructional strategies does one move to the next section: the design or modification of a specific game.

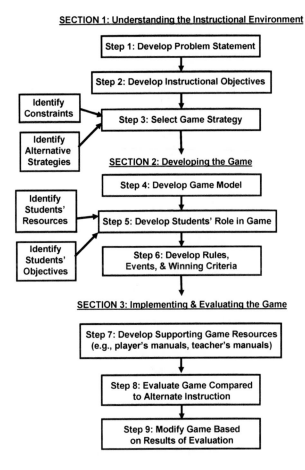

Figure 11.3:
A Systematic Approach to Instructional Game Design
and Use

The second section of Figure 11.3 shows the basic steps in developing an instructional game. The fourth step is to develop the game model. Like any model, it is a simplified representation of only certain elements of reality. The specific elements chosen for the game should be selected on the basis of how they will support the instructional objectives already identified. Step 5 is the identification of how the students will participate in the game.

Several questions, like the following, must be answered to support game design. Will each student play the same role or different roles? Will they play as individuals or as a team? Will learner actions affect the outcome of the game or do they just observe? These and other questions will lead to the development of specific rules and events in the game. Finally, the criteria for winning the game must be developed. Winning the game should involve improved learner performance on the instructional objectives. Sometimes an existing game can be modified for a new instructional situation. Even if an existing game is chosen, it must be modified to meet the specific requirements of the new instructional situation.

The third section of Figure 11.3 shows the three main steps involved in the implementation and evaluation of an instructional game. In addition to the game, supporting materials, like players' instructions and teachers' manuals must be developed. As indicated by the data from studies such as Leutner (1993) and Mayer, et al. (2002), instructional support that explains the purpose of the game and how to play it can enhance the instructional value of the game. In step 8, the instructional game is evaluated. Ideally this evaluation should compare the effectiveness of the game (as measured by learner performance) to the effectiveness of alternate instructional approaches. The final step in this process uses the results of the evaluation to modify the game to improve its instructional effectiveness.

In any systematic process, like the one depicted in Figure 11.3, it is necessary to make specific design decisions about the game. Malone (1981; 1982) reported the results of a series of studies that detailed the characteristics that made several simple video games enjoyable to students. As discussed earlier, he used his results to develop a general framework for analyzing the appeal of instructional environments, computer games, and computer interfaces (see Table 11.1). The framework was based on three categories: challenge, fantasy, and curiosity. Because this framework is consistent with the important characteristics of games and motivational instructional environments summarized earlier (e.g., Malone & Lepper, 1987; Lepper & Malone, 1987; Csikszentmihalyi, 1990; Leemkuil, et al., 2000), it has been adapted to provide recommendations about the design of effective and motivational instructional games (see Table 11.6).

Table 11.6:
Design Recommendations for Instructional Games

Design Category	Recommendations
Challenge	**A. Goal.** • There should be a clear goal to the game. • The goal should be consistent with the instructional objective. • Performance feedback should be provided about how close the learner is to achieving the goal.
	B. Uncertain Outcome. • The outcome of reaching the goal should be uncertain. The learner should have to exert effort to achieve the goal. • If the subject matter is complex, the game should include multiple levels of difficulty or complexity. Sub-goals should help the learner successfully complete enabling learning objectives.
	C. Competition. • A game can be made more challenging by introducing competition. • Competition can be against a live opponent, against a computer-controlled opponent, or against a criterion score. Achieving a criterion score can be one of the factors that allows a learner to advance to higher levels of difficulty. • Game scores should be clearly related to the achievement of learning objectives (e.g., not just how many shots are fired accurately or how many opponents are defeated).
Fantasy	**A. Emotional Appeal.** • The fantasy should embody emotional appeal for the learners (e.g., not everyone reacts positively to shooting weapons or conversely, to complex interpersonal situations).
	B. Fantasy Metaphor. • The metaphor used in the fantasy should embody physical or other characteristics that the learner already understands.

Table 11.6:
(continued)

Design Category	Recommendations
Curiosity	**A. Optimal Level of complexity.** • The game should provide an optimal level of informational complexity to meet the needs of the learners. • The level of complexity should increase as learners gain higher levels of expertise.
	B. Incorporation of Interesting Media. • The game should use interesting audio and visual effects to enhance the fantasy and emphasize instructional content. • The game can incorporate elements of randomness to avoid boredom for the learner.
Instructional Quality	**A. Logical Instructional Structure.** • The game should capitalize on the learner's desire to have "well-formed" knowledge structures. • Elements of the game should build on and reinforce each other to help build the learner's knowledge structures. • Learners should be able to easily see when their knowledge structures are incomplete. Feedback during the game should be used to help learners complete their knowledge structures.
	B. Incorporation into the Larger Instructional Program. • The game should not "stand alone." Rather, it should be part of a larger instructional program. • Debriefing and feedback should be provided after the game to help the learner understand how the experiences in the game support the learning objectives.

One thing that is fairly clear is that instructional games are not a panacea. Like any instructional medium or approach, games must provide a means for learners to engage in cognitive and/or motor interactions that directly support instructional objectives. Gratuitous use of games or the use of games with no clear instructional goals will probably increase the cost of the instruction without providing the instructional benefit that learners require (see the earlier discussion of de Jong & van Joolingen, 1998). If a game is chosen as an instructional approach, it is important that it includes instructional support, such as emphasizing important information in the game that addresses the instructional objectives (e.g., Leutner, 1993).

If designed with instructional goals in mind, games can provide effective instruction. Jacobs and Dempsey, J. V. (1993) expressed the opinion that "By facilitating learner involvement via simulation and gaming and incorporating sound instructional features, learning outcomes should show improvements relative to other training methods that are less engaging or that provide less effective means of instructional interaction" (p. 198). They suggest that instructional gaming design should take several factors into account. Instructional games should include relevant activities that make up the job or domain of interest. The relative "criticality" of the various activities should be determined and the most critical should be included in the game. Finally, the performance of learners in the game activities should be evaluated so learners are rewarded for performing correctly and given remediation to improve incorrect performance.

Conclusions and Recommendations

This review of empirical research on the effectiveness of instructional games leads to the following five conclusions and four recommendations. The *conclusions* are:

1. The empirical research on the effectiveness of instructional games is fragmented. The literature includes research on different tasks, age groups, and types of games. The research literature is also filled with ill-defined terms, and plagued with methodological flaws.

2. Although research has shown that some games can provide effective learning for a variety of learners for several different tasks (e.g., math, attitudes, electronics, and economics), this *does not tell us* whether to use a game for our specific instructional task. We should not generalize from research on the effectiveness of one game

311

in one learning area for one group of learners to all games in all learning areas for all learners.

3. There is *no evidence* to indicate that games are the *preferred* instructional method in all situations.

4. Instructional games should be embedded in instructional programs that include debriefing and feedback so the learners understand what happened in the game and how these events support the instructional objectives.

5. Instructional support to help learners understand how to use the game increases the instructional effectiveness of the gaming experience by allowing learners to focus on the instructional information rather than the requirements of the game.

The following four *recommendations* may help the instructional gaming industry produce more instructionally effective games.

1. The decision to use a game should be based on a *detailed analysis of the learning requirements* and an analysis of the *tradeoffs* among alternate instructional approaches.

2. Program managers and procurement personnel should *insist* that game developers clearly demonstrate how the design of a game will provide interactive experiences that *support properly designed instructional objectives* (see for example, Gagné & Briggs, 1979; Merrill, 1983; 1997 for guidance on the proper design of instructional objectives).

3. Instructors should view instructional games as adjuncts and aids to help support instructional objectives. Learners should be provided with debriefing and feedback that clearly explains how their experiences with the game help them meet these instructional objectives.

4. Instructor-less approaches (e.g., web-based instruction) must include all "instructor functions." These include performance evaluation, debriefing, and feedback.

Herbert Simon (2000) provided a succinct prescription for designing improved instruction. Although he was not speaking specifically about instructional games, his prescription applies equally well to instructional games as to other forms of instructional activities. As Simon put it, "A first step toward improved instruction is to examine the understanding we hope students will acquire, the things they should be able to do with

312

their knowledge... Next, we must design a series of experiences that will enable students to learn the relevant cues in the situations they encounter and to evoke from memory the actions that are effective and appropriate in specific situations" (pp. 117-118).

Section IV
The Science of Learning and the Art of Instruction

This final section includes two chapters that discuss some of the important issues that should be considered when designing, implementing or evaluating instruction. Chapter 12 presents discussions of methodological issues that should be considered when evaluating learning outcomes (the effectiveness of instruction). Chapter 13 presents several sets of scientifically-derived principles for the design and implementation of instruction. These principles are examined through the lens of the systems theory perspective and the empirical research presented throughout the book. The chapter also includes a summary of a successful instructional development project—the Virtual Environment for Submarine Ship Handling Training (VESUB), the first virtual environment training system fielded by the U. S. Navy. This project summary illustrates how the science of learning was used to support one cycle of the ISD process. Next, a brief description of the Instructional Quality Evaluation Tool, which can help determine if computer- and web-delivered instructional products are of high quality, is presented. The chapter ends with a few final remarks and recommendations.

Chapter 12
Evaluation of Learning Outcomes

Any instructional program (e.g., a course or instructional medium added to a course) must be evaluated to ensure that it enables learners to gain the knowledge and skills required to meet the goals of the program. Evaluation is also the basis for determining if an instructional program requires modification, whether a new instructional approach can be applied, or to compare the effectiveness of two instructional approaches. This chapter provides brief discussions of some of the major methodological issues and constraints that make instructional evaluations difficult to conduct and also difficult to interpret. These issues and constraints differ, depending on the specifics of the evaluation, such as where the evaluation is conducted (e.g., laboratory, school, or on the job), the purpose of the evaluation (e.g., student reactions, amount of information learned, the effects on the learner's organization), or the resources available for the evaluation. These issues and constraints must be understood if the results of instructional evaluations are to be meaningfully used to improve instruction.

Formative or Summative Evaluation

Two major types of evaluations are formative and summative evaluations. *Formative evaluations* are usually conducted during the development or initial implementation of an instructional program. During program development, a formation evaluation serves as an initial test of the adequacy of the instructional content and delivery methods chosen for the program. Some formative evaluations use subject matter experts to analyze and validate the correctness of the learning content. Others may target the delivery method or how a specific method is applied by testing a small sample of learners. Instructional program development should include a series of targeted formative evaluations. These should focus on important instructional issues as early as possible. The earlier instructional problems are identified, the easier and less costly they are to correct. Hays, Stout, and Ryan-Jones (2005) developed an evaluation tool that identifies specific criteria that

317

can be used for both formative and summative evaluations. Additional information on this tool is provided in Chapter 13.

Summative evaluations focus on the outcome of the instructional program. Kirkpatrick (1996) identified four levels of outcome evaluation:

1. *Reaction.* This level evaluates how well a learner liked a particular instructional program. It is a measure of the learner's feelings. It does not measure any learning that has taken place.
2. *Learning.* This level evaluates immediate learning of principles, facts, and techniques at the end of instruction.
3. *Behavior.* This level evaluates on-the-job behavior (transfer or learning to the job).
4. *Results.* This evaluates how the instructional program affected the larger organization. For example, did it result in lower costs, higher quality, increased production, or lower rates of employee turnover and absenteeism?

The issues and methods discussed in the remainder of this chapter are relevant to both formative and summative effectiveness evaluations.

General Instructional Evaluation Issues

Any instructional evaluation involves some form of measurement. When planning for an evaluation, there are at least three decisions that an instructional program evaluator must make: when to measure, what to measure, and how to measure.

When to Measure

Instructional evaluators must first decide when they will collect data about the effects of the program on learners. Measures of instructional programs can be obtained immediately or soon after learners have been presented the instructional content. These are sometimes called *proximal measures* (Goldstein, 1974). Proximal measures can be obtained at the end of lessons within the course, at the end of the entire course, or soon after the learner applies the learned information on the job. Proximal measures should not be confused with formative evaluation measures, which are obtained and used during instructional program development. Rather, they

318

are measures of learner performance after exposure to an implemented course. Most evaluations (e.g., transfer of training studies) collect proximal measurement data because of project schedules and the difficulty of tracking learners for longer periods of time. The data obtained using proximal measures may or may not reflect the long-term retention of knowledge and skills.

If learning outcomes are obtained after a longer period of time, they are often labeled *distal measures* (Goldstein, 1974). These measures are sometimes used to evaluate long-term retention of knowledge and skills and their effects on organizational effectiveness (e.g., Kirkpatrick's [1996] Level 4 evaluation). It is usually more difficult to obtain distal measures because of the complexity and cost of collecting data over long periods of time.

The choice of when to conduct instructional evaluations can influence the results of the evaluation, sometimes resulting in erroneous judgments about the instructional program. The following hypothetical examples illustrate how such erroneous judgments might be made. Figure 12.1 shows a hypothetical interaction between the evaluation score and the time the evaluation measures are obtained. If, in this hypothetical situation, the evaluation is conducted at time 1, instructional program A will be evaluated as more effective than program B. However, if the evaluation is conducted at time 2, instructional program B will be evaluated as more effective. A premature evaluation might result in the selection of program A, even though program B would result in better performance on the job.

Erroneous conclusions can also be drawn about the effectiveness of instructional programs if the measures are collected either too early or too late. Figure 12.2 shows an example of an evaluation that was collected too early. In this example, no difference was shown between the two instructional programs at time 1. If these data were used, either instructional program might be selected. However, if the data were collected at time 2, a large difference between the two programs would have been detected and Program A would probably be selected.

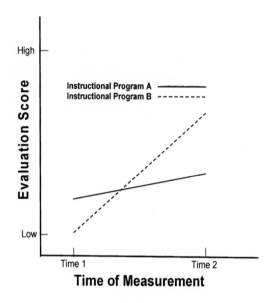

Figure 12.1:
Hypothetical Interaction between Time
and Instructional Program Effectiveness

Another example if the effect of time is shown in Figure 12.3. In this hypothetical example, the effectiveness of the two instructional programs seems very different at time 1, but appears essentially the same at time 2. If the data were collected at time 1, Program A would probably be selected. If the data were collected at time 2, either program could be chosen. In this case, other factors, like program cost or availability of facilities, would have to be used to make the choice between instructional programs.

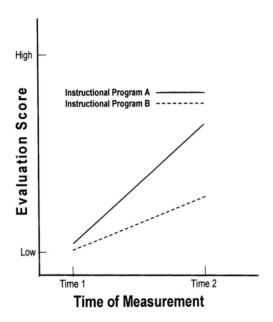

Figure 12.2:
Hypothetical Example of Evaluating Too Soon

It is impossible to say which, if any of these hypothetical examples might be encountered. However, it is clear that very different conclusions can be drawn depending on when the evaluation is conducted. The question of when to measure should be determined by the goals of the evaluation and the resources available for the evaluation.

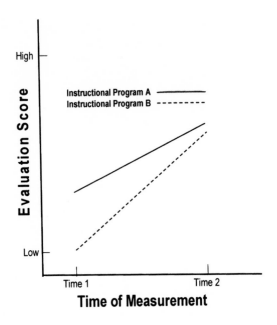

Figure 12.3:
Hypothetical Example of Two Evaluation Times

What to Measure

Instructional program evaluators must decide what specific performance data to collect in order to measure the effectiveness of the program. Measures can be characterized as falling on a continuum ranging from objective criteria to subjective criteria, although many evaluations use a combination of both. *Objective criteria* are quantifiable things such as the rate of production, the number of correct or incorrect answers, or the number of steps performed correctly. One problem with objective criteria is that other variables, like differences in learner experiences and aptitudes may mask the effect of the instruction.

Subjective criteria commonly use peer ratings or instructor evaluations to judge the effectiveness of the instructional program. The greatest problem with subjective criteria is that human estimation is very easily biased and may not accurately reflect the effectiveness of the instruction. An example of this type of bias is the favorable ratings that instructors might give for their favorite instructional approach or their favorite learner.

Another decision concerns how the effectiveness measures are referenced. Performance measures can be either criterion-referenced or norm-referenced (Goldstein, 1974). *Criterion-referenced measures* are tied to absolute standards, generally using specific objective behavioral items. *Norm-referenced measures* evaluate the learners' standing compared to their peers, a naive group, or possibly a group of experts.

In general, the most valuable evaluation data is generated by using objective, criterion-referenced measures. In this case, the data would provide information on how well the learners actually learned the required knowledge and skills as specified in the instructional program. Less valuable data would be generated from subjective instructor ratings that are only referenced to the learners in the evaluation. In this case, all the data could tell us is how the instructor thinks the learners performed with reference to their classmates. Even less valuable data are self-ratings of learning. As discussed in Chapter 6, Kruger and Dunning (1999) and Maki (1998) found that learners often overestimate how well they have learned material. Program evaluators should strive to collect objective performance data whenever possible.

Each instructional evaluation must be designed based upon the available resources such as time, funding, availability of objective measures, and access to experts. Within these constraints, evaluators should strive for objective, criterion-referenced measures whenever possible.

How to Measure

As important as the decision of what to measure is the determination of how to collect the effectiveness measures of the instructional program. As evaluators begin to design the evaluation plan, they must consider whether their measures are reliable and valid. *Reliability* refers to how consistent the test or measure is across repeated applications. A reliable measure would, for example, obtain the same answer from a learner every time it is collected. The goal of obtaining reliable measures is one reason for avoiding the use of purely subjective ratings. Even the best raters can vary on their responses over time and thus, raise questions about the data collected on any one occasion.

A reliable measure does not ensure that and evaluation will actually provide useful data about the effectiveness of an instructional program. Two examples illustrate this issue. A broken thermometer always shows the same temperature. It is reliable, but almost always wrong. Another example is the Thomas Quick Test of Intelligence, which asks one very reliable question, "What do you like on your hamburger?" (Matlin, 1979, p. 21). People who say they put nothing on their hamburger are given an intelligence score of zero and every ingredient added increases their score by one point. This question is reliable in that people are fairly consistent in their choices of condiments, but the relationship of their choices to intelligence is weak. In addition to being reliable, a measure must also be valid.

Ensuring that the measure used to evaluate instructional program effectives is valid is probably the most difficult part of any evaluation. In general, *validity* refers to whether the measure is actually measuring what is intended to be measured. There are two general classes of validity, internal validity and external validity. *Internal validity* is concerned with the controls designed into the evaluation. These controls involve issues such as the design of the evaluation, the number of learners measured, or how the performance of one group of learners is compared to the performance of another group. The evaluator must ensure that any inference he or she makes about the relationships between variables (e.g., the instructional intervention and learner performance) is supported by the appropriate experimental design and statistical interpretation of results. Table 12.1 lists and defines examples of confounding variables that can threaten the internal validity of any instructional program evaluation (Cook & Campbell, 1979; Eberts, Smith, Drays, & Vestwig, 1982).

Table 12.1:
Examples of Threats to Internal Validity

Type of Threat	Discussion of Threat
History	History is the effect of events that occur during the data collection that have no relationship to the instructional intervention variable. For example, some learners could be exposed to information by associating with other learners. It is impossible to determine how this exposure affected the learner's performance.
Maturation	Maturation occurs when the observed effect on performance is the result of changes in the learner (e.g., growing older, wiser, or stronger) during the data collection. Maturation is especially difficult to detect in longitudinal research where data on learner performance is collected over long periods of time.
Test-Retest Familiarity	Learning can occur when learners take a criterion test multiple times. It is difficult to determine how much learning is the result of the instruction. To guard against this confound, pre and posttest should avoid the same or similar procedures.
Instrumentation	Apparent changes in performance might be caused by: (1) Characteristics of the measuring instrument: for example, a scale with narrower intervals at the ends than in the middle. This could result in ceiling or floor effects. (2) Changes in the measuring instrument: For example, human observers might become more experienced between pre and posttests thus more discriminating when recording nuances in performance.
Statistical Regression	Statistical regression (sometimes called regression to the mean) occurs, when after repeated tests, high performers tend to perform less well and lower performers tend to perform better (closer to the average, or mean of the population). This can be a problem when pre-tests are used to classify learners into experimental groups. Later, the apparent effect of an instructional intervention could be influenced by regression to the mean.

Table 12.1:
(continued)

Type of Threat	Discussion of Threat
Selection	Initial differences between comparison groups (e.g., on abilities, interests, or knowledge of the subject matter) could cause the observed performance differences rather than as a result of the instructional intervention.
Mortality	Differential results might be obtained because different kinds of people dropped out of one or more groups during the course of the evaluation experiment. This leads to a selection effect since the groups would then be fundamentally different.
Amount of Instruction	This confound is related to the earlier discussion of when to measure. Results could differ depending on when performance data are collected. An instructional intervention (e.g., a simulation) that provides quick initial performance improvements might appear better than its alternative. The alternative might be shown to provide higher performance improvements if data were collected at a later time.

There are several methods that can be used to control the confounding variables that threaten internal validity:

1. The effects of a confounding variable may be controlled by holding it constant. This is done by ensuring that all groups are treated in exactly the same manner. Random assignment of trainees to groups is one method for hold confounding variables constant. One can assume that, through random assignment, any confounding variables are equally distributed throughout all groups.

2. A confounding variable can be controlled by measuring the variable to show that it has no effect. One way to do this is to use a pretest-posttest design to show whether the groups are initially the same. This requires avoiding instrumentation and test-retest familiarity problems.

3. A no-instruction control group can account for the effects of history, maturation, and instrumentation.

4. The effects of confounding variables may be measured and reduced or eliminated with statistical techniques such

as an analysis of covariance (e.g., Winer, 1962; Kirk, 1968).

5. The effects of a confounding variable may be controlled by making it an experimental variable. For example, an evaluation design might incorporate different levels of the confounding variable to determine if it has an effect on learner performance.

External validity refers to the inference that one causal relationship (e.g., the results of one evaluation) can be generalized to other settings, times, or groups of persons (Cook & Campbell, 1979). It is concerned with whether the evaluation actually measured a "real world" relationship. Do data collected in a laboratory with college students reflect a general class of instructional relationships that would also apply to children or military recruits? Do data on the attention span (vigilance) of radar operators apply to maintaining the attention of learners in an electronics technician course? These are the types of questions that must be asked about any instructional evaluation. This includes the research efforts summarized earlier.

Measuring Transfer

There have been a considerable number of discussions and disagreements about the transfer of learned knowledge and skills from the instructional to the real-world setting (see Chapter 6). Much of the work on measuring transfer has been conducted in the context of instructional (training) devices and simulators. However, most of the transfer evaluation designs can also be used to evaluate instructional innovations or to compare instructional programs. The issues and problems with various designs are similar, no matter what type of instructional product or approach is evaluated.

The Classic Transfer Evaluation Design. The classic transfer evaluation design is based on two assumptions (Caro, 1977). The first assumption is that the mastery of one skill will affect the acquisition of another similar skill. The second assumption is that the best way to evaluate the effect of instruction is to compare the outcome of one instructional approach to that of another matching instructional program that doesn't use the approach.

The classic transfer evaluation design (often called a transfer of training [TOT] design) involves two groups, which are treated in almost the same way. The control or baseline group experiences instruction in the current manner, without the instructional intervention being evaluated. The experimental or comparison group is provided the new instructional intervention or program that is being evaluated. The performance of learners in both groups is measured the same way and the performance measures are compared. If there is a difference between the average performance of the experimental and control groups, it can be assumed that it is the result of the instructional intervention.

The specific measures used to assess performance in a transfer evaluation depends on the type of task. For example, the evaluation of instruction on a cognitive task that requires the recall of specific facts (e.g., the names of organs in the body) might compare the number of errors when learners label the organs on a drawing of the body. On the other hand, a psychomotor task (e.g., hitting a target with a weapon) might compare the average distance from the center of the target. In any case, the measures of performance should be determined by the instructional objectives of the specific instructional program.

Transfer Comparison Formulas. The two best known transfer comparison formulas are based on the classic transfer design. The formulas compare the performance levels or instructional time across the two evaluation groups to generate a transfer score. The first formula is *percent transfer* (Micheli, 1972). Percent transfer is calculated to determine if an instructional intervention produces either an increase in proficiency or a decrease in the instructional time required to achieve a desired level of proficiency. The percent transfer score is computed according to Formula 1. In this

$$\% \text{ transfer} = ([T_C - T_E] / T_C) \times 100 \qquad (1)$$

formula, T_C refers to either the time in instruction or the proficiency level of the control group. T_E refers to the time in instruction or the proficiency level of the experimental group.

The second transfer comparison formula (Povenmire & Roscoe, 1973) is the *transfer effectiveness ratio* (TER). This formula is often used to evaluate the effectiveness of new instructional simulators by measuring and comparing the performance of the control and experimental groups on the actual equipment after instruction. It is therefore more directly relevant to long-term retention of skills and to on-the-job performance rather than just immediate proficiency in the school or laboratory (Atkinson, 1972). In the TER formula (see Formula 2), T_C refers to training time or trials spent on the actual equipment or under the current instructional approach to reach criterion performance. T_E is the same measure for the experimental group on the simulator or after experiencing a new instructional approach. X_E refers to the

$$TER = (T_C - T_E) / X_E \qquad (2)$$

same or a similar measure for the experimental group on the actual equipment after instruction in the simulator. The criterion level of performance is set to be the same for both groups so the TER can be used to directly compare the underlying costs of instruction for the actual equipment and simulator or the two instructional approaches.

<u>Variations on the Classic Transfer Design</u>. It is very difficult to conduct an evaluation using the classic transfer design, because it requires access to learners in both the instructional and transfer situations. This takes a long amount of time and extensive financial and other resources. Several evaluation designs can be applied when it is not possible to conduct the evaluation using the classic transfer design. The first three designs are derived from the classic transfer design, but differ in the way they deal with the control (baseline) groups. They are: the self-control design, the pre-existing control design, and the uncontrolled design.

The *self-control design* uses a pre-test on the proficiency measure as the basis of comparison with the proficiency measure taken after instruction. This design suffers from the problem of determining whether improvements in proficiency are due to the instruction or are derived from taking the same or similar tests.

The *pre-existing control design* uses pre-existing information, such as learner scores from previous groups to control for the test-retest problem. However, this design introduces other, equally serious problems. The reason for a control group is to ensure that only the instructional variable of interest (e.g., type of instructional approach) is different from the experimental group. All other variables are assumed to be shared by both groups and thus, any performance differences can be attributed to the effect of the instructional intervention. That assumed commonality may not exist between the earlier groups and the current evaluation group, so it is not possible to infer that performance improvements are due to the instructional intervention.

These problems, possible interfering variables and the inability to infer that proficiency improvements are the result of the instructional intervention, are compounded in the *uncontrolled design*. Here, one measures proficiency after instruction and assumes that any improvements are due to the instruction. Because performance could be influenced by so many uncontrolled variables, this assumption may be unwarranted.

The next two designs also suffer from some of the problems mentioned above. They are the device-to-device design and the instructional device improvement design. In the *device-to-device design*, no control group is used and the assumption is that the final measure of performance (on the second device) is equivalent to the performance that would be found on the actual equipment. In the *instructional device performance design*, the assumption is similar to that in the self-control design. Specifically, it is assumed that any improvement in learner performance is the result of the instructional intervention. In addition to suffering from no control group, neither of these designs measures performance on the actual equipment or job-situation. Using these designs, it is difficult or impossible to predict competence on the job.

The last group of designs are so different from the classic transfer design that there is little basis for comparisons. This group includes the backward transfer design, the device fidelity design, the instructional program analysis design, and the opinion survey design. The *backward transfer design* tests experts on the instructional device. It is assumed that if the experts can transfer their skills and proficiency from the actual equipment to the instructional device, then a person given instruction on the device should be able to transfer these skills to the actual equipment. There has been no empirical verification that such transfer works in both ways even though the assumption seems reasonable. A second assumption of this design is that the most effective instruction always comes from practice on the actual equipment. Thus, instructional devices would always try to closely approximate the physical and functional characteristics of the actual equipment. This assumption ignores the differences between experts and novices. Experts have already learned the necessary knowledge and skills and may not reflect how novices would react to instruction on the device. It and also ignores instructional approaches that build on small, simple learning steps or use instructional features of the device that are not available on the actual equipment (e.g., replay or restart).

The *device fidelity design* is also based on the assumption that the closer the instructional device approximates the actual equipment, the higher its effectiveness. Analytic tools were developed in the 1970s and 1980s, which attempted to assess effectiveness by comparing the characteristics of the instructional device to the actual equipment (e.g., Wheaton, Rose, Fingerman, Leonard, & Boycan, 1976; Swezey & Evans, 1980). These designs have seldom been validated in actual instructional settings.

The *instructional program analysis design* assumes that instruction will be effective if the program of instruction is well designed and uses good instructional techniques. This design is limited, just as the device fidelity design, because it only evaluates the instructional device or program in an analytic manner. It does not measure actual performance and therefore cannot determine whether skills and knowledge actually transfer to the real world.

The *opinion survey design* collects data on the opinions of experts, such as course developers, subject matter experts, instructors, and even learners. These opinions may be useful, but do not provide empirical data on the effectiveness of the instructional program. This design is most effectively used in conjunction with the classic transfer design or one of the designs that closely approximates it.

Summary

This chapter included discussions on some of the important issues that must be addressed when one wishes to evaluate the outcomes of instructional programs. These evaluations are not limited to the end of program development, but rather should be conducted throughout the development and implementation processes. Formative evaluations may be more important than summative evaluations because instructional program developers have the opportunity to improve the program of instruction (POI) based on the results of formative evaluations. The results of summative evaluations may be used to document a well-designed POI, but may not be able to influence changes in the POIs that are not optimally effective.

The chapter also included discussions of general evaluation issues such as the importance of choosing what to measure, when to measure, and how to measure. Emphasis was placed on the importance of measuring transfer to the learner's job or to the ultimate location where the knowledge and skills will be used. However, the difficulty of conducting transfer evaluations has led to the development of variations on the classic transfer design for use in applied settings. The strengths and weaknesses of these variations were also discussed.

Chapter 13
Applying the Science of Learning

Previous chapters included summaries of a large amount of research data on learning processes and instructional applications. This chapter summarizes some of the available guidance on applying these results to the design of effective instruction. This guidance is followed by an ISD process analysis of an example instructional development project. The project (VESUB) was the first virtual environment instructional simulation adopted by the U.S. Navy. This summary illustrates the important events and activities that must occur to successfully complete one ISD cycle. This is followed by a brief overview of a tool designed to evaluate the instructional quality of computer- and web-delivered instruction. Finally, a few concluding comments and recommendations are provided.

Teaching Specific Subject Matter

Richard Mayer (2004) proposed that the evolution of the science of learning (in his terms, the science of instruction) has proceeded through three stages. Each stage can be characterized by how it viewed the concept of transfer. Early learning theories were dominated by the concept of *general transfer*, "the idea that it is possible to improve the mind in general" (Mayer, 2004, p. 717). People thought that studying subjects like Latin or geometry would produce "proper habits of mind" that would improve learning on all tasks. Early research found no evidence for general transfer (e.g., Thorndike & Woodworth, 1901). This led to the concept of *specific transfer.*

"Specific transfer refers to the idea that previous learning helps on a new task only if the new task required exactly the same behaviors as was learned" (Mayer, 2004, p. 717). Thorndike's theory of identical elements (1913; 1931) is usually regarded as the exemplar of specific transfer theory. Transfer of identical elements and updated versions of the theory "have been challenged not on the grounds that specific transfer theory is incorrect but rather that it is incomplete" (Mayer, 2004, p. 717).

More modern theories of transfer maintain that learners "can apply a general principle or conception to new tasks that require the same principle or conception" (Mayer, 2004, p. 717). Mayer refers to this as "specific-transfer-of-general-knowledge" and regards it as the foundation for teaching specific subject matter.

Mayer (2004) recommended that the development of instruction be guided by the *specific-transfer-of-general-knowledge* approach. This involves first conducting a cognitive task analysis, "a description of the cognitive processes that a person would need to go through in order to accomplish the task" (p. 718). This cognitive analysis is part of the first phase of the ISD process. It is critical that this type of analysis, as well as other analyses such as equipment or procedure analyses, specify the requirements of the task so that instructional objectives and approaches can be designed to meet these specific requirements. Once the instructional objectives have been clearly specified, instructional methods and techniques can be designed to target underlying cognitive processes and supporting requirements. Mayer discussed several representative academic tasks (reading fluency, reading comprehension, writing, mathematics, and science) and the cognitive processes that underlie them. He then summarized the research, which provides insights into how to design instruction for each component cognitive process. Table 13.1 (synthesized from Mayer, 2004) lists and defines the component cognitive processes required to accomplish each of these tasks.

Once the components of a specific task have been identified, general instructional principles can be tailored to meet these requirements. The applicability of the general principles will depend on the specific task requirements, but there will be considerable applicability regardless of the task (e.g., the need for practice, need for performance assessment, and the need for performance feedback.) In the following sections, some general instructional principles are summarized.

Table 13.1:
Component Cognitive Processes in Several Tasks

Task	Component Process	Definition
Reading a word	Being aware of sound units	Recognizing, producing, and manipulating phonemes
	Decoding words	Converting a printed word into sound
	Accessing word meaning	Finding a mental representation of the word's meaning in one's memory
Comprehending a passage	Using prior knowledge	Activating and assimilating to existing schemas
	Using prose structure	Distinguishing important and unimportant material and organizing the material into a coherent structure
	Making inferences	Adding appropriate inferences to the material
	Using metacognitive knowledge	Determining whether the passage makes sense
Writing a Composition	Planning	Remembering or finding relevant information, deciding how to organize it, and setting goals for communicating with the audience
	Translating	Producing printed text on paper or screen
	Reviewing	Detecting and correcting errors in the text

Table 13.1:
(continued)

Task	Component Process	Definition
Solving an Arithmetic Word Problem	Translating	Converting each sentence into an internal mental representation
	Integrating	Building a coherent mental representation of the problem situation
	Planning/monitoring	Devising a solution plan and keeping track of how well it works
	Executing	Carrying out a solution plan
Understanding how a Scientific System Works	Recognizing an anomaly	Realizing that one's mental model is flawed
	Creating a new model	Mentally constructing a new mental model
	Using a new model	Using a mental model to test hypotheses in research

Scientifically-derived Principles for the Design and Implementation of Instruction

Many educational researchers (e.g., National Research Council, 1999a; Halpern & Hakel, 2003; deWinstanley & Bjork, 2002) have strongly advocated the use of scientifically-derived principles to guide the design and implementation of instructional approaches and policies. "Unfortunately, the research literature is usually ignored, while educational leaders and policy makers grasp at the ephemeral 'magic' of quick fixes" (Halpern & Hakel, 2003, p. 38). Some of the principles identified by these researchers include:

- Practice at retrieval of information is an important variable in promoting long-term retention and transfer. "Information that is frequently retrieved becomes more retrievable" (Halpern & Hakel, 2003, p. 38). This practice opens the learner's output screen and strengthens the associations in the learner's memory.

- Retrieval practice should be based on minimal cues, repeated over time with varied applications. This type of practice will help learners become more fluent in recall and more likely to recall information across different situations. "The benefits of retrieving information learned earlier to produce answers in response to new questions are among the most robust findings in the learning literature" (Halpern & Hakel, p. 39).

- Retrieval of information is enhanced if practice is spaced over multiple sessions rather than massed into fewer, longer sessions. "The spacing effect—that long-term recall is enhanced by distributing rather than massing the presentations of to-be-remembered information—is one of the most robust and general effects in experimental psychology" (deWinstanley & Bjork, 2002, p. 23).

- Some specific methods to promote practice at retrieval include:
  - Ask questions periodically to check understanding
  - Ask why learner chose his or her answer
  - Return to key concepts at several points in the lecture or course
  - Relate material to previously covered concepts, previous lectures or courses
  - Point out connections between concepts and other materials or applications
  - Provide cues for recall, with examples, context, or mnemonics

- "Varying the conditions under which learning takes place makes learning harder for learners but results in better learning" (Halpern & Hakel, p. 39). Variety reduces the effects of habituation and helps the learner develop additional associations between the new information and information already in memory. Some possible strategies to introduce variety in learning include:
  - Change the format of class time periodically.
  - Use different methods during laboratory times.
  - Use computer-based instructional methods or assignments.
  - Take learners on "field trips".

337

o Point out relevant cases from real world settings (e.g., hospitals, etc.).

- Learning is generally enhanced when learners are required to take information that is presented in one format and "represent" it in an alternative format. This principle is related to Dual-Coding Theory (Paivio, 1990), which postulates that information is easier to retrieve if it is encoded from both verbal and visuospatial representations. This dual coding helps develop multiple associations and strengthens existing associations. Some possible strategies that can be used to help learners reformat information include:

  o Providing skeletal outlines or diagrams of the lecture for learners to fill in on their own time.
  o Asking learners to rephrase a concept or explain it to each other.
  o Creating tables or charts for students to fill in to categorize or make contrasts between key concepts.
  o Asking learners to predict an outcome or diagnosis.
  o Asking learners to write a test question about what they perceive as an important concept.
  o Asking learners to compare or contrast concepts.
  o Asking learners to think of a real world application of a concept.
  o Using role-playing scenarios to probe understanding.

- What and how much is learned in any situation depends heavily on prior knowledge and experience. Learners build meaning into new information using what they already know. The new information is made meaningful through the formation of new associations and the strengthening of existing associations.

- Learning is influenced by both learners' and instructors' epistemologies. Individuals maintain many beliefs about the world and these beliefs are difficult to change (e.g., 21% of 2000 respondents to a phone interview believed the sun revolves around the earth). These beliefs affect learners' input screens. Learners should be informed about the effects of their beliefs on learning. For example, beliefs about learning itself and how learning works (e.g., the belief "I cannot do math" can lead to problems in other disciplines). Furthermore, people often have great confidence in their erroneous beliefs. "Confidence is not a reliable indicator of depth and quality of learning" (Halpern & Hakel, p. 40). Instructors' beliefs affect their output screens and the way they present instructional information. Instructors need to constantly review their beliefs to ensure that they do not negatively influence their presentation of instruction.

• Learning requires effort and may even be painful and aversive. Learners need to understand that they must expend effort to learn, but that this effort will result in better learning. Learners must consciously engage their decider to direct their attention to instructional information and to open their input screen so the information can enter their system and be associated with information in memory.

• Experience alone is a poor teacher. "What people learn from experience can be systematically wrong" (Halpern & Hakel, p. 40). For example, physicians may believe their intervention has worked when actually most patients improve no matter what the intervention. This illustrates the importance of practice, assessment, and feedback. Without assessment and feedback, practice may result in the strengthening of incorrect or inappropriate performance.

• Lectures work well for learning that is assessed with recognition tests, but work badly for understanding. Lecturing is not optimal to foster deep learning and reliance on recognition tests is not a reliable method to assess deep learning. "Understanding is an *interpretive* process in which students must be active participants" (Halpern & Hakel, p. 40, author's emphasis).

• The act of remembering itself may influence what a learner will and will not remember in the future. When learners are asked to remember specific pieces of information, this often leads to "selective forgetting" of information they were not asked to recall. All experience forms new associations. Thus it is important that learners experience events that strengthen all of the associations that support desired performance.

• Less can be more, especially when we think about long-term retention and transfer. To achieve a balance between how much and how well something is learned requires clearly articulated goal statements for both the learner and the instructor. Then learning activities can be matched to these goals.

- "What learners do determines what and how much is learned, how well it will be remembered, and the conditions under which it will be recalled" (Halpern & Hakel, p. 41). Performance requires the activation of associations in memory and the transfer of this information through the output screen to the motor or output transducer. The more often these processes are activated, the easier they can be activated in the future. Some "doing" activities include:
  - o   Case exercises
  - o   Dissection
  - o   Writing exercises
  - o   Charts or diagrams to fill in
  - o   Demonstrations or debates
- "We need to look constantly for concrete evidence when we evaluate claims about what works in education. Consequently, we urge you to develop a healthy skepticism about all educational claims" (Halpern, & Hakel, p. 41). This is one way of thinking more scientifically. Other ways to think scientifically were discussed in Chapter 1.

Learner-centered Psychological Principles

The American Psychological Association (APA) established a Learner-centered Principles Work Group under its Education Directorate's Center for Psychology in Schools and Education. This multidisciplinary group generated 14 principles about the learner and the learning process. The principles are based on a number of different theoretical perspectives and more than a century of research on teaching and learning. They focus on psychological factors that are mostly internal to and under the control of the learner. The principles are divided into those referring to cognitive and metacognitive factors, motivational and affective factors, development and social factors, and individual differences factors. Table 13.2 lists the principles with short descriptions. The following discussions of each principle are based on APA's discussions and the systems perspective of learning research discussed in previous chapters.

Table 13.2:
Learner-centered Psychological Principles

Cognitive and Metacognitive Factors	
1. Nature of the learning process.	The learning of complex subject matter is most effective when it is an intentional process of constructing meaning from information and experience.
2. Goals of the learning process.	The successful learner, over time and with support and instructional guidance, can create meaningful, coherent representations of knowledge.
3. Construction of knowledge.	The successful learner can link new information with existing knowledge in meaningful ways.
4. Strategic thinking.	The successful learner can create and use a repertoire of thinking and reasoning strategies to achieve complex learning goals.
5. Thinking about thinking.	Higher order strategies for selecting and monitoring mental operations facilitate creative and critical thinking.
6. Context of learning.	Learning is influenced by environmental factors, including culture, technology, and instructional practices.
Motivational and Affective Factors	
7. Motivational and emotional influences on learning.	What and how much is learned is influenced by the learner's motivation. Motivation to learn, in turn, is influenced by the individual's emotional states, beliefs, interests and goals, and habits of thinking.
8. Intrinsic motivation to learn.	The learner's creativity, higher order thinking, and natural curiosity all contribute to his or her motivation to learn. Intrinsic motivation is stimulated by tasks of optimal novelty and difficulty, relevant to personal interests, and that provide for personal choice and control.
9. Effects of motivation on effort.	Acquisition of complex knowledge and skills requires extended learner effort and guided practice. Without learners' motivation to learn, the willingness to exert this effort is unlikely without coercion.

Table 13.2:
(continued)

Developmental and Social Factors	
10. Developmental influences on learning.	As individuals develop, there are different opportunities and constraints for learning. Learning is most effective when differential development within and across physical, intellectual, emotional, and social domains is taken into account.
11. Social influences on learning.	Learning is influenced by social interactions, interpersonal relations, and communication with others.
Individual Differences Factors	
12. Individual differences in learning.	Learners have different strategies, approaches, and capabilities for learning that are a function of prior experience and heredity.
13. Learning and diversity.	Learning is most effective when differences in learners' linguistic, cultural, and social backgrounds are taken into account.
14. Standards and assessment.	Setting appropriately high and challenging standards and assessing the learners as well as learning progress–including diagnostic, process, and outcome assessment–are integral parts of the learning process.

Principles that Refer to Cognitive and Metacognitive Factors

The first set of principles involves the cognitive and metacognitive factors that focus on the development of richer knowledge structures, setting learning goals, and the application of strategies that help the learner monitor and evaluate their learning success.

Nature of the Learning Process

There is no single learning process. Different processes are involved in learning various types of knowledge and skills (Bloom, 1956; Gagné, 1985; Mayer, 2004). For example, learning a motor skill involves extensive practice and the development of habits or motor programs. On the other hand, learning cognitive knowledge requires the establishment and strengthening of associations to encode and retrieve the knowledge. No matter which specific skill or knowledge needs to be learned, the learner will be more successful if he or she is actively engaged in and takes responsibility for his or her own learning. This requires engagement of the learner's decider to coordinate attention and direct the associator to develop links between the new information and information in memory. Further activities like repetition or practice strengthen these associations and open the learner's output screen so he or she can perform

Goals of the Learning Process

Successful learning requires the learner to be goal-directed. It is necessary for learners pursue personally relevant goals in order to construct useful representations of knowledge and to acquire thinking and learning strategies that help their learning success (metacognitive skills). Learners may start with short-term, sketchy goals, but gradually, as they develop a better understanding of the subject matter, they can refine these and strive toward longer-term goals. As goals develop the learner takes greater and greater control of his or her learning. In other words the learner's decider takes more control to direct attention to new information and coordinate the associator to form and strengthen links between the new information and information in memory.

Construction of Knowledge

As learners build more and more associations between new information and experiences and their existing knowledge and skills base, they become deeper and more comprehensive. These associations can take a variety of forms, including adding to, modifying, or reorganizing the existing knowledge or skills. These different forms of association are due to different types of subject matter as well as the learner's memory. Unless new knowledge and skills become integrated with existing capabilities it will remain isolated and of little effective use for new tasks or situations. This integration of old and new knowledge can be assisted if instruction uses techniques such as concept mapping or categorizing. Associations must also be made between the information in memory and the learner's output processes. Practice, guided by assessment-based feedback helps the learner open his or her output screen and modify his or her performance to more closely meet task requirements.

Strategic Thinking

Successful learners approach learning, reasoning, and problem solving by applying strategic thinking strategies (metacognitive skills). They understand that the use of these strategies can help them achieve their learning and performance goals and enable them to apply what they have learned in new situations. They try to expand their repertoire of strategies by monitoring the effectiveness of the strategies and modifying them as appropriate. Learners can be assisted in developing, applying, and assessing their strategic learning skills.

Thinking about Thinking

The ability to reflect on how they think and learn is a characteristic of successful learners. They are able to set reasonable learning and performance goals, select learning strategies or methods, and monitor their learning progress. If they encounter learning problems, successful learners are able to generate alternative methods or reassess the appropriateness of their goals. Instructional methods can be applied to help learners develop these metacognitive strategies and take more responsibility for learning.

Context of Learning

Many environmental factors, such as culture, technology, and instructional methods influence learning. Learners bring their cultural and group influences to the learning situation. In systems terms, the learner is influenced by different suprasystems with different and sometimes competing goals. For example, a young learner may be encouraged to learn by his or her family, but discouraged by his or her peer group. These suprasystem influences may affect learners' motivation, orientation toward learning, and ways of thinking. Instructional technologies and practices may conflict with or support learners' cultural and group influences. For example, learners who are uncomfortable with computers may resist their use in an instructional program. The degree that the learning environment supports and nurtures the learner can counteract negative influences and enhance positive influences. It is important that instructors and instructional developers are aware of the influences of different suprasystems. This is true not only for learners' suprasystem, but also for organizational suprasystems that sometimes exert conflicting influences on the learning system.

Motivational and Affective Factors

This group of principles focuses on factors that influence the learner's motivation and feelings about learning.

Motivational and Emotional Influences on Learning

Beliefs about themselves and their expectations for success can enhance or interfere with a learner's motivation. Motivational and emotional factors can influence the learner's ability to think and process information. Positive emotions, like curiosity, can enhance motivation and help the learner focus his or her attention and energy on learning. Mild levels of anxiety can enhance the learner's attention. However, negative emotions, such as anxiety, panic, rage, or insecurity, and the negative thoughts they generate (e.g., worrying about failure, fearing punishment, or negative self-labeling) usually detract from motivation and interfere with successful learning. Some of the research on positive teaching behaviors was summarized in Chapter 6.

Intrinsic Motivation to Learn

Curiosity, creativity, and flexible thinking are indicators of the learners' intrinsic motivation to learn. Intrinsic motivation is enhanced by tasks that the learners perceive as interesting, meaningful, and relevant to their personal needs. It is also enhanced by tasks that are matched to the learner's abilities in terms of complexity and difficulty. If the task is too easy, the learner can become bored and lose the motivation to continue. If the task is too complex or difficult, the learner may believe they cannot succeed and stop trying in order to avoid failure. Real-world tasks that enable the learner to make choices and exercise control also facilitate intrinsic motivation. Instructional approaches that regularly assess the learners' perceptions about the learning tasks and modify them appropriately can help the learner maintain higher levels of intrinsic motivation.

Effects of Motivation on Effort

The level of effort that a learner applies to the learning task is a strong indicator of his or her motivation to learn. Learning complex knowledge and skills requires a substantial investment of energy, strategic effort, and persistence. Instructional strategies that include meaningful activities, practices that enhance positive emotions, and help the learner perceive the task as interesting and personally relevant help enhance motivation and result in increased effort.

Developmental and Social Factors

The next two principles involve matching the learning task with the learner's developmental level and his or her opportunities to engage with other learners in collaborative learning tasks.

Developmental Influences on Learning

Individual development varies across social, emotional, physical, and intellectual domains. Successful learning in these different domains can vary depending on the learner's level of development in each domain. Too much emphasis on one domain (e.g., reading readiness) can preclude learners from demonstrating capabilities in other areas (e.g., conceptual understanding). Educators must continuously assess learners' competencies as they mature. This will enable them to tailor their instructional approaches to enhance learning regardless of their current level of development.

Social Influences on Learning

Interaction and collaboration with other learners can facilitate learning. Instructional settings that allow interaction and collaboration give learners the opportunity to experience different perspectives and engage in reflective thinking. This, in turn, may lead to higher levels of social, moral, and cognitive development and also enhance learners' self-esteem. A community of mutually-supportive learners can provide relationships that enhance each learner's self-respect and self-acceptance, and provide stability, trust, caring, and sense of belonging. A positive learning climate can help learners feel comfortable when sharing ideas and help them more actively participate in the learning process.

Individual Differences Factors

The final three principles refer to factors that are different across learners.

Individual Differences in Learning

Learners bring different capabilities and talents to the learning situation. They have acquired their own preferences for how they like to learn and the pace at which they learn. However, learner preferences do not always help them reach their learning goals. The existence of different learning preferences does not mean that people learn differently. The same basic processes are involved in all learning (e.g., attention, motivation, repetition, practice, assessment, and feedback). Learners need help to examine their learning preferences and to develop ways to expand or modify them to support their learning goals.

Learning and Diversity

Related to the above principle, all learners are affected by the same basic principles of learning, motivation, and effective instruction. However, each learner's language, ethnicity, race, beliefs, and socioeconomic status can also influence learning. Learners need to feel that their individual differences and experiences are respected and can be accommodated in learning contexts. If the learners feel that they are valued and respected as themselves, their levels of motivation and achievement are enhanced.

Standards and Assessment

Assessment can provide important information to both the learner and the instructor at all stages of the learning process. As mentioned in several previous principles, the learner is more successful when he or she feels challenged to work towards meaningful goals. Ongoing assessment of the learner's progress and targeted feedback (for both learners and instructors) can help sustain motivation by demonstrating learning success and can also help the learner direct his or her efforts to the areas that need improvement. Assessments can be standardized to compare progress of learners with their peers. However, improved performance on standardized tests should not be the only learning goal. Self-assessments can be an important tool to improve the learner's metacognitive skills (e.g., self-appraisal and self-directed learning). In all cases, assessments should evaluate both learning processes and outcomes.

Learning In and For the Workplace

In the modern world, learning is a life-long process. Many people need to learn new information and update their existing knowledge for career advancement or even to keep their current job. Penuel and Roschelle (1999) discussed ways to more effectively design workplace learning. Their discussion was illustrated with examples from the Denver Project, an experimental learning program aimed at improving the skills of repair technicians. Their key principles can be summarized as follows:

1. *Learning takes place within communities of practice.* People learn every day at work by observing others who are more skilled than they are or by participating in tasks that allow them to learn about different aspects of the job.

2. *Novices learn to become experts through practice in solving a variety of problems in a domain.* The more one works, the more expertise he or she develops on a variety

of tasks and problems encountered on the job. For examples, salespersons become more likely to close a sale after they have dealt with a larger number of customers.

3. *Becoming an expert means applying learning to new contexts.* Learning that is too closely coupled to specific situations is less resistant to forgetting and is less likely to be applied in different contexts. Robust learning is more likely to occur from a combination of a variety of experiences similar to the target situation that help generate more general knowledge.

4. *Prior knowledge mediates learning.* Previous experience can help us learn new knowledge and skills or it can get in the way. In all cases, new learning must be incorporated into our existing mental representations.

5. *Learning is enhanced when thinking is made visible by collaboration and reflection among learners.* Active monitoring of their learning helps learners improve their comprehension and mastery of a particular topic. This monitoring can be enhanced when groups of learners can share their ideas and reflect on their learning experiences. Cognitive learning theories view learning as an active, constructive process that can be made more efficient through collaboration with other learners or persons with greater expertise in a field.

The principles summarized in the above sections are very general. Although a given instructor or instructional developer may understand and support the principles, they may be lost in the many activities involved in the development of an instructional program. The next section summarizes an example instructional project to highlight many of the processes and principles discussed throughout the book.

Process Analysis of an Example Instructional Project (VESUB)

In May of 1994, performance problems with the handling of submarines while surfaced were brought to the attention of the Navy. In November of 1994, an initial task analysis was conducted and a feasibility demonstration system was developed under the Navy's Virtual Environment Training Technology Program. A technology demonstration research project entitled "Virtual Environment for Submarine Ship Handling and Piloting Training (VESUB)" was initiated in October of 1994 and the feasibility demonstration system was transitioned to support this project. VESUB was funded as a Navy Manpower, Personnel, and Training Research and Development technology demonstration project with the goal to develop, demonstrate, and evaluate the training effectiveness of a virtual reality (VR)-based system for surfaced submarine Officer of the Deck (OOD) training. The submarine ship handling task was chosen as the task area for the technology demonstration for three reasons: 1) there was a clear Navy need for this training; 2) submarine ship handling is a visually dependent task; and 3) the visual modality was the most mature of the three areas of VR development. Based on the results of the VESUB technology demonstration effort, the Navy planned to procure several operational VESUB systems and install them at submarine training facilities throughout the United States. The author was assigned as the leader of the R&D team.

This section summarizes the VESUB technology demonstration project as an example of how the science of learning and the Instructional System Development (ISD) process can be applied to develop a new instructional approach or program. In Chapter 2 it was argued that the ISD process is an application of the scientific method. To be successful, each phase of ISD should follow the principles of science to ensure that the necessary information is accumulated and that this information is correct and valid. Only if this is the case should one move on to the next phase. Figure 13.1 shows the stages of ISD and lists some of the important events in the VESUB project. Each of these events is discussed in the following sections.

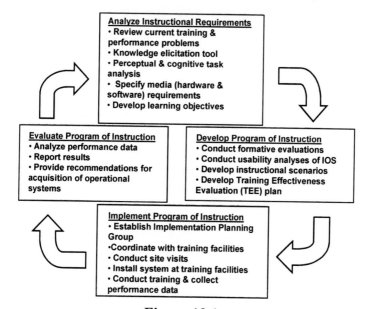

Figure 13.1:
ISD Stages and Important Events in the VESUB Project

Stage 1: Analyze Instructional Requirements

<u>Review Current Training and Performance Problems</u>

The analysis phase began with a review of the submarine surfaced ship handling problem and how training was currently delivered. Interviews with submarine Commanding Officers, Executive Officers, and senior enlisted personnel and reviews of submarine ship handling incidents (e.g., collisions, groundings, close calls with other ships, etc.) provided the initial data to document the need for a new training approach. This need can be summarized as follows. Land-based simulator facilities already existed for training Submarine Piloting and Navigation teams. However, these systems did not provide detailed harbor and channel ship handling training for the Officer of the Deck (OOD), the individual in charge of making critical ship handling decisions when surfaced. The OOD stands on the submarine bridge (on top of the tall conning tower) and issues commands to the helmsman to make

351

changes to the ships speed and direction based on what the OOD sees in the harbor channel. Other members of the navigation team (e.g., the navigator, contact coordinator, assistant navigator) also communicate with the OOD to provide important information. None of the other navigation team members can actually see the harbor (except through the periscope) because they are inside the submarine. Thus, the OOD's ship handling task is primarily perceptual (e.g., locating and identifying navigation aids) and cognitive (e.g., understanding the rules of the road for channel passage). It also requires sending and receiving correct communications with the navigation team.

Prior to this effort, OOD training was primarily obtained through on-the-job experience, which was adversely impacted by the operational constraints of the Submarine Force, and the limited surfaced steaming time of submarines. Therefore, an alternative, simulation-based training capability was needed. Figure 13.2 shows an artist's depiction of the planned VESUB system. It would consist of several components:

1. A simulated bridge, shown as the large box in which the trainee is standing.
2. A head-mounted display and head-tracking system, which could display a realistic, 360 degree representation of the harbor channel (shown in the large window on the left side of Figure 13.2).
3. An instructor/operator station, used to author training scenarios and monitor training sessions.

Knowledge Elicitation Tool

A rudimentary feasibility demonstration system that was developed in 1994 under another research project was used as a knowledge elicitation tool to help specify the requirements for the VESUB technology demonstration system. The feasibility demonstration system included a very simplified harbor scene, which was viewed through a low-resolution head-mounted display. Submarine experts were brought into the laboratory and afforded the opportunity to try out a virtual environment using the feasibility

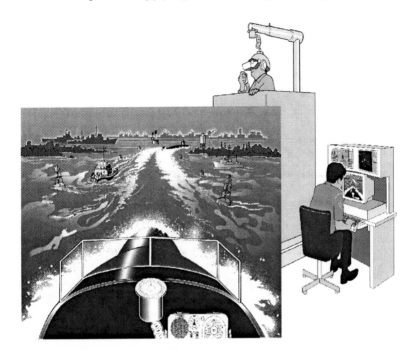

Figure 13.2:
Artist's Depiction of the VESUB system

demonstration system. After they experienced the virtual environment, detailed functional requirements for the VESUB system were elicited from these experts using questionnaires and interviews. This approach yielded baseline requirements, but did not provide enough details about the task and the media (hardware and software) necessary to support it. Therefore, a more extensive perceptual and cognitive task analysis was conducted.

Conduct Perceptual and Cognitive Task Analysis

A submarine, when surfaced, must perform according to the ship handling procedures followed by surface ships. Each submarine Commanding Officer (CO) must evaluate the performance of junior officers (JOs) prior to certifying them as qualified Officers of the Deck (OODs). Submarine COs were interviewed to help the research team understand how they determined that a JO was qualified as OOD. In almost every case, the COs responded that their personnel were qualified when they had developed the "Seaman's Eye." This concept was, therefore, used as the keystone for the analysis of the training task.

The way the submarine experts used the term "Seaman's Eye" made it clear to the research team that it was composed of both perceptual and cognitive components. Prior to interactions with additional submarine experts, the following definition of "Seaman's Eye" was developed to guide the perceptual and cognitive task analysis.

> *Seaman's Eye:*   The total situation
> *awareness of the ship handling*
> *environment and the ability to safely*
> *maneuver the vessel in all conditions.*

"Seaman's Eye" includes situation awareness as an integral component. Situation awareness has been defined as "the perception of the elements in the environment within a volume of time and space, the comprehension of their meaning, and the projection of their status in the near future" (Endsley, 1988, p. 97). This implies that in order to develop good situation awareness (e.g., "Seaman's Eye"), the individual must develop a mental model of his own ship, other ships, the environment, and the task (e.g., how to safely make a turn). Rouse and Morris (1986) define a mental model as a "mechanism whereby humans generate descriptions of system purpose and form, explanations of system functioning and observed system states, and predictions of future system states" (p. 360). To construct a mental model that is accurate and complete, the individual must perceive the information available in the environment (perception), and process the information to assess the current status of the environment and project the future status of the environment (cognition). The quality of an individual's situation awareness is directly dependent upon the degree of completeness and accuracy of the mental model that has been developed. The more accurate the mental model, the better the individual will be able to process critical information in an efficient and effective manner. Task performance follows a similar progression; a more accurate and complete mental model of the environment and task should lead to improved task performance. The goal of any training system (including VESUB) should be to enhance the individual's mental model of the task situation.

With this goal in mind, it was decided to use the definition of "Seaman's Eye" as the initial guide for the development of hardware, software, and instructional approaches for VESUB. However, the definition was still too general to meet this goal. Therefore, based on the results of focused group discussions with additional submarine experts, a listing of the perceptual and cognitive components that make up "Seaman's Eye" was developed. This listing is shown in Table 13.3.

Table 13.3:
Components of "Seaman's Eye"

PERCEPTUAL COMPONENTS
1P. Locating and Identifying Navigation Aids
2P. Judging Distance
3P. Identifying the Start and Completion of Turns
4P. Locating, Identifying, and Avoiding Obstacles
5P. Sense of Ship's Responsiveness
6P. Recognizing Environmental Conditions
7P. Recognizing Equipment Failures
8P. Detecting and Filtering Communications

COGNITIVE COMPONENTS
1C. Understanding the Relationship of Visual Cues to their Representations on Charts
2C. Understanding Relative Size and Height/Range Relationships, and Angle on the Bow (AOB)
3C. Understanding Advance and Transfer
4C. Understanding the Effects of Tides, Currents, Wind, and Seas
5C. Understanding Rules of the Road
6C. Understanding Relative Motion (Direction and Speed)
7C. Understanding Methods to Differentiate and Prioritize Traffic Contacts
8C. Understanding Ship's Operation Under Harbor Directives
9C. Understanding Methods to Deal with Uncooperative Traffic
10C. Understanding Correct Operation of Ship's Systems
11C. Understanding When and How to Take Corrective Actions
12C. Understanding Effective Communication Procedures

Specify Media Requirements

The information generated using the knowledge elicitation tool and the results of the perceptual and cognitive task analysis were used to specify the media (hardware and software) requirements for VESUB. The requirements (Tenney, Briscoe, Pew, Bradley, Seamon, & Hays, 1996) were used as guidance for the design and development of the VESUB technology demonstration system.

The perceptual components of "Seaman's Eye" were used to determine the hardware requirements for the system. For example, the requirements to locate and identify navigation aids (1P) and to judge distance (2P) required that the trainee be able to see the objects at great distances. This necessitated the use of a high-resolution head-mounted display. Because navigation aids are sometimes located behind the submarine, it was necessary to provide the trainee with a 360-degree visual environment. This required the use of head tracking and rapid refresh rate of the visual scene. Additional details on the determination of VESUB hardware and software components can be found in Hays, Castillo, Bradley, and Seamon (1997).

Develop Learning Objectives

The results of the perceptual and the cognitive task analysis (the components of "Seaman's Eye") were also used to develop and organize the learning objectives for trainees using the VESUB system. These learning objectives are shown in Table 13.4.

Stage 2: Development

Conduct Formative Evaluations

Formative evaluations of the VESUB system began when the first version was delivered and installed in the laboratory. Each improvement in the hardware or software was evaluated against the functional requirements (Tenney, et al., 1996) and the learning objectives. In addition, eleven submarine experts were brought to the laboratory for extensive exposure to the developing VESUB system. Their recommendations and those of the research team were

Table 13.4:
VESUB Learning Objectives

PERCEPTUAL COMPONENTS	LEARNING OBJECTIVES
1P. Locating and Identifying Navigation Aids	• The trainee shall be able to locate navigation aids when referenced by the Navigator. • The trainee shall be able to recognize navigation aids in the visual field and relate them to the chart.
2P. Judging Distance	• The trainee shall be able to accurately judge distances to: navigation aids, contacts, and landmarks. • The trainee shall be able to judge distances relative to track. • The trainee shall be able to verify known distances using environmental cues and chart work. • The trainee shall be able to maintain the ship within the acceptable limits of the channel.
3P. Identifying Start and Completion of Turns	• The trainee shall be able to determine relative and true directions on a compass. • The trainee shall be able to determine relative bearings to the navigational aid to be used for turn bearings. • The trainee shall check turn bearings when turning. • The trainee shall be able to recognize when the ship is clear to turn (e.g., when buoys are in line).
4P. Locating, Identifying, and Avoiding Obstacles	• The trainee shall look far enough ahead to evaluate contacts early. • The trainee shall be able to recognize new contacts prior to being informed of the contact. • The trainee shall be able to recognize relative directions and motions. • The trainee shall be able to locate, identify, classify, and differentiate between various types of contacts and other obstacles (e.g., debris, aquatic animals). • The trainee shall take early and effective actions to avoid obstacles or lessen their negative outcomes.

Table 13.4:
(continued)

PERCEPTUAL COMPONENTS	LEARNING OBJECTIVES
5P. Sense of Ship's Responsiveness	• The trainee shall understand the ship's capabilities and limitations, including: advance and transfer, speed at various engine orders, loss of steerage way, distance to stop or reverse course.
6P. Recognizing Environmental Conditions	• The trainee shall be able to accurately estimate: sea state, cloud cover, direction and velocity of current, wind direction and speed, and time of day. • The trainee shall be able to accurately judge the state of visibility.
7P. Recognizing Equipment Failures	• The trainee shall stay alert for equipment failures. • The trainee shall regularly monitor rudders, indicators, and other equipment.
8P. Detecting & Filtering Communications	• The trainee shall be able to recognize communication sources and proper or improper repeat backs.
COGNITIVE COMPONENTS	**LEARNING OBJECTIVES**
1C. Understanding the Relationship of Visual Cues to Chart(s)	• The trainee shall be familiar with all the navigation aids to be used. • The trainee shall understand how to read ranges (fore and aft). • The trainee shall understand how to determine if the ship is left/right of track versus left/right of range. • The trainee shall understand when to attempt to drive the ship in the center of the channel. • The trainee shall understand buoyage systems (e.g., IALA "A" and "B" systems). • The trainee shall understand the inaccuracy of buoys. • The trainee shall understand the accuracy/inaccuracy of Fix information.

Table 13.4:
(continued)

COGNITIVE COMPONENTS	LEARNING OBJECTIVES
2C. Understanding Relative Size and Height/ Range Relationships, and Angle on the Bow	• The trainee shall understand how to determine contact mast head height. • The trainee shall know his height of eye. • The trainee shall know how to determine: size and distance relationships to navigation aids, contact length, distance to the horizon, hull down, and angle on the bow.
3C. Understanding Advance and Transfer	• The trainee shall understand the concepts of advance and transfer. • The trainee shall understand ship characteristics like tactical diameter of own ship. • The trainee shall understand the criticality of turning the vessel the wrong way. • The trainee shall understand the principles of conning the ship through turns. • The trainee shall understand when to turn the ship based on the use of a slide bar. • The trainee shall understand the principles of compensation. • The trainee shall compensate for set and drift when making turns. • The trainee shall check that the next channel is clear prior to turning. • The trainee shall not drive based solely on the Navigator's recommendations.
4C. Understanding the Effects of Tides, Currents, Wind, and Seas	• The trainee shall understand how the wind affects the height of seas. • The trainee shall understand that current and tides tend in the direction of the natural geography. • The trainee shall understand the relationship of the estimated winds associated with various sea heights. • The trainee shall understand that sea height influenced by wind speed can give false indications of the actual direction of currents.

Table 13.4:
(continued)

COGNITIVE COMPONENTS	LEARNING OBJECTIVES
5C. Understanding Rules of the Road	• The trainee shall comprehend the criticality of Rules of the Road. • The trainee shall correctly exercise Rules of the Road by taking appropriate actions in: overtaking, meeting, passing, and crossing situations. • The trainee shall understand the rules for sound signals and responses. • The trainee shall take appropriate action when nearing a bend in the channel. • The trainee shall take appropriate actions to avoid collisions.
6C. Understanding Relative Motion (Direction & Speed)	• The trainee shall understand true and relative bearing and their significance. • The trainee shall be able to convert relative to true and true to relative. • The trainee shall be able to determine the relative direction of contacts. • The trainee shall be able to determine own ship's motion relative to fixed objects.
7C. Understanding Methods to Differentiate and Prioritize Traffic Contacts	• The trainee shall be able to classify, differentiate, and prioritize various types of contacts and other obstacles. • The trainee shall understand safe distances to hazards. • The trainee shall be able to effectively determine contacts of interest. • The trainee shall correctly assign master control numbers to contacts of concern. • The trainee shall maintain awareness of contacts in relation to own ship. • The trainee shall prompt personnel for supporting information. • The trainee shall drop contacts of interest when no longer of concern. • The trainee shall be able to correctly determine contact's angle on the bow.

Table 13.4:
(continued)

COGNITIVE COMPONENTS	LEARNING OBJECTIVES
8C. Understanding Ship's Operation Under Harbor Directives	• The trainee shall understand harbor, port limitations, restrictions, & regulations.
9C. Understanding Methods to Deal with Uncooperative Traffic	• The trainee shall take proper and effective actions to avoid encounters with uncooperative traffic.
10C. Understanding Correct Operation of Ship's Systems	• The trainee shall understand the correct operation of bridge equipment. • The trainee shall verify rudder orders by: visually checking the rudder and the bridge suitcase indicator. • The trainee shall verify engine orders by: checking the bridge suitcase indicator and observing screw wash.
11C. Understanding When and How to Take Corrective Actions	• The trainee shall understand emergency operating procedures.
12C. Understanding Effective Communication Procedures	• The trainee shall speak clearly. • The trainee shall use correct terminology. • The trainee shall effectively communicate with each station using required terminology. • The trainee shall acknowledge all reports and repeat backs. • The trainee shall inform appropriate personnel about his actions. • The trainee shall not clutter the circuits.

communicated to the hardware and software developers and implemented into subsequent versions of the system. The formative evaluations focused on both the functionality of the trainee interface (e.g., the fidelity of objects in the visual scene or the functionality of the voice recognition system) and the usability of the Instructor-Operator Station (see below). Although the initial hardware configuration of VESUB was not significantly changed, the formative evaluations led to many improvements in software and scenario authoring capabilities.

Conduct Usability Analyses of Instructor/Operator Station

The instructor/operator station (IOS) is a critical component of any simulation-based training system. The IOS is the tool for constructing instructional scenarios, monitoring learner performance, and providing instructional feedback to the learner. Thus, the usability of the IOS was an important consideration in the development of VESUB.

Students from a graduate level "Human-computer Interaction Design and Evaluation" class at the University of Central Florida assisted in the usability analysis of the VESUB IOS. Students worked in teams, evaluating the IOS using Nielsen's (1993) usability design criteria. These analyses and those of the research team identified both major and minor usability design violations. These violations were communicated to the system developer and documented in two reports (Hays, Seamon, & Bradley, 1997; Hays, 1999). Those violations that could be corrected within the budget and schedule of the project were completed. Other violations had to await the development of the operational VESUB systems after completion of the research effort.

Develop Instructional Scenarios

The development of the instructional scenarios to be used in the training effectiveness evaluation (TEE) followed an "event-based" training approach (Johnston, Cannon-Bowers, & Smith-Jentsch, 1995; Dwyer, Fowlkes, Oser, & Lane, 1997; Dwyer, Oser, Salas, & Fowlkes). "The cornerstone of event-based training is a process-based performance measurement system that is linked closely to training objectives that are embedded in pre-specified scenario events" (Johnston, et al., 1995, p. 275). This approach has been used for training tasks in a variety of areas, including: shipboard command teams (Johnston, et al., 1995), aviation team coordination (Fowlkes, Lane, Salas, Franz, & Oser, 1994), and multi-service team training, distributed among multiple remote sites (Dwyer, et al., 1997; 1999). A similar approach was followed in the development and construction of the scenarios used in the TEE.

The cognitive and perceptual components of "Seaman's Eye" (Table 13. 3) and the training objectives derived from them (Table 13.4) were used to develop the ship handling skill training events for the TEE scenarios. Seven performance skill areas were identified that would include the performance variables to be measured in the TEE. These seven skills areas were:

1. Position Determination
2. Contact Management
3. General Ship Handling
4. Emergency Operations
5. Incorrect Report Recognition
6. Communications
7. Rules of the Road

Three scenarios were developed. One scenario was designed to familiarize the learners with the capabilities of the VESUB system and help them become comfortable with the head-mounted display. This scenario also provided an opportunity for the learners to practice communication tasks and become familiar with the voice recognition and voice synthesis systems. Two comparable scenarios were developed (in-bound and out-bound) for training and testing of learners. Both of these scenarios included the same events (e.g., ferry boat crossing their path). They also included scripts for instructional interventions (used in the training scenario). Complete scripts can be found in Hays, Vincenzi, Seamon, & Bradley, 1998).

<u>Develop Training Effectiveness Evaluation (TEE) Plan</u>

The training effectiveness evaluation (TEE) of VESUB technology demonstration system was essential to secure support for development and installation of operational systems. Thus, the research team spent several months developing a plan for the TEE. The instructional objectives and the event-based scenarios to be used in the TEE had already been developed. The next step was to determine how to collect empirical performance data and create data collection forms.

<u>Operational Definitions of Dependant Variables</u>. Specific operational definitions of dependant variables were required so empirical data could be collected to demonstrate performance improvements as a result of instruction using VESUB. Table 13.5 shows the dependant variables for each of the seven skill areas listed above. The table provides the operational definition of each variable and also shows how each dependant variable was related to the perceptual and cognitive components of "Seaman's Eye." Each

Table 13.5:
Operational Definitions of Dependent Variables for VESUB TEE

Dependant Variable	Operational Definition of Variable	Related "Seaman's Eye" Components
	Position Determination	
Position of Own Ship Across Track	Difference between the actual starting position (right or left of track) and the reported position, as determined by use of navigation aids and range markers.	**1P**, **2P**, **1C**, 2C
Position of Own Ship Along Track	Rating of subject's determination of Own Ship's position along the track (satisfactory = within 200y of actual position).	**1P**, **2P**, **1C**, 2C
	Contact Management	
Contacts Found	Ratio of the total number of contacts found to the total number of contacts available.	2P, **4P**, 2C
Contacts "Of Concern"	Ratio of the total number of contacts identified as being of concern to the total number actually of concern, as determined by subject matter experts.	2P, **4P**, 2C, 5C, 6C, **7C**
	General Ship Handling	
Turning Commands	Ratio of the number of correct commands given by subject when making turns to the total possible number of correct turning commands for all turns during the entire scenario.	1P, 2P, **3P**, **5P**, 1C, **3C**, 4C, 10C, **12C**
Checking the Rudder	Ratio of the number of times the subject visually checked the rudder after giving a rudder order to the total number of possible visual checks after rudder orders during the entire scenario.	**10C**
Checking Ranges	Ratio of the number of times the subject visually checked the range markers to the total possible number of times ranges should have been checked during the entire scenario, as determined by subject matter experts.	**1P**, 10C

Table 13.5:
(continued)

Dependant Variable	Operational Definition of Variable	Related "Seaman's Eye" Components
Emergency Operations		
Man Overboard Reaction Time	Time to begin corrective actions after hearing report that a man was overboard.	8P, 6C, **11C**, **12C**
Man Overboard Commands	Number of correct commands given and actions performed during MOB event.	6C, **11C**, 12C
Yellow Sounding	Total number of correct actions taken by the subject during Yellow Sounding event.	**1P**, 2P, 8P, 4C, 10C, **11C**, 12C
Incorrect Report Recognition		
Incorrect Report Recognition	Total number of correct actions taken and commands issued by the subject when given an incorrect position report by the Navigator.	**1P**, 2P, **8P**, **11C**, 12C
Communications		
Commands to Get Underway	Ratio of number of correct commands given when getting own ship underway to the total possible number of correct commands to get own ship underway during the entire scenario.	5P, 4C, **10C**, **12C**
Acknowledge Reports	Ratio of the number of scheduled reports that are acknowledged by the subject to the total possible number of required acknowledgments	**8P**, 10C, **12C**
Use Station Identifiers	Number of times the trainee failed to use station identifiers when issuing commands.	10C, **12C**
Rules of the Road		
Ferry Passage	The total number of correct commands given during the crossing situation with the ferry.	2P, **4P**, 5P, 8P, 2C, **5C**, 6C, 7C, **8C**, 10C, 11C, **12C**

dependant variable involved multiple perceptual and cognitive components. The components that are most related to each dependant variable are shown in boldface.

Stage 3: Implementation

The implementation of the VESUB technology demonstration system was not intended to be permanent. It was temporarily installed to support the TEE. However, even this temporary installation illustrates some of the challenges that must be overcome to implement any instructional product or system.

Establish Implementation Planning Group

An Implementation Planning Group, consisting of active duty submarine personnel, government engineers, and instructional developers (either working at training facilities or higher echelon commands) was established. This group helped identify issues that had to be addressed and requirements that had to be met in order to install VESUB at Navy training facilities for the TEE. Regular project reports kept the group informed of important developmental and evaluation issues and solicited assistance when required. The group also helped develop plans for future implementation of operational VESUB systems. The group served as interface between the research team and the training facilities and helped develop the schedule for the TEE.

Coordinate with Training Facilities

The TEE plan called for installation and evaluation of VESUB at one or more Navy training facilities with active duty submarine personnel. Although the TEE only required the installation of the VESUB system for a short duration (3 weeks at each site), extensive coordination was required. Many of the installation and coordination issues for this short-term installation must also be addressed for the "permanent" installation of instructional systems.

The first step was to obtain permission from the Commanding Officer of each training facility to install the system and to obtain the time and expertise of instructional personnel at the facility. Permissions to conduct the TEE at two training facilities, the Navy Submarine Training Facility, Norfolk, VA and the Naval Submarine School, Groton, CT were obtained. The next step was to visit the facilities and determine where VESUB could be installed.

Conduct Site Visits

Several important supporting requirements had to be met in order to successfully install VESUB at the Navy training facilities. These included identification of enough space to install the system, relative isolation of this space to avoid distractions during the TEE, and access to 220v power. Two site visits were made to each site. During these visits, coordination was improved with training facility personnel and in-service engineers (responsible for the care and maintenance of all instructional simulators at each site). With the help of these individuals, a room that met the needs of the TEE was identified. Floor plans showing all power access points and locations for each VESUB component were drawn. These floor plans served as guide for the VESUB installation team at each site.

Install VESUB System

A team of computer scientists and engineers installed the VESUB system in the locations identified during the site visits. The installation and system testing required approximately two days at each site. Once the VESUB system was installed and fully tested, data collection could begin.

Conduct Training and Collect Performance Data

The TEE of the VESUB technology demonstration system was conducted at the Submarine Training Facility in Norfolk, VA during January of 1998 and at the Naval Submarine School in Groton, CT during March 1998.

Method. The VESUB research team consisted of two data collectors, two instructors, and one research coordinator. The data collectors recorded all subject actions on data collection forms (available in Hays, et al., 1998). The instructors operated the VESUB system and role played as members of the navigation team (except for the computer-generated virtual navigator) during all scenarios. They also provided instructional interventions at selected times during the training scenario, and provided debriefings after the training scenario. The research coordinator supervised the other members of the research team to ensure that all events occurred as specified in the research plan. Simulator side effects data were collected using a modified form of the simulation sickness questionnaire (Kennedy, Lane, Berbaum, & Lilienthal, 1993).

Forty-one uniformed Navy personnel, with various levels of experience (novice to expert) served as subjects for the TEE. Each subject first participated in an orientation scenario to become familiar with the virtual environment and to practice voice commands to the virtual navigator. Next, subjects were randomly assigned to receive training on either an in-bound or out-bound scenario. After the training scenario and scenario debrief, the subjects were tested on the alternate scenario. Data were collected on 15 ship handling variables grouped into the seven skill categories discussed previously.

Stage 4: Evaluation

At the conclusion of the TEE at each site, all data collection forms were packaged and shipped to the VESUB laboratory for analysis.

Analyze Performance Data

A mixed factorial analysis of variance (ANOVA) design, with experience as the between-subjects variable and scenario session (training and testing) as the within subjects variable, found significant learning (skill improvements) for all experience levels (0 to 14 years) on eleven of the fifteen variables ($p < .01$). For example, trainees improved:

- 39% in checking range markers
- 33% in visually checking the rudder
- 13% in issuing correct turning commands
- 57% in contact management skills
- 44% in reaction time during a man overboard (MOB) event
- 29% in using correct commands during the MOB event

♦ 40% in using correct commands during a yellow sounding event

No major simulator side effects problems were found during the TEE, even though trainees averaged almost two hours in the head-mounted display.

Report Results

The results of the VESUB TEE were documented in a technical report (Hays, et al, 1998) and a journal article (Hays & Vincenzi, 2000). A project summary report (Seamon, Bradley, Hays, Vincenzi, 1999) described important events and issues that could help guide future system developers.

Provide Recommendations for Acquisition of Operational Systems

The successful VESUB technology demonstration led Navy policy makers to fund the acquisition of five operational systems, called VESUB 2000. Five systems were developed and installed at the five major submarine training facilities. The results of the VESUB project were used as guides to help the acquisition team. The following recommendations from VESUB TEE and summary reports have been adapted for general workplace instruction:

1. *VESUB provided effective ship handling training.* Data from the TEE on eleven of fifteen variables showed significant learning in a variety of ship handling skill areas. It can be said with confidence that VESUB technologies can provided effective training for ship handling and related tasks. However, a training system is far more than just technologies. It cannot be stated too strongly that a training system will only be effective if it is used correctly. Care should be taken to implement instructional technologies, like those in VESUB, in a manner that is consistent with known learning principles.

2. *All experience levels benefited from VESUB training.* Data on almost every variable showed that trainees with every level of experience could benefit from training in VESUB. Very inexperienced trainees, those that had never been on the bridge of a

submarine, experienced the feelings and events of a real-time, high fidelity simulation that provided most of the cues that must be dealt with in the real world. The experienced trainees, even those with over 10 years experience, showed significant improvement in their ship handling skills. Thus, instructional media (like VESUB) can be used for both initial and refresher instruction. However, care must be taken to tailor the instruction to the needs of the learners, whatever their experience level.

3. *Event-based curriculum development was recommended.* Any training system will only be effective if it is used in a well-designed instructional curriculum. For the purposes of the TEE, an abbreviated curriculum was developed to target several important skill areas. An event-based approach was used to design scenarios that allowed the trainees to experience the critical cues required for ship handling tasks and to practice the skills required to successfully accomplish them. Curriculum developers (or instructors) should target the critical skills required to support all elements of the target task and they should provide the scenario events and the instructional interventions, which will allow trainees to learn and practice the required skills.

4. *Instructor training is essential.* We cannot expect workplace instructors to be expert instructors unless they are provided with the necessary support to reach this goal. A well-designed instructor/operator station can help by making the instructor's job easier (see Hays, et al., 1997). This alone is not enough. New instructional technologies come with new responsibilities for the instructor. They need to understand the capabilities of the instructional system and how to use these capabilities to achieve the best results. On-line help and advice can be a part of this training as can a well designed training system instructor's manual. However, these are not sufficient. Instructors must be trained to understand that learning is a multi-step process. Each learner must receive

instruction, be allowed to practice relevant skills, and be given constructive performance feedback. If instructors learn how to excel in all these areas, learning will be more effective.

The first VESUB 2000 system (Device 21F35) was delivered to the Navy Submarine School, Groton, CT in early 2001. Over the next three years four additional VESUB 2000 systems were delivered to four other submarine training facilities. The devices are now in use and have been enthusiastically accepted by the submarine training community.

A Tool to Evaluate Instructional Quality

Over the years, a variety of guidance documents have been produced to help instructional developers create high quality instructional products (e.g., Aagard & Braby, 1976; Merrill, 1997). It is often difficult to determine if these types of guidance documents achieve their goals. Recently, Hays, Stout, and Ryan-Jones (2005) developed a tool that can help instructional developers and instructional program managers determine the quality of their computer- and web-delivered instructional products. The Instructional Quality Evaluation Tool consists of a series of evaluation criteria and rating scales that address the major factors that influence the quality of instructional products. The evaluation criteria (listed in Table 13.6) are divided into two major sections: 1) instructional features evaluation criteria and 2) user interface evaluation criteria. Within each of these sections, criteria address specific instructional requirements. Likert-type rating scales for each criterion are used to help standardize evaluations. Two examples or the rating scales are shown in Figure 13.3.

The Tool is focused on computer-delivered instruction, without the presence of a live instructor. However, many of the criteria are also relevant to classroom instruction with a live instructor, as well as other forms of instruction, such as live, video-based lectures and demonstrations. Ongoing efforts are expanding the Tool to address these other forms of instruction.

Table 13.6:
Instructional Quality Evaluation Criteria

Instructional Features Criteria	User-Interface Criteria
1. Instructional Content 1.a. The content is presented in a logical manner 1.b. The purpose of the course is clearly stated 1.c. The instructional objectives are clearly stated 1.d. The content supports each and every instructional objective 1.e. The content is free of errors 1.f. The content is job-relevant 1.g. The "authority" for the content is clearly stated 1.h. there are clear indications of prerequisites 1.i. There are clear indications of completed topics 1.j. Sources for additional information are available	**5. Navigation and Operation** 5.a. User interface makes course structure explicit 5.b. tutorial is available to explain navigation and operation features 5.c. Help function is available to explain navigation and operation features 5.d. Includes all necessary navigation and operation controls 5.e. Navigation and operation controls are clearly and consistently labeled 5.f. Navigation and operation controls are located in a consistent place 5.g. Navigation and operation controls function consistently 5.h. Course is designed to show learner's location 5.i. Course is designed to show how learner arrived at location 5.j. Course is designed to show estimated time required for each module
2. Instructional Activities 2.a. Activities are relevant (all support learning objectives and job requirements) 2.b. The learner is required to interact with content 2.c. Instruction is engaging (attracts and maintains the learner's attention) 2.d. Instructional media directly support learning activities	**6. Content Presentation** 6.a. There are no sensory conflicts 6.b. All media are clear and sharp 6.c. Presentations are aesthetically pleasing 6.d. Multi-modal presentation of content is used 6.e. Multi-media presentation of content is used 6.f. Media are easy to use 6.g. External hyperlinks are kept to a minimum

Table 13.6:
(continued)

Instructional Features Criteria	User-Interface Criteria
3. Performance Assessment 3.a. Assessments are relevant 3.b. Assessments are logical 3.c. assessments are varied	**7. Installation and Registration** 7.a. Course does not require installation or learners can install the course without assistance 7.b. Minimal "plug-ins" are required 7.c. "Optimization" test is available 7.d. Technical support is available 7.e. Registration is simple and straightforward (or not required)
4. Performance Feedback 4.a. Feedback is timely 4.b. Feedback is meaningful 9related to objectives) 4.c. Positive reinforcement is provided for correct responses 4.d. remediation is provided for incorrect responses	

Concluding Remarks

The purpose of this book is to provide a scientific perspective on the science of learning by using systems theory to organize and integrate the large body of empirical data on learning processes and instructional approaches. It also provided an overview of the scientific method, scientific thinking, and applications of the scientific method to the study of learning and the development of instruction. A scientific approach to the learning enterprise is vitally needed because too many instructional programs are based on traditions, opinions, and anecdotes (Mayer, 2000; Richardson 2002).

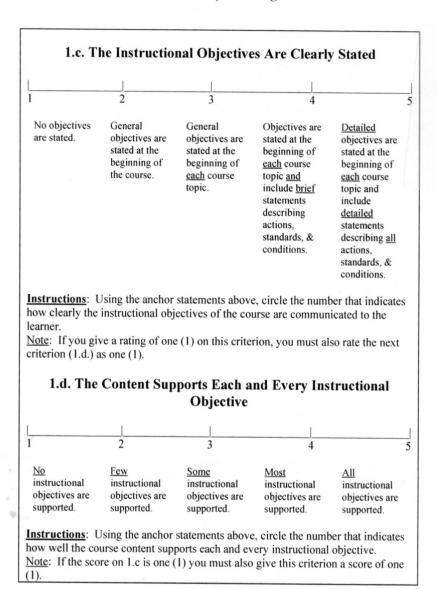

1.c. The Instructional Objectives Are Clearly Stated

1	2	3	4	5
No objectives are stated.	General objectives are stated at the beginning of the course.	General objectives are stated at the beginning of each course topic.	Objectives are stated at the beginning of each course topic and include brief statements describing actions, standards, & conditions.	Detailed objectives are stated at the beginning of each course topic and include detailed statements describing all actions, standards, & conditions.

Instructions: Using the anchor statements above, circle the number that indicates how clearly the instructional objectives of the course are communicated to the learner.

Note: If you give a rating of one (1) on this criterion, you must also rate the next criterion (1.d.) as one (1).

1.d. The Content Supports Each and Every Instructional Objective

1	2	3	4	5
No instructional objectives are supported.	Few instructional objectives are supported.	Some instructional objectives are supported.	Most instructional objectives are supported.	All instructional objectives are supported.

Instructions: Using the anchor statements above, circle the number that indicates how well the course content supports each and every instructional objective.

Note: If the score on 1.c is one (1) you must also give this criterion a score of one (1).

**Figure 13.3:
Two Example Scales from the Instructional Quality
Evaluation Tool**

The summaries of empirical data were organized and integrated using two system-based models: the systems model of the learner and the communication-oriented model of the learning system. These two systems were discussed as subsystems of various larger suprasystems that may exert conflicting forces on their processes and sometimes negatively compromise the effectiveness of instruction. The goal of these integrative summaries and discussions is to help the reader transform this large body of learning data into a "body of knowledge" that can help them develop the tools and world-view that will help them be more successful in whatever role they play in the instructional enterprise, whether they are scientists, instructors, instructional developers, or managers of instructional programs.

The following concluding remarks summarize some of the important points and recommendations made in the body of the book. It is hoped that the reader will apply the recommendations become an advocate for the use science and scientific thinking in all aspects of learning and instruction. The reader can become a positive force to improve the quality and effectiveness of instruction by using the scientific method and scientific thinking as their guide.

There is a Need for Scientific Approaches to Learning and Instruction

Many persons advocate scientifically based education reform (e.g., U.S. Congress, 2001; Slavin, 2002), but few understand science and how to apply the scientific method. Furthermore, many people do not think scientifically when they make decisions about learning and instruction (e.g., Mayer, 2000). The discussions of science and the scientific method (Chapter 1), ISD and systems theory (Chapter 2), and the system-based overviews of learning research illustrated how science and scientific thinking are used to help us understand learning and instruction. The summaries of instructional media research illustrate some of the tools that can help improve instructional communication by focusing on the learner and the barriers (screens) that can distort or block instruction.

Science is Both a Method and a Way of Thinking

If science is to have a positive effect on the educational enterprise, it is important that all persons involved in the development and evaluation of instruction or the generation of data on learning processes think more scientifically. This is of course true for the scientists who conduct learning research and evaluate the effectiveness of instructional approaches. These scientists need to be caretakers of the scientific method by ensuring that no corners are cut and that all the tools of science are applied. They also need to step back from their narrow "area of investigation" to view learning as part of multiple interacting systems.

It may be even more important for policy makers and instructional program managers to think scientifically. Program managers and policy makers are targets for various advocates, salespersons, and individuals with personal agendas about instructional products and approaches. They need to be skeptical about the effectiveness of these products and should require demonstrations of their effectiveness before they are adopted. They also need to understand that implementing a local change is rarely an effective approach to improve an instructional program. They need to be aware of the conflicting system forces that can distort or negate the effectiveness of any instructional program and ensure that these forces be identified and managed.

ISD is Derived from the Scientific Method and Works if it is "Worked" Scientifically

One of the myths discussed in Chapter 3 is that ISD doesn't work. As a derivative of the scientific method, ISD is an iterative, cyclic process that should be constantly evaluated, corrected, and improved. As illustrated in the VESUB example, ISD is effective if it is managed scientifically. This means that the data required in each ISD stage should be generated and evaluated using the scientific method. No ISD stage should be started until all of the necessary information has been transmitted from the preceding phase. When the "final" phase is completed, it should be regarded as the beginning of the next ISD cycle. Like science, no ISD product is ever finished. We can always improve instruction by using science and ISD to focus on the forces that distort or block instruction. Information about instructional approaches needs to be exchanged in an open, scientific manner. Collaboration is the essence of science and should also be embraced by everyone involved in the instructional enterprise.

Instruction is a Form of Communication

The learning system model (presented in Chapter 7) focused on instruction as a form of communication. The internal and external screens that can block or distort instructional information must be identified. Then these screens can be managed through the application of appropriate instructional strategies in the appropriate instructional context. Instructional can be delivered in classrooms, in the workplace, or in other locations. It can be delivered by an instructor, by a local computer, or distributed over the Internet. No matter which instructional context is chosen, the specific internal and external screens must be identified and managed.

The Learner is a System and is Part of a Larger Instructional System

The systems model of the learner illustrates how different learning processes interact within the learner. These interactions can support learning, but can also interfere with each other to the detriment of learning. The learner is also a subsystem of the larger instructional system. The communication of instructional information must be managed to reduce or eliminate internal and external screens that may block or distort the information. The application of instructional media can enhance the communication process, but only if these media are integrated into the instructional program.

Forces from different suprasystems influence the instructional system. These forces can either support or interfere with instructional communication. Awareness of the interactions at various system levels can help scientists, instructional developers, and program managers direct their attention and resources to make adjustments to these interactions that will support the learner.

In addition to understanding how the learner is influenced by various suprasystems, research is also needed to help us develop greater understanding of how the learner's various subsystem processes interact and influence each other. This understanding will help us manage the development and delivery of instructional information to enhance the learner's ability to incorporate the information into their personal memory structures. This, in turn, will help the learner improve his or her performance when using new skills and knowledge.

References

Aarntzen, D. (1993). Audio in courseware: Design knowledge issues. *Educational and Training Technology International, 30*(4), 354-366.

Aagard, J. A., & Braby, R. (1976). *Learning guidelines and algorithms for types of training objectives* (TAEG Report No. 23). Orlando, FL: Training analysis and Evaluation Group.

Adams, J. A., & Reynolds, B. (1954). Effect of shift in distribution of practice conditions following interpolated rest. *Journal of Experimental Psychology, 47*, 32-36.

Alba, J. W., & Hasher, L. (1983). Is memory schematic? *Psychological Bulletin, 93*(2), 203-231.

Alexander, P. A., Shallert, D. L., & Hare, V. C. (1991). Coming to terms: How researchers in learning and literacy talk about knowledge. *Review of Educational Research, 61*(3), 315-344.

American Psychological Association (1997). *Learner-centered psychological principles: A framework for school reform & redesign*. Retrieved on 1/11/2005 from http://www.apa.org/ed/lcpnewtext.html.

Andersen, J. F., & Andersen, P. A., & Jensen, A. D. (1979). The measurement of nonverbal immediacy. *Journal of Applied Communication Research, 7*, 153-180.

Andersen, P. A., & Andersen, J. F. (1982). Nonverbal immediacy in instruction. In L. Barker (Ed.), *Communication in the classroom* (pp. 98-120). Englewood Cliffs, NJ: Prentice Hall.

Anderson, J. R. (1993). Problem solving and learning. *American Psychologist, 48*, 35-44.

Anderson, J. R., & Bower, G. H. (1972). Recognition and retrieval processes in free recall. *Psychological Review, 79*(2), 97-123.

Anderson, J. R., & Bower, G. H. (1973). *Human associative memory*. Washington, DC: V. H. Winston & Sons.

Anderson, J. R., & Bower, G. H. (1974). A prepositional theory of recognition memory. *Memory and Cognition, 2*(3), 406-412.

Anderson, J. R., Greeno, J. G., Reder, L. M., & Simon, H. A. (2000). Perspectives on learning, thinking, and activity. *Educational Researcher, 29*(4), 11-13.

Anderson, R., Manoogian, S. T., & Reznick, J. S. (1976). The undermining and enhancing of intrinsic motivation in preschool children. *Journal of Personality and Social Psychology, 34*(5), 915-922.

Appleyard, D., & Craik, K. H. (1974). The Berkeley Environmental simulation Project: Its use in environmental impact assessment.

In T. G. Dickert & K. R. Domey (Eds.), *Environmental Impact assessment: Guidelines and commentary*. Berkeley, CA: University Extension, University of California.

Arnspiger, B. R., & Bowers, G. A. (1996, November). Integrated use of force training program. *FBI Law Enforcement Bulletin*, 1-7.

Aronson, E. (1968). Dissonance theory: Progress and problems. In R. P. Abelson, E. Aronson, W. J. McGuire, T. M. Newcomb, M.J. Rosenberg, & P. H. Tannenbaum (Eds.), *Theories of cognitive consistency: A sourcebook*. Chicago: Rand McNally.

Atkinson, F. D. (1977). Designing simulation/gaming activities: A systems approach. *Educational Technology, 17*(2), 38-43.

Atkinson, J. W. (1964). *An introduction to motivation*. New York: Van Nostrand Reinhold Co.

Atkinson, R. C. (1972). Ingredients for a theory of instruction. *American Psychologist, 27*, 921-931.

Atkinson, R. K. (2002). Optimizing learning from examples using animated pedagogical agents. *Journal of Educational Psychology, 94*(2), 416-427.

Atkinson, R. C., & Shiffrin, R. M. (1968). Human memory: A proposed system and its control processes. In K. W. Spence, & J. T. Spence (Eds.), *The psychology of learning and motivation: Advances in research and theory* (vol. 2), (pp. 89-195). New York: Academic Press.

Ausubel, D. P. (1960). The use of advance organizers in the learning and retention of meaningful verbal material. *Journal of Educational Psychology, 51*, 267-272.

Ausubel, D. P. (1963). *The psychology of meaningful verbal learning: An introduction to school learning*. New York: Grune and Straton.

Ausubel, D. P. (1968). *Educational psychology: A cognitive view*. New York: Holt, Rinehart, & Winston, Inc..

Ayres, J., Wilcox, A. K., & Ayres, D. M. (1995). Receiver apprehension: An explanatory model and accompanying research. *Communication Education, 44*, 223-235.

Babbie, E. R. (1975). *The practice of social research*. Belmont, CA: Wadsworth Publishing Company.

Baddeley, A. D. (1972). Retrieval rules and semantic coding in short-term memory. *Psychological Bulletin, 78*(5), 379-385.

Baddeley, A. D., (1986). *Working memory*. Oxford, England: Oxford University Press.

Baddeley, A. D. (1992). Working memory. *Science, 255*(5044), 556-559.

Baddeley, A. D. (1999). *Human memory*. Boston: Allyn and Bacon.

Bahrick, H. J. P., & Hall, L. K. (1991). Lifetime maintenance of high school mathematics content. *Journal of Experimental Psychology: General, 120*(1), 20-33.

References

Bandura, A. (1995). Exercise of personal and collective efficacy in changing societies. In A. Bandura (Ed.), *Self-efficacy in changing societies* (pp. 1-45). New York: Cambridge University Press.

Banich, M. T., & Heller, W. (1998). Evolving perspectives on lateralization of function. *Current Directions in Psychological Science, 7*(1), 1-2.

Barak, A., Engle, C., Katzir, L., & Fisher, W. A. (1988). Increasing the level of empathic understanding by means of a game. *Simulation & Games, 18*(4), 458-470.

Baranauskas, M. C. C., Neto, N. G. G., & Borges, M. A. F. (1999). Learning at work through a multi-user synchronous simulation game. In Proceedings of the PEG'99 Conference, Exeter, UK (pp. 137-144). Exeter, UK: University of Exeter. Retrieved on 8/15/2005 from http://www.ic.unicamp.br/~maborges/PEG99.htm.

Baron, R., Byrne, D., & Kantowitz, B. (1978). *Psychology: Understanding behavior*. Philadelphia: W. B. Saunders Company.

Barone, T. (2001). Science, art, and the predispositions of educational researchers. *Educational Researcher, 30*(7), 24-28.

Bartlett, F. C. (1932). *Remembering: A study in experimental and social psychology*. Cambridge: Cambridge University Press.

Baum, D. R., Riedel, S., Hays, R. T., & Mirabella, A. (1982). *Training effectiveness as a function of training device fidelity* (ARI Technical Report 593). Alexandria, VA: U.S. Army Research Institute.

Baylor, A. L., & Ryu, J. (2003). The effects of image and animation in enhancing pedagogical agent persona. *Journal of Educational computing Research, 28*(4), 373-394.

Beck, R. C. (1978). *Motivation: Theories and principles*. Englewood Cliffs, NJ: Prentice-Hall, Inc.

Belanich, J., Sibley, D. E., & Orvis, K. L. (2004). *Instructional characteristics and motivational features of a PC-based Game* (Research Report 1822). Alexandria, VA: U. S. Army Research Institute for the Behavioral and Social Sciences.

Bellman, R., & Zadeh, L. (1970). Decision-making in a fuzzy environment. *Management Science, 17*(4), B141-B164.

Bennell, C., & Jones, N. J. (2004). *The effectiveness of use of force simulation training: Final report*. Canada: Department of Psychology, Carleton University. Retrieved on 3/14/2005 from http://www.cprc.org/tr/tr_2005-01.pdf.

The Science of Learning

Benson, O. (1961). A simple diplomatic game. In J. N. Rosenau (Ed.), *International politics and foreign policy: A reader in research and theory* (pp. 504-511). New York: The Free Press of Glencoe, Inc.

Berlyne, D. E. (1960). *Conflict, arousal, and curiosity.* New York: McGraw-Hill.

Bertalanffy, L. v. (1968). *General systems theory.* New York: Braziller.

Beveridge, W. I. B. (1957). *The art of scientific investigation* (3rd ed.). New York: Vintage Books.

Bjork, R. A. (1975). Short-term storage: The ordered output of a central processor. In F. Restle, R. M. Shiffrin, N. J. Castellan, H. R. Lindeman, & D. B. Pisoni (Eds.), *Cognitive theory* (Vol. 1) (pp. 151-171). Hillside, NJ: Lawrence Erlbaum Associates.

Bjork, R. A., & Jongeward, R. H., Jr. (1975). *Rehearsal and mere rehearsal.* Unpublished manuscript.

Björk, S., & Holopainen, J. (2003, November). Describing games: An interaction-centric structural framework. Proceedings of the Level Up Conference. Utrecht, The Netherlands. Retrieved on 7/25/2005 from http://www.digra.org/dl/db/05150.10348.

Bilodeau, E. A., & Bilodeau, I. McD. (1961). Motor skills learning. *Annual review of Psychology, 12,* 243-280.

Bilodeau, E. A., Bilodeau, I. McD., & Schumsky, D. A. (1959). Some effects of introducing and withdrawing knowledge of results early and late in practice. *Journal of Experimental Psychology, 58*(2), 142-144.

Birch, H. G. (1945). The relation of previous experience to insightful problem-solving. *Journal of Comparative Psychology, 38,* 367-383.

Bishop, M. J., & Cates, W. M. (2001). Theoretical foundation for sound's use in multimedia instruction to enhance learning. *Educational Technology Research and Development, 49*(3), 5-22.

Bloom, B. S. (Ed.). (1956). *Taxonomy of educational objectives. Handbook I: Cognitive domain.* New York: David McKay.

Bloom, B. S. (1984). The 2 sigma problem: The search for methods of group instruction as effective as one-to-one tutoring. *Educational Researcher, 13*(6), 4-16.

Bousfield, W. A. (1953). The occurrence of clustering in the recall of randomly arranged associates. *Journal of General Psychology, 49,* 229-240.

Bousfield, W. A., & Cohen, B. H. (1955). The occurrence of clustering in the recall of randomly arranged words of different frequencies-of-usage. *Journal of General Psychology, 52,* 83-95.

References

Bower, G. H. (1981). Mood and memory. *American Psychologist, 36*(2), 129-148.

Bower, G. H. (2000). A brief history of memory research. In E. Tulving and F. I. M. Craik (Eds.), *The Oxford handbook of memory* (pp. 3-32). New York: Oxford University Press.

Boyd, S. (1992). *Training effectiveness of interactive video systems for the use of lethal force decision making.* Unpublished doctoral dissertation, University of San Francisco, CA.

Bradshaw, G. L., & Anderson, J. R. (1982). Elaborative encoding as an explanation of levels of processing. *Journal of Verbal Learning and Verbal Behavior, 21*, 165-174.

Bransford, J. D. (1979). *Human cognition: Learning, understanding and remembering.* Belmont, CA: Wadsworth.

Bransford, J. D., Barclay, J. R., & Franks, J. J. (1972). Sentence memory: A constructive versus interpretive approach. *Cognitive Psychology, 3*, 193-209.

Bransford, J. D., & Franks, J. J. (1971). The abstraction of linguistic ideas. *Cognitive Psychology, 2*, 331-350.

Branson, R. K., Rayner, G. T., Cox, J. L., Furman, J. P., King, F. J., & Hannum, W. H. (1975). *Interservice procedures for instructional systems development* (5 vols.), (TRADOC Pam 350-30 and NAVEDTR 106A). Ft. Monroe, VA: U.S. Army Training and Doctrine Command.

Bredemeier, M. E., Bernstein, G., & Oxman, W. (1982). BA FA BA FA and dogmatism/ethnocentrism: A study of attitude change through simulation-gaming. *Simulation & Gaming, 13*(4), 413-436.

Bredemeier, M. E., & Greenblat, C. S. (1981). The educational effectiveness of simulation games: A synthesis of findings. *Simulation & Games, 12*(3), 307-332. Also in C. S. Greenblat & R. D. Duke (Eds.). (1981). *Principles and practices of gaming-simulation.* (pp. 155-169). Beverly Hills, CA: Sage Publications.

Brewer, W. F., & Treyens, J. C. (1981). Role of schemata in memory for places. *Cognitive Psychology, 13*, 207-230.

Brewster, J. (1996). Computers in teaching: Teaching abnormal psychology in a multimedia classroom. *Teaching of Psychology, 23*(4), 249-252.

Bridgeman, P. W. (1927). *The logic of modern physics.* New York: Macmillan.

Briggs, G. E. (1954). Acquisition, extinction, and recovery functions in retroactive inhibition. *Journal of Experimental Psychology, 47*(5), 285-293.

Briggs, G. E. (1957). Retroactive inhibition as a function of the degree of original and interpolated learning. *Journal of Experimental Psychology, 53*(1), 60-67.

Bright, G. W., & Harvey, J. G. (1984). Computer games as instructional tools. *Computers in the Schools, 13*, 73-79.

Britton, B. K., Stimson, M., Stennett, B., & Gülgöz, S. (1998). Learning from instructional text: Test of an individual-differences model. *Journal of Educational Psychology, 90*(3), 476-291.

Broadbent, D. E. (1958). *Perception and communication.* Oxford: Pergamon Press.

Broadbent, D. E. (1963). Flow of information within the organism. *Journal of Verbal Learning and Verbal Behavior, 2*, 34-39.

Brown, L. T., & Weiner, E. A. (1979). *Introduction to psychology.* Cambridge, MA: Winthrop Publishers, Inc.

Brown, R., & McNeill, D. (1966). The "tip-of-the-tongue" phenomenon. *Journal of Verbal Learning and Verbal Behavior, 5*, 325-337.

Brown, S. J., Lieberman, D. A., Gemeny, B. A., Fan, Y. C., Wilson, D. M., & Pasta, D. J. (1997). Educational video game for juvenile diabetes: results of a controlled trial. *Medical Informatics, 22*(1), 77-89.

Browning, R. F., Ryan, L. E., Scott, P. G., & Smode, A. F. (1977). *Training effectiveness evaluation of Device 2F87F, P-3C Operational Flight Trainer* (TAEG report No. 42). Orlando, FL: Training Analysis and Evaluation Group.

Bryan, J. H., Redfield, J., & Mader, S. (1971). Words and deeds about altruism and the subsequent reinforcement power of the model. *Child Development, 42*(5), 1501-1508.

Byrne, D., Baskett, G. D., & Hodges, L. (1971). Behavioral indicator of interpersonal attraction. *Journal of Applied Social Psychology, 1*(2), 137-149.

Cabeza, R., & Nyberg, L. (2000). Imaging cognition II: An empirical review of 275 PET and FMRI studies. *Journal of Cognitive Neuroscience, 12*, 1-47.

Caftori, N. (1994). Educational effectiveness of computer software. *Technical Horizons in Education (T.H.E.) Journal, 22*(1), 62-65.

Caftori, N., & Paprzycki, M. (1997). The design, evaluation and usage of educational software (web version). Originally in J. D. Price, K. Rosa, S. McNeil, & J. Willis (Eds.). *Technology and teacher education annual, 1997* (CD-ROM edition). Charlottesville, VA: Association for the Advancement of Computing in Education. Retrieved on March 12, 2003.from http://www.webcom.com/Journal/Caftori.html

References

Caillois, R. (2001). *Man, play and games* (M. Barash, Trans.). Urbana and Chicago: University of Illinois Press. (Original work published 1958)

Calder, B. J., & Staw, B. M. (1975). The interaction of intrinsic and extrinsic motivation: Some methodological notes. *Journal of Personality and Social Psychology, 31*(1), 76-80.

Campbell, S. C., Feddern, J., Graham, G., & Morganlander, M. (1977). *A-6E systems approaches to training Phase I final report* (NAVTRAEQUIPCEN 75-C-0099-1). Orlando, FL: Naval Training Equipment Center.

Carlson, J. G., & Hill, K. D. (1982). The effect of gaming on attendance and attitude. *Personnel Psychology, 35*, 63-73.

Carney, R. N., & Levin, J. R. (2002). Pictorial illustrations still improve students' learning from text. *Educational Psychology Review, 14*(1), 5-26.

Caro, P. W. (1973). Aircraft simulators and pilot training. *Human Factors, 15*(6), 502-509.

Caro, P. W. (1977). *Some factors influencing Air Force simulator training effectiveness* (Tech. Rep. AFOSR-TR-77-0971). Washington, DC: Bolling Air Force Base, Air force Office of Scientific Research (NL).

Caro, P. W. (1979). The relationship between flight simulator motion and training requirements. *Human Factors, 21*(4), 493-501.

Caro, P. W., Corley, W. E., Spears, W. D., & Blaiwes, A. S. (1984). *Training effectiveness evaluation and utilization demonstration of a low cost cockpit procedures trainer* (Technical Report NAVTRAEQUIPCEN 78-C-0113-3). Orlando, FL: Naval Training Equipment Center.

Carron, A. V. (1972). Motor performance and learning under physical fatigue. *Medicine and Science in Sports, 4*(2), 101-106.

Chandler, P., & Sweller, J. (1991). Cognitive load theory and the format of instruction. *Cognition and Instruction, 8*(4), 293-332.

Cherry, E. C. (1953). Some experiments on the recognition of speech, with one and with two ears. *Journal of the Acoustical Society of America, 25*(5), 975-979.

Chesebro, J. L., & McCroskey, J. C. (1998). The relationship of teacher clarity and teacher immediacy with students' experiences of state receiver apprehension. *Communication Quarterly, 46*, 446-456.

Chi, M. T. H., Feltovich, P. J., & Glaser, R. (1981). Categorization and representation of physics problems by experts and novices. *Cognitive Science, 5*, 121-152.

Chi, M. T. H., Siler, S. A., Jeong, H., Yamauchi, T., & Housmann, R. G. (2001). Learning from human tutoring. *Cognitive Science, 25*, 471-533.

Churchman, C. W. (1968). *The systems approach.* New York: Delacorte.

Cicchinelli, L. F., Harmon, K. R., Keller, R. A., & Kottenstette, J. P. (1980). *Relative cost and training effectiveness of the 6883 three-dimensional simulator and actual equipment* (AFHRL-TR-80-24). Brooks Air Force Base, TX: Air Force Human Resources Laboratory.

Cicchinelli, L. F., Harmon, K. R., & Keller, R. A. (1982). *Relative cost and training effectiveness of the 6883 F-111 converter/flight control system simulators as compared to actual equipment* (AFHRL-TR-82-30). Brooks Air Force Base, TX: Air Force Human Resources Laboratory.

Clark, J. M., & Paivio, A. (1991). Dual coding theory and education. *Educational Psychology Review, 3*(3), 149-210.

Clark, L. V. (1960). Effect of mental practice on the development of a certain motor skill. *Research Quarterly, 31*, 560-569.

Clark, R. C. (2003). *Building expertise: Cognitive methods for training and performance improvement* (2nd ed.). Washington, DC: International Society for Performance Improvement. ISBN 1-890289-13-2

Clark, R. C., & Mayer, R. E. (2003). *E-learning and the science of instruction: Proven guidelines for consumers and designers of multimedia learning.* San Francisco, CA: John Wiley & Sons, published by Pfeiffer.

Clark, R. E. (1983). Reconsidering research on learning from media. *Review of Educational Research, 53*(4), 445-459.

Clark, R. E. (1994). Media will never influence learning. *Educational Technology Research and Development, 42*(2), 21-29.

Clark, R. E., & Salomon, G. (1986). Media in teaching. In M. Wittrock (Ed.), *Handbook of research on teaching* (3rd ed.) (pp. 464-478). New York: Macmillan.

Clark, R. E., & Voogel, A. (1985). Transfer of training principles for instructional design. *Education Communication and Technology Journal, 33*(2), 113-123.

Coffield, F., Moseley, D., Hall, E., & Ecclestone, K. (2004a). *Learning styles and pedagogy in post-16 learning: A systematic and critical review.* London: Learning and Skills Development Agency. (ISBN 1 85338 918 8)

Coffield, F., Moseley, D., Hall, E., & Ecclestone, K. (2004b). *Should we be using learning styles? What research has to say to practice.* London: Learning and Skills Development Agency. (ISBN 1 85338 914 5)

References

Cohen, K. J., & Rhenman, E. (1961). The role of management games in education and research. *Management Science, 7*(2), 131-166.

Collins, A. M., & Loftus, E. F. (1975). A spreading activation theory of semantic processing. *Psychological Review, 82*(6), 407-428.

Cook, T. D., & Campbell, D. T. (1979). *Quasi-experimentation: Design and analysis issues for field settings.* Chicago: Rand McNally.

Corkin, S. (1984). Lasting consequences of bilateral media temporal lobectomy: Clinical course and experimental findings in H. M. *Seminars in Neurology, 4*, 249-259.

Costabile, M. F., De Angeli, A., Roselli, T., Lanzilotti, R., & Plantamura, P. (2003). Evaluating the educational impact of a tutoring hypermedia for children. *Information Technology in Childhood Education Annual*, 289-308.

Costikyan, G. (2002). I have no words & I must design: Toward a critical vocabulary for games. In, F. Mäyrä (Ed.), *Proceedings of the Computer Games and Digital Cultures Conference* (pp. 9-33). Tampere, Finland: Tampere University Press. Retrieved from on August 1, 2005 from http://www.digra.org/dl/db/05164.51146.

Craik, F. I. M., & Lockhart, R. S. (1972). Levels of processing: A framework for memory research. *Journal of Verbal Learning and Verbal Behavior, 11*, 671-684.

Craik, F. I. M., & Watkins, M. J. (1973). The role of rehearsal in short-term memory. *Journal of Verbal Learning and Verbal Behavior, 12*, 599-607.

Crookall, D. (1992). Editorial: Debriefing. *Simulation & Gaming, 23*(2), 141-142.

Crown, S. W. (2001). Improving visualization skills of engineering graphics students using simple JavaScript web based games. *Journal of Engineering Education.* Retrieved on 8/4/2005 from http://www.findarticles.com/p/articles/mi_qa3886/is_200107/ai_n8988842/print.

Csikszentmihalyi, M. (1990). *Flow: The psychology of optimal experience.* New York: Harper & Row, Publishers.

Darwin, C. (1952). The origin of species. In R. M. Hutchins (Ed.), *Great books of the western world* (vol. 49). Chicago, IL: Encyclopedia Britannica.

Dauvergn, P. (2000). The case for chess as a tool to develop our children's minds. Retrieved on 8/3/2005 from http://www.auchess.org.au/articles/chessmind.htm.

Davenport, T. H., & Prusak, L. (1998). *Working knowledge: How organizations manage what they know.* Boston, MA: Harvard Business School Press.

Day, R. L. (1962). *Marketing in action: A dynamic business decision game.* Homewood, IL: Richard D. Irwin, Inc.

de Felix, J. W., & Johnson, R. T. (1993). Learning from video games. *Computers in the Schools, 9*(2/3), 119-134.

de Jong, T., & van Joolingen, W. R. (1998). Scientific discovery learning with computer simulations of conceptual domains. *Review of Educational Research, 68*(2), 179-201.

Dekkers, J., & Donatti, S. (1981). The integration of research studies on the use of simulation as an instructional strategy. *Journal of Educational Research, 74*(6), 424-427.

Demaree, R. G., Norman, D. A., & Matheney, W. G. (1965). An experimental program for relating transfer of training to pilot performance and degree of simulation (NAVTRADEVCEN Tech. Rep. 1388-1). Port Washington, NY: Naval Training Device Center.

Dember, W. N., & Earl, R. W. (1957). Analysis of exploratory, manipulatory, and curiosity behaviors. *Psychological Review, 64*(2), 91-96.

Dempsey, J. V., Lucassen, B., Gilley, W., & Rasmussen, K. (1993-1994). Since Malone's theory of intrinsically motivating instruction: What's the score in the gaming literature? *Journal of Educational Technology Systems, 22*(2), 173-183.

Dempsey, J. V., Rasmussen, K., & Lucassen, B. (1996). *The instructional gaming literature: Implications and 99 sources* (Technical Report 96-1). College of Education, University of South Alabama. Retrieved on 8/5/2005 from https://www.southalabama.edu/coe/coe/programs/TechReports/tr96_1.pdf.

Department of Defense. (1997, Dec.). *DoD Modeling and Simulation (M&S) Glossary* (DoD 5000.59-M). Alexandria, VA: Defense Modeling and Simulation Office.

Department of Defense. (2001). *Handbook: Instructional Systems Development/Systems Approach to Training and Education* (part 2 of 5 parts) (MIL-HDBK-29612-2A).

Department of Education. (2003, Dec.). *Identifying and implementing educational practices supported by rigorous evidence: A user friendly guide.* (Prepared by the Coalition for Evidence-Based Policy). Washington, DC: Institute of Education Sciences National Center for Education Evaluation and Regional Assistance.

deWinstanley, P. A., & Bjork, R. A. (2002). Successful lecturing: presenting information in ways that engage effective processing. In D. F. Halpern and M. D. Hakel (Eds.), *Applying the science of learning to university teaching and beyond: New directions for teaching and learning, No. 89,* 19-31. San Francisco, CA: Jossey-Bass.

References

Dickinson, J. (1978). Retention of intentional and incidental motor learning. *Research Quarterly, 49*(4), 437-441.

Dillon, A., & Gabbard, R. (1998). Hypermedia as an educational technology: A review of the quantitative research literature on learner comprehension, control, and style. *Review of Educational Research, 68*(3), 322-349.

Donovan, M. S., Bransford, J. D., & Pellegrino, J. W. (Eds.). (2000). *How people learn: Bridging research and practice.* Washington, DC: National Academy Press.

Dorn, D. S. (1989). Simulation games: One more tool on the pedagogical shelf. *Teaching Sociology, 17*(1), 1-18.

Drever, J. (1964). *A dictionary of Psychology* (revised by H. Wallerstein). Middlesex, England: Penguin Books Ltd.

Driscoll, M. P. (2002). Psychological foundations of instructional design. In R. A. Reiser, & J. V. Dempsey (Eds.), *Trends and issues in instructional design and technology* (pp. 57-69). Upper Saddle River, NJ: Merrill Prentice Hall.

Driskell, J. E., & Dwyer, D. J. (1984, February). Microcomputer videogame-based training. *Educational Technology,* 11-16.

Driskell, J. E., Olsen, D. W., Hays, R. T., & Mullen, B. (1995). *Training decision-intensive tasks: A constructivist approach* (Technical Report 95-007). Orlando, FL: Naval Air Warfare Center Training Systems Division (Defense Technical Information Center No. ADA 303 694).

Dwyer, D. J., Fowlkes, J. E., Oser, R. L., & Lane, N. E. (1997). Team performance measurement in distributed environments: The TARGETs methodology. In M. T. Brannick, E. Salas, & C. Prince (Eds.), *Team performance assessment and measurement: Theory, methods, and applications* (pp. 137-153). Hillsdale, NJ: Lawrence Earlbaum Associates.

Dwyer, D. J., Oser, R. L., Salas, E., & Fowlkes, J. E. (1999). Performance measurement in distributed environments: Initial results and implications for training. *Military Psychology, 11*(2), 189-215.

Eberts, R., Smith, D., Drays, S., & Vestwig, R. (1982). *A practical guide to measuring transfer from training devices to weapon systems* (Final Report 82-SRC-13). Minneapolis, MN: Honeywell.

Egenfeldt-Nielsen, S. (2003, November). Review of the research on educational usage of games. Retrieved on July 25, 2005 from http://www.it-c.uk/people/sen/papers/Reviewing%20the%20literature%20on%simulations%20games%20for%20learning_v0.5.doc.

Einstein, G. O., & Hunt, R. R. (1980). Levels of processing and organization: Additive effects of individual-item and relational processing. *Journal of Experimental Psychology: Human learning and Memory, 6*, 588-598.

Eisner, E. W. (1997). The promise and perils of alternative forms of data representation. *Educational Researcher, 26*(6), 4-10.

Ellis, H. C. (1965). *The transfer of training.* New York: Macmillan.

Ellis, N. C., Lowes, A. L., Matheny, W. G., & Norman, D. A. (1968). *Pilot performance, transfer of training and degree of simulation: III. Performance of non-jet experienced pilots versus simulation fidelity* (Tech Rep. NAVTRADEVCEN 67-C-0034-1). Orlando, FL: Naval Training Device Center.

Elwell, J. L., & Grindley, G. C. (1938). The effect of knowledge of results on learning and performance: I. A co-ordinated movement of the two hands. *British Journal of Psychology, 29*, 39-54.

Endsley, M. R. (1988). Design and evaluation for situation awareness enhancement. In *Proceedings of the Human Factors Society 32nd Annual Meeting* (pp. 97-101). Santa Monica, CA: Human Factors Society.

Ericsson, K. A., & Lehmann, A. C. (1996). Expert and exceptional performance: Evidence of maximal adaptation to constraints. *Annual Review of Psychology, 47*, 273-305.

Estes, W. K. (1988). Learning. In E. R. Hilgard (Ed.), *fifty years of psychology: Essays in honor of Floyd Ruch* (pp. 75-92). Glenview, IL: Scott, Foresman and Company.

Exline, R. V., & Winters, L. C. (1965). Affective relations and mutual glances in dyads. In S. S. Tomkins & C. E. Izard (Eds.), *Affect, cognition, and personality: Empirical studies* (pp. 319-350). New York: Springer.

Faria, A. J. (1989). Business gaming: Current usage levels. *Journal of Management Development, 8*(2), 58-66.

Fernald, L. D., & Fernald, P. S. (1979). *Basic psychology* (4th ed.). Boston: Houghton Mifflin Co.

Festinger, L. (1957). *A theory of cognitive dissonance.* Evanston, IL: Row, Peterson.

Fisher, J. E. (1976). Competition and gaming: An experimental study. *Simulation & Games, 7*(3), 321-328.

Fitts, P. M. (1964). Perceptual-motor skill learning. In A. W. Melton (Ed.), *Categories of human learning.* New York: Academic Press.

Fitts, P. M., & Posner, M. I. (1967). *Human performance.* Belmont, CA: Brooks/Cole.

Flanagan, J. C. (1984). The American institutes for research. *American Psychologist, 38,* 1272-1276.

Fleishman, E. A. (1967). Performance assessment based on an empirically derived task taxonomy. *Human Factors, 9,* 349-366.

Fleishman, E. A. (1972). On the relationship between abilities, learning, and human performance. *American Psychologist, 27,* 1017-1032.

Fleishman, E. A. (1978). Relating individual differences to the dimensions of human tasks. *Ergonomics, 21,* 1007-1019.

Fleishman, E. A., & Quaintance, M. K. (1984). *Taxonomies of human performance.* Orlando, FL: Academic Press (Harcourt Brace Javanovich).

Fleishman, E. A., & Rich, S. (1963). Role of kinesthetic and spatial-visual abilities in perceptual-motor learning. *Journal of Experimental Psychology, 66*(1), 6-11.

Fowlkes, J. E., Lane, N. E., Salas, E., Franz, T., & Oser, R. (1994). Improving the measurement of team performance: The TARGETs methodology. *Military Psychology, 6,* 47-61.

Fox, J. R. (2004). A signal detection analysis of audio/video redundancy effects in television news video. *Communication Research, 31*(5), 524-536.

Fraas, J. W. (1982). The influence of student characteristics on the effectiveness of simulations in the Principles Course. *The Journal of Economic Education, 13*(1), 56-61.

Fredericksen, N. (1974). Toward a taxonomy of situations. In R. H. Moos & P. M. Insel (Eds.), *Issues in social ecology: Human milieus* (pp. 29-44). Palo Alto, CA: National Press Books.

Fritzsche, D. J. (1981). The role of simulation games: Supplement or central delivery vehicle? *Journal of Experiential Learning and Simulation, 2,* 205-211.

Gagné, R. M. (1954). Training devices and simulators: Some research issues. *American Psychologist, 9*(3), 95-107.

Gagné, R. M. (1973). The domains of learning. *Interchange, 3,* 1-8.

Gagné, R. M. (1985). The conditions of learning and theory of instruction (4th ed.). New York: Holt, Rinehart and Winston.

Gagné, R. M., & Briggs, L. J. (1979). *Principles of instructional design* (2nd ed.). New York: Holt, Rinehart and Winston.

Gagné, R. M., Reiser, R. A., & Larsen, J. (1981). *A learning-based model for media selection: Description* (Research Product 81-25a). Alexandria, VA: U. S. Army Research Institute for the Behavioral and Social Sciences.

Gagné, R. M., & Rohwer, W. D., Jr. (1969). Instructional psychology. *Annual review of Psychology, 20,* 381-418.

Gaines, B. R. (1978). Progress in general systems research. In G. J. Klir (Ed.), *Applied general systems research*. New York: Plenum.

Garcia-Berthou, E., & Alcaraz, C. (2004). Incongruence between test statistics and P values in medical papers. *BMC Medical Research Methodology, 4*(13). Retrieved from http://www.biomedicalcentral.com/1471-2288/4/13 on June 4, 2004.

Garner, W. R., Hake, H. W., & Eriksen, C. W. (1956). Operationalism and the concept of perception. *The Psychological Review, 63*(3), 149-159.

Garris, R., Ahlers, R., & Driskell, J. E. (2002). Games, motivation, and learning: A research and practice model. *Simulation & Gaming, 33*(3), 441-467.

Gazzaniga, M. S. (1967). The split brain in man. *Scientific American, 217*(2), 24-29.

Gazzaniga, M. S. (1970). *The bisected brain*. New York: Apppleton.

Gentile, A. M. (1972). A working model of skill acquisition with application to teaching. *Quest* Monograph XVII: 3-23.

Gibson, J. J. (1966). *The senses considered as perceptual systems*. Boston: Houghton Mifflin Co.

Gick, M. L., & Holyoak, K. J. (1980). Analogical problem solving. *Cognitive Psychology, 12*, 306-355.

Gick, M. L., & Holyoak, K. J. (1983). Schema induction and analogical transfer. *Cognitive Psychology, 15*, 1-38.

Gillund, G., & Shiffrin, R. M. (1984). A retrieval model for both recognition and recall. *Psychological Review, 91*, 1-67.

Glaser, R. (1982). Instructional psychology: Past, present, and future. *American Psychologist, 37*(3), 292-305.

Glaser, R, & Bassok, M. (1989). Learning theory and the study of instruction. *Annual Review of Psychology, 40*, 631-666.

Godwin, M. A., & Schmidt, R. A. (1971). Muscular fatigue and discrete motor learning. *Research Quarterly, 42*(4), 374-383.

Goldman, D. (1995). *Emotional intelligence: Why it can matter more than IQ*. New York: Bantam.

Goldstein, I. L. (1974). *Training: Program development and evaluation*. Monterey, CA: Brooks/Cole.

Gopher, D., Weil, M., & Bareket, T. (1994). Transfer of skill from a computer game trainer to flight. *Human Factors, 36*(3), 387-405.

Gould, J. L. (1986). The biology of learning. *Annual Review of Psychology, 37*, 163-192.

Graham, K. R. (1977). *Psychological research: Controlled interpersonal interaction*. Belmont, CA: Wadsworth Publishing Company, Inc.

References

Grant, B. M., & Hennings, D. G. (1971). *The teacher moves: An analysis of nonverbal activity.* New York: Teachers College Press.

Gray, J. A., & Wedderburn, A. A. I. (1960). Grouping strategies with simultaneous stimuli. *Quarterly Journal of Experimental Psychology, 12,* 180-184.

Gray, T. H. (1979). *Boom operator part-task trainer: test and evaluation for the transfer of training* (AFHRL-TR-79-37). Brooks Air Force Base, TX: Air Force Human Resources Laboratory.

Gredler, M. E. (2005). *Learning and instruction: Theory into practice* (5th ed.). Upper saddle River, NJ: Pearson Prentice Hall.

Greenblat, C. S. (1981). Teaching with simulation games: A review of claims and evidence. In C. S. Greenblat & R. D. Duke (Eds.), *Principles and practices of gaming-simulation* (pp.139-153). Beverly Hills, CA: Sage Publications.

Greenblat, C. S. (1987). Communicating about simulation design: It's not only (sic) pedagogy. In D. Crookall, C. S. Greenblat, A. Coote, J. H. G. Klabbers, & D. R. Watson (Eds.), *Simulation — gaming in the late 1980s: Proceedings of the International Simulation and Gaming Association's 17th International Conference, Université de Toulon et dur Var, France, 1-4 July 1987* (pp. 23-33). Oxford, UK: Pergamon Press.

Greenblat, C. S., & Duke, R. D. (Eds.). (1981). *Principles and practices of gaming-simulation.* Beverly Hills, CA: Sage Publications.

Greenblat, C. S., & Urestsky, M. (1977). Simulation in social science. *American Behavioral Scientist, 20*(3), 411-426.

Gremmen, H., & Potters, H. (1995). *Assessing the efficacy of gaming in economics education.* Retrieved on 9/12/2005 from http://arno.uvt.nl/show.cgi?fid=3278.

Guilford, J. P. (1959). Three faces of intellect. *American Psychologist, 14,* 469-479.

Haber, R. N. (1969). Introduction. In R. N. Haber (Ed.), *Information processing approaches to visual perception.* New York: Holt.

Hagin, W. V., Durall, E. P., & Prophet, W. W. (1979). *Transfer of training effectiveness evaluation: U.S. Navy Device 2B35* (Seville Technical Report TR 79-06). Pensacola, FL: Chief or Naval Education and Training.

Hagman, J. D., & Rose, A. M. (1983). Retention of military tasks: A review. *Human Factors, 25*(2), 199-213.

Hall, W. E., & Cushing, J. R. (1947). The relative value of three methods of presenting learning material. *The Journal of Psychology, 24,* 57-62.

Halpern, D. F., & Hakel, M. D. (2003). Applying the science of learning to the university and beyond: Teaching for long-term retention and transfer. *Change,* July/August, 36-41.

Hansen, F. C. B., Resnick, H., & Galea, J. (2002). Better listening: Paraphrasing and perception checking—A study of the effectiveness of a multimedia skills training program. Co-published simultaneously in *Journal of Technology in Human Services, 20*(3/4), 317-331 and H. Resnick & P. S. Anderson (Eds.), *Human services technology: Innovations in practice and education* (pp. 317-331). Haworth Press, Inc.

Harlow, H. F. (1949). The formation of learning sets. *Psychological Review, 56*, 51-65.

Harp, S. F., & Mayer, R. E. (1997). The role of interest in learning from scientific text and illustrations: On the distinction between emotional interest and cognitive interest. *Journal of Educational Psychology, 89*(1), 92-102.

Harp, S. F., & Mayer, R. E. (1998). How seductive details do their damage: A theory of cognitive interest in science learning. *Journal of Educational Psychology, 90*(3), 414-434.

Harrow, A. J. (1971). *A taxonomy of the psychomotor domain.* New York: David McKay.

Haskell, R. E. (2001). *Transfer of learning: Cognition, instruction, and reasoning.* San Diego, CA: Academic Press.

Hattie, J. (1999). *Influences on student learning. Inaugural lecture: Professor of Education.* University of Auckland.

Hays, R. T. (1992). Systems concepts for training systems development. *IEEE Transactions on Systems, Man, and Cybernetics, 22*(2), 258-266.

Hays, R. T. (1999). User-oriented design analysis of a virtual environment training system. In E. Salas (Ed.), *Human/technology interaction in complex systems (vol. 9)* (pp. 1-30). Stamford, CT: JAI Press Inc.

Hays, R. T. (2001). *Theoretical foundation for advanced distributed learning research* (NAWCTSD TR 2001-006). Orlando, FL: Naval Air Warfare Center Training Systems Division. (Defense Technical Information Center No. ADA 390 504)

Hays, R. T., Castillo, E., Bradley, S. K., & Seamon, A. G. (1997). A virtual environment for submarine ship handling: Perceptual and hardware trade-offs. In M. J. Chinni (Ed.), *Proceedings of the 1997 Simulation MultiConference: Military, Government, and Aerospace Simulation (April 6-10, 1997). Simulation Series 29*(4), (pp.217-222). San Diego, CA: The Society for Computer Simulation International.

Hays, R. T., Jacobs, J. W., Prince, C., & Salas, E. (1992). Flight simulator training effectiveness: A meta-analysis. *Military Psychology, 4*(2), 63-74.

References

Hays, R. T., Seamon, A. G., & Bradley, S. K. (1997). *User-oriented design analysis of the VESUB technology demonstration system* (NAWCTSD TR 97-013). Orlando, FL: Naval Air Warfare Center Training Systems Division. (Defense Technical Information Center No. ADA 332 570)

Hays, R. T., & Singer, M. J. (1989). *Simulation fidelity in training system design: Bridging the gap between reality and training.* New York: Springer-Verlag.

Hays, R. T., Stout, R. J., & Ryan-Jones, D. L. (2005). *Quality evaluation tool for computer- and web-delivered instruction* (NAWCTSD TR 2005-002). Orlando, FL: Naval Air Warfare Center Training Systems Division. (Defense Technical Information Center No. ADA 435 294)

Hays, R. T., & Vincenzi, D. A. (2000). Fleet assessments of a virtual reality training system. *Military Psychology, 12*(3), 161-186.

Hays, R. T., Vincenzi, D. A., Seamon, A. G., & Bradley, S. K. (1998). *Training effectiveness of the VESUB technology demonstration system* (NAWCTSD TR 98-003). Orlando, FL: Naval Air Warfare Center Training Systems Division. (Defense Technical Information Center No. ADA 349 219)

Healy, A. F., & McNamara, D. S. (1996). Verbal learning and memory: Does the Modal Model still work? *Annual Review of Psychology, 47*, 143-172.

Hebb, D. O. (1949). *The organization of behavior: A neuropsychological theory.* New York: John Wiley & Sons.

Heiser, M. W. (1972). An investigation of instructor use of space. *Dissertation Abstracts International, 33*, 3044A. (University Microfilms No. 72-30, 905).

Helsen, W. F., & Starkes, J. L. (1999). A new training approach to complex decision making for police officers in potentially dangerous interventions. *Journal of Criminal Justice, 27*(5), 395-410.

Herbert, M. J., & Harsh, C. M. (1944). Observational learning by cats. *Journal of Comparative and Physiological Psychology, 37*, 81-95.

Higgins, N., & Reiser, R. A. (1985). Selecting media for instruction: An exploratory study. *Journal of Instructional Development, 8*(2), 6-10.

Hinde, R. A. (1954). Factors governing the changes in strength of a partially inborn response, as shown by the mobbing behaviour of the chaffinch (Fringila coelebs): I The nature of the response, and an examination of its course. *Proceedings of the Royal Society of Biology, 142*, 306-331.

Hoehn, A. J. (1960). The development of training programs for first enlistment personnel in electronic maintenance MOS's: III— How to design the handbook materials (HumRRO research Memorandum). Alexandria, VA: The George Washington University, Human Resources Research Office.

Hogle, J. G. (1996). Considering games as cognitive tools: In search of effective "edutainment." Department of Instructional Technology, University of Georgia. Retrieved on 7/25/2005 from http://twinpinefarm.com/pdfs/games.pdf.

Holding, D. H. (1965). *The principles of training*. Oxford: Pergamon Press.

Holding, D. H. (1987). Concepts of training. In G. Salvendy (Ed.), *Handbook of human factors*, (pp. 939-962). New York: John Wiley & Sons.

Holman, G. H. (1979). *Training effectiveness of the CH-47 flight simulator* (Research Report 1209). Alexandria, VA: U.S. Army Research Institute.

Horton, D. L., & Mills, C. B. (1984). Human learning and memory. *Annual Review of Psychology, 35*, 361-394.

Hritz, R. J., & Purifoy, G. R. (1980). *Maintenance training simulator design and acquisition* (AFHRL-TR-80-23). Brooks AFB, TX: Air Force Human resources Laboratory.

Hull, C. L. (1943). *Principles of behavior*. New York: Appelton-Century-Crofts.

Hull, C. L. (1952). *A behavior system: An introduction to behavior theory concerning the individual organism*. New Haven, CT: Yale University Press.

Hunt, J. McV. (1963). Motivation inherent in information processing and action. In O. J. Harvey (Ed.), *Motivation and social interaction: Cognitive determinants* (pp.35-94). New York: Ronald Press.

Hunt, J. McV. (1965). Intrinsic motivation and its role in psychological development. In D. Levine (Ed.), *Nebraska symposium on motivation*. Lincoln: University of Nebraska Press.

Humphrey, G. (1930). *The nature of learning*. New York: Kegan Paul.

Iseke-Barnes, J. M. (1996). Issues of educational uses of the internet: Power and criticism in communications and searching. *Journal of Educational Computing Research, 15*(1), 1-23.

Jacobs, J. W., & Dempsey, J. V. (1993). Simulation and gaming: Fidelity, feedback, and motivation. In J. V. Dempsey & G. C. Sales (Eds.), *Interactive instruction and feedback* (pp. 197-227). Englewood Cliffs, NJ: Educational Technology Publications.

Jacobs, J. W., Prince, C., Hays, R. T., & Salas, E. (1990). *A meta-analysis of the flight simulator training research* (Technical Report 89-006). Orlando, FL: Naval Training Systems Center.

References

Jacobs, R. S., Williges, R. C. & Roscoe, S. N. (1973). Simulator motion as a factor in flight-director display evaluation. *Human Factors, 15*(6), 569-582.

James, W. (1890). *Principles of psychology* (2 vols.). New York: Henry Holt and Co.

James, W. (1892). *Psychology: Briefer course.* New York: Henry Holt and Co.

Jenson, J., & de Castell, S. (2002). *Serious play: Challenges of educational game design.* Paper presented at AERA Annual Meeting, New Orleans, LA, April 1-5, 2002. Retrieved on May 6, 2003 from http://www.yorku.ca/jjenson/papers/aera2002.htm.

Johnson, M. K., & Hasher, L. (1987). Human learning and memory. *Annual Review of Psychology, 38*, 631-668.

Johnson, S. L. (1981). Effect of training device on retention and transfer of a procedural task. *Human Factors, 23*(3), 257-272.

Johnston, J. H., Cannon-Bowers, J. A., & Smith-Jentsch, K. A. (1995). Event-based performance measurement system for shipboard command teams. *Proceedings of the First International Symposium on Command and Control Research and Technology* (pp. 274-276). Washington, DC: The Center for Advanced Command and Technology.

Ju, E., & Wagner, C. (1997). Personal computer adventure games: Their structure, principles, and applicability for training. *The DATA BASE for Advances in Information Systems, 28*(2), 78-91.

Justice and Safety Center. (2002). *The evaluation of a mobile simulation training technology-PRISim™.* Richmond, KY: Justice and Safety Center, Eastern Kentucky University.

Kahneman, D. (1973). *Attention and effort.* Englewood Cliffs, NJ: Prentice Hall.

Kalyuga, S. (2000). When using sound with a text or picture is not beneficial for learning. *Australian Journal of Educational Technology, 16*(2), 161-172. Retrieved on March 12, 2003 from http://www.ascilite.org.au/ajet/ajet16/kalyuga.html.

Kalyuga, S., Chandler, P., & Sweller, J. (1999). Managing split-attention and redundancy in multimedia instruction. *Applied Cognitive Psychology, 13*, 351-371.

Kalyuga, S., Chandler, P., & Sweller, J. (2000). Incorporating learner experience into the design of multimedia instruction. *Journal of Educational Psychology, 92*(1), 126-136.

Kandel, E. R. (1976). *Cellular basis of behavior.* San Francisco, CA: Freeman.

Kandel, E. R., & Schwartz, J. H. (1982). Molecular biology of learning: Modification of transmitter release. *Science, 218*, 433-442.

Kane, J. J., & Holman, G. L. (1982). *Training device development: Training effectiveness in the army system acquisition process* (SAI Report 82-02-178 prepared for the Army Research Institute). McLean VA: Science Applications, Inc.

Karmiloff-Smith, A. (1979). Problem-solving procedures in children's construction and representations of closed railway circuits. *Archives de Psychologie, 47*(XLVII), 37-59.

Katz, R., & Kahn, R. L. (1978). *The social psychology or organizations* (2nd ed.). New York: John Wiley & Sons.

Kaufman, R. (1990). "Technicians," "physicists," and educational technology. *Educational Technology, 30*(1), 32-33.

Kawai, M. (1965). Newly acquired pre-cultural behavior of the natural troop of Japanese monkeys on Koshima Islet. *Primates, 6,* 1-30.

Keller, J. M. (1979). Motivation and instructional design: A theoretical perspective. *Journal of Instructional Development, 2*(4), 26-34.

Keller, J. M. (1983). Motivational design of instruction. In C. M. Reigeluth (Ed.), *Instructional-design theories and models: An overview of their current status* (pp. 383-434). Hillsdale, NJ: Lawrence Erlbaum Associates, Publishers.

Keller, J. M. (1987). Development and use of the ARCS model of motivational design. *Journal of Instructional Development, 10*(3), 2-10.

Kendler, H. H. (1959). Learning. *Annual Review of psychology, 10,* 43-88.

Kendon, A. (1967). Some functions of gaze direction in social interaction. *Acta Psychologica, 26,* 22-63.

Kennedy, R. S., Lane, N. E., Berbaum, K. S., & Lilienthal, M. G. (1993). A simulator sickness questionnaire (SSQ): A new method for quantifying simulator sickness. *International Journal of Aviation Psychology, 3*(3), 203-220.

Kennedy, T. E., Hawkins, R. D., & Kandel, E. R. (1992). Molecular interrelationships between short- and long-term memory. In L. R. Squire & N. Butters (Eds.), Neuropsychology of memory (2nd ed.). New York: Wiley.

Kershaw, J. A., & McKean, R. N. (1959). *Systems analysis and education.* Santa Monica, Ca: Rand Corporation.

Kieras, D. E., & Bovair, S. (1984). The role of a mental model in learning to operate a device. *Cognitive Science, 8,* 255-273.

Kinkade, R. & Wheaton, G. (1972). Training device design. In H. Vancoff and R. Kinkade (Eds.), *Human engineering guide to equipment design* (pp. 667-699). Washington, DC: American Institutes for Research.

Kirk, R. E. (1968). *Experimental design: Procedures for the behavioral sciences.* Belmont, CA: Brooks/Cole Publishing Co.

References

Kirkpatrick, D. L. (1996). Techniques for evaluating training programs. *Training & Development*. Retrieved on June 20, 2003 from http://www.astd.org/CMS/templates/index.html?template_id=1&articleid=20840.

Klatsky, R. L. (1975). *Human memory: Structures and processes.* San Francisco, CA: W. H. freeman and Company.

Klein, J. D., & Freitag, E. (1991). Effects of using an instructional game on motivation and performance. *Journal of Educational Research, 84*(5), 303-308.

Koestler, A. (1969). Beyond atomism and holism—The concept of the holon. In A. Koestler & J. R. Smythies (Eds.), *Beyond reductionism: New perspectives in the life sciences* (pp. 192-231). Boston, MA: Beacon.

Köhler, W. (1925/1973). *The mentality of apes* (2nd ed.). New York: Harcourt Brace Jovanovich.

Koran, L. J., & McLaughlin, T. F. (1990). Games or drill: Increasing the multiplication skills of students. *Journal of Instructional Psychology, 17*(4), 222-230.

Kort, B., Reilly, R., & Picard, R. W. (2001). External representation of learning process and domain knowledge: Affective state as a determinate of its structure and function. Paper presented at the AI-ED 2001 (Artificial Intelligence in Education) Conference. M.I.T. Media Laboratory. Retrieved on May 4, 2004 from http://affect.media.mit.edu/AD_research/1c/.

Koumi, J. (1994). Media comparison and deployment: A practitioner's view. *British Journal of Educational Technology, 25*(1), 41-57.

Kozma, R. B. (1991). Learning with media. *Review of educational research, 61*(2), 179-211.

Kozma, R. B. (1994). Will media influence learning: Reframing the debate. *Educational Technology Research and Development, 42*(2), 7-19.

Krathwohl, D. R., Bloom, B. S., & Masia, B. B. (1964), *Taxonomy of educational objectives. Handbook II: Affective domain.* New York: David McKay.

Kraut, R. E., & Johnston, R. E. (1979). Social and emotional messages of smiling: An ethological approach. *Journal of personality and Social Psychology, 37*(9), 1539-1553.

Kruger, J., & Dunning, D. (1999). Unskilled and unaware of it: How difficulties in recognizing one's own incompetence lead to inflated self-assessments. *Journal of Personality and Social Psychology, 77*(6), 1121-1134. Web version retrieved on April 20, 2004 from http://www.apa.org/journals/psp/psp7761121.html.

Kuhn, T. S. (1962/1970). *The structure of scientific revolutions* (2nd Ed.). Chicago: The University of Chicago Press.

Laffey, J. M., Espinosa, L., Moore, J., & Lodree, A. (2003). Supporting learning and behavior of at-risk young children: Computers in urban education. *Journal of Research on Technology in Education, 35*(4), 423-440.

Latham, G. P., & Locke, E. A. (1987). Goal setting—A motivational technique that works. In R. M. Steers and L. W. Porter (Eds.), Motivation and work behavior (4th ed.) (pp. 120-135). New York: McGraw-Hill Book Company.

Laszlo, E. (1972). *The systems view of the world.* New York: George Braziller.

Lave, C. A., & Marsh, J. G. (1975). *An introduction to models in the social sciences.* New York: Harper & Row Publishers.

Lederman, L. C. (1992). Debriefing: Toward a systematic assessment of theory and practice. *Simulation & Gaming,* ʾ3(2), 145-160.

LeDoux, J. (1996). *The emotional brain: The mysterious underpinnings of emotional life.* New York: Simon & Schuster.

Lee, J. (1999). Effectiveness of computer-based instructional simulation: A meta-analysis. *International Journal of Instructional Media, 26*(1), 71-85.

Leemkuil, H., de Jong, T., & Ootes, S. (2000). Review of educational use of games and simulations (Knowledge management Interactive Training System Project No. IST-1999-13078). The Netherlands: University of Twente. Retrieved on 8/1/2005 from http://kits.edte.utwente.nl/documents/D1.pdf.

Lepper, M. R., & Greene, D. (1975). Turning play into work: Effects of adult surveillance and extrinsic rewards on childrens' intrinsic motivation. *Journal of Personality and Social psychology, 31,* 479-486.

Lepper, M. R., & Malone, T. W. (1987). Intrinsic motivation and instructional effectiveness in computer-based education. In R. E. Snow & M. J. Farr (Eds.), *Aptitude, learning, and instruction volume 3: Conative and affective process analyses* (pp. 255-286). Hillsdale, NJ: Lawrence Erlbaum Associates, Publishers.

Leutner, D. (1993). Guided discovery learning with computer-based simulation games: Effects of adaptive and non-adaptive instructional support. *Learning and Instruction, 3,* 113-132.

Levie, W. H., & Dickie, K. E. (1973). The analysis and application of media. In R. M. W. Travers (Ed.), *Second handbook of research on teaching* (pp. 858-882). Chicago: Rand McNally.

Lewin, K. (1935). *A dynamic theory of personality.* New York: McGraw-Hill.

References

Lintern, G. (1980). Transfer of landing skill after training with supplementary visual cues. *Human Factors, 22*(1), 81-88.

Lippman, L. G. (1973). Learning theory. In *Encyclopedia of Psychology* (pp. 144-147). Guilford, CT: The Dushkin Publishing Group, Inc.

Locke, E. A. (2000). Motivation, cognition, and action: An analysis of studies of task goals and knowledge. *Applied Psychology: An International Review, 49*(3), 408-429.

Locke, E. A., & Bryan, J. F. (1966). Cognitive aspects of psychomotor performance: The effects of performance goals o level of performance. *Journal of applied Psychology, 50*(4), 286-291.

Locke, E. A., Cartledge, N., & Koeppel, J. (1968). Motivational effects of knowledge of results: A goal-setting phenomenon. *Psychological Bulletin, 70*(6), 474-485.

Loftus, E. F. (1979). *Eyewitness testimony*. Cambridge, MA: Harvard University Press.

Loftus, E. F. (1992). When a lie becomes memory's truth: Memory distortion after exposure to misinformation. *Current Directions in Psychological Science, 1*(4), 121-123.

Loftus, E. F., & Palmer, J. C. (1974). Reconstruction of automobile destruction: An example of the interaction between language and memory. *Journal of Verbal learning and Verbal Behavior, 13*, 585-589.

Loman, N. L., & Mayer, R. E. (1983). Signaling techniques that increase the understandability of expository prose. *Journal of Educational Psychology, 75*(3), 402-412.

Lubar, J. F. (1973). Chaining. In *Encyclopedia of Psychology* (p. 41). Guilford, CT: The Dushkin Publishing Group, Inc.

Lumsdaine, A. A. (1963). Instruments and media of instruction. In N. Gage (Ed.), *Handbook of research on teaching* (pp. 583-682). Chicago: Rand McNally.

Lundin, R. W. (1972). *Theories and systems of psychology*. Lexington, MA: D. C. Heath and Company.

Magill, R. A. (1980). *Motor learning: Concepts and application*. Dubuque, IA: Wm. C. Brown Company Publishers.

Maki, R. H. (1998). Test predictions over text materials. In D. J. hacker, J. Dunlosky, & A. C. Graesser (Eds.), *Metacognition in educational theory and practice* (pp. 117-144). Mahwah, NJ: Erlbaum.

Malone, T. W. (1981). Toward a theory of intrinsically motivating instruction. *Cognitive Science, 4*, 333-369.

Malone, T. W. (1982). Heuristics for designing enjoyable user interfaces: Lessons from computer games. In *Proceedings of the 1982 conference on Human Factors in Computing Systems,*

Gathersburg, MD (pp. 63-68). Association for Computing Machinery.

Malone, T. W., & Lepper, M. R. (1987). Making learning fun: A taxonomy of intrinsic motivation for learning. In R. E. Snow & M. J. Farr (Eds.), *Aptitude, learning and Instruction volume 3: Conative and affective process analyses* (pp. 223-253). Hillsdale, NJ: Lawrence Erlbaum Associates, Publishers.

Malouf, D. B. (1987-1988). The effect of instructional computer games on continuing student motivation. *The Journal of Special Education, 21*(4), 27-38.

Marcus, N., Cooper, M., & Sweller, J. (1996). Understanding instructions. *Journal of Educational Psychology, 88*(1), 49-63.

Markham, S. (2004). *Learning styles measurement: A cause for concern* (Draft Technical Report). Computing Educational Research Group. Retrieved on 11/9/2005 from http://cerg.csse.monash.edu.au/techrepps/learning_styles_revie w.pdf.

Markle, D. G. (1967). *The development of the Bell System First Aid and Personal Safety Course: An exercise in the application of empirical methods to instructional system design.* Palo Alto, CA: American Institutes for Research.

Martin, E. L. (1981). Training effectiveness of platform motion: Review of motion research involving the Advanced Simulator for Pilot Training and the Simulator for Air-to-air combat (AFHRL-TR-79-51). Brooks Air Force Base, TX: Air Force Human Resources Laboratory.

Martin, E. L., & Waag, W. L. (1978). *Contributions of platform motion to simulator training effectiveness: Study I – basic contact* (Tech. Rep. AFHRL-TR-78-15). Brooks Air Force Base, TX: Air Force Human Resources Laboratory.

Matlin, M. W. (1979). *Human experimental psychology.* Monterey, CA: Brooks-Cole Publishing Company.

Mautone, P. D., & Mayer, R. E. (2001). Signaling as a cognitive guide in multimedia learning. *Journal of Educational Psychology, 93*(2), 377-389.

Mayer, R. E. (1989). Systematic thinking fostered by illustrations in scientific text. *Journal of Educational Psychology, 81*(2), 240-246.

Mayer, R. E. (2000). What is the place of science in educational research? *Educational Researcher, 29*(6), 38-39.

Mayer, R. E. (2001a). Resisting the assault on science: The case for evidence-based reasoning in educational research. *Educational Researcher, 30*(7), 29-30.

References

Mayer, R. E. (2001b). *Multi-media learning.* Cambridge, UK: Cambridge University Press.

Mayer, R. E. (2002). *The promise of educational psychology: Volume II: Teaching for meaningful learning.* Upper Saddle River, NJ: Pearson Education, Inc.

Mayer, R. E. (2003). What works in distance learning: Multimedia. In H. F. O'Neil (Ed.), *What works in distance learning* (Office of Naval Research Award Number N00014-02-1-0179) (pp. 32-54). Los Angeles: University of Southern California, Rossier School of Education.

Mayer, R. E. (2004). Teaching of subject matter. *Annual Review of Psychology, 55,* 715-744.

Mayer, R. E., & Anderson, R. B. (1991). Animations need narrations: An experimental test of a dual-coding hypothesis. *Journal of Educational Psychology, 83*(4), 484-490.

Mayer, R. E., & Anderson, R. B. (1992). The instructive animation: Helping students build connections between words and pictures in multimedia learning. *Journal of Educational Psychology, 84*(4), 444-452.

Mayer, R. E., Bove, W., Bryman, A., Mars, R., & Tapangco, L. (1996). When less is more: Meaningful learning from visual and verbal summaries of science textbook lessons. *Journal of Educational Psychology, 88*(1), 64-73.

Mayer, R. E., & Chandler, P. (2001). When learning is just a click away: Does simple user interaction foster deeper understanding of multimedia messages? *Journal of Educational psychology, 93*(2), 390-397.

Mayer, R. E., & Gallini, J. K. (1990). When is an illustration worth ten thousand words. *Journal of Educational Psychology, 82*(4), 715-726.

Mayer, R. E., Heiser, J., & Lonn, S. (2001). Cognitive constraints on multimedia learning: When presenting more material results in less understanding. *Journal of Educational Psychology, 93*(1), 187-198.

Mayer, R. E., Mathias, A., & Wetzell, K. (2002). Fostering understanding of multimedia messages through pre-training: Evidence for a two-stage theory of mental model construction. *Journal of Experimental Psychology: Applied, 8*(3), 147-154.

Mayer, R. E., Mautone, P., & Prothero, W. (2002). Pictorial aids for learning by doing in a multimedia geology simulation game. *Journal of Educational Psychology, 94*(1), 171-185.

Mayer, R. E., & Moreno, R. (1998). A split-attention effect in multimedia learning: Evidence for dual processing systems in working memory. *Journal of Educational Psychology, 90*(2), 312-320.

Mayer, R. E., & Moreno, R. (2003). Nine ways to reduce cognitive load in multimedia learning. *Educational Psychologist, 38*(1), 43-52.

Mayer, R. E., & Sims, V. K. (1994). For whom is a picture worth a thousand words? Extensions of a dual-coding theory of multimedia learning. *Journal of Educational psychology, 86*(3), 389-401.

Mayer, R. E., Sims, V. & Tajika, H. (1995). A comparison of how textbooks teach mathematical problem solving in Japan and the United States. *American Educational Research Journal, 32*, 443-460.

Mayer, R. E., Sobko, K., & Mautone, P. D. (2003). Social cues in multimedia learning: Role of speaker's voice. *Journal of Educational Psychology, 95*(2), 419-425.

McClelland, J. L. (1992). Parallel-distributed processing models of memory. In L. R. Squire (Ed.), *Encyclopedia of learning and memory*. New York: Macmillan.

McClelland, J. L. (2000). Connectionist models of memory. In El. Tulving & F. I. M. Craik (Eds.), *The Oxford handbook of memory* (pp. 583-596). New York: Oxford University Press.

McConnel, J. V. (1962). Memory transfer through cannibalism in planarians. *Journal of Neuropsychiatry, 3*, 42-48.

McConnell, J. V. (1973). The biochemistry of memory. In R. C. Teevan (Ed.), *Readings in introductory psychology*. Minneapolis: Burgess.

McDonald, L. B., Waldrop, G. P., & White, V. T. (1983). *Analysis of fidelity requirements for electronic equipment maintenance* (Technical Report NAVTRAEQUIPCEN 81-C-0065-1). Orlando, FL: Naval Training Equipment Center.

McGaugh, J. L. (2000). Memory: A century of consolidation. *Science, 287*, 248-251.

McGaugh, J. L., Roozendall, B., & Cahill, L. (2000). Modulation of memory storage by stress hormones and the amygadaloid complex. In M. S. Gazzaniga (Ed.), *The new cognitive neurosciences* (2nd ed., pp. 1081-1098). Cambridge, MA: MIT Press.

McKechnie, G. E. (1977). Simulation techniques in environmental psychology. In D. Stokols (Ed.), *Perspectives on environment and behavior: Theory, Research, Applications* (pp. 169-189). New York: Plenum Press.

References

Medin, D. L. (1972). Role of reinforcement in discrimination learning sets in monkeys. *Psychological Bulletin, 77*(5), 305-318.

Mehrabian, A. (1968). Relationship of attitude to seated posture, orientation and distance. *Journal of Personality and Social Psychology, 10*(1), 26-30.

Mehrabian, A. (1969). Some referents and measures of nonverbal behavior. *Behavioral Research Methods and Instruments, 1*(6), 203-207.

Mehrabian, A. (1981). *Silent messages: Implicit communication of emotion and attitude.* Belmont, CA: Wadsworth.

Melnick, M. J. (1971). Effects of overlearning on retention of a gross motor skill. *Research Quarterly, 42*(1), 60-69.

Melton, A. W., & Irwin, J. M. (1940). The influence of degree of interpolated learning on retroactive inhibition and the overt transfer of specific responses. *The American Journal of Psychology, 53*(2), 173-203.

Merrill, M. D. (1983). Component display theory. In C. M. Reigeluth (Ed.), *Instructional design theories and models: An overview of their current status* (pp. 279-333). Hillsdale, NJ: Erlbaum.

Merrill, M. D. (1997). Instructional strategies that teach. *CBT Solutions*, Nov./Dec., 1-11. Retrieved from http://www.id2.usu.edu/Papers/Consistency.PDF on June 16, 2004.Merrill, M. D. (1997).

Merrill, M. D. (2002). Instructional strategies and learning styles: Which takes precedence? In R. A. Reiser & J. V. Dempsey (Eds.), *Trends and issues in instructional technology* (pp. 99-106). Upper Saddle River, NJ: Prentice Hall.

Merrill, M. D., Drake, L., Lacy, M. J., Pratt, J., & the ID2 Research Group. (1996). Reclaiming instructional design. *Educational Technology, 36*(5), 5-7.

Mestre, J. P. (2001). *Testimony before the Subcommittee on Research of the House Committee on Science, May 10, 2001.* Retrieved on March 22, 2004 from http://www.house.gov/science/research/may10/mestre.htm.

Meyer, D. E., & Schvaneveldt, R. W. (1976). Meaning, memory structure, and mental processes. *Science, 192*, 27-33.

Micheli, G. S. (1972). *Analysis of the transfer of training, substitution and fidelity of simulation of training equipment* (TAEG Report No. 2). Orlando, FL: Training Analysis and Evaluation Group.

Mielke, K. W. (1968). Questioning the questions of ETV research. *Educational Broadcasting Review, 2*, 6-15.

Miller, C. S., Lehman, J. F., & Koedinger, K. R. (1999). Goals and learning in microworlds. *Cognitive Science, 23*(3), 305-336.

Miller, G. A. (1956). The magical number seven, plus or minus two: Some limits on our capacity for processing information. *Psychological Review, 63,* 81-97.

Miller, G. A., Heise, G. A., & Lichten, W. (1951). The intelligibility of speech as a function of the context of the test materials. *Journal of Experimental Psychology, 41,* 329-335.

Miller, J. G. (1978). *Living systems.* New York: McGraw-Hill Book Company.

Miller, R. B. (1954). *Some working concepts of systems analysis.* Pittsburg, PA: American Institutes for Research.

Milner, B., Corkin, S., & Teuber, H. (1968). Further analysis of the hippocampal amnesic syndrome: 14-year follow-up study of H. M. Neuropsychologia, 6, 215-234.

Montemerlo, M. D., & Tennyson, M. E. (1976). *Instructional systems development: Conceptual analysis and comprehensive bibliography* (Technical Report NAVTRAEQUIPCEN IH-257). Orlando, FL: Naval Training Equipment Center.

Morange, M. (2006), What history tells us VI. The transfer of behaviors by macromolecules. *Journal of Bioscience, 31*(3), 323-327.

Moray, N. (1959). Attention in dichotic listening: Affective cues and the influence of instructions. *Quarterly Journal of Experimental Psychology, 11,* 56-60.

Moray, N. (1981). Feedback and the control of skilled behavior, in D. H. Holding (Ed.), *Human Skills.* New York: John Wiley & Sons.

Moray, N., Bates, A., & Barnett, T. (1965). Experiments on the four-eared man. *Journal of the Acoustical Society of America, 38,* 196-201.

Moreno, R., & Mayer, R. E. (1999). Cognitive principles of multimedia learning: The role of modality and contiguity. *Journal of Educational Psychology, 91*(2), 358-368.

Moreno, R., & Mayer, R. E. (2000). A coherence effect in multimedia learning: The case for minimizing irrelevant sounds in the design of multimedia instructional messages. *Journal of Educational Psychology, 92*(1), 117-125.

Moreno, R., & Mayer, R. E. (2002). Verbal redundancy in multimedia learning: When reading helps listening. *Journal of Educational Psychology, 94*(1), 156-163.

Moreno, R., & Mayer, R. E. (2004). Personalized messages that promote science learning in virtual environments. *Journal of Educational Psychology, 96*(1), 165-173.

Moreno, R., Mayer, R. E., Spires, H. A., & Lester, J. C. (2001). The case for social agency in computer-based teaching: Do students learn more deeply when they interact with animated pedagogical agents? *Cognition and Instruction, 19*(2), 177-213.

References

Morris, C. (1938/1969). Foundations of the theory of signs. In O. Neurath, R. Carnap, & C. Morris (Eds.), *Foundations of the unity of science: Toward an international encyclopedia of unified science* (vol. 1, Nos. 1-10), (pp. 79-137). Chicago: University of Chicago Press.

Morris, R. (1976). Simulation in training – Part 4: Business games are not funny. *Industrial Training International, 11*(7-8), 241-243.

Morris, R., & Holman, J. (1976). Simulation in training – Part 5. *Industrial Training International, 11*(9), 267-271.

Morris, R., & Thomas, J. (1976). Simulation in training – Part 1. *Industrial Training International, 11*(3), 66-69.

Mousavi, S. Y., Low, R., & Sweller, J. (1995). Reducing cognitive load by mixing auditory and visual presentation modes. *Journal of Educational Psychology, 87*(2), 319-334.

Murray, H. A. (1938). *Explorations in personality.* New York: Oxford University Press.

Najjar, L. J. (1998). Principles of educational multimedia user interface design. *Human Factors, 40*(2), 311-323.

National Research Council (1991). D. Druckman & R. A. Bjork (Eds.), *In the mind's eye: Enhancing human performance.* Washington, DC: National Academy Press.

National Research Council (1999). J. D. Bransford, A. L. Brown, & R. R. Cocking (Eds.), *How people learn: Brain, mind, experience, and school.* Committee on Developments in the Science of Learning. Washington, DC: National Academy Press.

Naylor, J. C., & Briggs, G. E. (1963). Effects of task complexity and task organization on the relative efficiency of part and whole training methods. *Journal of Experimental Psychology, 65*(3), 217-244.

Nebes, R. D. (1974). Hemispheric specialization in commissurotomized man. *Psychological Bulletin, 81*(1) 1-14.

Newell, A., & Simon, H. A. (1972). Human problem solving. Englewood Cliffs, NJ: Prentice-Hall, Inc.

Nielson, J. M. (1958). *Memory and amnesia.* Los Angeles: San Lucas.

Nier, C. J. (1979). Educational autobiographies: Explorations of affective impact. *Teacher Educator, 15*, 14-20.

Nitsch, K. E. (1977). *Structuring decontextualized forms of knowledge.* Unpublished doctoral dissertation, Vanderbilt University, Nashville.

Norman, D. A. (1976). *Memory and attention: An introduction to human information processing* (2nd ed.). New York: John Wiley and Sons, Inc.

Notz, W. W. (1975). Work motivation and the negative effects of extrinsic rewards: A review with implications for theory and practice. *American Psychologist, 9*, 884-891.

407

Nussbaum, J. F. (1984, April). *The Montana program to systematically modify teacher communicative behavior.* Paper presented at the annual meeting of the American Educational Research Association, New Orleans. (ERIC Document Reproduction Service No. ED 243 832).

Nyberg, L. (1998). Mapping episodic memory. *Behavioral Brain Research, 90,* 107-114.

Oblinger, D. G. (2004). The next generation of educational engagement. *Journal of Interactive Media in Education, 8,* 1-18.

Osgood, C. E. (1949). The similarity paradox in human learning: A resolution. *Psychological Review, 56,* 132-143.

Oxendine, J. B. (1969). Effect of mental and physical practice on the learning of three motor skills. *Research Quarterly, 40,* 755-763.

Oxford, R. L., Harman, J., & Holland, V. M. (1987). Advances in the development of hand-held, computerized game-based training devices. In D. Crookall, C. S. Greenblat, A. Coote, J. H. G. Klabbers, & D. R. Watson (Eds.), *Simulation — gaming in the late 1980s: Proceedings of the International Simulation and Gaming Association's 17th International Conference, Université de Toulon et dur Var, France, 1-4 July 1987* (pp. 65-72). Oxford, UK: Pergamon Press.

Pajares, F. (1996). Self-efficacy beliefs in academic settings. *Review of educational Research, 66*(4), 543-578.

Paivio, A. (1990). *Mental representations: A dual-coding approach.* New York: Oxford University Press.

Pange, J. (2003). Teaching probabilities and statistics to preschool children. *Information Technology in Childhood Education Annual,* 163-172.

Palmer, S. E. (1975). Visual perception and world knowledge: Notes on a model of sensory-cognitive interaction. In D. A. Norman, D. E. Rumelhart, and the LNR Research Group (Eds.), *Explorations in cognition.* San Francisco, CA: Freeman.

Parchman, S. W., Ellis, J. A., Christinaz, D., & Vogel, M. (2000). An evaluation of three computer-based instructional strategies in basic electricity and electronics training. *Military Psychology, 12*(1), 73-87.

Parker, L. E., & Lepper, M. R. (1992). Effects of fantasy contexts on children's learning and motivation: Making learning more fun. *Journal of Personality and Social Psychology, 62*(4), 625-633.

Patterson, M. L., & Sechrest, L. B. (1970). Interpersonal distance and impression formation. *Journal of Personality, 38,* 161-166.

Penfield, W. (1958/1967). *The excitable cortex in conscious man.* Liverpool University Press.

References

Penfield, W., & Perot, P. (1963). The brain's record of auditory and visual experience. *Brain, 86,* 595-696.

Penuel, B., & Roschelle, J. (1999). Designing learning: Cognitive science principles for the innovative organization (SRI Project 10099). Prepared for Lotus Research Corporation by SRI International. Retrieved on 2/1/05 from http://domino.research.ibm.com/cambridge/research.nsf/0/e13476a/01cbf7de85256920006aaf9a/$FILE/DesigningLearning.PDF.

Peterson, L. R., & Peterson, M. J. (1959). Short-term retention of individual verbal items. *Journal of Experimental Psychology, 58*(3), 193-198.

Pierfy, D. A. (1977). Comparative simulation game research: Stumbling blocks and stepping stones. *Simulation and Games, 8*(2), 255-268.

Pintrich, P. R., Cross, D. R., Kozma, R. B., & McKeachie, W. J. (1986). Instructional psychology. *Annual Review of Psychology, 37,* 611-651.

Pohlmann, L. D., & Reed, J. C. (1978). Air to air combat skills: Contributions of platform motion to initial training (Tech. Rep. AFHRL-TR-78-53). Brooks Air Force Base TX: Air Force Human Resources Laboratory.

Pollock, E., Chandler, P., & Sweller, J. (2002). Assimilating complex information. *Learning and Instruction, 12,* 61-86.

Postman, L., Bronson, W., & Gropper, G. L. (1953). Is there a mechanism of perceptual defense? *Journal of Abnormal and Social Psychology, 48,* 215-224.

Postman, L., Stark, K., & Fraser, J. (1968). Temporal changes in interference. *Journal of Verbal Learning and Verbal Behavior, 7,* 672-694.

Postman, L., & Underwood, B. J. (1973). Critical issues in interference theory. *Memory and Cognition, 1,* 19-40.

Poulton, E. C. (1957). On prediction in skilled movements. *Psychological Bulletin, 54*(6), 467-478.

Povenmire, H. K., & Roscoe, S. N. (1973). Incremental transfer effectiveness of a ground-based general aviation trainer. *Human Factors, 15*(6), 534-542.

Prensky, M. (2001). *Digital game-based learning.* New York: McGraw-Hill.

Quillian, M. R. (1969). The teachable language comprehender: A simulation program and theory of language. *Communications of the Association for Computing Machinery, 12*(8), 459-476.

Racine, R. J., & deJonge, M. (1988). Short-term and long-term potentiation in projection pathways and local circuits. In P. W. Langfield & S. A. Deadwyler (Eds.), *Long-term potentiation: From biophysics to behavior.* New York: Liss.

Ramey, C. T., & Ramey, S. L. (1998). Early intervention and early experience. *American Psychologist, 53*(2), 109-120.

Randel, J. M., Morris, B. A., Wetzel, C. D., & Whitehill, B. V. (1992). The effectiveness of games for educational purposes: A review of recent research. *Simulation & Gaming, 23*(3), 261-276.

Reid, L. S., Brackett, H. R., & Johnson, R. B. (1963). The influence of relationships among items to be recalled upon short-term retention. *Journal of Verbal Learning and Verbal Behavior, 2,* 86-92.

Reigeluth, C. M., & Stein, F. S. (1983). The elaboration theory of instruction. In C. M. Reigeluth (Ed.), *Instructional design theories and models: An overview of their current status.* Hillsdale, NJ: Lawrence Erlbaum.

Reiser, R. A. (1994). Clark's invitation to the dance: An instructional designer's response. *Educational Technology Research and Development, 42*(2), 45-48.

Reiser, R. A. (2001a). A history of instructional design and technology: Part I: A history of instructional media. *Educational Technology Research and Development, 49*(1), 53-64.

Reiser, R. A. (2001b). A history of instructional design and technology: Part II: A history of instructional design. *Educational Technology Research and Development, 49*(2), 57-67.

Reiser, R. A., Gagné, R. M., Wager, W. W., Larsen, J. Y., Hewlett, B. A., Noel, K. L., Winner, J. L., & Fagan, C. (1981). *A learning-based model for media selection: Media selection flowchart and user's guide* (Research Product 81-25c). Alexandria, VA: U. S. Army Research Institute for the Behavioral and Social Sciences.

Renaud, L., & Stolovitch, H. (1988). Simulation gaming: An effective strategy for creating appropriate traffic safety behaviors in five-year-old children. *Simulation & Games, 19*(3), 328-345.

Ricard, G. L., Parrish, R. V., Ashworth, B. R., & Wells, M. D. (1981). The effects of various fidelity factors on simulated helicopter hover (Technical Report: NAVTRAEQUIPCEN IH-321). Orlando, FL: Naval Training Equipment Center.

Ricci, K., Salas, E., & Cannon-Bowers, J. A. (1996). Do computer games facilitate knowledge acquisition and retention? *Military Psychology, 8*(4), 295-307.

Richardson, A. (1967). Mental practice: A review and discussion. *Research Quarterly, 38*(1)—Part I: pp. 95-107; Part II: pp. 263-273.

References

Richardson, J. (2002, October). The science of learning choices. *Results.* National Staff Development Council. Retrieved on February 23, 2004 from http://www.nsdc.org/library/publications/results/res10-02rich.cfm.

Richmond, V. P., Gorham, J. S., & McCroskey, J. C. (1987). The relationship between selected immediacy behaviors and cognitive learning. *Communication Yearbook 10* (pp. 574-590). Newbury Park, CA: Sage. Retrieved on April 28, 2004 from http://www.jamescmccroskey.com/publications/140.htm.

Ricketson, D. S., Schulz, R. E., & Wright, R. H. (1970). *Review of the CONARC systems engineering of training program and its implementation at the United States Army Aviation School.* Fort Rucker, AL: Human Resources Research Organization.

Rieber, L. P. (1990). Using computer animated graphics in science instruction with children. *Journal of Educational Psychology, 82*(1), 135-140.

Rieber, L. P. (1996). Seriously considering play: Designing interactive learning environments based on the blending of microworlds, simulations, and games. *Educational Technology Research and Development, 44*(2), 43-58.

Rieber, L. P., & Noah, D. (1997). Effect of gaming and visual metaphors on reflective cognition within computer-based simulations. Paper presented at the 1997 AERA conference in Chicago, IL. Retrieved on 9/14/05 from http://it.coe.uga.edu/~lrieber/gaming-simulation/Rieber-gaming-simulation.pdf.

Rieber, L. P., Smith, L., & Noah, D. (1998). The value of serious play. *Educational Technology, 38*(6), 29-37.

Rilling, M. (1996). The mystery of the vanished citations: James McConnell's forgotten 1960s quest for planarian learning, a biochemical engram, and celebrity. *American Psychologist, 51,* 589-598.

Ritchie, G. H., & Beal, C. R. (1980). Image detail and recall: Evidence for within-item elaboration. *Journal of Experimental Psychology: Human learning and Memory, 6,* 66-76.

Robinson, J. A., Anderson, L. F., Hermann, M. G., & Snyder, R. C. (1966). Teaching with Inter-Nation simulation and case studies. *American Political Science Review, 60*(March), 53-64.

Rogers, C. A., Jr. (1974). Feedback precision and postfeedback interval duration. *Journal of experimental Psychology, 102*(4), 604-608.

Rogoff, B., Paradise, R., Arauz, R. M., Correa-Chávez, M. & Angelillo, C. (2003). Firsthand learning through intent participation. *Annual Review of Psychology, 54,* 175-203.

Rolls, E. T. (2000). Memory systems in the brain. *Annual Review of Psychology, 51*, 599-630.

Ronen, M., & Eliahu, M. (2000). Simulation—a bridge between theory and reality: The case of electric circuits. *Journal of Computer Assisted Learning, 16*, 14-26.

Rosas, R., Nussbaum, M., Cumsille, P., Marianov, V., Correa, M., Flores, P., Grau, V., Lagos, F., López, X., López, V., Rodriguez, P., & Salinas, M. (2003). Beyond Nintendo: Design and assessment of educational video games for first and second grade students. *Computers & Education, 40*, 71-94.

Rose, A. M., & Martin, M. F. (1988). *Implementation of ASTAR: Evaluation of the Combat Talon II maintenance trainer* (AIR Report 49901-TR3-02/88). Washington, DC: American Institutes for Research.

Roscoe, S. N., & Williges, R. C. (1975). Motion relationships in aircraft attitude and guidance: A flight experiment. *Human Factors, 17*(4), 374-387.

Rosenfeld, H. M. (1966). Instrumental affiliative functions of facial and gestural expressions. *Journal of Personality and Social Psychology, 4*(1), 65-72.

Rosenthal, R. (1966). *Experimenter effects in behavioral research.* New York: Appleton-Century-Crofts.

Rouse, W. B., & Morris, N. M. (1986). On looking into the black box: Prospects and limits in the search for mental models. *Psychological Bulletin, 100*, 359-363.

Rowe, J. C. (2001). An experiment in the use of games in the teaching of mental arithmetic. *Philosophy of Mathematics Education Journal, 14*. Retrieved on 8/1/2005 from http://www.ex.ac.uk/~PErnest/pome14/rowe.htm.

Rowland, K. M., & Gardner, D. M. (1973). The uses of business gaming in education and laboratory research. *Decision Sciences, 4*, 268-283.

Royer, J. M. (1979). Theories of the transfer of learning. *Educational Psychologist, 14*, 53-69.

Rubenstein, R. A., Laughlin, C.D., Jr., & McManus, J. (1984). *Science as cognitive process: Toward an empirical philosophy of science.* University of Pennsylvania Press.

Rubin, H. J. (1978). A note on PARADIGM: A simulation model of the competition of ideas in evolving groups. *Simulation and Games, 9*(2), 173-184.

Ruesch, J. (1969). A general systems theory based on human communication. In W. Gray, F. J. Duhl, and N. D. Rizzo (Eds.), *General Systems Theory and psychiatry* (pp. 141-157). Boston: Little, Brown and Company.

References

Rumelhart, D. E., & Norman, D. A. (1981). Analogical processes in learning. In J. R. Anderson (Ed.), *Cognitive skills and their acquisition* (pp. 335-359). Hillsdale, NJ: Lawrence Erlbaum.

Rundus, D. (1971). Analysis of rehearsal processes in free recall. *Journal of Experimental Psychology, 89*(1), 63-77.

Rushton, J. P. (1975). Generosity in children: Immediate and long-term effects of modeling, preaching, and moral judgment. *Journal of Personality and Social Psychology, 31*(3), 459-466.

Ryan, L. E., Scott, P. G., & Browning, R. F. (1978). The effects of simulator landing practice and the contribution of motion simulation to P-3 pilot training (TAEG Rep. No. 63). Orlando, FL: Training Analysis and Evaluation Group.

Scharr, T. M. (2001). Interactive video training for firearms safety. *Federal Probation, 65*(2), 45-51.

Schiffman, H. R. (1976). *Sensation and perception: An integrated approach.* New York: Wiley.

Schneider, W. (1985). Training high-performance skills: Fallacies and guidelines. *Human Factors, 27*(3), 285-300.

Schoenfeld, A. H. (1987). What's all the fuss about metacognition? In A. Schoenfeld (Ed.), *Cognitive Science and Mathematics Education* (pp. 189-215). Hillsdale, NJ: Lawrence Erlbaum Associates.

Schramm, W. (1977). *Big media, little media: Tools and technologies for instruction.* Beverly Hills, CA: Sage Publications.

Seamon, A. G., Bradley, S. K., Hays, R. T., & Vincenzi, D. A. (1999). *VESUB technology demonstration: Project summary* (TR 1999-002). Orlando, FL: Naval Air Warfare Center Training Systems Division. (Defense Technical Information Center No. ADA 362 565)

Serrano, E. L., & Anderson, J. E. (2004). The evaluation of food pyramid games, a bilingual computer nutrition education program for Latino youth. *Journal of family and Consumer Sciences Education, 22*(1). Retrieved on 8/3/2005 from http://www.natefacs.org/JFCSE/v22no1/v22no1Serrano.pdf.

Shannon, C. E., & Weaver, W. (1949). *The mathematical theory of communication.* Urbana, IL: University of Illinois Press.

Shavelson, R. J., & Towne, L. (Eds.). (2002). *Scientific research in education.* National Research Council, Division of Behavioral and Social Sciences and Education, Committee on Scientific Principles for Education Research. Washington, DC: National Academy Press.

Shepard, R. N. (1967). Recognition memory for words, sentences, and pictures. *Journal of Verbal Learning and Verbal Behavior, 6,* 156-163.

Shrestha, L. B. (1990). *Computer based training: The effects of game characteristics on motivation and learning.* Unpublished master's thesis, University of Central Florida, Orlando.

Shulman, H. G. (1972). Semantic confusion errors in short-term memory. *Journal of Verbal Learning and Verbal Behavior, 11,* 221-227.

Siiter, R. (1973). Associationism. In *Encyclopedia of Psychology* (pp. 18-19). Guilford, CT: The Dushkin Publishing Group, Inc.

Simkin, M. V., & Roychowdhury, V. P. (2003). Read before you cite! *Complex Systems, 14,* 269-274. Retrieved from http://www.arxiv.org/abs/cond-mat/0212043 on June 6, 2004.

Simon, H. A. (2000). Observations on the sciences of science learning. *Journal of Applied Developmental Psychology, 21*(1), 115-121.

Simons, D. J., & Chabris, C. f. (1999). Gorilla in our midst: Sustained inattentional blindness for dynamic events. *Perception, 28,* 1059-1074.

Simons, K. L. (1993). New technologies in simulation games. *System Dynamics Review, 9*(2), 135-152.

Simpson, E. J. (1972). The classification of educational objectives in the psychomotor domain. In *Contributions of behavioral science to instructional technology: 3 The Psychomotor Domain: A resource book for media specialists* (pp. 43-56). Washington, DC: Gryphon House.

Singer, R. N. (1980). *Motor learning and human performance.* New York: Macmillan.

Skinner, B. F. (1938). *The behavior of organisms: An experimental analysis.* New York: Appleton-Century-Crofts.

Skinner, B. F. (1954). The science of learning and the art of teaching. *Harvard Educational Review, xxiv*(2), 86-97. Reprinted in Rosenblith, J. F., Allinsmith, W., & Williams, J. P. (1962). *The causes of behavior* (1st ed.). Boston: Allyn & Bacon, Inc.

Slamecka, N. J. (1968). An examination of trace storage in free recall. *Journal of Experimental Psychology, 76*(4), 504-513.

Slamecka, N. J., & Graf, P. (1978). The generation effect: Delineation of a phenomenon. *Journal of Experimental Psychology, 4*(6), 592-604.

Slavin, R. E. (2002). Evidence-based educational policies: Transforming educational practice and research. *Educational Researcher, 31*(7), 15-21.

Sleet, D. A., & Stadsklev, R. (1977). Annotated bibliography of simulations and games in health education. *Health Education Monographs, 5* (supplement 1), 74-90.

Smith, H. (1982/1989). *Beyond the post-modern mind* (rev. ed.). New York: The Crossroads Publishing Co.

References

Smith, L., & Land, M. (1981). Low inference verbal behaviors related to teacher clarity. *Journal of Classroom Interaction, 17*(1), 37-42.

Smolensky, P. (1995). On the proper treatment of connectionism. In C. Macdonald, & G. Macdonald (Eds.), Connectionism: Debates on psychological explanation. Cambridge, USA: Blackwell.

Smoll, F. L. (1972). Effects of precision on information feedback upon acquisition of a motor skill. *Research Quarterly, 43*(4), 489-493.

Sokolov, E. N. (1960). Neuronal models of the orienting reflex. In M. A. B. Brazier (Ed.), *The central nervous system and behavior: Transactions of the third conference.* New York: Josiah Macy, Jr., Foundation.

Song, S. H., & Keller, J. M. (2001). Effectiveness of motivationally adaptive computer-assisted instruction on the dynamic aspects of motivation. *Educational Technology Research and Development, 49*(2), 5-22.

Southerland, S. (1989). *The international dictionary of psychology.* New York: The Continuum Publishing Co.

Spence, K. W. (1956). *Behavior theory and conditioning.* New Haven, CT: Yale University Press.

Sperling, G. (1960). The information available in brief visual presentations. *Psychological Monographs: General Applied, 74*(11), (Whole No. 498), 1-29.

Sperry, R. W. (1968). Hemisphere deconnection and unity in conscious experience. *American Psychologist, 23*, 723-733.

Squire, K. (2005). *Game-based leaning: Present and future state of the field.* Masie Center e-Learning Consortium, February, 2005. Retrieved on 8/26/2005 from http://www.masie.com/xlearn/Game-Based_Learning.pdf.

Squire, L. R. (1987). *Memory and brain.* New York: Oxford University Press.

Squire, L. R., Knowlton, B., & Musen, G. (1993). The structure and organization of memory. *Annual Review of Psychology, 44*, 453-495.

Staddon, J. E. R., & Cerutti, D. T. (2003). Operant conditioning. *Annual Review of Psychology, 54*, 115-144.

Stahl, S. A. (1999, Fall). Different strokes for different folks? A critique of learning styles. *American Educator*, 1-5.

Stark, R., Mandl, H., Gruber, H., & Renkl, A. (2002). Conditions and effects of example elaboration. *Learning and Instruction, 12*, 39-60.

Stelmach, G. E. (1970). Learning and response consistency with augmented feedback. *Ergonomics, 13*(4), 421-425.

Stein, B. S., & Bransford, J. D. (1979). Constraints on effective elaboration: Effects of precision and subject generation. *Journal of Verbal Learning and Verbal Behavior, 18,* 769-777.

Steinberg, E. R., Avner, R. A., Call-Himwich, A., Klecka, J. A., & Misselt, A. L. (1977). *Critical incidents in the evolution of PLATO projects* (MTC Report No. 12). Urbana, IL: University of Illinois, Computer-Based Education Research Laboratory.

Steinmetz, J. E. (1998). The localization of a simple type of learning and memory: The cerebellum and classical eye blink conditioning. *Current Directions in Psychological Science, 7*(3), 72-77.

Sternberg, R. J. (1996). Attention and consciousness. In *Cognitive psychology* (pp. 68-107). Fort Worth, TX; Harcourt Brace College Publishers.

Stevenson, R. J. (1981). Depth of comprehension, effective elaboration, and memory for sentences. *Memory and Cognition, 9*(2), 169-176.

Streufert, S. (1986). *Assessment of task performance via a quasi-experimental simulation technology.* Unpublished report, Pennsylvania State University, College of Medicine, University Park, PA.

Swaak, J., & de Jong, T. (2001). Discovery simulations and the assessment of intuitive knowledge. *Journal of Computer Assisted Learning, 17,* 284-294.

Sweller, J., & Chandler, P. (1994). Why some material is difficult to learn. *Cognition and Instruction, 12*(3), 185-233.

Sweller, J., Chandler, P., Tierney, P., & Cooper, M. (1990). Cognitive load as a factor in the structuring of technical material. *Journal of Experimental Psychology: General, 119*(2), 176-192.

Swezey, R. W., & Evans, R. A. (1980). *Guidebook for users of TRAINVICE II.* McLean, VA: Science Applications, Inc.

Szafran, R. F., & Mandolini, A. F. (1980). Test performance and concept recognition: The effect of a simulation game on two types of cognitive knowledge. *Simulation & Games, 11*(3), 326-335.

Tart, C. T. (1973). States of consciousness and state-specific sciences. In R. E. Ornstein (Ed.), *The nature of human consciousness: A book of readings* (pp.41-60). San Francisco: W. H. Freeman and Company.

Tenney, Y. J., Briscoe, H., Pew, R. W., Bradley, S. K., Seamon, A. G., & Hays, R. T. (1996). *Virtual environment submarine officer of the deck simulation and training: Preliminary requirements recommendation* (NAWCTSD SR 96-002). Orlando, FL: Naval Air Warfare Center Training Systems Division.

Tessmer, M. N. (1995). Formative multimedia evaluation. *Training Research Journal, 1,* 127-149.

References

Thayer, S., & Schiff, W. (1974). Observer judgment of social interactions: Eye contact and relationship inferences. *Journal of Personality and Social Psychology, 30,* 110-114.

Thomas, R., Cahill, J., & Santilli, L. (1997). Using an interactive computer game to increase skill and self-efficacy regarding safer sex. *Health Education and Behavior, 24*(1), 71-86.

Thompson, D. M., & Tulving, E. (1970). Associative encoding and retrieval: Weak and strong cues. *Journal of experimental psychology, 86*(2), 255-262.

Thompson, M. (2003). Does the playing of chess lead to improved scholastic achievement? *Issues in Educational Research, 13.* Retrieved on 8/3/2005 from http://education.curtin.edu.au/iier/lier13/Thompson.html.

Thompson, R. A., & Nelson, C. A. (2001). Developmental science and the media: Early brain development. *American Psychologist, 56,* 5-15.

Thompson, R. F. (1989). A model system approach to memory. In P. R. Solomon, G. R. Goethals, C. M. Kelley, & B. R. Stephens (Eds.), *Memory: Interdisciplinary approaches.* New York: Springer-Verlag.

Thompson, R. F. (1992). Memory. *Current Opinion in Neurobiology, 2,* 203-208.

Thorndike, E. L. (1898). Animal intelligence: An experimental study of the associative process in animals. *The Psychological Review: Series of Monograph Supplements, 2*(4), (Whole # 8).

Thorndike, E. L. (1913). *Educational psychology.* New York: Columbia University Press.

Thorndike, E. L. (1931). *Human learning.* New York: Century.

Thorndike, E. L. (1932). *The fundamentals of learning.* New York: Columbia University Press.

Thorndike, E. L., & Woodworth, R. S. (1901). The influence of movement in one mental function upon the efficiency of other functions. *Psychological Review, 8,* 247-261.

Thornton, G. C., III, & Cleveland, J. N. (1990). Developing managerial talent through simulation. *American Psychologist, 45*(2), 190-199.

Thorpe, W. H. (1963). *Learning and instinct in animals* (2nd ed.). London: Methuen.

Tolman, E. C. (1959). *Principles of purposive behavior.* In S. Koch (Ed.), Psychology: A study of a science (Vol. 2). New York: McGraw-Hill.

Toulmin, S. (1953). *The philosophy of science: An introduction.* London: Hutchinson.

417

Tracey, W. R. (1984). *Designing training and development systems*. New York: American Management Association (AMACOM).

Travers, R. M. W. (1972*). Essentials of learning* (3rd ed.). New York: MacMillan.

Treisman, A. M. (1964). Verbal cues, language and meaning in selective attention. *American Journal of Psychology, 77*, 206-219.

Treisman, A. M. (1969). Strategies and models of selective attention. *Psychological Review, 76*(3), 282-299.

Trowbridge, M. H., & Cason, H. (1932). An experimental study of Thorndike's theory of learning. *Journal of General Psychology, 7*, 245-260.

Trussell, E. (1965). Prediction of success in a motor skill on the basis of early learning achievement. *The Research Quarterly, 36*(3), 342-347.

Tulving, E. (1962). Subjective organization in free recall of "unrelated" words. *Psychological Review, 69*(4), 344-354.

Tulving, E. (1964). Intratrial and intertribal retention: Notes toward a theory of free recall verbal learning. *Psychological Review, 71*(3), 219-237.

Tulving, E. (1972). Episodic and semantic memory. In E. Tulving & W. Donaldson (Eds.), *Organization and memory* (pp. 381-403). New York: Academic Press.

Tulving, E. (2002). Episodic memory: From mind to brain. *Annual Review of Psychology, 53*, 1-25.

Tulving, E., & Thompson, D. M. (1973). Encoding specificity and retrieval processes in episodic memory. *Psychological Review, 80*, 352-373.

Underwood, B. J. (1948). Retroactive and proactive inhibition after five and forty-eight hours. *Journal of Experimental Psychology, 38*, 29-38.

Underwood, B. J. (1983). *Attributes of memory*. Glenview, IL: Scott Foresman.

U. S. Congress (2001). *No Child Left Behind Act of 2001*. Washington, DC: Author.

Valiela, I. (2001). *Doing science: Design, analysis, and communication of scientific research*. New York: Oxford University Press.

Valverde, H. H. (1973). A review of flight simulator transfer of training studies, *Human Factors, 15*(6), 510-523.

Van Eck, R., & Dempsey, J. (2002). The effect of competition and contextualized advisement on the transfer of mathematics skills in a computer-based instructional simulation game. *Educational Technology Research and Development, 50*(3). Retrieved on 8/3/2005 from http://www.gamespace.nl/content/MAThesis_DBNieborg.pdf.

References

van Gigch, J. P. (1978). *Applied General System Theory.* New York: Harper and Row.

VanSickle, R. L. (1986). A quantitative review of research on instructional simulation gaming: A twenty-year perspective. *Theory and Research in Social Education, XIV*(3), 245-264.

VanLehn, K. (1996). Cognitive skill acquisition. *Annual Review of Psychology, 47,* 513-539.

Virvou, M., Katsionis, G., & Manos, K. (2005). Combining software games with education: Evaluation of its educational effectiveness. *Educational Technology & Society, 8*(2), 54-65.

Vitro, F. T. (1973). Programmed learning. In *Encyclopedia of Psychology* (p. 210). Guilford, CT: The Dushkin Publishing Group, Inc.

von Neumann, J. (1956). The general and logical theory of automata. Reproduced in part in W. Buckley (Ed.), *Modern systems research for the behavioral scientist* (pp. 97-107). Chicago, IL: Aldine.

Waag, W. L. (1981). *Training effectiveness of visual and motion simulation* (AFHRL-TR-79-72). Brooks Air Force Base, TX: Air Force Human Resources Laboratory.

Wallace, W. (1971). *The logic of science in sociology.* Chicago: Aldine-Atherton.

Wang, M. C., Haertel, G. D., & Walberg, H. J. (1993). Toward a knowledge base for school learning. *Review of Educational Research, 63*(3), 249-294.

Wasserman, E. A., & Miller, R. R. (1997). What's elementary about associative learning? *Annual Review of Psychology, 48,* 573-607.

Webster's new collegiate dictionary. (1977). Springfield, MA: G. &. C. Merriam Company.

Weineke, C. (1981). The first lecture: Implications for students who are new to the university. *Studies in Higher Education, 6*(1), 85-89.

Weiten, W. (2004). *Psychology Themes and variations* (6th ed.). Belmont, CA: Wadsworth/Thomson Learning.

Wellington, W. J., & Faria, A. J. (1996). Team cohesion, player attitude, and performance expectations in simulation. *Simulation & Gaming, 27*(1), 23-40.

Welsch, M. A. (1963). Prediction of motor skill attainment from early learning. *Perceptual and Motor Skills, 17,* 263-266.

Westbrook, J. I., & Braithwaite, J. (2001). The Health Care Game: An evaluation of a heuristic, web-based simulation. *Journal of Interactive Learning Research, 12*(1), 89-104.

Wheaton, G. R., Rose, A. M., Fingerman, P. W., Leonard, R. L., Jr., & Boycan, G. G. (1976). *Evaluation of the effectiveness of training devices: Validation of the predictive model* (ARI Tech. Rep. TR-76-A2). Alexandria, VA: U.S. Army Research Institute. (Defense Technical Information Center Number ADA 040 911)

Wheeless, L. R. (1975). An investigation of receiver apprehension and social context dimensions of communication apprehension. *The Speech Teacher, 24*, 261-268.

Wheeless, L. R., Preiss, R. W., & Gayle, B. M. (1997). Receiver apprehension, informational receptivity, and cognitive processing. In J. A. Daly, J. C. McCroskey, J. Ayres, T. Hopf, & D. M. Ayres (Eds.), *Avoiding communication: Shyness, reticence, and communication apprehension* (2nd ed.) (pp. 151-187). Cresskill, NJ: Hampton Press.

White, B. Y. (1984). Designing computer games to help physics students understand Newton's laws of motion. *Cognition and Instruction, 1*(1), 69-108.

Whitehill, B. V., & McDonald, B. A. (1993). Improving learning persistence of military personnel by enhancing motivation in a technical training program. *Simulation & Gaming, 24*(3), 294-313.

Wickens, C. D. (1976). The effects of divided attention in information processing in tracking. *Journal of Experimental Psychology: Human Perception and Performance, 2*(1), 1-13.

Wickens, C. D. (1984). *Engineering psychology and human performance.* Columbus, OH: Charles E. Merrill Publishing Company.

Wickens, C. E., & Hollands, J. G. (2000). *Engineering psychology and human performance* (3rd ed.). Upper Saddle River, NJ: Prentice Hall.

Wickens, D. D., & Clark, S. (1968). Osgood dimensions as an encoding class in short-term memory. *Journal of Experimental Psychology, 78*, 580-584.

Wiebe, J. H., & Martin, N. J. (1994). The impact of a computer-based adventure game on achievement and attitudes in geography. *Journal of Computing in Childhood Education, 5*(1), 61-71.

Wiener, N. (1948). *Cybernetics.* Cambridge, MA: Technology.

Wikipedia. (2005). Game classification. In Wikipedia, the free encyclopedia. Retrieved on July 29, 2005 from http://en.wikipedia.org/wiki/Game_classification.

Wilkinson, R. T. (1963). Interaction of noise with knowledge of results and sleep deprivation. *Journal of Experimental Psychology, 66*, 332-337.

Williams, R. H. (1980). Attitude change and simulation games: The ability of a simulation game to change attitudes when structured in accordance with either the cognitive dissonance or incentive models of attitude change. *Simulation & Games, 11*(2), 177-196.

Wilson, E. B., Jr. (1952). *An introduction to scientific research.* New York: McGraw-Hill Book company, Inc.

Winer, B. J. (1962). *Statistical principles in experimental design.* New York: McGraw-Hill Book Company, Inc.

Wishart, J. (1990). Cognitive factors related to user involvement with computers and their effects upon learning from an educational computer game. *Computers and Education, 15*(1-3), 145-150.

Wolfle, D. (1951). Training. In S. S. Stevens (Ed.), *Handbook of experimental psychology* (pp. 1267-1286). New York: John Wiley & Sons.

Wolfe, J. (1997). The effectiveness of business games in strategic management course work. (Special Issue: Teaching Strategic Management). *Simulation & Gaming, 28*(4), 360-376.

Wolfe, P., & Brandt, R. (1998). What do we know from brain research? *Educational Leadership, 56*(3), 8-13.

Wood, L. E., & Stewart, P. W. (1987). Improvement of practical reasoning skills with a computer game. *Journal of Computer-Based Instruction, 14*(2), 49-53.

Woodward, A. (1993). Do illustrations serve an instructional purpose in U.S. textbooks? In B. K. Britton, A. Woodward, & M. Binkley (Eds.), *Learning from textbooks: Theory and practice* (pp. 115-134). Hillsdale, NJ: Lawrence Erlbaum Associates.

Wright, R. (1989). *System thinking: A guide to managing in a changing environment.* Dearborn, MI: Society of Manufacturing Engineers.

Wurtz, R. H., & Kandel, E. R. (2000). Central visual pathways. In E. R. Kandel, J. H. Schwartz, & T. M. Jessell (Eds.), *Principles of neural science.* New York: McGraw-Hill.

Yerkes, R. M., & Dodson, J. D. (1908). The relation of strength of stimulus to rapidity of habit-formation. *Journal of comparative Neurology and Psychology, 18*, 459-482.

Author Index

423

Subject Index